Soft Skills

The software developer's life manual

John Z. Sonmez

MANNING

SHELTER ISLAND

For online information and ordering of this and other Manning books, please visit
www.manning.com. The publisher offers discounts on this book when ordered in
quantity. For more information, please contact:

Special Sales Department
Manning Publications Co.
20 Baldwin Road
PO Box 761
Shelter Island, NY 11964
Email: orders@manning.com

Manning Publications Co.   Development editor: Cynthia Kane
20 Baldwin Road   Copyeditor: Jodie Allen
PO Box 761   Proofreader: Melody Dolab
Shelter Island, NY 11964   Illustrator: Višeslav Radović
                                         Typesetter: Marija Tudor
                                    Cover designer: Leslie Haimes

ISBN: 9781617292392
Third, corrected printing, September 2015

Printed in the United States of America
6 7 8 9 10 – EBM – 19 18 17

To all developers who strive for continuous self-improvement...

Who are not satisfied with good enough

Who always seek every opportunity to expand their horizons and explore the unknown

Whose thirst for knowledge is never fully quenched

Who believe that software development means more than just writing code

Who know that failure is not the end, but merely a step in the journey

Who struggle at times, and sometimes fall, but always get back up again

Who have the will and determination to seek the harder path in life

And, most importantly, who are willing to help others along the way

Brief contents

Contents

Foreword

I've long been an advocate for soft skills. Coding is so harsh and cold. Everything is so easily measured in the hard world of code. How many lines of code can you write? How productive can you be? Did those tests pass? It's easy to get caught up in the measurement of it all and lose sight of the human aspect of technology.

Are you liked? Are you appreciated? Are you kind and welcoming? Do you inspire with your positivity and supportive demeanor, or just with your ruthless competence? Are you taking care of yourself, your back, your buns, and your brain? I've been coding for well over 25 years and, let me tell you, things break down if you don't take care of them.

Perhaps you're a consultant, as many of us are. Are you taking care of your finances? Money doesn't compile quite the same way as code, as much as you'd wish it did. All of these skills and so many more make up the so-called soft skills. What John has done for us with this book is to compile all of the things one needs to know to form, well, a well-rounded software professional! After many years of fail-fast, fail-often, John speaks from vast experience about what works and what doesn't. *Soft Skills* is a near complete brain dump from a successful engineer and it gives you useful, practical, and actionable advice on a wide array of topics.

I'd also recommend you check out my free video documentary, "Get Involved in Tech" at http://www.getinvolvedintech.com for a video discussion of what it means to be a social developer, just like John talks about in Section 2 of this very book! John and I think similarly about these things which is why I'm thrilled to be writing this foreword.

Enjoy this book. Take it a little at a time, jump around, absorb, and return to it. Continuous integration and continuous improvement work in wetware as well as software!

SCOTT HANSELMAN
SOFTWARE ARCHITECT, ENGINEER, AUTHOR, TEACHER

Foreword

Late in the evening of Friday, December 5, 2014 (my 62nd birthday), I received an email from John Sonmez, the author of this book. He wrote, asking me to write a foreword by Monday, December 8. In John's email was a zip file with several dozen Word files—I found this presentation of the manuscript to be inconvenient and annoying, and I didn't have time to generate a PDF of the whole book.

I wasn't pleased to get such a request. My wife had just had double knee replacements and was in rehab. I had a flying lesson Saturday morning and planned to spend the rest of the day with my wife. I was scheduled to board a plane to London Saturday evening and teach courses Monday through Friday. So there was no way, not by Monday. John hadn't given me enough time, and I told him so.

Just before driving to the airport, I found John had sent me a Christmas package of cheeses and ham. It included a card, thanking me for considering writing the foreword. Also, I received another email from John in which he said he had begged his publisher for another day, so he could give me until Tuesday. He sent me several other imploring emails, but I told him that there was no reasonable chance, and that he should expect nothing from me.

I drove to the airport, boarded the plane, slept through the flight, and took a taxi to my favorite London hotel. I was wiped out by the travel and played Minecraft in a stupor until I finally crashed. On Monday I taught a full day, and then had to do some work on the SMC Compiler for Episode 30 of my Clean Code video series on http://cleancoders.com.

Today is Tuesday, December 9. It's the second day of my class, and I just started the students working on a two-hour exercise. I checked my email and found that John had sent me another message with a simple PDF of the whole book. Okay, that would make things easier. I could just open that file and scroll up and down the book. Nice.

Note what I'm telling you: John did what was necessary. He *thought* about what I might need and want. He followed his original request with inducements and helpful aids. He clearly spent a lot of time and effort working to make my job easier, on the off-chance that it would make it possible for me to write this foreword. Even after I'd declined and told him it was almost certainly impossible, he continued to find ways to induce and aid me. He didn't give up. He didn't back down. As long as there was a chance, he continued to search for a way.

And *that* is what this book is about. It's about getting to success. It's about the habits and strategies, procedures and mindsets, and tricks and hacks that you can use to push yourself ever closer to success. John's actions toward me, after his original request, are an example, and he is an exemplar, of what he has written in this book.

So, with two hours to kill while the students did their exercise, I cracked the PDF open and began to read. Whoa! Look at the topics! He talks about physical fitness. He talks about options trading. He talks about real estate. He talks about spiritual balance. He talks about quitting your job, starting a consulting business, joining a startup, building a product, climbing the corporate ladder, marketing yourself, and the list goes on…

Knowing I'd never be able to read the entire book in two hours, and that I wasn't going to write the foreword anyway, I read and skimmed, and read and skimmed again. But as I did, I started to get the feeling that John had a message and that it was a good one! It was a holistic message, one that every software developer (and everybody else, for that matter) ought to hear.

Do you know how to write a resume? Do you know how to negotiate your salary? Do you know how to set your rates as an independent consultant? Do you know how to weigh the risks of quitting your job to become a contractor? Do you understand how to get funding for a startup? Do you understand the cost of watching TV? (Yes, you read that right.)

These are the things this book talks about, and can teach you. They're things you need to know. I haven't read the whole book, but I've read *in* the book and skimmed a lot of it, and that was enough, because here I am, writing this foreword, after all. My conclusion is that if you're a young software developer trying to find your way in this complex industry, then you're holding a book that will give you a lot of insight and good advice.

John figured out a way to get me to write this foreword, despite a bumpy beginning, an impossible schedule, and the overall difficulty of the situation. He applied the principles that he writes about in this book, and, once again, gained success!

ROBERT C. MARTIN (UNCLE BOB)
UNCLE BOB CONSULTING LLC

Preface

I'd love to be able to give you a fantastic story about how I came to write this book. I'd like to tell you that I was meditating in the desert when an eagle flew down, landed on my shoulder, and whispered in my ear, "You must write a book about soft skills for software developers." I'd like to tell you that the book came to me in a dream; that I was awakened by a vision of the outline of the book in the middle of the night and that I started frantically writing chapters, trying to capture what I had seen.

But the truth is that I wrote the book because I felt that I had to.

Throughout my life as a software developer, I've been on many different journeys. I've taken some right paths, some wrong paths, and some paths that I'm still not sure about. Along the way, I haven't had much help or guidance. I've never felt like there was someone who had cut a trail for me that I could follow. I've never felt like there was someone who could show me how to be the most successful software developer I could be — not just in writing code — but in life in general.

Sure, there have been plenty of people who have influenced my life, and plenty of people who've taught me all kinds of things about software development and more. I certainly owe what I've accomplished in life, in part, to those people. But I've never found a single person or guide that condensed all this information into one place. Things like

- Not only how to manage my career, but how to make the right choices about my career

- How to learn in a better and more efficient way and how to be as productive as possible, and what to do when I feel unmotivated and discouraged

- The basics of finance, physical and mental health, and how all those things affect me in my role as a software developer and as a person living on this planet.

I wrote this book because I wanted to provide that guide—or at least to do the best job I could of providing it with what I've learned from my personal experience and from the experiences of other successful software developers, financial experts, fitness gurus, and motivational speakers that I've had the pleasure of meeting and interacting with. I wrote this book because I felt that it would be a waste to not share what I have learned and what I have experienced.

I wrote this book, for you

…to make your journey a little easier

…to help you become a better version of yourself

…and, most importantly, to help you not feel so alone in your journey through life as a software developer.

Did reading this make you feel inspired?

Good. Let's begin the journey!

Acknowledgments

If I have seen further than others, it is by standing upon the shoulders of giants.

—Isaac Newton

Few books are written without the help of many people. Certainly, no books are published and distributed without the help of a whole lot of people. This book is no different, so I'd like to take a moment to thank the "giants" in my life.

First, I want to thank all the people who've positively impacted my life and have helped me become the person I am today—and who have helped me realize that I still have a long way to go.

I'd like to thank my coworkers and bosses, throughout my career, who've challenged me, mentored me, given me enough rope to hang myself, and have helped me cut down the rope before something truly bad happened. There are too many of you to name, but you know who you are.

I'd like to thank the authors of the many books I've read who have made me a better person and given me new perspectives in life. Again, too many to name, but if I was hard pressed to name a few, Robert C. Martin (Uncle Bob), Steven Pressfield, and Dale Carnegie come to mind as some of the most influential authors I've read.

So I am especially grateful and honored that Robert C. Martin found the time in his busy schedule to contribute a foreword to my book, even though I asked him way too late. I am also thrilled that Scott Hanselman penned a second foreword, also at the last minute, and that he shares many of my views on the soft skills developers need. My sincere thanks to both of them for endorsing my book.

I'd like to give a special thanks to my family—especially my wife Heather and my daughter Sophia—who had to deal with my mood swings, my over-commitment of time, and the overall craziness of writing a book. My wife was also my proofreader who read every chapter and corrected it before it was sent to the editor—making me look a lot smarter than I am.

I'd also like to thank my dad, Sahin, who taught me the value of hard work, without which this book would have never been written in the first place, and there'd be nothing to write about anyway!

And I can't forget my mom, Laura, who, more than anyone else, taught me to believe in myself, regardless of what anyone else says—an indispensable quality for an entrepreneur.

I'd also like to thank Derick Bailey, Josh Earl, and Charles Max Wood, also known as the Entreprogrammers (http://entreprogrammers.com), who are part of my weekly mastermind group and have encouraged, motivated, inspired, and challenged me at every step of writing this book.

Of course, I need to thank everyone at Manning Publications, without whom this book wouldn't have been published—or perhaps it would have been published in some completely unrecognizable form.

First, Marjan Bace, the publisher of Manning, who had the foresight to realize that a book of this kind was exactly what software developers needed.

Next, I'd like to thank my editor, Robin de Jongh, who brought me into the Manning fold, helped me come up with the concept for *Soft Skills,* and provided support and encouragement during the process of writing the book.

I'd like also like to thank my development editor, Cynthia Kane, who reviewed the earliest versions of the manuscript and provided invaluable feedback and advice in a way that made me feel more inspired to keep writing, rather than discouraged.

Thanks to Candace Gillhoolley, who did an excellent job of marketing the book and who taught me a few tricks about marketing that I'll be using in the future.

A big thanks to Jodie Allen and Mary Piergies, who had the difficult job of coordinating everything that went along with getting this book through production, and again to Jodie for copyediting the entire manuscript.

Another big thanks to Rebecca Rinehart for coordinating the MEAP (Manning Early Access Program) release of *Soft Skills* and for dealing with my extreme pickiness regarding the cover of the book, although in the end Manning conducted a survey of customers who had pre-ordered the book and let them choose the final cover, which features one of the historical figures typical of so many Manning books.

Thanks also to graphic artist Višeslav Radović, who perfectly illustrated the visuals I tried to convey in the book. And a thank you to all the other staff at Manning who made this book possible.

Special thanks to the reviewers who read the manuscript in its early drafts and whose comments helped to improve the book: Heather Campbell, Ionel Condor, Luke Greenleaf, Robert Hanson, Rebecca Jones, Anita Lugomer, Matthew Margolis, Javier Muñoz Mellid, Edward G. Prentice, Alvin Scudder, Craig Smith, David Stanek, Lourens Steyn, and Jerry Tan.

Finally, I'd like to thank the Simple Programmer audience. Many of you have contributed by asking questions, providing feedback, and inspiring and encouraging me in everything I do.

About This Book

Hey, I'm glad you picked up this book, but you're probably wondering what it's about. What the heck is a "software developer's life manual" anyway? That's an excellent question, and I'll try to answer it here—briefly.

Think of it this way: there are a lot of good books out there that will teach you how to write better code, learn a new technology, or do things like work on a team or run a software project. You might even find some books that talk about your career and how to improve it, or simply how to pass interview questions. But have you ever found a book that told you how to become a better version of the software developer you already are?

Have you ever found a book that told you not only how to get a better job and make more money, but what to do with that money and how to eventually leave that job to become an entrepreneur—if you so desire?

Have you ever found a book that told you the steps to successfully build a reputation for yourself in the software development industry and at the same time taught you how to become stronger and healthier physically, mentally, and spiritually?

I haven't either, so that's why I decided to write a book about all that …and more.

Regardless of who you are, this book is written for *you*. And I don't say that lightly. There are chapters in this book that cover everything from hacking the interview process and crafting a killer resume, to creating a wildly successful blog and building your own personal brand, to being extremely productive and learning how to deal with burnout, and even investing in real estate and losing weight.

And you'll also find an entire section dedicated to my special technique for learning things quickly—the same one I used to create over 55 online courses in less than two years for the online training company Pluralsight.

Seriously, no matter who you are, or where you are in your software development career, there's something in this book for you. There is even a chapter devoted to meeting that special person—you know what I mean!

Chapter 1 will tell you more about what you'll find in the book and how it's organized, but before you get into it, I want to point to a few online resources that might be helpful to you as you read the book. You'll find links to useful websites sprinkled throughout the chapters, but below are a few staples you're sure to find useful.

Online Resources

- The Simple Programmer Blog: http://simpleprogrammer.com

Here you'll find a huge collection of blog posts that have to do with many of the topics in this book. It's also the best way to get in contact with me and find other valuable information that I post for free on a weekly basis. (While you're there, make sure you sign up for my email list and you'll get all kinds of freebies and other good stuff that I produce each week.)

- My YouTube channel: http://youtube.com/jsonmez

Here I post videos about many of the topics you'll find in this book—and it's all for free. If you're interested in learning about a topic I cover in this book, try doing a search on my YouTube channel—there's a good chance you'll find a video I did on it.

- How to Market Yourself as a Software Developer Course: http:// devcareerboost.com/m

If you're interested in the section in this book on marketing yourself, go to this site to buy the full course that goes into detail about building a personal brand and making a name for yourself in the software development industry. This is the most popular thing I've ever produced, by far.

I'll even give you a special discount because you purchased this book. Use the code SOFTSKILLS to get $100 off the complete package.

- 10 Steps to Learn Anything Quickly Course: http://simpleprogrammer .com/ss-10steps

This is another in-depth course that goes into detail about what I teach you in the Learning section of this book. If you enjoy that section and want a little more in-depth treatment of the subject, check out the course to find out more.

- Entreprogrammers: http://entreprogrammers.com

If you're interested in becoming an entrepreneur or starting your own business, check out this free, weekly podcast that I prepare with three other developers/entrepreneurs (developerneurs).

- Get Up and CODE: http://getupandcode.com

Finally, if the Fitness section appeals to you, you'll probably enjoy this free podcast I produced about fitness for software developers and IT professionals.

Author Online

Purchase of *Soft Skills* includes free access to a private web forum run by Manning Publications where you can make comments about the book, ask questions, and receive help and feedback from the author and other users. To access the forum and subscribe to it, point your web browser to www.manning.com/SoftSkills.

This page provides information on how to get on the forum once you're registered, what kind of help is available, and the rules of conduct on the forum. The Author Online forum and the archives of previous discussions will be accessible from the publisher's website as long as the book is in print.

About the Author

John Sonmez is the founder of Simple Programmer (http://simpleprogrammer.com), where he tirelessly pursues his vision of transforming complex issues into simple solutions. He has published over 50 courses on topics such as iOS, Android, .NET, Java, and game development for the online developer training resource Pluralsight. He also hosts the Get Up and CODE podcast, where he talks about fitness for programmers (http://getupandcode.com), and the Entre-  programmers podcast, where he and three other developers/entrepreneurs share their real stories of building their online businesses (http://entreprogrammers.com).

John is a life coach for software developers, and helps software engineers, programmers, and other technical professionals boost their careers and live a more fulfilled life. He empowers them to accomplish their goals by making the complex simple.

1

Why this book is unlike
any book you've ever read

Most software development books are about…software development—this one isn't. There are plenty of books out there about writing good code and using various technologies, but I've been hard-pressed to find a book that told me how to be a good software developer.

When I say "good software developer," I'm not talking about being good at writing code, solving problems, or hacking out unit tests. Instead, I'm talking about being a good software developer in terms of managing your career, reaching your goals, and enjoying your life. Sure, all those other skills are important, but I'm going to assume that you can go elsewhere to figure out how to implement a good sorting algorithm in C++ or write the kind of code that doesn't make the next person who maintains it want to run you over with their car.

This book isn't about what you can do. This book is about…you. That's right. It's about your career, your life, your body, your mind, and—if you believe there is such a thing—your soul. Now, I don't want you to think I'm some kind of lunatic. I'm not a transcendentalist monk sitting on the floor meditating while eating peyote buttons, trying to help you ascend to a higher state of consciousness. On the contrary, I think you'll find I'm a pretty down-to-earth kind of guy who just happens to think that being a software developer is about a whole lot more than writing code.

I embrace a holistic approach to software development. This means that I think that if you want to be a better software developer—a better

1

anything, really—you need to focus on the entire person, not just one or two areas of your life.

That's both where this book came from and what it's designed to do. Now, obviously I can't cover everything there is to cover about life in this short book—nor would I have the experience or wisdom to tackle such a broad subject—but what I can do with this book is focus on the main areas of a software developer's life that I have some experience and expertise in and that will probably benefit you the most.

In the pages of this book you'll find quite a few seemingly unrelated topics strung together, but there is some semblance of reasoning behind this madness. This book is divided into seven sections, each focusing on a different aspect of your life as a software developer. If you wanted to categorize and group these sections it would be easiest to look at them as career, mind, body, and spirit.

We'll start off by talking about your career, because I feel that this is one of the most important areas to focus on for most software developers. I've found that very few software developers really give much thought to actively managing their career. In section 1, "Career," I'm going to help remedy that problem—at least in your case—as I teach you exactly how you can actively manage your career to reach the outcome you're looking for, whether that may be climbing the corporate ladder, starting your own consulting business, or even becoming an entrepreneur and creating your own product. I've done all three, and I've interviewed countless software developers who have as well, so you'll learn from our collective mistakes and avoid some of the black eyes we got along the way. I'll also cover some important skills you need to have regardless of your career goal, like creating an eye-catching resume, mastering interviews, working remotely, and getting those good ol' people skills everyone is talking about these days.

In section 2, "Marketing yourself", we'll touch on a topic that's near and dear to my own heart—selling yourself. "Marketing"—how does that word make you feel? Most software developers get uncomfortable and possibly a bit queasy when I mention the word, but by the end of this section, you'll get a whole new appreciation for the word and understand why it's so important. Everyone is a salesperson; some of us just do a lousy job of selling. In this section, I'll help you learn how to become a better salesperson and to know exactly what it is you're selling. This won't involve any slimy tactic or sending spam mail offering get-rich-quick schemes. Instead, it will contain practical advice about how to build a personal brand, how to create a successful blog, and how to get your name out there by speaking, teaching, writing, and a whole bunch of other ways you've probably never even considered. With these skills in place, you'll be able to take what you learned from section 1 and multiply it to achieve an even greater result.

With the career stuff out of the way, it will be time to transition into the realm of your mind, when we get to section 3, "Learning." Learning is a critical part of any software developer's life. I probably don't need to tell you that one of the most common things a software developer or any IT professional does is learn. Learning how to learn, or rather how to teach yourself, is one of the most valuable skills you can acquire, because the skill of self-teaching is a skill that literally enables you to do just about anything you can imagine. Unfortunately, most of the educational systems we've had forced upon us while growing up are broken, because they rely on a false premise that says you must have a teacher to learn and that learning only flows in one direction. I'm not saying teachers or mentors aren't important, but in this section, I'll show you how to first rely on your own abilities and common sense mixed with a little courage and curiosity to achieve a greater result than you can by listening to a boring lecture and furiously scribbling down notes. I'll take you through the 10-step self-learning process I developed over my career and the same process that helped me learn everything I needed to know in record time to produce over 50 complete online developer training courses in just over two years for an online training company, Pluralsight. I'll also cover some critical topics like finding a good mentor, being a mentor, and whether or not you need a traditional education and degree to be successful.

Continuing with the theme of mind, section 4, "Productivity," is all about—you guessed it—being more productive. This section is designed to kick you in the behind and put your butt in gear. Productivity is a great struggle for many software developers and it's one of the single biggest things that hold you back from being as successful as you can be. You can have everything else fine-tuned in your life, but if you don't know how to overcome the hurdles of procrastination, disorganization, and just plain laziness, you'll have a hard time getting out of first gear. I've done my fair share of gear-grinding, but I eventually figured out a system that has me cruising down the highway at top speed. In this section, I'll share that system with you. I'll also tackle some difficult topics like burnout, watching too much TV, and finding motivation to dig in and do some plain old-fashioned hard work.

In section 5, "Financial," we'll handle one more mental topic that often gets completely ignored, personal finance. You can be the most successful software developer in the world, but if you can't effectively manage all that money you're making, some day you might end up on a street corner holding up a sign that says "Will code for food." In this section, I'll take you on a wild ride through the world of economics and personal finance and give you the basics you need to know to be able to make smart financial decisions and actually start planning out your financial future. I'm not a financial planner or professional stock trader, but in addition to being a software developer, I've been a professional real estate investor since I was 18, so I have a pretty good idea of what I'm talking about. We won't go too far into this topic, because the topic is deep enough to fill volumes of books, but I'll teach you the basics of managing your income, how the stock market really works, how to do real estate investing, and avoiding debt. As an additional bonus, I'll share with you my story and how I used these principles to effectively retire at the age of 33 without hitting it big selling a startup. (It's really not that hard and just about anyone can do it.)

Now we get to the fun part and work on your body. Are you ready for boot camp? In section 6, "Fitness," I'll teach you everything you need to know about how to lose fat, gain muscle, and get in shape. Most software developers I know are overweight, have poor health, and feel powerless to do anything about it. Well, knowledge is power, and as a software developer who has competed in bodybuilding competitions and hosted a podcast about fitness for programmers, I'm excited to share what I've learned to equip you with the knowledge you need to finally take control of your life. In this section, I'll take you through the basics of diet and nutrition and explain how what you eat affects your body. I'll also show you how to set up a successful fitness plan and diet to lose weight, gain muscle, or do both. I'll even cover some tech-specific topics like standing desks and fitness gear for geeks.

Finally, in section 7, "Spirit," we'll head into the metaphysical world and look for the illusive "ghost in the machine." Even though the title is "Spirit," don't let this section fool you; I'll give you some real, practical advice about topics that affect your emotional state and attitude. I suppose you could call this the self-help section of the book—although I'm not particularly fond of that phrase. In this section, I'll focus mainly on helping you rewire your brain to create the positive attitude necessary for success. I'll also briefly cover love and relationships, because this area is a difficult one for many of those who excel in technology. I'll also give you my personal success book list: a list of books I've compiled over the years by simply asking every famous or hypersuccessful person I've ever met to tell me the one book they'd recommend everyone read.

So go ahead and make yourself comfortable, give your analytical mind the day off for a change, and get ready to dive into a quite different book about software development.

Career

The biggest mistake that you can make is to believe that you are working for somebody else. Job security is gone. The driving force of a career must come from the individual. Remember: Jobs are owned by the company, you own your career!

—Earl Nightingale

Few software developers actively manage their careers. But the most successful developers don't arrive at success by chance. They have a goal in mind and they create a solid and well-thought-out plan to achieve that goal. If you really want to succeed in the competitive world of software development, you need to do more than just polish your resume and take whatever job you happen to get. You need to think things through and decide what actions you should take, when you should take them, and how you should go forward with them.

In this section, I'll take you through the process of deciding what you want to get out of your software development career and out how to get it.

2

Getting started with a "BANG!": Don't do what everyone else does

Imagine sitting in a field in the middle of summer enjoying a nice fireworks show. All around you screaming rockets burst into explosions of blue, red, purple, and yellow. You watch as one particular rocket soars high up into the sky and then…nothing. No bang, no explosion, just a fizzle. Which firework do you want your software development career to be like? The one that explodes high in the air with a loud bang, or the one that reaches altitude and then quietly falls back to the ground?

Having a business mindset

Most software developers starting out in their careers make a few huge mistakes. The biggest of those mistakes, by far, is not treating their software development career as a business. Don't be fooled; when you set out into the world to write code for a living, you're no different than the blacksmith of old times setting up shop in a medieval town. Times may have changed, and most of us work for a company, but our skills and our trade belong to us and we can always choose to set up shop somewhere else.

This kind of mindset is crucial to managing your career, because when you start to think of yourself as a business, you start to make good business decisions. When you're used to getting a regular paycheck that isn't really dependent on your performance, it can be easy to develop a mindset that you're just an employee of a company. While it's true that you may be an employee of a particular company at any given time in your career, it's important to not let that particular role define you and your career.

It's better to think of an employer as a customer for your business of developing software. Sure, you might only have a single customer, and all of your revenue may be coming from that single customer, but viewing the relationship this way moves you from a position of powerlessness and dependency to one of autonomy and self-direction. (In fact, many "real" companies have one big client that makes up a majority of their revenue.)

> TIP   This is the first thing you must do in your career: switch your mindset from that of an indentured servant to a business person who is running their own business. Just having this mindset at the start will change the way you think about your career and cause you to be mindful and present in the active management of it.

How to think like a business

Now, just thinking of yourself as a business doesn't really do you much good. You have to understand what it is to think in this fashion if you want to get any benefit from it. Let's talk about how to think about yourself as a business and what exactly that means.

We can start off by thinking about what makes up a business. Most businesses need a few things to be successful. First, you need to have a product or a service. A business without something to offer doesn't have a way to make money, because they have nothing to sell. What do you have to sell? What is your product or service?

You may very well have an actual digital product to sell as a software developer—we'll talk about that in chapter 13—but most software developers are selling the service of developing software. Developing software is a wide term that can cover a variety of different activities and individual services, but in general, software developers are selling their ability to take an idea and make it into a digitized reality.

> NOTE   The service you provide is to create software.

Just thinking about what you offer as a business in this way has a pro-found impact on how you view your career. Businesses are constantly revising their products and improving them. You should too. The ser-vice you provide as a software developer has a tangible value, and it's your job to communicate not only what that value is, but what makes it different than the offerings of thousands of other software developers out there.

That brings us to marketing, which we'll cover more extensively in the next section. It's important to at least realize that having a product or service by itself is not enough. You've actually got to be able to let potential customers know about that product or service if you want to make any money. Companies all over the world realize this key truth about business and that's why they spend so much money and effort on marketing. As a software developer offering your service, you also have to be concerned with marketing. The better you market your offerings, the higher price you'll be able to charge for your services and the more customers you'll potentially be able to attract.

You can imagine that most software developers starting out don't think about their careers in this way. Instead of starting out with a bang, they enter the scene with a barely audible pop. So don't do what they do.

Instead

- Focus on what service you're providing and how to market that service.

- Think about ways you can improve your offering.

- Think about how you can specialize the service you're providing to serve the needs of a particular type of client or industry.

- Focus on being a specialist who provides a very specialized set of services to a very particular type of client. (Remember, as a software developer looking for a good job, you only really need to land one client.)

Also think about how best to spread the word about your service and find your customers. Most software developers create a resume and blast it out to companies and recruiters. But, when you think about your career as a business, do you really think that is the best and only way to prospect potential clients? Of course not. Most successful companies figure out how to get customers to come to them to buy their products or services; they don't go out chasing customers one by one.

You can do the same thing by making yourself a more marketable software developer through many of the techniques we'll discuss in section 2 of this book. Even without getting into the specifics, the point is to think outside the box and start thinking like a business. What is the best way you can attract customers and how can you tell them about the service you have to offer? If you can answer this simple question, you'll start off your career with a bang.

Taking action

- Think about a business that has a product or service they offer. How do they differentiate and advertise that product or service?
- If you had to describe the specific service you can provide a perspective employer or client in a single sentence, what would it be?
- How does treating your career like a business affect the way you
    - Do your work?
    - Handle finances?
    - Look for a job or new clients?

3

Thinking about the future: What are your goals?

Now that you're thinking about your software development career as a business, it's time to start defining the goals you have for this business.

Not everyone is alike. You might have a very different set of goals for your career than I do, but if you're ever going to achieve any of those goals, you have to know what they are. This is, of course, easier said than done. I've found that most people, software developers included, drift through life without really having a concrete realization of what their goals are or what they're trying to accomplish in life. This is the natural state of most human beings. We don't tend to give enough thought to what to focus on and as a result our steps lack purpose or direction.

Think about sailing a ship across the ocean. You can get into a ship and raise your sails, like most people do. But if you don't have a clear destination picked out and you don't take steps to steer the ship in that direction, you'll just drift aimlessly at sea. Perhaps you'll end up sailing your ship by chance to an island or other land mass, but you'll never really make any solid progress until you define where you want to go. Once you know your destination, you can use all of the tools at your disposal to actively steer the ship in the direction that will take you there.

It seems pretty obvious, yet so few software developers ever define goals for their career—why? I can only guess, but I'd say that most software developers are afraid of committing to a long-term vision for their career. They want to leave all options open to them because they're afraid of choosing one path and going down that path. *What if it's the wrong path? What if I don't like where it takes me?* These are scary questions indeed.

Some developers haven't even given it much thought at all. Left to our own devices, we tend to follow the path that's laid out for us. It's a much more difficult job to create our own path, so we just don't do it. Instead, we take the first job we get an offer for and stay at that job until a better opportunity comes along or we get fired—I mean "laid off."

Whatever your reason may be for not defining goals for your career, now is the time to do it. Not tomorrow, not next week, but right now. Every step you take without a clear direction is a wasted step. Don't randomly walk through life without a purpose for your career.

How to set goals

Okay, so now that I've convinced you that you need to set goals, how do you do it? It's easiest to start out with a big goal in mind and then create smaller goals along the way that will help you get to the bigger goal. A big goal is usually not very specific, because it's hard to clearly define something that's potentially very far off. But, that's okay. You don't have to be specific when you define a big, far-off goal. Your big goal has to be specific enough to give you a clear direction in which to travel. Going back to the ship analogy, if I want to sail to China, I don't have to know the exact latitude and longitude of the port I want to get to right away. I can get in my ship and start heading in the direction of China, and when I get closer, I can always get more specific. All I need to know to get started out is whether I'm getting closer to China or further from it.

Your big goal should be something not too specific, but clear enough that you can know if you're steering toward it or not. Think about what you want to ultimately do with your career. Do you want to become a manager or executive at a company? Do you want to go out and start your own software development business some day? Do you want to become an entrepreneur creating your own product and bringing it to market? For me, my goal was always to eventually be able to get out on my own and work for myself.

It's really up to you to define what your big goal is. What do you want to get out of your career? Where would you like to see yourself in 5 or 10 years? Go ahead and spend some time thinking about this—it's really important.

Once you've figured out what your big, far-off goal is, the next step is to chart a course to get there by making smaller goals along the way. Sometimes it helps to think backwards from your big goal to your present situation. If you had already achieved your big goal, what would have been some of the milestones along the way? What path could you imagine tracing backwards from your big goal to your present situation?

At one time, I had a big goal of losing about 100 pounds of weight. I had let myself get out of shape and I wanted to get back on track. I set for myself smaller goals of losing 5 pounds every two weeks. Every two weeks that I was able to reach my smaller goal, it moved me forward toward my big goal.

If you can make small goals that gradually move you forward in the direction toward your bigger goals, you'll eventually reach your destination. It's important to have various sizes of goals that lead you in the direction of your big goal. For example, you might have a yearly goal of reading so many technical books or learning a new programming language. That yearly goal might be a smaller goal that will lead you toward your bigger goal of becoming a senior-level developer. But that yearly goal might

Steps for setting goals

be broken up into smaller goals of reading a single book each month or making some defined amount of progress each day.

The smaller goals keep you on track and motivated so that you keep heading in the direction of your bigger goals. If you set out to accomplish a big goal and don't have smaller goals along the way, you don't end up having time to course-correct when you're off track. Smaller goals also give you frequent rewards that help motivate you. Small victories each day and each week help us feel like we're making progress and accomplishing things, which makes us feel good about ourselves and helps us keep moving forward. Smaller goals also don't seem as daunting as a big goal.

Consider my writing this book. Right now I have a goal for writing so much of this book each day and each week. I'm not trying to tackle the huge goal of writing the entire book, but instead I'm looking at it from the perspective of what my goal is for each day, knowing that by doing what I need to do each day, I'll eventually reach my big goal of completing the entire book.

If you haven't given much time to think about your future and you don't have at least one clear and definite goal you're aiming toward, put down this book and define some goals for yourself. It's not easy, but you'll be glad you did it. Don't be a ship floating aimlessly in the ocean. Chart a course before you set sail.

Tracking your goals

Periodically, you should track and update the goals you have set for yourself—and adjust them if necessary. You don't want to travel miles off course before you discover your mistake, and you probably don't want to travel far down a path that turns out to be the wrong one, either.

I'd recommend setting regular intervals for checking up on your goals. This will help you to make adjustments when needed and keep you accountable. You might want to review the goals you set for each week at the end of that week before you plan out the next week. The same goes for every month, quarter, and year.

It can be helpful to reflect on what you accomplished during small and large time periods so that you can figure out if you're making the right amount of progress or you need to make some kind of adjustment.

Taking action

- Sit down and write out at least one major goal for your career.
- Break down that major goal into smaller goals that correspond to
  - Months
  - Weeks
  - Days
- Write down your major goal where you can see it each day to remind you of what you're striving for.

4

People skills: You need them more than you think

To some degree this book is all about people skills or "soft skills." As someone reading this book, you're probably at least somewhat aware of their importance in your life and your career. But in this chapter, I want to dive in a little deeper and talk about why people skills are so important and some of the things you can do to acquire them.

Leave me alone, I just want to write code!

I used to be under the impression that the job of a software developer was just to write code. I know I'm not alone in having been guilty of thinking that way.

The fact is that a majority of our time in the software development field is spent dealing with people, not with computers. Even the code we write is written first for human consumption and only secondarily for the computer to understand. If that were not the case, we'd all be directly writing our code as machine language — 1s and 0s. If you want to be a good software developer, you have to learn to deal effectively with people (even if writing code is the part of your job you enjoy the most).

Think about how much of your time at your job is actually spent interacting with people and you immediately begin to see the value of improving your interactions with them. When you sit down to do your work in the morning, what is one of the first things you do? That's right, check email. And who sends you email? Is it computers? Does your code send you an email asking you to finish it or to make it better? No. People do.

Do you go to meetings during the day? Do you converse with cowork-ers about problems you're working on and strategize on how to solve them? When you do finally sit down to code, what do you code? Where do the requirements come from?

If you think your job is to write code, you had better think again. Your job as a software developer, and in just about any profession, is to deal with people.

Learning how to deal with people

Many excellent books have been written on the subject of dealing with people, and I'll give you my personal list of what I think are the best ones in section 7, so I'm not going to attempt to cover everything there is to know on the subject in this short chapter. But I do want to cover some of the basic concepts you should know that will perhaps give you the best bang for your buck. I'll borrow heavily from one of my all-time favorite books on the subject, *How to Win Friends and Influence People* by Dale Carnegie (Gallery Books, Reprint, 1998).

Everyone wants to feel important

Perhaps one of the most important concepts you should know when dealing with people is that, at their core, every single person wants to feel important. It's one of the deepest and most desperate desires of the human race and the primary motivation for most great achievements in society and life.

Every time you interact with another person, you should remember and be aware of how you're affecting this basic human need. If you belittle or make a person and their accomplishments feel diminished in some way, fully expect them to react with the ferocity and desperation of a person whose oxygen supply has been cut off.

It's very easy to make the mistake of quickly dismissing a coworker's idea so that you can present your own, but when you commit this grievous error in judgment, you'll often find them deaf to your own ideas because you've made them feel unimportant. If you want people to accept your ideas and think them valuable, you have to extend the same courtesy first. You can never win a person's heart if you do not leave their pride intact.

Never criticize

In regards to this first concept, you should immediately be able to realize that criticism will rarely be a tool that will achieve your intended result. I used to be a big criticizer. I used to think that punishment was a much more effective motivator than rewards, but I was completely wrong.

Time and time again, studies have shown that rewarding a positive behavior is much more effective than punishing a negative behavior. If you're in a position of leadership or management, this is an especially important principle to observe. You have to learn to bite your tongue and only speak words of encouragement if you want to inspire people to perform their best or you want to effect change.

Perhaps you're currently working for a boss or have worked for a boss who lacks the understanding of this principle and responds to all faults with outright and harsh criticism. How does it make you feel? Does it make you feel motivated to do a better job? Do not expect others to react in a much different way. If you want to motivate and inspire, use praise instead of criticism.

Think about what the other person wants

The key to successfully dealing with people is to stop thinking in terms of you and what you want and start thinking in terms of what is important to the other person and what she wants. By shifting your mindset in this way, you'll avoid making another person feel less important and you'll be less likely to criticize her. A person who is handled in this manner is much more likely to deal with you in a favorable way and see your ideas as valuable.

When you first enter a dialog with a coworker or boss, try to shift your focus from you to them. Try thinking about things from their perspective. What is it you think they're trying to get out of this conversation? What is it that's important to them? Listen attentively and then when it's your time to talk, phrase your dialog in ways that appeal to the desires of the other person. (In fact, rehearse this scenario in advance. Be prepared ahead of time for how the conversation will go.)

It does no good telling your boss why you would like to implement a feature a certain way. It's much better to phrase the suggestion from the frame of mind of why implementing a feature the way you suggest will be useful to your boss. Perhaps it will cause the software to be more stable or more likely to be shipped on time.

Avoiding arguments

As software developers, we sometimes tend to think that all people think about things from a logical perspective. It's easy to fall into the trap of falsely believing that solid reasoning is enough to compel another person to accept your way of thinking.

The truth of the matter is that even though we like to pride ourselves on our intellectual prowess, we're all very emotional creatures. We're like little babies who are walking around wearing suits and ties and pretending to be all grown up. A slight or injury is just as likely to cause us to cry or throw a tantrum, but we've learned to control and hide those emotions out of sight.

For this reason, it's imperative to avoid arguments at all costs. Logic and pure reason do little to convince a screaming toddler that it indeed makes sense for him to go to sleep so that he'll be well rested for the day ahead, and it will do just about as much good in convincing a slighted coworker that your way of doing things is best.

> *I have come to the conclusion that there is only one way under high heaven to get the best of an argument—and that is to avoid it. Avoid it as you would avoid rattlesnakes and earthquakes.*
>
> Dale Carnegie, *How to Win Friends and Influence People*

If you have a disagreement about how something should be done, in many cases your best course of action is to first determine whether or not that particular point is a hill that's worth dying on—especially if you know it is for the other person involved. Any opportunity that you can find to give up your side and admit that you're wrong on a small matter that doesn't mean much to you, but perhaps a great deal to the other person, will win you unmeasurable respect with them and store up for you future credit that can be redeemed when the tables are turned.

If you've never taken the time to work on your people skills, there's no better time than now to start. You'll find your life much more enjoyable when you learn how to interact and deal with others in a pleasant way, and the benefits you'll accrue from learning those skills now will be lifelong and difficult to put a price on.

Landmine: Dealing with "poisonous" people

Sometimes, you'll find that there are people you just can't get along with no matter what. Some people are just looking for opportunities to bring others down and generally have a negative view of everything in life. I call these kinds of people caustic, and you would do well to avoid them.

If you recognize someone as being caustic, don't try to change them, and don't try to deal with them; just stay out of their way and limit your interactions as much as possible. You can recognize the signs of a caustic person by the trail of destruction they leave behind them. Some people seem to always be involved in some kind of drama and have bad things happen to them. They often try to play themselves off as the victim. If you recognize this pattern, run—run away as fast as you can.

But what can you do if this kind of person is your boss or a coworker you have to interact with? Not much. You might either have to suck it up or you might have to look into moving to a new department or even a new job. Whatever you do, don't get sucked into their trap. If you have to interact with them, do it in a minimal, nonemotionally invested way.

Taking action

- ☉ In a single day at your work, keep track of every encounter you have with another human being. At the end of the day, count up how many interactions you had during that day, including answering emails or phone calls.
- ☉ Get a copy of the book *How to Win Friends and Influence People* by Dale Carnegie. The book is in public domain, so you can find it very cheap. Read it—more than once.
- ☉ The next time you're being sucked into an argument, think about ways you can turn it around. For an interesting test, try just giving in. In fact, don't just give in, but emphatically take your opponent's side. The outcome of doing this may surprise you.

5

Hacking the interview

Although resume writing is a skill you can delegate to someone else, interviewing is something only you can do, so it's a critical skill to master. It can also be one of the most intimidating things you do when looking for a new job. Interviews are somewhat unpredictable. You can't know for sure what questions you're going to be asked and you might be asked to write code on the spot—a scary proposition for many. But what if there was a way to "hack" the interview so that it was basically a formality?

You might expect for me to go in-depth into the strategy for passing a technical interview in this chapter, but instead I'm going to focus on something much more important. I'm going to help you gain an advantage that will make it so the cards are in your favor before you even get into the interview. Skeptical? Read on.

The quickest way to "pass" an interview

Imagine this scenario: you walk into a job interview, shake the interviewer's hand, and as he looks at you, his face lights up with a moment of recognition. "Hey, I know you. I recognize your picture from your blog. I've read a lot of your blog posts."

If that happens during an interview, what do you think your chances of getting offered the job are? Now, I know what you're probably thinking: "Well, that's great, but I don't have a super popular blog, so it's unlikely any interviewer will have ever heard of me." The key point is that contrary to popular belief, most interviewers decide to hire people based on all kinds of nontechnical factors. (I'll actually show you how to make it so you do have a popular blog in section 2, when I tell you about how to market yourself, but for now, that isn't the point.)

> NOTE   I've seen the most technically competent, yet arrogant and unfriendly people lose out on a job to a much less skilled but likable person.

Now, don't get me wrong, I'm not saying you can get hired for a job by representing skills you don't have and just being famous or friendly, but what I am saying is that there are many technically competent developers applying for a single job, and the biggest factor that determines which one of them gets it isn't technical aptitude.

To put it simply, the quickest way to pass an interview is to get the interviewer to like you. There are many ways to go about doing this, most of which can be done before the interview even starts.

How I got my last job

For the job I held before going out on my own, I determined ahead of time that I wanted to work for this particular company because they seemed like a very good company and they allowed their developers to work from home. I spent some time researching the company and found that some of the developers for that company maintained blogs. I started following all of the blogs of the developers who worked for that company and began putting thoughtful and relevant comments on many of their blog posts.

Over time, many of the developers working at that company began to recognize my name and started to know who I was based on my comments on their blog. Some of them even started reading my blog.

The next time that company was hiring for a developer and I applied, how hard do you think it was for me to get the job? I still did an interview, but as long as I didn't completely blow it, I was pretty much a shoe-in for getting an offer (and a much higher one than I would have gotten if I had not gone about applying for the job in the way I did).

Thinking outside the box and building rapport

The key to "hacking" the interview is to start thinking about a strategy for the interview before the interview starts. Sure, it's possible to be absolutely charming during an interview and sweep your interviewer off their feet. But, I'm going to assume that most of us don't have that kind of charisma. If you do, you probably don't need to read this chapter at all.

A majority of job hires come from personal referrals. You should try to make sure that any job you apply for is applied for through a referral. When you go into an interview as a referral, the interviewer automatically is in a position to think more highly of you, because you're borrowing the social credibility of the person referring you. The reputation and rapport the person referring you has with the interviewer is partially extended to you as the interviewee. You're walking into the interview with the interviewer

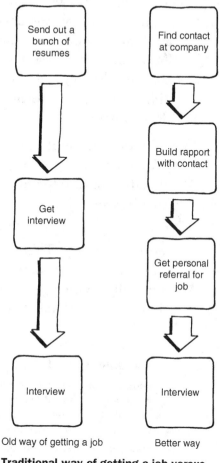

Traditional way of getting a job versus the better way

having a partial bias toward liking you already because you were referred by someone they like and trust.

But what if you don't know anyone at the company you're applying to? How do you get a referral? In my example, I found the blogs of developers who were already working for the company and built a relationship with them. When a position opened up, it was easy to get a personal referral.

You have to be willing to think out of the box a little bit and come up with ways that you can build relationships with contacts within the company. I know one developer who looked up the hiring manager for a job and found out that the hiring manager belonged to a particular local club in the area that met weekly. This smart developer joined that club and became friends with the hiring manager. I'm pretty sure he didn't even have a formal interview when he was offered a position at the company.

With the advent of social media and the internet, it's easy to find information about any company and to make connections with employees already working for that company. You just have to be willing to do a little legwork ahead of time.

If you want to build a bunch of relationships at one time, try joining a local user group. There are many user groups for developers that meet on a weekly or monthly basis. If you become a regular attendee—and especially if you give a few presentations—you'll quickly build relationships with developers and hiring managers from many local companies.

Landmine: What if you need a job *now*?

Perhaps you agree with everything I'm saying, but you only have one problem—it's too late. You just got laid off and now you need to find a new job, but you don't have time to build a network or reputation online or even "stalk" a potential employer. What can you do in this case?

Your best bet in this situation is to try to make contact with the interviewer ahead of time if possible and do as much following up as possible. See if you can get a pre-interview before you interview by asking to meet to talk about the company or ask a few questions before you sit down for the real interview. Ask for five minutes of a person's time for a quick call to touch base. Come up with as many excuses as possible to put yourself in front of as many people who have some influence on the hiring decision.

I know this technique sounds crazy—and you're better off taking the longer road—but in a pinch, this works. A good friend of mine who runs a startup company called Health Hero used this exact approach to get the company accepted to three different startup accelerator programs, which are notoriously difficult to get into. He simply set up pre-interviews with all the key decisions makers, and by the time he went to the real interview, everyone knew who he was and liked him.

But what about the actual interview itself?

Hopefully, by the time you walk into the interview, the interviewer already knows who you are, but either way, you need to know what to do in the interview. Now, obviously, you need to be technically competent to pass a technical interview. But assuming you have the skills to pay the bills, so to speak, the next thing to focus on is demonstrating confidence in your ability to know what needs to get done and do it.

Think about it from an employer's perspective. Hiring an employee is an investment. It costs money and time to hire an employee, and you want to see a good return on that investment. Employees who are autonomous and can do what needs to be done without asking them to do it are employees who almost always add to the bottom line—plus, they are a lot less of a headache, because they require very little of your own resources to manage.

I'd rather hire a developer who knows a little less but knows how to figure out what needs to be done and how to do it, than someone highly skilled who requires constant hand-holding to be productive. When you're in an interview—to the extent that it's in your control—focus on demonstrating why you're the kind of employee who gets things done without being asked to do them.

You'll still have to prove that you're actually technically competent, but if you can convince the interviewer that you are a go-getter who doesn't let any obstacle stop you, not only will they probably like you, but there is a good chance they'll hire you as well.

What can you do right now?

Whether you're actively looking for a job right now or just trying to keep your options open, there's no better time than now to start preparing for your next job interview.

The first thing you should do is make sure you're keeping up on your technical skills. All the interview tricks in the world won't help you get a job you aren't qualified for. Make sure you're reading technical books and blog articles and putting time into developing your skills.

You can also start developing your network before you need it. Start reaching out to employees at different companies in your area and making connections that can help you later. Read and comment on blogs and get to know other developers and even recruiters in your area. Try to figure out ways to expand your circle.

And don't forget to practice. You might want to interview for jobs just to get practice doing interviews—even if you have no interest in a new job right now. The more practice you get, the more comfortable you'll be in an interview that counts.

You'll also benefit greatly from focusing on marketing yourself, but we'll cover that in the next section.

Taking action

- Even if you aren't actively looking for a job right now, make a list of companies that you'd potentially like to work for and who you know at those companies.
- If there are companies on your list that you'd like to work for, but you don't know anyone at those companies, come up with a plan to meet at least one person working at one of those companies and build a relationship with them.
- Find at least one local user group in your area and attend a meeting. Introduce yourself to as many people as possible.

6

Employment options: Enumerate your choices

It's easy to fall into the trap of just doing what everyone else does and follow the path laid out for you. While it's true that most software developers will work as an employee for most of their careers, it isn't your only option. There are many profitable ways to put your programming skills to good use.

You might not even be aware that there are other options besides traditional employment—I know I wasn't. In this chapter, I'll lay out your options so you can better decide what you want for your future. Later in this section, we'll look at each one of these options and learn what it takes to succeed down each employment path.

Option 1: The employee

This is the default and obvious employment choice that a majority of software developers pursue. I was an employee for most of my software development career, partially because I didn't know there were any other options and partially because it's the easiest route to take. I probably don't need to define for you what exactly being an employee is, but it's worth taking a look at some of the benefits and detriments to choosing this employment option.

By far the biggest benefit to being an employee is stability. I don't mean stability in one particular job or working for one particular employer; instead, I'm referring to stability in terms of having a predefined way to make a living that you know will succeed. As an employee, as long as you have a job, you will get a paycheck. You may lose that job in the future and have to look for new work, but you at least have some period of relative stability where you can depend on a set level of income each month.

Being an employee also is an easier road to pursue than other choices because you have a limited scope of responsibility and that path is pretty clear. There is a well-defined process for finding and applying for jobs. It isn't up to you to figure out what you need to do to get paid.

As an employee, you also usually have paid vacation and—in the United States at least—some help with medical insurance.

The negative side to being an employee mainly involves your freedom. As an employee, you'll spend a majority of your time doing work for your employer. You don't have much of a choice in the kind of work that you do, and you might not always get to do the kind of work that you enjoy. You're also usually expected to conform to some kind of schedule defining how many hours per week and what days you need to work.

And while being an employee means that your income is defined ahead of time, it also means that is it "capped" to some degree. As an employee, you'll eventually hit what is known as the "glass ceiling" in terms of your income and advancement opportunities. You'll eventually reach a point where you can't make significantly more income and you can't advance up the ranks any further without switching career paths.

Table 6.1 outlines the benefits and drawbacks of being an employee.

Table 6.1   Benefits and drawbacks of being an employee

Benefits	Drawbacks
Stability	Lack of freedom
Easier road to pursue	Income capped
Paid vacation	
Possible medical insurance assistance	

Option 2: The independent consultant

Many software developers make their living by being independent consultants. An independent consultant is just a software developer who doesn't work for one particular employer, but instead does work for one or more clients. If you've ever had a side job where you did some programming work for a client who either paid you an hourly rate or a fixed price for that work, you know what consulting is.

I consider an independent consultant to be a software developer who makes a majority of his or her income doing this kind of work. This is very different from being a contractor who works for a single client and is paid hourly to do only their work. A contractor is more of an employee relationship. An independent consultant usually has his own company that he contracts out to do work for clients, but isn't bound to any one single client.

I spent a few years in my career as an independent consultant and I still do some independent consulting work today. I always had the dream of getting out on my own and working for myself, and I imagined being an independent consultant would be the fulfillment of that dream. I thought about how nice it would be to be my own boss instead of working for someone else, but I had no idea that being an independent consultant really meant trading one boss for many bosses.

Not to say that being an independent consultant is all bad. There are some definite perks to not having a single employer whom you have to report to. As an independent consultant you can set your own hours, for the most part, and you have the freedom to choose what jobs you want to work on—assuming you have enough work to be picky. You can come and go as you please and have a flexible schedule, but clients will expect to be able to get ahold of you and to have their work completed in a timely fashion.

The biggest benefit, by far, is probably earning potential. As an independent consultant, you can make a much higher hourly wage than you can working for someone else. I currently bill clients $300 per hour for work I do for them, and I know some independent consultants whose bill rates are even higher.

That doesn't mean you'll necessarily make a fortune just by becoming an independent consultant. You won't start off at a $300-per-hour bill rate—although in section 2 on marketing, I'll give you some practical ways to boost your bill rate. You also won't typically book out 40 hours' worth of work per week, each and every week. Even though it can seem like you're making a ridiculous amount of money as an independent consultant, a large amount of that time will be spent looking for clients and on other overhead related to running a business. When you're an independent consultant, you're literally a business (not just in mindset). You're responsible for your taxes, legal counsel, sales, healthcare, and everything else associated with running a business.

Table 6.2 outlines the benefits and drawbacks of being an independent consultant.

Table 6.2   Benefits and drawbacks of being an independent consultant

Benefits	Drawbacks
More freedom (set your own hours)	Have to find your own work
Constantly have new projects to work on	Overhead of running a business
Potential to make more money	Trading one boss for many bosses

Option 3: The entrepreneur

The entrepreneur route is probably the most difficult, most undefined, yet potentially most rewarding route you could go with your career. That's a lot of adjectives to describe a single career choice, and for good reason. I equate being an entrepreneur to being a professional gambler. There is very little, if any, stability in being an entrepreneur, but if you hit it big, you could hit it *really* big.

So what exactly does it mean to be an entrepreneur? Your guess is as good as mine. It's a pretty vague definition and can mean many different things. For the most part, though, I consider a software developer entrepreneur to be someone who develops their own business or product using their software skills. While an employee and an independent consultant trade dollars for hours, an entrepreneur trades their time for no pay up front, but a chance at a much bigger future payoff.

I'd consider myself in the entrepreneur category right now. I spend most of my time developing training and other products that I sell, either directly or indirectly through partners, to make my living. I still write code, but I don't usually write code for any particular client. I'm either writing code for a particular product or service I'm creating or developing training materials to teach others what I know.

In fact, this very book is an example of an entrepreneurial effort. I'm taking a pretty big gamble, spending a large number of hours writing this book. I'll get a small advance from the publisher, but it won't pay for the time that I'll spend working on the book. I'm hoping to either sell enough copies of the book and get paid royalties to compensate me for the effort, or to use it as promotional material that will help me draw customers in others areas of my business. It's quite possible that this entire book could fail and it will have been a wasted effort (although slightly less likely considering you're reading the book now).

Other software developer entrepreneurs operate in completely different ways than I do. Some of them form startup companies and look for large funding from outside investors called VCs, or venture capitalists. Others build small software-as-a-service (SaaS) companies and make their money by selling subscriptions to their services. For example, the founders of the popular developer training company Pluralsight started out with classroom training. But later, they found that they could do much better by providing a totally online service and then moved into a SaaS model when they started offering a subscription-based service.

I'm sure you can guess by now what the two biggest advantages of being an entrepreneur are: complete freedom and completely uncapped earning potential. As an entrepreneur, you don't have any boss, besides yourself—although you can be the harshest one. You can come and go completely as you please and you're entirely responsible for your own future. You could also make millions of dollars or more if you build something that's extremely successful. You're able to apply leverage to your time to make the returns from it grow in potentially exponential ways.

But being an entrepreneur isn't all limousines and parties. It's probably the toughest and riskiest career choice you can embark upon. There is no guarantee of any income at all, and you could go deep into debt chasing your brilliant ideas. The life of an entrepreneur is filled with rollercoasters. One day customers are buying your product and you're on top of the world; the next day your project falls flat and you wonder how you're going to afford to pay your rent.

Being an entrepreneur also requires you to invest heavily in other skills that you might not need to worry about as a software developer working for someone else or doing client work. Entrepreneurs have to learn both sales and marketing as well as many other aspects of business and finance that are critical to being successful. (I'll cover some of these topics later in the book. In section 2 we'll discuss marketing yourself, which is a similar concept to marketing a product, and in section 5 we'll get into some finance topics you'll find useful even if you aren't planning on becoming an entrepreneur.)

Table 6.3 outlines the benefits and drawbacks of being an entrepreneur.

Table 6.3   Benefits and drawbacks of being an entrepreneur

Benefits	Drawbacks
Complete freedom	Very risky
Huge earning potential	Completely on your own
Work on what you want	Requires many other skills
No boss	Might end up working very long days

Which should you pick?

For most software developers, especially when starting out, it makes sense to be an employee. That option has the least risk and doesn't require you to already have a large amount of experience under your belt. I tend to view being an employee like being an apprentice. Even if you have aspirations of making it out on your own, it's a good place to start to learn the craft and hone your skills.

With that said, if you're just starting out and have the opportunity to be an independent consultant or entrepreneur and you can tolerate the risk involved, you can get all of the inevitable failings and mistakes out of the way early and set yourself up for a nice career later on.

The choice is really up to you and you can always switch paths later. In fact, in chapter 11 I'll show you how to make the transition from employee to self-employed. It's not an easy road, but it's possible.

Taking action

- ○ Try to come up with a list of software developers you know or have heard of who fit each of the three categories.
- ○ If you're interested in becoming an independent consultant or entrepreneur, set up a meeting with someone you know who is already on that career path and ask him or her what it's like. (Too many developers jump in without knowing what they're getting themselves into.)

7

What kind of software developer are you?

Have you ever had to hire a lawyer? What was the first thing you did? If you've never hired a lawyer, what do you think would be the first thing you'd do?

If you guessed that you'd need to figure out what kind of lawyer you needed, then you're correct. You don't want to just call any lawyer; you want to call a specific lawyer who deals in the area in which you have a problem. Lawyers have expertise and they usually make that expertise known from the start. There are criminal lawyers, accident lawyers, real estate lawyers, and so on.

You wouldn't want to have a divorce lawyer represent you for a tax or real estate problem, so specialization is important. A lawyer doesn't come out of law school and decide they just want to be a "lawyer," but unfortunately that's exactly what most software developers do when it comes to their profession.

Specialization is important

There are plenty of software developers out there who don't have a specialization. In fact, most software developers will completely define their specialization by what programming language they program in. You'll commonly hear "I'm a C# developer," or "I'm a Java developer." This kind of specialization is too broad. It doesn't really say enough about the kind of software development work you can do. A programming language doesn't tell me anything about what kind of developer you are and what you can actually do. It only tells me one tool that you use to do your job.

You might be scared to specialize in one area of software development because you're afraid that you'll become pigeon-holed into one specialty and that will exclude you from many jobs and opportunities. While it's true that specialization will close you off from some opportunities, it will open many more for you that you wouldn't have otherwise had.

Think about the lawyer situation again. If you became a lawyer and had no specialization, technically every person seeking a lawyer could be your client. But the problem is that very few people would want to hire a generalist lawyer. Most potential clients would seek to hire a specialist.

Even though it would appear that you had a bigger pool of potential clients, the reality would be that by being a generalist, you'd have greatly reduced your pool of clients to only those who weren't savvy enough to realize they needed a specialist.

By being a specialist you have a smaller pool of potential employers and clients, but you become a much more attractive prospect to them. As long as your specialty is big enough and it's not overcrowded, you'll have a much easier time finding a job or getting a client than you would if you just called yourself a software developer.

Getting specific about specialties

If calling yourself a C# developer or Java developer isn't specific enough, what is? This isn't an easy question to answer, because the real answer is "It depends." It depends on what you're trying to achieve and how big the market is in that area.

Let me give you an example. Earlier in my career I billed myself as a software developer who specialized in printers and printer languages. This was a pretty specific specialty. I only had a handful of major employers that I could look to for employment. But can you imagine how difficult it is for a printer manufacturer to find a software developer who specializes in printers and printer languages?

My specialty made me very valuable to a small number of potential employers. These employers didn't have a presence in most cities, so if my market was the entire world or even the United States, I had a pretty big market where my specialty would be very useful. But, if I didn't want to move out of the place I was currently living, my market would have been too small for that specialty. (How many local companies need a software developer who specializes in printers?) Fortunately, at the time, I was willing to work just about anywhere in the United States, so the specialty worked out well for me.

> NOTE The rule of specialization is that the deeper you specialize, the fewer potential opportunities you'll have, but the more likely you'll be to get those opportunities.

Let's go back to your situation. Suppose you're looking for a job in your local area, and that you're a Java developer. In most metro areas there's a pretty big demand for Java developers, so you'll start out with a nice healthy-sized pool—there are plenty of jobs you could potentially get. But you don't need to get all those jobs, you only need one.

Let's pretend, at any given time, that there are 500 available Java developer jobs in your area. Now suppose you decide to specialize to narrow down your market and give you a better chance at getting one of those jobs, so you specialize as a Java web developer. Perhaps this

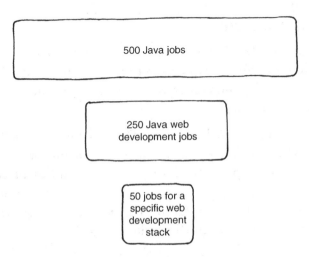

500 Java jobs

250 Java web development jobs

50 jobs for a specific web development stack

Being specific narrows down your job pool, but increases your chances of getting hired.

eliminates 250 of the jobs, but leaves you with 250 that you could potentially get. Still plenty, right? Remember, you only need one.

Now you decide to specialize a little further, and, without getting into the details of Java web development stacks, let's say that you pick a Java web development stack to specialize in. Perhaps this knocks your job pool down to 50 jobs. Still plenty of jobs to choose from, but now your chances of getting one of those 50 just went way up, because you now are specifically targeting those jobs with your skills and your message.

Kinds of specialties for software developers

There are many different kinds of specialties for software developers. Obviously there are language specialties and platform specialties, but there are also specialties in methodologies and specific technologies or industries.

One of the first things you should figure out, though, is what kind of software development it is you want to do. Do you want to work on the frontend of applications, creating and programming user interfaces? Do you want to work on the middleware of an application, implementing business rules and logic? Do you want to work on the backend of an application, working with databases or low-level operations? You can even pick all three and be a full-stack developer, but in that case you should definitely specialize in a specific stack of technologies. (For example, a full-stack web developer might specialize in creating ASP.NET MVC websites, using C# and SQL Server.)

You can also specialize in areas like embedded systems development where you work close to hardware devices and write code that runs on computers inside of a device. Embedded systems programmers have to deal with a whole different set of problems than web developers do.

Operating systems is another area of specialty, although not very important when dealing with web development. Many developers specialize in writing applications for a specific operating system, like Windows, UNIX, or Mac.

Mobile application development or even a specific mobile operating system is another potential area for specialization. There is a huge demand for iOS or Android developers who specialize in writing mobile applications for either platform.

Some developers specialize really deep and become experts in a very specific platform or framework. These developers have few potential clients, but they can demand a high hourly rate because of their specialty. You'll find that low-level specialties are most common around very expensive software suites or frameworks. Consider the giant German software company SAP. Some very highly paid developers specialize in developing customer solutions to integrate with this expensive software system.

SPECIALIZATION AREAS

- Web development stack
- Embedded systems
- Specific operating system
- Mobile development
- Framework
- Software system

Picking your specialty

Most software developers I talk to about specializing agree with me, but I'm often asked about how to actually pick a specialty. Picking a specialty often can seem like an overwhelming task.

Here are a few tips to help you pick your specialty:

- What were some of the major pain points in your current or previous company? Can you become a person who specializes in solving those pain points?
- Is there a particular kind of work that nobody wants to do or that lacks skilled people? Become the person who is an expert in that area, and you'll have plenty of business.
- What kind of topics most commonly come up at conferences and user groups?

- What kind of questions do you answer the most, either for coworkers or on sites like Stack Overflow (http://stackoverflow.com)?

Whatever you do, make sure you pick some kind of specialty. The size of your market will determine how specific it is, but try to make it as specific as possible. You'll be in much higher demand in your specific market if you do so. And don't worry; you can always change your specialty later if you need to. Obviously, I'm not specializing in developing software for printers anymore, and I know many other developers who have had great success moving around to different specialties during their careers. For example, a good friend of mine, John Papa, used to specialize in Microsoft Silverlight. After Silverlight went away, he changed his specialty to Single Page Applications (SPAs).

What about the polyglot programmer?

Whenever I bring up the topic of specialization, I always encounter at least some resistance. I think it's important to clarify that even though I recommend specializing and having a specialty, it doesn't mean I think you shouldn't also have a wide variety of skills.

Although those two things may seem contradictory, they don't have to be. Being a well-rounded and versatile software developer is great. Being able to use multiple technologies and programs and many different programming languages can only help your career and can make you a much more valuable software developer than someone who only knows one specific technology or programming language. But it's very difficult to market yourself as a jack-of-all-trades.

It's nice to have a developer who can do anything on the team, but rarely do companies or clients set out to find that kind of person. Even though you may be awesome at all kinds of different technologies and know 50 different programming languages, you still will be better off picking some specialty—even if it changes from time to time.

Learn as much as you can and become as flexible as possible, but also have a specialty that makes you unique and stand out. If you have to choose between the two options, start with specialization and branch out later.

Taking action

- List all the different kinds of software developer specialties you can think of. Go from broad to specific and see how specific you can get.
- What is your current specialty? If you don't have one, think about what area of software development you could specialize in.
- Go to a popular job search website and look for jobs in your market for your specialty. Try to get an idea of whether or not further specialization would benefit you or would limit your choices too much.

8

Not all companies are equal

Your experience as a software developer can be radically different depending on what type of company you choose to work for. It's important to decide for yourself whether you want to work for a small company just starting up, a large corporation with massive budgets and shareholders, or somewhere in between.

Not only does the size of the company greatly affect your experience, but all companies have their own individual cultures that can have a dramatic impact on your overall happiness and how much you feel that you fit in and belong where you are.

It's important to take this into consideration before accepting a job offer. It's easy to evaluate a potential employment opportunity based solely on salary and benefits, but in the long run the work environment will likely be much more important to you.

In this chapter, we'll examine the pros and cons of each type of company—small, medium, and large—and talk about how to decide what type of company you want to work for.

Small companies and startups

Most small companies are startups, so they have a very distinctive startup mentality. This startup mentality is usually focused on rapid growth and doing everything you can to get the company to a profitable situation or reach some other pressing goal.

As a software developer working in a company like this, you'll most likely have to wear many hats. You won't just be writing code. Because there are fewer employees, roles will be less defined and you'll have to be more flexible. If you just want to sit at your desk and write code, you might not like having to set up a build server or help out with testing. But if you're the kind of person who thrives on energy and excitement and is always up to face a new challenge, you might find this kind of environment very engaging.

In a small company, what you do is often much more impactful. This can be both good and bad. If you like to blend into the crowd and just do your job, you probably won't like working at a small company—it's very hard to fly under the radar. But if you're the kind of person who likes to see the impact of the work you're doing, a small company is by far the best place for this. With a small number of employees, each person's contributions directly affect the bottom line and are noticed. This means your great achievements are magnified, but so are your screw-ups.

Small companies also usually offer much less stability than a larger company, but a potentially bigger reward in the long run. A small company is much more likely to go out of business or not be able to make payroll and have to cut staff. But at the same time, if you can ride out the storms, being one of the first employees at a small company that has grown significantly can be very rewarding. It can be difficult to reach a director-level position at a big company by climbing the corporate ladder, but at a small company, your upward mobility is much greater because new employees tend to come in underneath you already.

Many developers work for startups taking low salaries and working ridiculous hours hoping to get rich on the stock options if the company goes public or gets acquired, but I consider that a pretty risky bet. I wouldn't recommend choosing to work for a startup just because you might hit the lottery someday. Taking that approach, you're likely to burn out fast and have nothing to show for it. A better reason to work for a small company or startup is because you like that kind of fast-paced exciting environment and you want to be part of building something and watching it grow.

Medium-size companies

Most companies are medium-size companies. So this is the most likely place you'll end up working, or you may be working for one now. Medium-size companies are usually companies that have been around for some time and have profitable business, but don't have the momentum to make it into the fortune 500 list.

In a medium-size company, roles are usually a bit more defined and you have quite a bit more stability. I'd say that medium-size companies often offer more stability than large companies, which often have large workforce reductions and periodic reorganizations. If you like stability, you'll probably find a medium-size company suits you best.

Working at a medium-size company, you'll probably find the pace a bit slower, although it's still hard to hide among the reeds. Your contributions might not cause the company to sink or swim, but they will be noticed. In a medium-size company, slow and steady often wins the race. The fast-paced do-or-die mentality of a startup usually drives decisions quickly and embraces cutting-edge technologies, but most medium-size companies are risk-averse and move quite a bit slower. If you like working on the bleeding edge, you'll find it a tough sell to your boss at a medium-size company, because it will be hard to justify the risk.

Large companies

Large companies are pretty interesting. Each large company is very different from another. Large companies usually have very deep company cultures that permeate every aspect of the company. Many large companies are publicly held and have CEO celebrities you aren't likely to ever interact with.

Perhaps the biggest thing you'll notice when working for a large company is the amount of procedure and process that's in place. When you interview for a large company, you usually go through a series of interviews and follow a very formal process. And when you work at a large company, you'll probably have to conform to an established way of doing things. Cowboys and renegades are usually not welcome in the corporate culture. If you like process and you like structure, you'll probably enjoy working for a large company.

One neat thing about large companies, though, is the opportunities you have when working for one. When I worked for a Fortune 500 company, I had many different training opportunities and just about every software product at my disposal. Many large companies offer career guidance to help you grow and learn within their organization. You also may get the chance to work on some cool stuff. Small and medium-size companies don't have the budgets for massive, world-changing projects. But for many large companies, technological innovations are common. You might not be able to have a noticeable impact on one of these large-scale initiatives, but you could be part of a team that brings something truly remarkable to the market.

For many developers, large companies are frustrating, because they feel that their individual contributions don't matter. You're likely to be working on a small piece of functionality in a large code base. If you're the kind of developer who likes to get your hands into all aspects of a software system, you might not like working at a large company.

It's very easy to go off the radar working at a large company. I've worked at several large companies where some developers basically did nothing all day long and no one really noticed until there was a major round of company-wide layoffs. This kind of autonomy can be put to good use, though. Sometimes it's nice to be able to work on projects that you think are important or interest you without having the pressure of having to produce.

A final note about large companies: politics. Large companies usually have complex political systems that can rival large governments. You can try to avoid politics as a software developer in a large company, but even if you do, other people's political maneuvers are sure to affect you in some way. And, as we'll talk about in the next chapter, to climb the corporate ladder, you'll have to learn how to navigate your way through the complex political climate of any large company you work for. If politicking isn't your thing and you want to avoid it completely, look for a small company with a flat management structure.

Table 8.1 shows some pros and cons of working for small, medium, and large companies.

Table 8.1 Pros and cons of small, medium, and large companies

Company size	Pros	Cons
Small	Get to wear lots of hats; flexible roles	Might not get to just sit down and code
	Higher impact work	Can't hide under the radar
	High potential for rewards	Low stability
Medium	Stability	Slow pace for change
	Less crazy hours	Might not get to work on cutting-edge technology
Large	Established processes and procedures	Lots of red tape
	Training opportunities	Probably will work in a very small area of codebase
	Large impactful projects	Difficult to get noticed

Software development companies versus companies with software developers

Another major factor you should consider when deciding what kind of company to work for is the difference between companies that have software developers to work on their internal software or part of some product they're producing versus companies that actually produce software or do software development as their core offering.

Companies that don't focus on software development, but instead hire software developers to work on some aspect of their system, treat software developers in a much different way than companies whose primary focus is software development. When a company's focus isn't software, typically software developers aren't given as much respect and leeway. These companies are much more likely to have loose software development practices.

On the other hand, companies whose livelihood is based on developing software are much more likely to put a high value on the software developers they hire. It doesn't mean necessarily that the work environment will be better, but it's usually very different.

You'll also probably find that software development companies are a bit more cutting-edge when it comes to technologies and tools than companies that have a different focus but hire software developers. If you want to work on newer technologies, you'll probably want to find a company that develops software directly.

The difference between these two types of companies becomes very apparent when dealing with Agile software development methodologies. Companies whose primary focus isn't software tend to have much more difficulty adopting Agile processes because Agile processes are usually driven by the development teams. Agile processes require adoption from the top down, so it's often a difficult sell to make a whole company change the way it does things just because some developers think it's a good idea.

Choose carefully

These are just some general guidelines about the different kinds of companies you might work for as a software developer, but every company is different. It's up to you to decide what kind of working environment suits you best and what kind of company culture you best fit in to. It's always a good idea to talk to developers already working for a company before accepting a job there so that you can get a more realistic feel for what it would be like to work at that company.

Taking action
- Take some time to think about what kind of environment you prefer working in. What company size matches your ideal working environment?
- Make a list of companies in your area or companies you have worked for and decide which category each fits into.

9

Climbing the corporate ladder

I know quite a few people in the IT industry who just can't seem to ever move up in the world. Year after year they have the same exact job and job title. I wonder if they ever even get a raise. Do you know someone like that? It's surprisingly common. If you don't want to end up on that dead-end path, you've got to do something about it. In this chapter, I'm going to give you some advice on how to climb the corporate ladder so that you don't get stuck in the same position, never advancing.

Taking responsibility

The most important thing you can do to go up in the ranks at any company is to take on more responsibility.

> TIP   It may seem obvious, but often in your career you'll be faced with choices between more money and more responsibility. The right choice—at least in the long term—is almost always more responsibility.

Money always catches up to responsibility. Any time you're offered more responsibility, take it.

But what if you aren't offered more responsibility? What can you do to gain it yourself? Sometimes you have to go out and look for opportunities where you can take charge of an initiative or head up a project. There is almost always some neglected area of business that you can find to contribute your talents to—you just might have to dig to find it.

One of the best places to search is in areas that no one else wants to get involved in. Perhaps there's a legacy application that no one wants to touch or a certain module in your codebase that is particularly nasty. These are landmasses to add to your growing empire, because no one will want them, so you won't be up for much of a fight. But if you can turn those swamplands into fertile ground, you can really show your value.

Another way to indirectly take on responsibility is to become a mentor for others on your team. Volunteer to help the new person get up to speed. Always offer help to anyone who needs it. Not only will you learn more by encountering and solving other people's problems, in addition to your own, but over time you'll develop the reputation of being the "go-to" person on the team. Eventually this reputation is likely to land you a team-lead position or management position, if you want to go that route.

> **HOW YOU CAN TAKE ON MORE RESPONSIBILITY**
>
> - Is there a project that has been neglected that you could take charge of?
> - Can you be the person who helps new team members get up to speed?
> - Can you take the role of documenting processes and keeping those documents up to date?
> - What job does no one else want to do that you could take on and make easier or automate?

Becoming visible

It doesn't matter if you're the brightest, best, and hardest-working developer on a team if no one knows who you are and what you've achieved. All of your hard work can easily go to waste if you can't find a way to let your boss and upper management know what you're doing.

One of the first things I did whenever I started a new job was to start keeping a daily account of where I spent my time and what I accomplished during the day. I'd then take that information and compile a weekly summary every Friday to send to my manager. I called this my "weekly report," and when I'd send out my first report at each new job, I'd include some information to let my manager know that I understand how important it is to know what your direct reports are doing, and so I was sending a weekly summary of my activities to make his or her job easier.

This weekly report ensured that every single week I'd show up on my manager's radar and I could talk about what I accomplished that week without outright bragging. It was a great way to gain visibility and it often appeared that I was much more productive than my peers simply because my manager was hearing about all the work I was doing, but not much about the work other developers were doing.

Not only was this weekly report valuable for my visibility, but it was also an excellent resource for myself when review time came around. I could go back through my weekly reports and pick out my key accomplishments for the year. When it came time to fill out reviews, I knew exactly what I had accomplished during the year and I had dates to prove it.

I'd definitely recommend sending an unsolicited weekly report, but there are also many other ways to become more visible in your organization. One of the best ways is to offer to give presentations on some topic or problem your team is facing. Pick a topic you can present on and offer to present that topic to your team. You can even offer to do it as a lunch-and-learn where you present an educational topic during lunch instead of on company time. This is a great way to gain visibility and show how knowledgeable you are in a particular area. Plus, there's no better way to force yourself to learn something than to know that you have to present it in front of other people. I've done my best learning under that kind of pressure.

HOW TO BE MORE VISIBLE

- *Keep a daily log of your activities* — Send this log as a weekly report to your manager.
- *Offer to give presentations or trainings* — Pick a topic that would be useful to your team.
- *Speak up* — Do this at meetings and any time you get the chance.
- *Be seen* — Set up regular meetings with your boss. Make sure you are seen often.

Educate yourself

Another really good way to advance is to keep increasing your skills and knowledge. It's hard to stagnate when you're constantly improving your education level. Educating yourself makes it easy to justify a raise or promotion, because you can clearly show that you're more valuable now than you were before.

You can, of course, take traditional higher-education courses—especially if your company will pay you to get a degree—but there are many alternative ways to educate yourself that can pay off in the future. You should always be learning something new or advancing your skills in some way. Sign up for training courses or seek out certifications that will show that you are committed to continually improving.

At one point, early in my career, I felt like my upward mobility was somewhat limited, so I decided to start getting Microsoft certifications. I studied hard and took all the tests I needed to get one of the top-level Microsoft certifications. It wasn't easy, but I quickly saw the benefits in my career. The extra effort showed my manager that I was serious about advancing my career and opportunities were quickly opened for me.

In section 3 we'll talk more about how to learn things quickly, but it's definitely a skill you should master. The faster you can advance your knowledge, the more you'll be able to learn and the more opportunities that will come your way.

Also, don't just learn about software development. Take some time to learn about leadership, management, and business if you have your sights set on higher-level and possibly executive positions.

And don't forget to share what you're learning. We've already talked about how you can offer to give presentations to share your knowledge, but you can also create your own blog, write magazine articles or books, and speak at community events or conferences. The outside exposure will help establish you as an authority in your area of expertise and will make you seem more valuable to the company you're working for.

Be the problem solver

In any organization there are always plenty of people who will tell you why some idea won't work or some problem is too hard. People like that are a dime a dozen. Don't be one of them. Instead, be the person who always has a solution to a problem and is able to execute that solution to get results.

One of the most useful kinds of people to have around in any company is the kind of person who never seems to find an obstacle that they can't overcome. Building a reputation for being that kind of person is a sure way to get promoted. Forget the political games and posturing for position—if you can solve problems that other people can't or aren't willing to tackle, you'll easily become the most valuable person at any company.

> **Landmine: I don't have any opportunity for advancement**
>
> Most companies offer some kind of opportunity for advancement, but perhaps you've followed all the advice in this chapter, and, for whatever reason, you just don't see any opportunities ahead of you. What do you do then?
>
> Quit. Make sure you have another job lined up first, but sometimes you just have to realize that you're in a dead-end job and you need to find a better opportunity. Perhaps your work environment is caustic and mentally unhealthy, perhaps nepotism ensures you'll always stay where you are; whatever the reason, you might need to move on.

What about politics?

You can't really have a chapter about advancing in a corporate culture without at least mentioning politics. I'm addressing this one last, because I think it's the least important thing to focus on when trying to advance your career. I'm not naïve; I realize that most organizations have quite a bit of politics and you have to be aware of them, but I don't think you should invest too much time in playing political games.

Sure, you can advance up the corporate ladder by deft maneuvers and ruthless ambition, but when you advance that way, you're likely to fall just as easily. Some will disagree with me, but I've always found it better to build a solid foundation based on being a valuable employee rather than appearing to be one.

With that said, you should still be aware of the political climate of whatever organization you're in. You can't completely avoid politics, so you have to at least know what's going on, what kinds of people you need to avoid, and which ones you should never cross.

Taking action

- What is one way you can take on more responsibility at your current job right now?
- How visible are you to your current boss or manager? What is one concrete action you can take in the next week to become more visible?
- What are you doing to educate yourself? Decide what would be the most valuable thing to educate yourself on and create a plan to get that education over the next year.

10

Being a professional

In one of my favorite books of all time, *The War of Art* (Black Irish Books, 2002), Steven Pressfield expounds upon the difference between being a professional and being an amateur:

> *Turning pro is a mindset. If we are struggling with fear, self-sabotage, procrastination, self-doubt, etc., the problem is, we're thinking like amateurs. Amateurs don't show up. Amateurs crap out. Amateurs let adversity defeat them. The pro thinks differently. He shows up, he does his work, he keeps on truckin', no matter what.*

Being a professional is all about showing up, doing your work, and not letting adversity defeat you. Being a professional requires you to overcome your vices so that you can sit down and produce the best work possible.

In this chapter, we're going to focus on what it means to be a professional and how you can be a professional in your software development job whether you work for someone else directly or produce work for clients.

As a software developer, professionalism will be one of your greatest assets. Not only will learning how to act like and be perceived as a professional help you to get better jobs and more clients, but it will also help you feel better about the kind of work you're doing and to have pride in that work—a critical component of long-term success.

What is a professional?

Simply put, a professional is someone who takes their responsibilities and career seriously and is willing to make the tough choices that have to be made—often at their own expense—for the purpose of doing what they know is right.

For example, imagine what you'd do in a situation where you've been asked to cut your normal quality standards and ship some code as quickly as possible. How do you react in this situation? What if you're repeatedly asked to work in this way? Can you stand up and do what is right, even if it may end up costing you your job? What principles do you stand for? What quality bar do you personally set for your work?

A professional is what we should all strive to be. A professional is someone you can count on to get a job done and do it right, but a professional also doesn't just tell you what you want to hear. A professional will let you know when something isn't possible or the path you want to proceed down is wrong.

A professional is someone who may not have all the answers, but thoroughly studies their craft and seeks to hone their skills. A professional will freely admit when they don't know the answer, but you can count on a professional to find it.

Perhaps most importantly, a professional is consistent—stable. A professional has a high-quality standard for their work and you can expect a professional to adhere to it each and every day. When a professional doesn't show up, you had better call emergency dispatch, because there is certainly something wrong.

Table 10.1 outlines some differences between professionals and amateurs.

Table 10.1   Professionals versus amateurs

Professionals	Amateurs
Have principles that they abide by	Do whatever is asked
Are focused on getting the job done right	Are focused on getting the job done

Table 10.1 Professionals versus amateurs

Professionals	Amateurs
Aren't afraid to admit when they are wrong or don't know	Pretend to have knowledge they don't possess
Consistent and stable	Unpredictable and unreliable
Take responsibility	Avoid responsibility

Being a professional (forming good habits)

It's easy to identify a professional, but how do you become one? What is it about you and your work that reeks of amateur, and how do you neutralize the odor?

It starts with habits. Habits are an essential part of becoming a professional, because a large portion of what we do every day is completely habitual. We get up, we go to work, and we perform our daily routines each and every day, mostly without thinking about it. If you want to change your life, you need to start with changing your habits. This is, of course, easier said than done. Bad habits are exceedingly difficult to break and new habits aren't easy to form.

But if you want to become a professional, you need to develop the habits of a professional. At one time when I was working on a team following the Scrum process, where we would have a daily stand-up meeting stating what we had done, what we had planned to do, and what was impeding us, there was one developer in particular who always had a written version of exactly what he was going to say. Every single day before the Scrum meeting he would prepare his statement, instead of coming up with it during the meeting like most of us did. This is the kind of habit a professional develops.

Another strong habit to develop as a professional is time-management skills. How good are you at managing your time right now? Do you know what you're going to work on each day before you work on it? Do you have a good handle on how long routine tasks will take? Get in the habit of effectively managing your time by planning out your day in advance. A professional knows what work must be done each day and roughly how long it will take to do the work.

These are just two examples of the kinds of habits that are important to develop as a professional software developer. You'll have to decide for yourself what habit you need to form to reach your own standard of professionalism in your work, but habits are critical because they build consistency, and consistency is what makes you reliable. (For a great book on the subject of habits, check out *The Power of Habit* [Random House, 2012] by Charles Duhigg.)

Doing what is right

As a software developer, you're often faced with many difficult challenges, both technical and ethical. If you want to be a professional, you need to be able to make the correct choices in both of these cases. Often the technical challenges you face are more objective. There are right ways to solve technical problems. It's easy to prove one solution over another. But the ethical challenges can be much more difficult. There isn't always a clear-cut right answer.

One of the biggest ethical challenges software developers face is that of going forward with decisions they know are correct and in the best interest of their client even if making those decisions could jeopardize their own well-being or stability.

One of my favorite software developers and authors, Bob Martin, wrote an excellent article on saying "No," which addresses this very issue (http://simpleprogrammer.com/ss-no). In this article, Bob compares a software developer to a doctor. He talks about how absurd it would be for a patient to tell a doctor how to do their job. In his example, a patient tells the doctor that his arm hurts and that he needs to cut it off. Of course, the doctor says "No" in this case. But in many cases, software developers in a similar situation, fearing the wrath of higher-ups, will say "Yes" and perform an amputation on their code.

A professional needs to know when to say "No," even to their own employers, because, as Bob Martin put it, professionals have certain lines they won't cross. It might even mean getting fired, but sometimes that's the price to pay if you want to call yourself a professional. In the short term, it may be painful, but consistently choosing to do the thing you know is right over the course of your career is much more likely to pay off than the alternative—plus you can sleep better at night.

Sometimes professionals have to make tough decisions about the priorities of what they work on. Unprofessional developers will often waste time by gold-plating things, because they can't decide what to work on next or they'll constantly have to ask someone else to set their priorities. A professional assesses the work that has to be done, prioritizes it, and gets to work.

Landmine: What if I can't afford to say "No"

It's easy for me to sit back in my chair and tell you that you just have to say "No" sometimes, but not everyone has the luxury of being able to risk their job. I understand that you may be in a position where you literally can't say "No," because doing so could be catastrophic for your future.

My advice in this situation is to go ahead and do what you need to do to get by, but never let yourself get in this kind of situation again. It's easy to get trapped into situations where you need a job, but when you get trapped in those situations you limit your own options and allow people to exercise great power over you.

If you're in this kind of a situation, try to get out of it as fast as possible. Save up some money so that you don't have to worry so much about losing your job. You might even consider looking for another job where you won't be required to make so many ethical decisions or where your opinion is more highly valued.

When it comes down to it, you have to do what you have to do, but always try to put yourself in positions where you have the upper hand or are at least on equal footing, whenever possible.

Seeking quality and self-improvement

As a professional you must strive to constantly improve and increase the quality of the work you produce. You won't always be able to produce the quality of work you desire, but over time, with consistency, you'll reach your standards. The big mistake many software developers make is to lower their standards when they seem out of reach instead of seeking to improve themselves to rise up to meet the challenge.

It's important to apply quality to every detail of your work, not just the parts that seem most important. A real professional has high-quality standards for all areas of his or her work, because a professional knows that, as T. Harv Eker put it, "how you do anything is how you do everything" (*Secrets of the Millionaire Mind*, HarperCollins Publishers, 2005). If you lower your standards in one area, you'll inadvertently find them dropping in other areas as well. Once you've crossed the line of compromise, it can be difficult to go back.

And don't forget to play to your strengths. You can, of course, improve your weaknesses, but it's a good idea to know what your individual strengths are and use them to your advantage. A professional has a good, accurate, and realistic self-assessment of their own abilities—and weaknesses.

The way a professional meets the high-quality expectations they have is by continuous self-improvement. If you want to be a professional, you need to dedicate yourself to always improving your skills and learning more about your craft. Make sure that you have an education plan that you can follow to expand your skills and learn new things that will help you do a better job. Don't ever be happy with good enough—always strive to become a better version of yourself.

Taking action

- Would you define yourself as a professional today? If so, why? If not, why not?
- What are your habits? Observe your day and try to identify as many habits as possible. List your habits in two categories, good and bad. Now identify some good habits you need to develop. Come up with a plan for developing those habits.
- When was the last time you had to say "No"? If you've never encountered this situation, think about what you'd do if your boss asked you to do something that you knew was wrong. How would you react?

11

Freedom: How to quit your job

For the longest time my dream was to one day quit my day job and work for myself. I felt trapped working in the corporate world, and I knew that I could do better if I could just get out on my own. The problem was, "How?"

I didn't know anyone who had successfully made it out of the rat race, so I didn't know what I needed to do. I just knew that I wasn't completely happy working for someone else.

Now, you may not want to work for yourself. You may want to continue to enjoy the benefits of being an employee—and there is nothing wrong with that. But if you're like me and have always dreamed of working for yourself and becoming your own boss, read on.

Going about things the smart way

Want to know the easy way to quit your job and work for yourself? Just go into your boss's office tomorrow and tell them you quit. That's it. That's all you have to do. I hope you have quite a bit of money saved up in the bank, because once you do that you'll be completely on your own. Good luck.

This might not be the smartest way to go about gaining your freedom, though. It's easy to be a bit impatient and not see another way to escape, so you might be tempted to do exactly that—I know I've been. You might be able to quit your day job with just a few months of savings, lacking a solid plan, and jump right into the ocean of entrepreneurship or independent consulting and make it, but is it worth taking the risk?

It's not a pretty sight. Usually, after just a few months, there is blood everywhere. Checking accounts are bleeding, credit cards are hemorrhaging, and what seemed wonderful and beautiful suddenly got extremely violent. It's really difficult to create a business when there is a gun to your head. You just can't make good decisions and you're paralyzed by fear.

I'm not saying this to scare you—although I hope it does if you're considering leaping before you look—but instead I'm saying this to help you understand that you need an actual plan if you want to quit your job and work for yourself. You have to figure out a way to build up enough side income to support yourself while you get the new thing working.

I'd be a hypocrite if I told you that I never attempted to make the leap myself without having a solid plan. I've been tempted down that path and have succumbed before. But eventually I got smarter. I figured out that the only way I was really going to be able to make a jump was to figure out how to start building my new business on the side and make it successful enough to support me while I made the transition, even if it meant a big pay cut.

Before you think about quitting your job you need have a solid plan in place. I'd highly recommend starting whatever business you want to create on the side first and only transitioning to doing it fulltime when you're generating enough income from it to support yourself. I know this is the slow and painful way to quit your day job, but it's important to do things this way for more than just financial reasons.

Landmine: I already quit my job and I didn't save any money...now what?

Whoops. I just hope you're reading this chapter before you put a second mortgage on your house. If you're already in the situation where you've quit and gone out on your own, you'll just have to face up to reality a little quicker.

My advice in this situation is to start working really hard and develop some good productivity habits to give yourself the best chance of success. You should also cut as many expenses as possible. That probably means getting rid of cable. You want to give yourself as much runway as possible.

(continued)

But also be realistic. Think carefully about how long you can survive and what you can do to stretch that time out. Have a plan for when you need to throw in the towel and go back to being an employee if things don't work out. You can always try again later. Just make sure not to jeopardize your whole future by taking out massive credit card debt, mortgaging your house, or borrowing money from friends and family.

Also, perhaps it helps to know you're not alone. The first two times I tried to make it on my own, I didn't do things the smart way and I had to go crawling back to regular employment.

Preparing to work for yourself

Working for yourself is harder than you thought—probably much harder. We've already talked about how it's important to start your new business as a side business before quitting your job, so that you aren't strapped financially, but perhaps a more important reason for doing this is to prepare you for what it's like to work for yourself.

When you're commuting to the office every day and spending your hours making someone else rich, it can seem like working for yourself would be a much easier and pleasurable way to spend your time. Now, while working for yourself is rewarding, it's also a lot of work, especially when you're just getting started.

The trouble with working for yourself is that you can't really get an idea of how much work it's going to be until you've already quit your job, and by that point it's too late. That's why I strongly recommend starting up your new venture on the side and making it successful before you dive into it fulltime. Working at your new venture on the side will give you an idea of the kind of hours you'll have to pull working for yourself. Many aspiring entrepreneurs have no idea how difficult it can be to run a business and how much extra work is involved to deal with all the overhead and nondevelopment aspects of running your operation.

By starting your business on the side while you still have your fulltime job, you'll get an idea of what it feels like to work longer days and to run the new venture. You'll also avoid the risk that causes ulcer-inducing stress and early gray hairs, because your survival won't depend on this thing succeeding. If you fail at your business, you'll still have the income from your job to rely on.

If you're still not convinced, one of the most solid reasons I can give you for doing things this way is that your business—especially your first one—is likely to fail. A majority of new businesses do. It might take you more than a few tries to create a successful business that can sustain you. Would you rather spend years saving up enough money to take one shot at it and hope that it pans out, or have enough runway to give several tries until you finally get something that sticks?

How much do you really work?

I'm going to be completely candid and honest with you here when I tell you that even though I was a great employee for most of the companies I worked at, I didn't work half as hard during the day as I could have.

I'd have never figured this out if I didn't start my own business and start tracking my time. When I first started working for myself, I couldn't believe how much harder it was to get through an 8-hour day. I was working 8- to 10-hour days at my regular job every single week, so why was it suddenly so hard to sit down and work 8 hours when I was working for myself? And why was I getting way less than 8 hours of work done in that time?

I discovered the answer to this question by carefully measuring my time. I set up a mechanism to log and track my hours during the day so that I could see where my time was going. When I did this, I found that I was usually getting only around 4 hours of actual work done during a day. I wouldn't have believed it if someone else had told me—I still could hardly believe it, but the numbers didn't lie. Here I was working harder than ever, but I was producing only half of my potential capacity each day.

I immediately began to wonder how much work I was actually getting done during a day at my regular job, before I quit. I thought back through my typical working day and I tried to figure out how I was spending my time.

I started with eight hours. Then I subtracted from those eight hours about one hour a day for work- and nonwork-related socialization. Generally I found that I'd get pulled into various conversations throughout the day, usually in small chunks, but adding up to an average of one hour a day. Some of this was work-related of course, but I don't consider this to be productive work.

Now I'm left with seven hours. From those seven hours I can subtract another two hours for general overhead related to checking and answering emails, reading bulletins and memos, and attending pointless meetings where real work isn't being done and I don't really need to be there.

Finally, I'll take off one more hour for what I'll call general laziness. We all goof off from time to time and check our Facebook messages, answer personal emails, and so on. There is no sense denying it and it probably adds up to about an hour each day.

So, what does that leave me with? Four hours. Out of an eight-hour day at work, most of us probably only work about four hours. And I'm sure that on some days it's even less. But there's another factor to consider. How hard do we work during those four hours?

I like to think of it this way. Imagine the difference between jogging down the street and running for your life because a man-eating lion is chasing you. That's the difference between the kind of work you do when you're working for someone else and when you're working for yourself. When you're working for yourself, you tend to work much harder, because you only make money when you're working.

Taking that into account, we could probably estimate that, on average, we only work half as hard when working for someone else. What I came to realize was that in a typical day of work at my regular job, I might have been just putting in the equivalent of 2 hours of real, hard, productive work. (And sometimes I stayed late and worked 10 hours to do it.)

What is my point in telling you this? It's two-fold. First, I want you to realize that when you work for yourself, you'll be working much harder than you do working for someone else, even if you technically put in the same amount of time—you need to prepare for this and be used to this kind of workload. While it may be true that you may be

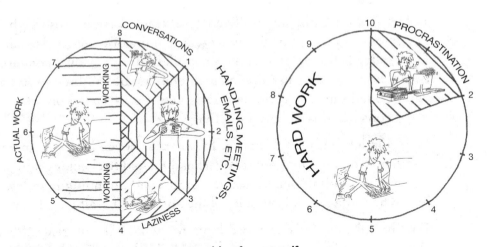

Working for someone else versus working for yourself

more motivated working for yourself because you're passionate about what you are doing, don't count on that passion lasting. Passion tends to fizzle out over time and is somewhat fickle. (For a good book on this subject, check out *So Good They Can't Ignore You* by Cal Newport [Business Plus, 2012].)

Second, it's important to realize that you can't necessarily plan eight hours' worth of work into your working day when you work for yourself. When I first quit my regular job to work fulltime on my side business, I figured I'd be giving myself an extra eight hours a day to get things done. Because I was working three to four hours each evening on my side business while holding down my regular job, I thought I could work just eight hours a day and now get twice as much work done. I was completely wrong and it almost caused me to become discouraged and give up.

Before you quit your job, it's important to have realistic expectations of how much work you actually get done and to train yourself ahead of time to handle a much heavier workload. At your current job, you can start tracking your time during the day and see if you can get to the point of producing six hours of productive work consistently. Also, working on your side job during the evening will prepare you for what it will be like to spend a full eight or more hours working on it each day.

Cutting the cord

Okay, so you've made the decision. You want to be independent. You're tired of working for "the man," but how do you do it? I can't offer you a one-size-fits-all solution, but here's a fictional example of how a software developer might make the transition to self-employment.

Joe has been a software developer for about ten years. He likes his job, but he really wants to become a freelancer and work for himself. He likes the idea of having the flexibility and freedom of choosing his clients and deciding what to work on and when.

Now, Joe has been thinking about making the jump for quite a while. The first thing Joe did was to start cutting his monthly expenses and stashing away cash. Joe wants to have some breathing room when he transitions to self-employment, so he has saved up an entire year's worth of living expenses to cover him at least through the first year.

Joe figures that if he can make half of what he needs to live during the first year of his freelancing, he'll have enough savings to last him two years. That's plenty of time to get his new business going or to realize it isn't going to work out. (Note: Joe didn't save a year's worth of salary, but a year's worth of expenses—what he needs to live, not what he needs to live comfortably. He's willing to make that sacrifice to pursue his dream.)

Joe also started devoting about 15 hours each week to freelancing while he still kept his regular job. He spends about the first 2 hours of each day doing freelance work. He spends 5 hours each week working on getting new business and advertising, and 10 hours doing billable work. Joe made sure to start doing this six months before he planned on quitting his job so that he'd be sure that he'd have some guaranteed income coming in and not feel so much pressure when he quit his job.

Joe calculated the exact day he'd quit in advance and has had it on his calendar for over a year. When that day comes, Joe hands in his two-week notice and begins his dream. He's financially and mentally prepared for the transition.

Landmine: Dangerous employment contracts

I have to caution you that the advice in this chapter might get you into trouble. I've seen some pretty nasty employment contracts that say whatever you're working on belongs to the company you're working for.

Before you start a side project that might eventually become a full-time job for you, make sure you check to see what you agreed to when you took your current position. If the wording of your employment agreement says anything about the company owning what you produced, you might want to check with a legal professional to find out how to properly handle that situation.

Now, I'm not a legal professional, so this isn't legal advice, but I'll give you my opinion on what I think you should do. First, if you have an employment contract that basically states that everything you create belongs to your company whether you do it on your own time or not, I'd suggest either asking to have that clause removed from your contract or finding a new job. I don't believe in slavery, and to me a contract like that is draconian. I can understand a business being concerned about you creating your own company on their time using their resources, but I don't think any employer should restrict what you do in your own time (just my opinion).

If your employment contract has a clause saying that what you create on company time or using company resources belongs to them, things could be a bit more tricky, because they aren't so straightforward. In that case, personally, I'd be pretty upfront about what I was doing, and I'd carefully document the hours I worked on my side project and the resources that were used. If you have a log book that shows that you worked on everything on your own time and you used your own resources, I'd think you'd be in pretty good shape. Still, in this case you want to tread carefully. It couldn't hurt to get a lawyer involved.

The bottom line is if you think you're going to have a problem with your employer, you probably will. You can either choose to keep everything you're doing on the side very secret or make it very transparent—either way has risks of its own. My best overall advice, though, is to carefully document and log the work you spend on your side business so that there's no question about the ownership.

Taking action

- Calculate exactly how much money you'll need to earn each month to live. You might be surprised to find out how high it is right now. If you want to get "free" quicker, you'll need to figure out a way to reduce that amount so that your side business will need to bring in less income.
- Start tracking your time every day at work. Get an idea of how you're spending your time currently each day. Now, figure out how much of that time is actual productive time where you're actually doing real hard productive work—you might be surprised by the results.

12

Freelancing: Going out on your own

One way to get out on your own and start your own business is through freelancing or becoming an independent consultant. A freelancer is someone who doesn't work for a single client, but instead hires out their work to multiple clients either for a fixed price or an hourly rate.

For many software developers the idea of becoming a freelancer is very appealing, but it can be difficult to get started. For much of my career, when I was working as an employee, I dreamed of being a freelancer, but I struggled with not knowing how to make the transition. I knew that many developers were making their living working as freelancers, but I didn't know how they managed to find clients and spread the word about their services.

In this chapter, I'll give you the advice I wish I had when I was first starting out. I'll give you a practical plan you can put into place to become a freelancer or enhance your business if you already are one.

Getting started

If you read the last chapter on quitting your job, you know that I recommend starting a side business before trying to start a new business full-time. This especially applies to freelancing, because it can be very difficult to get started freelancing and get a steady stream of business.

One of the greatest fears of freelance developers is that they will not have work and so they will not get paid. It's very stressful to know that you don't have enough work to fill your time or that after you complete some work for a client you'll have to go out and hunt for more. It's much better to have work lined up ahead of time and to be in a situation where you have to turn work down.

The only way to get to this point is to build up your business over time. You need to have existing long-term clients that you can count on for future business and you need a steady stream of new clients coming in the door. It's pretty difficult to just hang your shingle out one day and expect both of these things to happen. You have to cultivate these two situations over time.

Ask someone you know

How do you get started? How do you actually get your first client? The best way to get a client is through someone you already know. Someone you already know is more likely to trust you, especially starting out. Without quitting your day job, put out messages on your social networks letting your friends and acquaintances know that you're starting a new freelancing business and you're looking for work. Make sure you're specific about what exactly you can do for them and what problems you can solve. (Specialization will help greatly here. Check out chapter 7 for more on that.)

Make a list of all the people you know who would be potentially be interested in your services and email them personally. Tell them exactly what you can do for them and why they should hire you to do the work. The more prospects you have, the more likely you are to get work. Getting work is mostly a numbers game. Don't be afraid to send out follow-up emails every so often to keep letting people know about your services. Over time this diligence will pay off.

Your goal should be to get to a point where you're filling up all of the part-time hours you have allocated to this side business and you actively have to turn people away because you can't take on any more work. If you can't get to this point running your business on the side, you really have no business trying to do it fulltime. It will be much more difficult to fill up 40 hours of work a week than it will be to fill up 10 or 20.

Best way to get clients

You'll probably find that you only have so many friends and acquaintances who need your services—you might even find that you don't have any. But don't worry, there are other ways to get clients rather than just reaching out to people you know.

There are plenty of freelancers who advertise their services on various job boards and even use paid advertising to pick up clients, but I'm going to tell you a much easier way that requires a lot less overhead— the only drawback is that it will require patience and some hard work.

What you really want to focus on is what is called *inbound marketing*. (We'll cover this in much more detail in section 2.) Inbound marketing is basically getting potential clients to come to you instead of you going out to find them. The primary way you do this is by offering something of value for free.

I harp on this quite a bit, but most developers should have a blog. A blog is an excellent way to do inbound marketing, because you can publish articles on your blog that get people to go there and read your content. Once potential clients are on your blog reading your content, you can try to directly convert them to customers by offering your consulting services at the end of your blog post or through some navigation on your site, or you can offer them something else of value in exchange for their email address.

Email marketing is one of the best and most effective ways to market your products or services. Once you have a list of people who are interested in what you have to offer, you can slowly send them more information about you and what you can do for them and eventually convert them to customers.

You can also do inbound marketing by offering free webinars, writing books, speaking at conferences, appearing on podcasts, running your own podcast, and just about anything that is giving someone valuable (and mostly free) content related to the service you're providing.

The only problem with inbound marketing is that it can take some time to start working. You have to have enough content out there to attract

Ideas for inbound marketing

enough potential customers to fill up your pipeline with work. That's a good reason to start now and to not quit your day job just yet. But in the long term, inbound marketing will bring you much more business and make it easier for you to raise your rates—which we'll talk about next.

Setting your rate

Okay, so you've got some clients that are interested in your services, or perhaps you already have been doing some work for clients, but what do you charge them?

This is one of the most difficult problems, besides acquiring clients, that freelancers face. Most freelancers greatly underestimate both the amount they can charge a client and the amount they need to charge a client.

First, let's talk about how much you need to charge a client. Let's say that you're currently working a job where you make $50 per hour. This is a pretty decent wage in the United States, but you can't charge that same amount as a freelancer and have anywhere near the same standard of living. Let me explain.

As an employee you're probably getting some benefits on top of that $50 an hour you're being paid. Perhaps you're getting medical benefits and some vacation time. Plus, in the United States, if you work for yourself, you have to pay what is called self-employment tax—yes, the government charges you extra for creating your own job. (Well, actually that isn't entirely accurate. Right now your employer is paying this tax for you, but that's beside the point.) The $50 an hour you're making might actually really be about $65 an hour after everything is said and done.

Now, let's consider the overhead of running a business. Normally your employer pays for nice things like electricity, computer equipment, internet, etc. But as a freelancer, you'll have to pay for all this stuff yourself. You'll probably also need to hire an accountant or bookkeeper and perhaps have some legal fees and other overhead involved with running a small business. All this can add up, so you'll need to make more money to cover this overhead.

Finally, let's talk about booking. When you're employed by someone else, you usually get paid for 40 hours a week—at least here in the United States. You don't really have to worry about filling up your time, because whether there is work or not, as long as you're at your desk, you'll get a paycheck. Not so for the freelancer. As a freelancer you'll most likely have some downtime each year, perhaps even each week. In addition, you won't be able to bill your clients for things like checking and responding to emails, installing an OS on your computer, or any of those other things you might need to do during the day that aren't directly billable work.

When all is said and done, you might need to make $75–$100 an hour as a freelancer to have the same net pay you would make as an employee. Many freelancers start out charging what they were making as an employee or just slightly higher and find that they are barely getting by—and until they do all those calculations I ran through, they have no idea why.

As a general rule of thumb, you need to bill at about twice the hourly rate you have as a fulltime employee when you're a freelancer (see table 12.1). Unfortunately, though, that's not how you set your rates.

Table 12.1   Employee versus freelancer rates

Paid as employee	Paid as freelancer
$50/hour	$100/hour
- Nothing	- Self-employment tax
	- Utilities and office
	- Accountant and/or bookkeeper
	- Nonbillable time
= $50/hour	= $50/hour

You see, you don't get to arbitrarily throw out a rate based on what you think you need to make and automatically have people pay it. Instead, the rate you can charge is what the market allows you to charge. This is one of the reasons why I stress inbound marketing so much. The bigger your reputation in the industry and the more clients coming to you, the more you can charge for your services.

You still need to know what number you need to charge to be able to make a living, but it's up to you to get to the point where you can justify that number—or a higher one—to the market. You do this by focusing not on the rate itself, but what your work is worth to your clients. You can treat what you do like a commodity or you can treat it as a service that increases the profitability of your clients. If you decide to treat what you do as a commodity, you can go out there and bid with other developers—many with much lower income expectations—for jobs. In that case, the market will push the buyer to accept the freelancer with the lowest rate.

But if you market your services based on what you can save your client or how you can increase their business, you can base your fee on what value your services would bring to the client. This is why it's so important to specialize.

I'll give you an example. I provide consulting services specifically in regards to creating automation test frameworks. When I talk to potential clients about those services, I talk about how much money it costs to build out an automation framework and how expensive it is to make mistakes and have to start over. I talk about how I have experience building many automation frameworks and that I know exactly what to do.

I show the potential client how hiring me for $300 an hour will save them much more money than hiring a regular developer who may have never written an automation framework before. I tell them how 1 hour of my guidance might save them 20 hours of work possibly going in the wrong direction.

I'm not lying, either. I can make the pitch so effectively, because I really believe it's true. The key is that I'm focusing on how my services will easily pay for themselves and more by the value I'm providing. It becomes an easy decision to hire me instead of someone cheaper who just talks about what he or she can do technically.

WHICH DO YOU THINK IS A BETTER PITCH?

"I can design you a new website for your business. I am highly skilled at HTML5, CSS, and web design, and have successfully built many websites for other companies similar to yours."

Or

"Is your current website generating the most traffic it can and converting that traffic to customers? If you're like most small businesses, the answer is 'no.' But don't worry, I can help you by creating a top-notch custom-designed website that's specifically designed to increase your traffic and conversion rates. I've helped many other small businesses double and even triple their customers and I can help you too."

One last piece of advice on setting your rate: if you're never having any potential client tell you "No" or that your rate is too high, raise it. Keep raising your rate until you start getting "Nos." You might be surprised how much a client would be willing to pay for your services. I know some freelancers who have more than doubled their rates by using this technique combined with inbound marketing and structuring their offer in terms of the value they can bring a client.

Taking action

- Make a list of all the people you know who could potentially use your services or may know someone who can.
- Come up with an email template that you can send to everyone from the list you just created. (Remember to talk about what value you can bring, not just what you can do from a technical perspective.)
- Send out a message on your social networks and send your email to a small portion of the list you created and see what kind of response you get. Once you get some feedback, alter your email and send it out again to more people.

13

Creating your first product

As a software developer, you're in a unique position to be able to be an entrepreneur who not only imagines a concept or new idea, but can also create it yourself. Many software developers choose to become entrepreneurs and create because of this reason. Other entrepreneurs have to hire people to create their ideas—and as you know, developing custom software can be expensive.

Not only can you create a software product as a software developer, but you can also create an information product like a book or a video.

In this chapter, I'm going to help you learn what you need to know to create your own first product and start down the long and bumpy road of entrepreneurship. But be warned, the path you're about to embark upon isn't an easy one.

Finding an audience

Many software developers first venturing into the realm of entrepreneurship make the common mistake of building a product before they've found an audience for that product. Although it might seem sensible to start by building a product, you want to avoid falling into this trap; otherwise, you risk creating a solution to a problem that doesn't exist.

Every product created—including this book—solves a particular problem. A product has no purpose without a problem to solve, and a product with no purpose has no customers, which means no money for you. Some products solve very specific problems for a very specific group of people—for example, a software product to help dentists manage their patients or a book to help software developers learn how to use the .NET Unity framework. Other products solve a general problem like boredom. Entertainment products like television shows and video games might fall into this category. But regardless of what problem a product solves, that problem, and the audience that has the problem, must be identified before the product is created.

If you want to create a product, the first step should be to identify a specific audience that you want to target a solution for. You might have a general idea of what the problem you want to solve for that audience is, but in many cases it will take some research to find a common problem that's either not being solved or isn't being solved very well.

Go where your audience goes and interact with the communities your audience participates in to get an idea of what kind of problems are common. What are the pain points that you're seeing over and over?

Products need customers

I started to notice a trend of software developers asking me how to build a reputation in the industry and how to get their name out there or get noticed. Many developers that were visiting my blog were asking me questions related to these topics. I could see that there was a real problem that software developers had with learning to market themselves. (In my case, my audience was coming to me through my blog and directly telling me their problems, so it made things easier—again, another reason to have a blog.)

I decided to create a product to solve that problem. I created a program called "How to Market Yourself as a Software Developer" (http://devcareerboost.com/m). The product solves a very specific problem that my target audience had, so I knew it would be successful before I even invested the time to create it. (I also had another method of verifying its success ahead of time, but we'll get to that in a minute.)

Many developers start backwards and create a product that doesn't yet have an audience and then they try to shop the product around to find an audience. When you do things that way, you're taking a big risk, because it's much more difficult to start with the answer and look for the question.

When I created "How to Market Yourself as a Software Developer," my audience came to me beforehand and told me what their problems were. This is an excellent way to get started that makes selling your product easier later on. Instead of trying to find an audience, build one. We'll get more into marketing yourself in section 2, but if you use the techniques in that section to get your name out there and create an audience centered around you and the content you produce, you'll find that you'll already have customers eager to buy whatever product you create.

Many famous celebrities use this technique to create and sell products. They already have an audience that they've built up. They know the needs and problems of that audience. When they launch a product into that audience it's automatically successful. Take someone like Glen Beck, for example. Political views aside, this guy can sell *New York Times* best-selling books, just because of his audience. He doesn't have to go and find an audience, because he created one. Just about everything he produces will automatically have buyers eagerly waiting to buy it up.

If you want to achieve the same kind of success with your products (although, perhaps, not nearly on that scale), build a successful blog first and use other media like podcasts, speaking engagements, video, and more to build an audience. Then, once you have an audience, you'll be able to sell products to that audience. You may have even bought this book because you were already a follower of my blog, or came across it because you were following some other work I did, or had heard about me on a podcast. That's the power of building your own audience.

Testing the market

Once you've determined the audience for your product and how it's going to solve a problem they have, there's still one more step you should take before you build a product. You should verify the product by testing the market and seeing if your potential customers are actually willing to pay for it.

Remember I said that I had another method of verifying my success for my "How to Market Yourself as a Software Developer" product before I actually created it? Well, here's a little secret: I got people to pay for it before I even started to work on it.

How did I do this, you might ask? Well, to put it simply: I just asked them to. When I was thinking about creating my product, I decided that before investing several months in doing the work involved, I'd say what the product I was going to create was and offer it at a big discount to my target audience if they would pay me for it before I created it. It seems a little crazy—and to some degree it was—but it was a good way to prove whether or not someone would actually pay for what I was planning to produce before I spent all the time producing it. I knew that if I could get developers to give me their money three months or more before it was released, then when it actually was released, selling it would be no problem.

So here's what you can do: set up a simple sales page where you talk about the product you're creating and what problem it's going to solve. Talk about what will be in the product and when you'll actually produce it. And give a discounted price so that someone who is interested can preorder the product and get it as soon as it's released. Offer a money-back guarantee so that potential customers know that if you don't deliver on the product or they aren't happy with it, they can get their money back.

But what will happen if you only sell a few preorders? Well, at that point you can decide if you want to change the product or the offering, because you aren't solving the right problem, or you could simply refund the money back to the few people who bought and apologize, telling them there wasn't enough interest. Not a fun thing to do, but much better than spending three months or more building a product only to find out no one wants to buy it.

For my product, it turned out that on the first day I put the pre-sales page up, I sold seven copies of the program. This gave me enough confidence to know that I could move forward and that I wouldn't be wasting my time. I also had a group of very interested customers who I could ask for feedback to help improve the product as I was building it.

Start small

I keep harping on you about not just quitting your job and jumping into an entrepreneurial pursuit, but I'm going to harp on you one more time when I tell you to start small. Too many budding entrepreneurs pick a much too aggressive target for their first product and leave everything behind to pursue their new dream.

You have to understand and realize that your first entrepreneurial pursuit will probably fail. And likely your second will, and perhaps your third. You might not actually see real success until you've gone through quite a few failures. If you throw everything you've got into one big undertaking, betting your entire future on its success, you might end up putting yourself in a position where you don't have the resources— or even the will—to try again. Don't do that. Start small instead and work on your first product on the side.

You want to make the learning curve as short as possible, so you need to reduce the cycle time between when you take actions and see the results. The problem with a large product is that you may not see the actual results until you're very far along and have spent considerable effort building that product.

Getting started

Perhaps everything in this chapter sounds great, but you have no idea how to get started. Don't worry; I was in the same boat when I created my first product. I was clueless about how to find out what kind of product I could create and how I could sell it.

I'm not going to lie and tell you that it's easy. There is quite a bit to learn, but it's easy to get started. Today, it's easier than ever to sell something online and there are a ton of resources to help you do it.

I'd start out by reading a few books on the subject. You might want to check out Ramit Sethi's blog at http://www.iwillteachyoutoberich.com/, because he's an expert on the topic and has helped many want-to-be-entrepreneurs become successful.

I'd also recommend checking out the book *The Lean Startup* by Eric Ries (Crown Business, 2011) to get some ideas of small businesses you could create and how to get started with them.

But a good amount of your education is going to come through trying and failing. To some degree, you have to do what you think is right, find out why it didn't work, and then try something different. Most entrepreneurs who create successful products do exactly that.

Taking action

- Come up with some target audiences you could investigate to create a potential product for.
- Pick one of these audiences and find out where members of that audience congregate, online or otherwise. Join some of their communities and listen to their problems. See if you can pick out one or two potential areas for a product that can solve a pain they have.
- Check who else may already be solving this problem. You don't want to enter a market with too much competition.

14

Do you want to start a startup?

One of the most appealing dreams of many software developers is to start their very own startup. A startup has a huge potential for reward, but is also extremely risky. I know many software developers who've devoted years of their lives to creating a startup, only to eventually fail and be worse off than when they started.

But if you've got a good idea—and perhaps, more importantly, the passion and drive to follow through with it—you might find it's worth the risk of starting your own company from the ground up.

In this chapter, we'll explore what exactly startups are, how you can get started with one, and some of the potential risks and rewards involved in becoming a founder (the name given to someone who creates a startup company).

Startup basics

A startup is a new company that's trying to find a successful business model it can use to scale and eventually become a medium-size or large, profitable company. If you start a company today, it will essentially be a startup.

Now, even though technically any new company could be considered a startup, there are generally two kinds of startup companies. First are the startups that are created with the intent of getting investments from outside investors to help them grow quickly. These startups are probably the most common kind of startups that you hear about. Many large, successful technology companies started out as startups that took money from investors to grow and become successful. Most of the terminology and discussion related to startups refers to these kinds of companies.

The other category of startups is bootstrapped startups. A bootstrapped startup is completely funded by its founders. If you're creating a bootstrapped startup, you aren't going out to try to raise money from investors and you might not care about getting so big. These companies usually end up being smaller than the startups that take funders, but they're also less likely to fail—because they usually have much less overhead—and the founders have much more control over the business, because they haven't given away large portions of the company.

Because there are already chapters in this book that talk about starting your own bootstrapped business, here we're mostly going to talk about startups that have the goal of acquiring outside investments to grow. From here on out, when I say startup, I'll be referring to a startup that intends to get outside investment.

Go big or go home

The goal of most startups is to make it big. The whole reason for taking outside investments is to be able to scale and grow rapidly. Most founders of startups have what is called an exit strategy. The typical exit strategy might be to grow to a certain size and then hopefully become acquired, resulting in a nice big payday for the founders and investors and a complete reduction of risk of the future of the company.

It's really important to think about the future when starting a startup. You might intend to create a company that you're going to stick with for the long haul, but you have to realize that most investors who invest in your startup are going to want to eventually cash out and see a return on their investment.

Getting acquired isn't the only way to get a nice return, though. Another common exit strategy is to go public. When a company goes public, it sells shares that represent the equity in the company to the public. The sales of those shares can result in a pretty big payday for founders and investors alike.

Regardless of what your overall exit strategy is, it's important to understand that startups that take outside investments generally have the goal of a big payday somewhere down the road. Typically, you aren't going to create one of these kinds of startups and be very conservative. Startups usually swing for the fences.

As you can imagine, this kind of mentality has a potential for some huge rewards, but along with it there are some huge risks. Most startups fail. Some estimates show that as many as 75% of startups that have gotten outside investments end up failing (http://simpleprogrammer.com/ss-startupsfail). I don't know about you, but to me that's pretty scary. Before you start a startup, you really need to think about dedicating years of your life and working insane hours, only to eventually close the doors with nothing to show for all your hard work except some hard-earned experience.

A typical startup lifecycle

There is a whole subculture dedicated to startups and plenty of books have been written on how they function, so there's a lot more to cover than I possibly can in this short chapter. But in this section, I'll try to give you my best overview of how a typical startup works, step by step.

Typically, when you set out to create a startup, you have an idea for a company you want to create. Usually that company is based on some kind of unique intellectual property that's going to make it very difficult for a bigger competitor to come in and simply do what you're doing. A good candidate for a startup would be a new technology or way of doing something that can be patented or protected in some way. A bad candidate for a startup might be a restaurant or other service that isn't unique in a way that can't be copied. A good startup also has the potential to scale very big. Think Twitter, Dropbox, Facebook, and so on.

Once you have an idea, you'll have to decide if you want to be a solo founder or if you want to take on a cofounder. There are some advantages and disadvantages to each, but in general, most startups have at least two cofounders. If you want to get into a startup accelerator or incubator—which we'll talk about next—you probably want to have at least one cofounder.

Accelerators

One good way to obtain some extra help getting started with a startup is to apply for a startup accelerator program. Accelerators are programs that help a startup get started and give them a small amount of funding in exchange for some equity in the company. You can find a big list of accelerators at http://www.f6s.com/accelerators. One of the most popular startup accelerator programs is Y Combinator (http://www.ycombinator.com/). Y Combinator has helped many famous startups like Dropbox get started.

There's usually a pretty lengthy application process to get into an accelerator, but it can be well worth the effort. An accelerator program is an intensive program that usually lasts a few months and helps get a startup off the ground. Most accelerators are run by successful entrepreneurs who've already created a startup or two of their own and can offer excellent advice and mentorship to a startup just starting out. Accelerators usually also help startups prepare for pitching their ideas to investors to get funding and often arrange a demo day for startups in their program. During a demo day, startups are given a chance to pitch to a room of potential investors.

Personally, I wouldn't start a startup today without getting accepted into an accelerator program. The competition is just too fierce, and the advantage of being in an accelerator program is just too great to try to make it completely on your own. I actually was a cofounder of a startup that was accepted into a couple of accelerator programs, but after some careful deliberation, I decided to bow out of the company, because I decided I wasn't at a point in my life where I wanted to go through the rigorous startup lifestyle.

Getting funded

Whether or not you get into an accelerator program, the first major milestone for a startup—arguably the one that decides whether the startup actually even has a breath of life in it—is when it gets its first round of funding. The first round of funding is usually called seed funding, and typically angel investors will invest in these very early startups. Angel investors are usually individual investors who invest in very early startups. It's a very risky investment, but it can carry a high reward. Now, angel investors won't just invest in your company for nothing; they're going to usually expect some percentage of equity in the company.

Landmine: How do I deal with equity?

You'll want to be very careful with giving away equity in your new company. Equity is the lifeblood of your startup. Without equity, you don't have the potential for a reward for all your hard work and you also don't have anything to offer investors. Be careful with how much equity you give away and to whom you give it.

Many startup founders have found themselves in the horrible position of giving away equity to a dead-beat cofounder who ends up not contributing to the company, but instead becomes a permanent drain on the company as a freeloader who eats up valuable equity.

Just make sure you make equity decisions very carefully and realize what it is you're giving away when you give away the equity in your company. Giving away equity is un-avoidable—you're going to have to give away at least some equity—but make sure you carefully think about it before you do it.

Once a startup has some seed money, it's time to get started. Actually, you should have gotten started before then, but once you have some seed money, you can probably hire some employees and start scaling things up. It's expected that most startups aren't going to be profitable at this state. In fact, it's likely that you're going to get pretty deep into the hole as you burn up the initial seed money building out your business model and proving it.

Once you run out of seed money, if the idea is still viable, it will be time to get some serious investments. The first round of investment after the seed round is typically called series A. In this round, venture capitalists usually get involved. When you hear about pitching to "VCs," it means to pitch your company to venture capitalists hoping to get a large investment from them so that you can grow. VCs usually contribute a large amount of capital to a startup in exchange for a large amount of equity. Don't be surprised if after a series A round of funding, a venture capitalist owns more of your company than you do—especially if you have more than one cofounder.

After the series A is complete, most startups go through several other rounds of funding as they exhaust the initial funding and struggle to get to profitability and scale. You basically continue this cycle of getting more funding until you can't get any more funding, become successful and profitable, or get acquired.

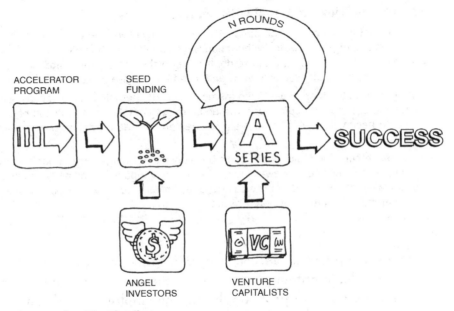

Stages of getting funding

This is, of course, a simplification of the whole process, but hopefully this chapter has given you a good idea of what the process of creating a startup is like.

Taking action

- Look up the history of one or two of your favorite startups. Pay attention to how they got started and how they got funded.
- Did they have a single founder or multiple founders?
- Had the founders successfully founded other companies?
- When did the company get funding? How much finding did they get?
- Did the startup go through an accelerator program?

15

Working remotely survival strategies

Today more and more software development teams are allowing their developers to work remotely from their own homes. Some teams are even completely virtual and don't actually have an office. If you decide to become an independent consultant or entrepreneur, you'll likely find yourself in the situation of working alone at home.

Although working remotely may seem like a fantasy come true, the reality of working in your PJs might not be quite as appealing as you had imagined. There are many struggles and challenges that the at-home worker must face. In this chapter, you'll get a better idea of what it's like to work from home and how to deal with problems like isolation, loneliness, and self-motivation.

The challenges of being a hermit

When I got my first work-from-home job I was thrilled. I couldn't imagine a better way to work than rolling out of bed in the morning, strolling across the hall, and sitting down in my own nice, comfortable chair. Although I still think working from home is great, I soon found there were also many challenges that I hadn't anticipated.

Challenge 1: Time management

First, we'll deal with the most obvious: time management. When you work from home, there are all manners of distractions that don't exist in an office environment. If you decide to click over to your Facebook window and hang out on Facebook all day long, no one is looking over your shoulder to notice. The mailman comes to the door to deliver a package, and you think "Hmm, maybe I should get a snack." Your kids or spouse come in to ask you a question or steal you for "just a minute." Before you know it, your whole day can be gone without anything to show for it.

Many work-from-home newbies think they will deal with this problem by working odd hours and getting work done when they can. They figure they can enjoy the nice day and get work done later that evening. This kind of thinking is a recipe for disaster, because when evening comes, there is always a new set of distractions or you end up too tired to sit in front of a computer.

The real solution to this problem is careful time management. You can work whatever hours you'd like to work, but set a schedule for each week and stick to it. The more regular and routine the schedule, the better. My wife and friends often joke with me about why I work a typical 9-to-5 schedule when I work from home and for myself, but that schedule is exactly what ensures that I'm not distracted and take my work seriously. We can't trust ourselves to try not to be distracted or to manage our time wisely; we have to plan it in advance, or we'll succumb to temptation repeatedly—trust me, I know. I have a whole string of failed attempts behind me.

Challenge 2: Self-motivation

I'm just going to say this now to get it out of the way. If you struggle with discipline and self-control, you probably should reconsider working from home. Next to time management, self-motivation is probably the single biggest "killer" of stay-at-home workers. It's closely related to time management, but even if you can manage your time effectively, sooner or later, you won't feel like doing any work.

When you get into this mood at an office job, you're immediately cured of it by the imminent threat of being fired. If your boss sees you lying down at your desk fast asleep or playing games on your phone when you're supposed to be working, you'll probably be handed a cardboard box and walked right out the door. But when you're working from home, there are no prying eyes to see what you're doing. You alone are accountable for your own motivation and the discipline required to keep on working when all your motivation is gone. (For a better understanding of motivation, check out *Drive* by Daniel Pink [Riverhead Hardcover, 2009].)

Like I said before, if you lack self-discipline, I really think it's a lost cause. I could teach you all the tricks to motivate yourself, but the temptation of turning on the TV, playing a videogame, or browsing Facebook all day is just going to be too great. On the other hand, if you do have some self-discipline to draw on, read on. It's possible to deal with self-motivation problems if you're willing to put the work in to do it.

Schedule and routine is very important to rely on for those times when you aren't feeling all that motivated. We've already covered that, so I won't go over it again, but make sure you do set up some sort of a schedule or routine. When you don't feel like doing work, having a time-boxed period for when you need to work can help you stay motivated enough to get it done and get it over with. The same goes for routine. If you can, develop a routine. Habit can help carry you through motivation dips. There are many times I feel too tired to brush my teeth in the evening, but habit compels me to do it anyway.

You should also remove as many distractions and temptations as possible away from your working environment. If the TV is right there next to you, the temptation to turn it on when you get bored is just too great. Never rely on your own willpower to overcome temptation—this lesson will serve you well in many areas of life. Instead, remove temptations and you'll have a much easier life. (We'll definitely talk more about this in section 6: "Fitness.")

And when you're feeling absolutely unmotivated, one very simple solution that I employ all the time—in fact, don't tell anyone, but I'm employing it right now—is to sit down, set a timer for 15 minutes, and start working. During that 15-minute timer, you have to work. You can't allow yourself to become distracted; you must focus on the task at hand. After 15 minutes of clear, focused work, you'll probably find it's much easier to keep moving forward. It turns out that once we give our undivided attention to something for that long, we end up getting drawn into what we're doing and we have some motivation to continue. I call this momentum.

Challenge 3: Loneliness

At first, working from home can seem like a relief. No one to bother you. You can just sit down and do your work. It's actually very true, too. When I first started working from home, it became very apparent to me how much of my day in the office was actually wasted by idle conversation. When I started working from home—once I learned to focus—I was able to get much more work done in a shorter period of time.

But after a while, that peace and quiet can become a bit unnerving. You may find yourself peering out the window looking for any signs of life. "Oh look, a person walking a dog. Maybe I should run outside and talk to her." (Don't forget to put on your pants first…not that I'm talking from personal experience.) Okay, so maybe I'm being a little dramatic here, but sitting at your desk alone all day, week after week, can eventually start to take a toll on you.

Most software developers who work from home never anticipate that they'll actually become lonely from the lack of social interaction—after all, as a group we can tend to be kind of reclusive. But just trust me on this one: after about a year or so, if you haven't figured out a way to get some kind of social interaction in your life, you're probably going to feel like you're going nuts.

Think about one of the worst ways rowdy prisoners are punished in prison. They put them in isolation. A day or two "in the hole" is a pretty bad punishment for anyone, because as human beings we are social creatures.

So how can you cure this? I've got a simple answer here—get out! Make sure you're setting up activities in the week that will take you out of the house and give you opportunities to see other human beings. Your spouse and kids don't count. Try joining a local software developer group that meets on a weekly or monthly basis. For a change of scene, head to a coffee shop or café. I go to the gym three times a week, and I'd of course recommend something like that as well. I also find that going to conferences and other networking events gives me a chance to unleash my geek talk to willing recipients. Sometimes it's pent up for months at a time.

You can also utilize some resource to help you feel a little less detached. Skype calls or Google Hangouts can give you a chance to talk to and even see your coworkers.

If you can overcome these three challenges, you'll be a successful remote worker, but if you can't, you might consider whether working from home is the thing for you. Some remote workers who just can't deal with these issues have found a solution by utilizing what are called coworking spaces. You can think of these spaces as small offices formed of remote workers and entrepreneurs. It's sort of like working in a regular office environment, only your coworkers don't actually work with you.

Landmine: I want to work remotely, but I can't find a remote job

For a long time I tried to find a job that would let me work from home, but I couldn't find one. They aren't all that easy to come by and there's often fierce competition. If you're looking for a remote job but you can't find one, there are two things I'd recommend:

1   You might want to see if you can work remotely from your current job. Perhaps start out on a trial basis. You might ask to work one or two days a week from home. Have a good argument for it, like that you can get more work done and focus. If you're given the chance, really show extra productivity when you're working from home.

2   You can start tracking companies that allow remote work or have completely distributed teams and start making connections with those companies. It may take some time, but if you're focusing on specific companies that you know allow remote work, you can increase your chances of getting a job at one of these companies. Get to know the developers who work there already, speak to the hiring managers, express your interest in the company, and when a job opening comes up, apply for it.

Taking action

- Take an honest self-assessment. After learning about these three challenges, how do you think you'd deal with time management, self-motivation, and loneliness?
- If you're working from home or planning on working from home, come up with a schedule that you'll stick to each week. Decide what your working hours will be and what days you'll work.

16

Fake it till you make it

In your career as a software developer, you're bound to come across many situations that you aren't qualified to handle. We all often find ourselves presented with challenges and obstacles we aren't prepared for. What you do at those times, though, will be the primary factor in determining your success.

Many people, when faced with adversity, will choose to hightail it and head for the hills. But other people, when faced with the same challenge, will rise up to face it head on. Do all the people who choose to stay and fight have confidence in their ability to succeed and overcome? No, but many of them do have one thing in common, though—they're able to fake it till they make it.

What it means to fake it until you make it

The phrase "Fake it till you make it" is pretty common, but it's also a fairly overused phrase. Different people will have different interpretations for what exactly it means. So, it's important to clarify how I'm using this phrase in this chapter.

When I say "Fake it till you make it," I'm not suggesting that you lie and pretend to have some knowledge or ability that you don't currently possess. Instead, I'm suggesting that you should act as if you've already succeeded at accomplishing a task or feat before you even begin it. When I say "Fake it till you make it," I'm talking about acting "as if:"

- As if you already possess the skills and talent you need to succeed
- As if you're already the kind of person you want to be

- As if the battle is already over and you have emerged victorious, because you know deep down that if you keep trying, you'll eventually prevail

- As if the unknown road you're about to embark upon has already been traversed by you many times before

When you act in this manner—and the key word is "act"—you eventually bend reality to conform with the image you're presenting. It might seem like magic and transcendental nonsense, but the truth is that our minds are very powerful. In section 7, we'll dive much deeper into the power of the mind to control and shape your reality, but for now, it's enough to know that if you act as if something were already true, and you can convince your mind of the same, it will take a great force to prevent that reality from actually coming into being.

Faking it till you make it is all about putting on such a great act that you convince your own mind and body to make that act a reality. Faking it till you make it is the opposite of being unconfident. It's acting with confidence in all that you undertake, even when you're in way over your head, because you have a supreme belief in yourself to overcome all obstacles.

Putting it into practice

Faking it till you make it is all about purposely putting yourself in situations that are over your head and forcing yourself to learn how to swim. It really is a mindset you carry forward with you in life that propels you into the unknown, confident that new challenges will bring new opportunities. If you want to learn how to fake it till you make it, you have to be willing to jump into the deep end.

Have you ever been in a situation where you felt like you didn't know what you were doing? A situation that made you feel very uncomfortable, perhaps a bit embarrassed, and maybe even a little incompetent? How did you react in that situation? Did you try to figure out how you could get out of it? Did you make excuses for why you might fail or not perform well?

It's natural to react to an uncomfortable situation or obstacle with fear, embarrassment, and excuse-making, but if you can overcome those tendencies and see the truth that the new or challenging situation you're currently in will someday become the regular and routine, you are well on your way to learning how to fake it till you make it.

Remember the first time you tried to write some code or learn a programming language? It was hard, wasn't it? Perhaps it may still be hard for you. But wherever you are now, you can always look back to a time when anything you consider easy was difficult and might have even seemed impossible to you. The key is to be able to see ahead to how easy some task or situation will be in the future and act now as if it were then.

One common place where this applies to software developers is in the job interview. It's almost impossible to be an expert at all of the technologies any particular job requires. There are just too many different technologies out there for you to be a master of all of them, so most job interviews you go into will be for jobs where some of the skills that you'll need to do the job aren't yet in your possession.

They key phrase in that sentence is "aren't yet." Many developers go into a job interview with an apologetic and nervous demeanor that projects a lack of confidence, because they have some doubts about their own ability to do a job dealing with some technologies they haven't yet mastered or encountered. Their vision is short-sighted, because they're looking at things from the perspective of now. Now is fleeting. Look at it and it's already gone. It's much better to have your eyes set on the future.

Sure, it may be true that at the precise moment when you're interviewing for a job you may not possess all the skills required to be excellent at that job. But unless you're a seasonal worker, an employer isn't hiring you for the short term. Just about every other developer interviewing for the job is also going to lack skills or experience in a certain area—perhaps ones different than yours. For that reason, it's better to project an aura of confidence and capability, knowing that you've faced challenges in the past, you rose up to meet them, and there's no reason to believe you won't do the same in the future.

Don't confuse this with lying, though. I'm not suggesting you misrepresent your skills to a prospective employer and claim competency where there is none. Instead, I'm suggesting that you be perfectly open and honest about your ability or lack thereof, but at the same time carry forward the attitude and posture of someone who has already overcome the obstacles that are before you, because you know that the only thing that stands between the present you and the future you is time.

Your confidence—careful here, not arrogance—will be contagious. When you carry around this "can-do" attitude, when you have a true belief in yourself that isn't inflated or exaggerated, but based on knowing that you eventually will succeed at anything you set your mind to, you'll find that others will believe this too. Walk into an interview with this attitude and you'll understand the power of faking it till you make it.

Taking action

- Honest assessment time. What is your attitude in difficult situations? How do you deal with encountering the new and unfamiliar? Think about the last time you were in a difficult or unfamiliar situation and how you reacted.
- How can you create a more confident attitude without appearing arrogant? What is the difference? What steps can you take right now to improve your ability to fake it till you make it?

Bonus: Practice your strategy by going out and purposely putting yourself into a situation that is "over your head."

17

Resumes are BORING— Let's fix that

Have you ever gone on a vacation and seen those racks that are filled with dozens of colored brochures about all the local attractions in the area? Ever picked up one of those brochures and looked at it? Most of them are full color, three-page, beautifully designed works of art. I'm not kidding. You can tell that quite a bit of work went into designing that pamphlet to convince you to spend $100 to go parasailing or rent a ski jet.

Now, contrast that with the average developer's resume: a single-font, double-spaced, five-page monstrosity, complete with grammatical errors, typos, and poorly structured sentences full of phrases like "spearheaded" and "results focused."

Make no mistake about it, both are trying to adver-tise and ultimately get

A typical resume doesn't compare to an advertising brochure.

someone to spend money on something. In one case, the advertisement is trying to get you to spend perhaps $100 on some vacation excursion. In the other case, the advertisement is trying to get a hiring manager to fork over $60,000, $80,000, or more to rent a software developer for a year.

It seems a bit crazy to me that someone trying to sell a $100 item would put so much work and effort into an advertising vehicle, but someone trying to sell a $60,000+ item would produce such a substandard version. Now, don't get me wrong. I'm not saying your resume is "crap," but chances are, if you're like most software developers, it probably could use a little work.

You aren't a professional resume writer

There's a reason your resume … stinks. It's pretty simple, actually—you aren't a professional resume writer. You don't write resumes for a living. I can just about guarantee you, though, that the guy or gal who created that beautiful brochure trying to convince you to rent a jet ski does create brochures or other advertising material for a living.

And while many career-coaching books and programs will try to tell you how to create a better resume, I'm not going to even bother. Why? Because you shouldn't have to be a professional resume writer. It's a waste of your time and talents. Writing a resume is a skill that you'll only use a handful of times in your career. It makes absolutely no sense for you to invest heavily in that area when there are thousands of professionals who already can do a better job of writing resumes than you could probably ever hope to do.

Think about it this way. The CEO of the company you work for probably doesn't write software. Sure, your CEO could probably sit down at the computer and crank up an IDE and learn how to code to write the software needed to run the company. But it makes a whole lot more sense to hire you to write the software instead. So why would you waste your time learning the skills of a professional resume writer instead of hiring one?

Hiring a resume writer

Hopefully by now I've convinced you that you need to hire a professional to write your resume. But how do you do it?

There are quite a few professional resume writers out there. A quick search on the internet will produce plenty of them, but you do have to be careful in choosing one. Writing a resume for a software developer is a bit more challenging than writing a resume for many other professions, because there are so many buzzwords and technologies related to our work (see table 17.1). (If you're looking for a good one that I'd personally recommend, check out Information Technology Resume-Service [http://simpleprogrammer.com/ss-resumewriter] and don't forget to mention this book.])

Table 17.1   What to look for in a professional resume writer

Familiarity with the tech industry	It does no good to hire a professional resume writer who doesn't know how to sell your development skills.
Has sample resumes to show you	The best way to know what kind of work you're likely to get is to look at the work a resume writer has already produced.

I have to warn you, resume-writing services—at least good ones—aren't cheap, but they're worth paying for, because a good resume can easily pay for itself by helping you land a higher-paying job much faster. Expect to pay somewhere around $300–500 for a quality, professionally written resume. Again, an expensive price, but if you can get a job that just pays 2 to 3% more, you can easily more-than make up for the price within the first year.

Also, before you hire a professional resume writer, make sure you have all the information that person will need to do a good job. Garbage in, garbage out. You don't want to pay someone to write a professional resume that has inaccurate information because you were too lazy to look up the correct dates of your previous employment or you didn't give her an accurate description of your skills and responsibilities. When you hire a professional resume writer, you are primarily hiring them to do two things for you:

- Write good and compelling "copy" to advertise your services and present you in the best light possible.
- Package it in a visually appealing, aesthetically pleasing format.

You aren't hiring them to be a research assistant or to fact-check your information. You need to give them as much information as possible and they'll take that information and condense it into a highly refined format that will effectively market your services.

Landmine: I don't feel right about hiring someone to write my resume

This is the most common objection I get to the advice of hiring someone to write your resume. Many people feel it's somehow "wrong" and deceptive to hire someone to write their resume; they feel that they should write their own resume. I can understand this viewpoint—and you're welcome to write your own resume—but how is hiring someone to write your resume any different than hiring someone to design your website or decorate your house? In fact, many celebrities employ ghost-writers to write books for them, in which they put themselves as the author. My point is that it's not as big of a deal as you might think. Just because you've always thought that developers should write their own resumes, doesn't mean that it's true. You don't have to share that you had a professional resume writer write your resume. And if you really feel uncomfortable about it, write your own resume and hire someone to "improve" it.

Going the extra mile

The title of this chapter indicates that traditional resumes are boring, and that's true. Although a conventional resume is important for any software developer looking to get a better job, it isn't the only way to present the same information to a potential employer.

You can, and should, take the information from your resume and put it online. You should have a LinkedIn profile that has the information from your resume on it, and you should have an online version of your resume so that you can send someone a link to it. Applying for a web developer job without an online version of your resume is sort of like being a professional carpenter who doesn't have their own tools.

Even the format of a resume is subject to revision. Try doing something unique with your resume and present it in a way that really grabs the reader's attention. You can either ask a resume-writing service to create something unique for you, or you can take the resume you get from them and hand it over to a graphic designer to make it really "pop."

I once saw a resume of a videogame programmer who had created an online version of his resume that was an actual playable videogame (http://simpleprogrammer.com/ss-interactiveresume). I'm pretty sure he doesn't have a hard time finding a job. And here's a list of really nice-looking, creative resumes that you can get some inspiration from: http://simpleprogrammer.com/ss-beautiful-resumes.

You don't have to have the fanciest-looking resume, but it's important for a software professional to have a professional-looking resume. If you think that old Word doc resume you wrote ten years ago that's filled with typos and awkward sentences is going to cut it, think again. If you're looking for a new job, one of the best investments you can make is in a professional resume.

What if you don't want to hire a professional?

I can understand if you still would rather create your resume yourself. Perhaps you aren't ready to make the financial investment or you feel like it's something you have to do yourself.

If you do choose to create your own resume, table 17.2 has some tips that you might find helpful.

Table 17.2   Tips for improving your resume

Tip	Benefit
Put your resume online.	Makes it easier for an employer to access your resume and is important if you're applying for a web developer position.
Present your resume in a unique way.	You can grab the attention of someone scanning resumes by making yours stand out from the crowd.
Use action–result language.	Your resume should show what action you did and what result it produced. This will show a perspective employer not only what you can do, but what results you've been able to achieve and how they might likewise benefit from hiring you.
Proofread.	Even if you hire a professional resume writer, make sure your resume is thoroughly proofread. A typo or spelling mistake can make you look careless.

Taking action

- Whether you're looking for a job or not, send a copy of your current resume to some recruiters and ask for their opinion on it. Recruiters see a large number of resumes and often are the best people to tell you if your resume needs work.
- Investigate some professional resume-writing services and look at some samples of the resumes they produce. How do those resumes compare to yours?

18

Don't get religious about technology

I don't know if you're a religious person or not. Regardless of which side you fall on, I'm sure you can agree with me that many of the most bloody and grim wars in history were fought, to some degree, over religion.

I don't say this to knock religion or to in some way suggest that religion itself is inherently good or bad, but to make you acutely aware of the fact that adherence to dogmatic beliefs tends to be quite inflammatory.

The same is true about software development. Religious beliefs about software development and technology tend to be just as inflammatory as religious beliefs about the origin of life or the existence of a supreme deity. Although we typically don't kill people because they prefer iOS over Android, we do have a tendency to batter them around a bit and perhaps give them a quick punch in the stomach when we think no one is looking.

I'm a firm believer that you'll go much further in your career if you can keep yourself from becoming religious about technology. In this chapter, we'll examine why this is the case.

We are all religious about technology

It's true. You might as well admit it. You have some bias toward some technology or programming language that you think is the best—at least, most programmers do. It's completely natural. We're enthusiastic about what we do, and any time there's enthusiasm and passion, there will be highly charged opinions. Just take a look at professional sports.

The problem with being religious about technology is that most of us are religious about a particular technology because that technology is what we know. It's natural to believe that what we've chosen is the best possible choice, so we often feel slighted by any suggestion to the contrary. We can't possibly know enough about all the technologies out there to make the best and most informed decision about which one is best, so we tend to choose what we know and assume it must be the best—life is too difficult to handle otherwise.

But this course of action, although built-in and natural, is also destructive and limiting. When we dogmatically hold onto beliefs that are only based on our own experience, we tend to associate with only the kinds of people who also hold those beliefs and shun all others. We end up segregating ourselves into communities where the same ideas are circulated over and over and over again. We reach a point where we stop growing, because we've already found all the answers.

I spent a good deal of my career being overly religious about operating systems, programming languages, and even text editors before I knew better and started to learn that I didn't have to just choose one technology that was the best and consider all the others inferior.

Everything is good

Not all technologies are great, but most technologies with widespread adoption are at least "good." It's hard for a thing that isn't at least good to become successful and to become widely known or used. Of course, circumstances change over time, but it's important to realize that, at least at some point in history, just about every technology was at one time good or even considered great.

Having this perspective will help you understand that in many cases there isn't just one good or best solution for a problem. There isn't just one good and best programming language, framework, operating system, or, yes...even text editor. You may like a particular technology more than others, and you may find you're even more productive using one programming language over another, but that still doesn't necessarily make it the best.

My conversion

I had a hard time believing this for a long time. I'd spend countless hours arguing why Windows was so much better than Mac. I'd yell and rant about how C# and other statically typed languages were far superior to dynamic languages like Perl or Ruby. I'd even at times—although I'm ashamed to admit it—berate other developers who thought otherwise. How could they dare believe something different about technology than I did?

The eye-opening experience for me was when I was first asked to be a team lead for a Java project. Up until that point, I had been primarily a .NET developer focused on C#. (Well, that's not entirely true. I was pretty religious about C++ until .NET came along.) I couldn't stomach the idea of working with Java. Java was such a dirty language compared to the elegance of C#. How could I possibly enjoy writing Java code when I couldn't even use lambda expressions?

I eventually decided to take the job, because it was just too good of an opportunity and I figured that because it was a contract, I could stomach it for a year or so. Well, it turned out that taking that job was one of the best decisions I made in my career. Working with a technology I hated made me see all technologies in a different light. It turned out Java wasn't so bad at all. I could see why some developers actually preferred it over C#.

I learned more over the few years I worked on that Java project than I had during my entire career up to that point. I suddenly had a huge toolbox full of tools that I could use to attack any problem instead of the few overused tools I had restricted myself to before.

From that point forward I adopted the same kind of open mindset I had given to Java to other programming languages—even dynamic ones—and I was able to use what I was learning from each to become a better programmer at them all. I also backed off of my opinions about operating systems and frameworks, trying out new things before I judged them. I probably wouldn't even be writing this book if I hadn't had this experience—or rather, it might be called *Why C# Is the Best and Everything Else Sucks.*

Don't limit your options

The real point here is to not limit your options. There is no good reason to vehemently insist that your choice of technology is the best at the expense of ignoring or belittling all others. It will only hurt you in the end by deciding to hold onto that viewpoint.

On the other hand, if you're willing to have an open mind about technology and not simply hold onto what you already know, claiming it to be the best, you'll find many more opportunities will open up to you.

Taking action

- Make a list of all your favorite technologies or technologies you feel are superior to others.
- For each item on that list, think about why you're drawn to that technology and what comparison you're using to justify its position. Do you have actual experience using its competitor?
- Pick one technology you hate and find someone who loves it. Ask open and honest questions about why they're excited about that particular technology. For bonus points, try using it yourself.

Section 2

Marketing yourself

Marketing is a contest for people's attention.

—Seth Godin

Marketing gets a bad rap in the software development industry. The world in general frowns on marketers, because so many marketers engage in less than trustworthy practices to make a quick buck. It seems that every day there's a new scam being peddled by unscrupulous marketers who have only their own best interests at heart.

But in reality, marketing itself isn't bad. It's how you do the marketing that determines whether it's for the benefit or detriment of the person being marketed to. Marketing is required to get people's attention, to get them to notice you or your product. Good marketing connects a need or want with a product or service that can fulfill that desire. It seeks to give value first before asking for anything in return.

In section 1 we talked about how you should treat your career as a business, and of course, all businesses need some kind of marketing to be successful. In this section, I'll take you through a crash-course on marketing yourself. You'll learn exactly what marketing is and how to do it in a way that doesn't offend people and "rip them off," but instead offers them real concrete value and keeps them coming back for more.

19

Marketing basics for code monkeys

Have you ever been to a nightclub and heard a cover band play a song that sounded just as good as the original artist—if not better? Have you ever wondered why that cover band is up there playing a gig in a small nightclub while another band that doesn't seem to have any more talent is touring the world and making platinum records?

Obviously both bands are talented, but talent alone will only take you so far in life. The real difference between great musicians and superstars is nothing more than marketing. Marketing is a multiplier for talent. The better marketing you have, the more it magnifies your talent. That's why it's critical for you, as a software developer, to learn this crucial skill.

What marketing yourself means

At its core, marketing is just connecting a product or service with someone who wants or needs that product or service. So marketing yourself is really connecting people who want what you have to offer with you. Even though marketing often has gotten a bad rap, there's nothing wrong with marketing yourself if you're able to do it in the right way.

The right way to market yourself is to provide value to others. We'll talk more about this in chapter 21, but the key to successfully marketing yourself in a way that makes others like you and want to work with you is to do it in a way that provides them value. Consider how well someone like Scott Hanselman does it. Scott provides developers quite a bit of value through his blog (http://www.hanselman.com/), speaking engagements, and podcasts. But before we get into the details, let's talk about what marketing yourself looks like in practice. How can you as a software developer market yourself?

Whether you realize it or not, you're marketing yourself all the time. Anytime you're trying to convince someone of your idea, you're essentially selling it to them, and as we talked about in chapter 17 on people skills, we know that how you package an idea is often more important than the idea itself.

When you apply for a job, your resume is essentially an ad that is marketing your services. Even the things you post on social media or your blog—if you have one—are giving out some kind of marketing message about you and what you have to offer.

The problem is that even though we're all marketing ourselves, most of us aren't doing it at a conscious level. We're leaving things up to chance, letting other people and circumstances define us and our message.

Marketing yourself is all about learning how to control the message you're sending out and the image you're portraying and amplifying the reach of that message. When you're marketing yourself, you're actively managing your career by purposefully choosing how you want to represent yourself and actively promoting that representation to people who are interested in hearing what you have to say, hiring you, or buying a product or service from you.

Think about how the advertising campaign for a new blockbuster movie is orchestrated. There's usually some overarching message that's communicated through all kinds of different advertising mediums. The trailer for the movie paints a specific and clear picture—it has a message. That message is amplified by all the different advertising channels.

Why marketing yourself is important

In the first example in this chapter, I talked about how a cover band might be just as talented as a famous rock band, but there's a great disparity between their overall success levels. I attribute this disparity mainly to marketing. The extremely successful rock band usually does a better job of marketing themselves than the cover band playing random gigs wherever they can.

Now, we can't know for sure that the cover band didn't do a good job of marketing themselves, but if we assume the talent level is pretty close, then aside from plain luck, that's the factor that they have control over. Marketing yourself doesn't guarantee success, but it's a very important element that you can control.

You can find the same type of pattern in many other fields as well. Take professional chefs. There are many chefs who possess a high level of talent and can cook exceptionally well, but most of them are relatively unknown. Yet there are some celebrity chefs like Gordon Ramsay or Rachel Ray who make millions of dollars, not because they're necessarily more talented, but because they've learned how to market themselves correctly to take advantage of their talent.

Don't think the field of software development is any different. You could be the most talented software developer in the world, but if no one knows that you exist, it won't matter much. Sure, you'll always be able to find a job, but you'll never reach your full potential unless you can learn how to market the skills you possess.

At some point in your career, you'll likely find that you've reached a skill level that's on par with many of the top developers. Many software developers can reach this level in their career in about 10 years. Once you reach that point, it can become very difficult to advance, because you're grouped in with the rest of the pack. Your individual talents become much less important, because you're competing against all the other software developers who possess similar skills.

But there is a way to break away from the pack. By learning how to market yourself you can stand out from the crowd, and just like a famous rock star or celebrity chef, earn a much higher income and have many more opportunities than you would otherwise.

Landmine: I'm not an expert at anything; I've got nothing to market

Just because you don't consider yourself an expert doesn't mean you can't start marketing yourself. In fact, trying to figure out how to market yourself can push you in the direction of becoming an expert or specializing in a particular area of software development.

Almost every developer has something to offer. You might have a unique perspective or you might come from a different background than other software developers. Perhaps you have passions or other hobbies that other software developers or clients would relate to. Even being a complete beginner or amateur can be an advantage if you market it well—plenty of people want to learn from someone who's just a few steps ahead of them, because they can relate to that person.

The point is, don't let not being an expert be an excuse for not marketing yourself. No matter where you are in your career, you can benefit from trying to control and shape your brand and from spreading the word about it.

How to market yourself

Hopefully I've already convinced you that marketing yourself is important, but now you may be wondering how you actually do it. How can you become the Gordon Ramsay of software development?

I'm not going to pretend it's easy. Success isn't something that's achieved overnight—at least not long-lasting success. But any developer can do it, and if you're willing to do the work, it can seem easy. I'll briefly mention all of the key concepts here, and in the following chapters we'll go over each one in much more detail.

Marketing yourself begins with developing a personal brand—something that you represent. You can't be all things to everyone, so you have to make conscious decisions about what you want to be and how you want to present that image to the world. You also want to create a sense of familiarity when someone is exposed to you or something you created multiple times. Branding helps you do that.

Once you have a brand of some sort and you know what message you're trying to convey, you need to find a way to convey that message. There are many different mediums you can use to get your message out there, but one of the most prominent ones I recommend for software developers is a blog. I consider a blog to be your home base on the internet. It's the one place where you completely control the message and you aren't at the mercy of someone else's platform or rules.

I adopted a strategy from an entrepreneur I follow and highly respect, Pat Flynn (http://www.smartpassiveincome.com/). Pat has a strategy called the "Be everywhere" strategy. The basic idea of this strategy is to be everywhere you can in the space you're trying to market yourself in. Whenever anyone in your target audience looks around they should have a good chance of seeing you. You might show up on their Twitter feed. They might hear a podcast that you were on. They might see your video online. Everywhere they look, they can't help but run into you. Table 19.1 shows several options for marketing yourself.

Table 19.1   Channels for marketing yourself

Blog posts	Either through your own blog or guest posts on other people's blogs.
Podcasts	Create your own podcast or be interviewed on an existing podcast.
Videos	Create topical videos or screencasts and tutorials on sites like YouTube.
Magazine articles	Write an article for a software development magazine.
Books	Write a book, like this one, or self-publish your own book.
Code camps	Most code camps will allow anyone to speak.
Conferences	A great way to network, and if you can speak at one of these events, even better.

This strategy takes time and consistency to execute. Over time, every blog post you write, every podcast you're interviewed on, and every book or article you produce contribute to your marketing effort and the recognition of your personal brand. You eventually become an authority in your area and build a following. And that reputation translates to bigger and better opportunities and ultimately a more successful career.

I mentioned it before, and we'll talk about it more in depth, but I want to emphasize that this all depends on your ability to bring value to others. The primary mechanism that you'll use to get people to follow you and to want to hear what you have to say will be by bringing value to them—giving them answers to their problems or even entertainment. If you attempt to do constant self-promotion without bringing value to others, you won't get very far, because everyone will just tune you out.

Taking action

- If you don't already have a blog, think about starting one. What kind of topic would you focus on?
- Come up with at least 20 possible blog posts for your new blog.
- Now put a schedule in place to actually get your blog started and create content for it.

20

Building a brand that gets you noticed

Brands are all around us. Everywhere you turn, you see Pepsi, McDonald's, Starbucks, HP, Microsoft...the list goes on and on.

But brands are more than just images. Most people associate brands with a logo. Think of the famous golden arches of McDonald's. But a brand is much more than a logo—it's a promise. A brand sets an expectation that you, as a consumer, expect to have delivered.

In this chapter, we'll talk about what exactly makes up a brand, and I'll show you how you can create your own brand that will help you get noticed in your marketing efforts.

What is a brand?

Think about some of the popular brands that exist today. Let's take Starbucks, for instance. Starbucks is a well-known brand that most people would recognize. At first glance, it might seem that the Starbucks brand is merely the all-too-familiar Starbucks logo, but that couldn't be further from the truth. The Starbucks logo is a visual reminder of the brand, but it isn't the brand itself.

When you walk into a Starbucks, what do you expect to see and hear? How do you expect the lighting to be? What kind of layout and furniture do you expect in the building? You could probably close your eyes right now and imagine what the inside of a Starbucks looks like—what it feels like.

How about when you go to the counter to order a drink? What do you expect the barista to look like? How do you expect the barista to address you and what questions do you expect them to ask you? Are you familiar with the menu? Do you have an expectation of what the prices will be and the quality level of the beverage?

You see, a brand is more than just a logo. A brand is a set of expectations about a product or service. A logo is just a visual reminder of a brand. The key to the brand isn't just the visual element, but what that brand makes you feel and what you expect when you interact with that brand. A brand is a promise: a promise to deliver some sort of value that you expect in the way that you expect it.

What makes up a brand?

You need four things to have a brand: a message, visuals, consistency, and repeated exposure. All of these four components are required to create a successful brand. Let's go over each one of them so you can see how you can create your own personal brand using these concepts.

First, and most importantly, is the message. A brand without a message doesn't have a purpose. A message is what you're trying to convey and the feelings you're trying to invoke with your brand. When you create

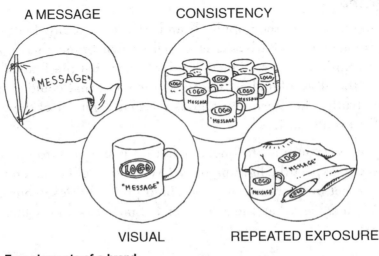

Four elements of a brand

your own personal branding, you need to have a central message that represents your brand. What is it that your brand is about? What are you about? For example, my branding of Simple Programmer is based around the message of making the complex simple. My message is that I take complex concepts, break them down, and make them simple so that anyone can understand them.

Second, you need visuals. While visuals aren't the brand itself, they're important to a brand. Obviously, a brand should have a logo, because it's a simple visual representation of that brand, but a good brand will use visuals everywhere it can. A set of colors and a style that represents that brand help to make a brand recognizable and promote the message that represents it.

Even if your brand is your own name, you can create a logo out of it. A great example of this is from my friend John Papa. If you go to his blog at http://johnpapa.net, you'll see that he has a logo that has been created from his name.

Next, there's consistency. You can have a great message and visuals, but if you don't have consistency, you'll never develop an expectation about your brand—or worse yet, you'll constantly betray it. Imagine what would happen if you went into McDonald's and every location had a different menu and different prices. A large amount of the value of the McDonald's brand would be lost. When you go to McDonald's, you have certain expectations about what your experience will be like. If that experience is constantly changing, if it isn't consistent, the brand starts to become meaningless.

Many developers trying to create their own personal brand make the mistake of not being consistent. They either aren't consistent in the message they're presenting or they lack consistency in how or when they deliver that message. The more consistent you can be, the more successful your personal brand will be at getting your laser-focused message across to as many people as possible and the more likely they will be to remember it.

This brings us to the final component of a brand: repeated exposure. If you do everything else correctly, but someone is only exposed to your brand once, it won't do you much good. Your logo might look nice and it might be eye-catching, but if someone only sees it once, what good did it do you? The whole point of a brand is to establish a set of expectations so that when someone sees your logo again or hears your name, they can instantly remember who you are and what you represent.

You have to actively work to spread the word and get your name out there as much as possible. You do this by blogging, writing articles, speaking, creating videos, podcasting, or using any other medium you can to get your name out there. The more you're able to get your brand out there and the more exposure you get for it, the more likely someone will be to remember it and to remember who you are.

Creating your own brand

When you set out to create your own personal brand, your first step should be to define your message. To define your message, you'll need to decide what you want to represent. You can't be all things to all people, so you need to narrow down your audience and pick a niche. This is pretty much the same concept we talked about in chapter 7 when we discussed specialization. Basically, you need to pick some smaller market that you're going to target or some unique spin you're going to apply to your brand.

One of my favorite examples of a software developer doing this correctly is Marcie Robillard, a.k.a. the DataGrid Girl. Marcie chose to make her niche the ASP.NET Datagrid control and to brand herself as the DataGrid Girl. This is a very narrow and focused niche and it worked very well for her. She got numerous speaking engagements, was on popular podcasts like .NET Rocks, and, I'm sure, enjoyed a massive amount of search traffic around the topic of ASP.NET Datagrids.

Pick some kind of niche and build your brand around it—the more specific the better. You'll be able to speak directly to your audience and you'll have a much easier time building up brand recognition if you can be narrowly focused.

Deciding on a niche isn't always easy. You can choose based on what you're passionate about, but that may change over time. Often, the best way to make the decision is from a purely strategic perspective. What advantage do you have that you can exploit through a specific niche? Take some time and think about this. Don't be afraid to change your niche later if you have to.

STEPS FOR CREATING A BRAND
- Define your message.
- Pick your niche.
- Create a tagline.
- Create an elevator pitch.
- Create visuals.

Once you have your niche figured out, it's time to work on your message. You should start with a tagline that represents your brand in just a single sentence or two. For example, my tagline is "Making the complex simple." Someone can quickly figure out what I'm about by reading my tagline.

Next, you should put together what's known as an elevator pitch. An elevator pitch is a quick description of what you do and what you are about that could be delivered in the time it takes to ride an elevator. Think about it as what you would tell someone when they ask what you do at a dinner party or actually during a ride on an elevator.

To create your elevator pitch, think about what exactly is the value you provide. What is it that uniquely defines you? What can someone expect of you? In your elevator pitch you want to clearly communicate what it is that you do and the unique value you bring.

Having this elevator pitch thought out ahead of time will ensure that you're consistent with your branding efforts and that you always convey the same message when you talk to people about your brand or you represent your brand in whatever medium you're using to promote it.

Only after you've figured out the core of your brand is it time to create visuals for the brand. The visuals you create should represent everything about the brand that you've defined so far. They should help to convey the message and serve as a visual reminder of what your brand represents.

You don't have to spend a large amount of money to get visuals for your brand, but I'd also recommend not trying to do it yourself, unless you happen to have very good graphical design skills. I have several brands I've created for different products and services, and for many of those brands, I've been able to get logos created for as cheap as $5 using one of my favorite services, Fiverr (http://simpleprogrammer .com/ss-fiverr). It's amazing the kind of talent you can find cheaply. You can also use a service like oDesk (http://simpleprogrammer.com/ ss-odesk) to hire a freelancer to do the work for you. I've had great success using both of these methods to get logos and other design work done for cheap.

And that's it. If you take the time upfront to work on creating a clear and consistent brand with a narrow focus and a thought-out message, you'll be far ahead of the game already. But like I said before, just having a message and visuals isn't enough. You need consistency and repeated exposure to really make a brand that has impact. In the next few chapters we'll look at how to add some consistency to your brand and spread the message through mediums like blogging, social networks, speaking engagements, and more.

Taking action

- Make a list of some of the popular brands you're familiar with. Pick one or two to study in depth. Try to determine what their message is and look for how they use their logo and other visual elements to convey it.
- Brainstorm a list of niche ideas for your own personal brand. Come up with at least 10 to 15 ideas and then narrow down the list to your top 2 or 3. Try to come up with one that you'll use for your personal brand.

21

Creating a wildly successful blog

As a software developer, one of the best mediums you can use to market yourself is a blog. It's my firm belief that every software developer who cares about their career should invest in creating a blog.

You can only meet so many people in person, so you need another primary way to market yourself and network. Think about how many people you've met in the tech industry over the past year. That number might approach several hundred, or even a thousand, but a successful blog could introduce you to hundreds of thousands of people.

A blog is a cheap and easy way to market yourself and it's extremely valuable for getting your name out there. A successful blog can attract hundreds or even thousands of visitors per day, which can give you many opportunities ranging from job offers to consulting gigs or even an audience to sell a product to.

Quite honestly, I owe most of the success I've experienced in my career to my blog. If I hadn't created a blog and figured out how to make it successful, it's unlikely that you'd be reading this book.

Why are blogs so important?

When you apply for a job, your resume typically is only going to be about two pages long. When you go into an interview, you're typically going to talk to an interviewer for about an hour or possibly two. It's very difficult to assess the skills of software developers from their resume and a short interview, so many employers have a difficult time knowing whether or not someone is a right fit for a job.

But imagine what happens if a software developer has a blog that has been updated regularly. That blog might contain a wealth of information about that developer, including code samples and in-depth technical analysis of various aspects of software development. I can tell more about a software developer by reading his or her blog than I can in almost any other way.

If that were the only reason for creating a blog—and maintaining it—it would be reason enough. But it isn't! Not only can having a blog help you to land a better job, it can also help you become a better software developer and communicator, and it can bring all kinds of opportunities you might have never imagined.

Think about famous developers like Scott Hanselman, Uncle Bob Martin, or Kent Beck—they all have blogs.

If you're a freelancer or you're interested in doing freelance work (see chapter 12), you'll find that a successful blog can bring many clients your way instead of you having to go out and look for them. Clients that come to you directly will be much more willing to pay a higher rate and will take much less convincing to hire you for a job.

And if you get enough blog traffic, you can use it as a platform to sell your own product (see chapter 13). If you have a steady stream of visitors to your blog, you can build a product around their interests and convert that traffic directly into customers.

Let's not forget the reputation a successful blog can bring you in the industry. Many famous software developers got their fame directly from the success of their blog. One good example is Jeff Atwood, one of the founders of Stack Overflow and Stack Exchange. His blog, Coding Horror (http://codinghorror.com), became wildly successful and the audience he built from that blog directly contributed to the success of Stack Overflow. The blog itself opened up the door for him to partner with Joel Spolsky (also a successful blogger, http://joelonsoftware.com).

And even if you discount all the financial benefits blogging can bring you, one intangible benefit that isn't easily dismissed is the improvement in your communication skills. Organizing your thoughts and putting them down into words is a difficult but valuable skill. Regularly writing helps you hone that skill, and the benefits you gain from being a better communicator will help you in many areas of your life. Plus, if you force yourself to blog on a regular schedule, you'll also be constantly forced to refresh your skills and stay up to date in your area of expertise.

As a software developer, learning how to write might actually help you to write better code, because you'll have an easier time communicating your intent. It will also help you to communicate your ideas and make them seem more compelling.

Creating a blog

Are you convinced you need a blog yet? Good. Then your next question might be how to get started.

Getting started is pretty easy nowadays. You can create a blog in about five minutes using a free service like Wordpress (http://wordpress.com) or Blogger (http://blogger.com). But before you go ahead and sign up for those services, there are a few things you'll want to consider.

A free service is the cheapest and easiest way to set up a blog, but it might not be the best way. One issue with free services is that they typically don't give you much control over the theme and layout of your blog. You can do some customizations, but you might not be able to add paid advertisements or shopping carts or other things to your blog. Those things might not be important to you right now, but later down the road, as your blog becomes more popular, you might want to have the capabilities you can't get from a free service.

Fortunately, there's an easy alternative to the completely free hosting platform. You can find many paid hosting services that allow you to easily host a blog with the popular Wordpress.org software (http://simpleprogrammer.com/ss-wordpress) for prices as cheap as $8 to $10 a month. (By the way, I'd highly recommend using the Wordpress.org software for your blog, because it's so widely used and it has a huge ecosystem. You can find plugins to extend your blog and themes to customize its look very easily if you choose Wordpress.org.) These paid hosting services offer you much more flexibility for a fairly cheap price.

You might start your blog on the free Wordpress.com service. (This is not to be confused with Wordpress.org, which is the actual software you'd use to host your blog on a paid hosting service.) For a while, being on Wordpress.com might be fine, but eventually you might reach the point where you want to customize your blog by adding plugins and want to be able to advertise on it. You might end up having to move to paid hosting to do this, and it could be somewhat of a hassle, so you might be better off starting with a cheap paid hosting service.

If you go the paid hosting route, you can find many services that will allow you to do a single-click install of the Wordpress.org software and you can be up and running in minutes. It isn't any more difficult than free hosting and you get much more power to customize your blog as you see fit.

You can also host your blog on a virtual private server (VPS). A VPS basically gives you a full operating system in the cloud that you can install on your blog yourself. It's the cheapest option in terms of what you get for what you pay, but it's also the most difficult option. I currently host my blog, Simple Programmer (http://simpleprogrammer.com), on a VPS, but I wouldn't recommend it if you're just starting out.

If you do decide to go with free hosting, I have one word of caution: make sure you register your own domain name. By default, free hosting services will give you an address to your blog that's part of their domain. You'll want to register your own domain and pay the fee to have your blog use it instead of the default one. A large portion of the traffic you eventually get to your blog will probably come from search engines like Google.

Google assigns what they call a page rank to certain web pages and domains on the internet based mainly on how many sites are linking to that domain. If you switch your blog to paid hosting in the future, you'll want to make sure you're able to carry that search engine relevance, or page rank, with you, so definitely make sure you start out with your own custom domain. (It's possible to work around this issue later on, but it isn't worth the hassle. It's much easier to start out doing things correctly.)

STEPS TO CREATE A BLOG
- ☼ Decide on hosting: free, paid, or VPS.
- ☼ Set up or install the blogging software.
- ☼ Configure any themes or customizations.
- ☼ Start writing!

Keys to success

Okay, so you've got your blog set up and you've written a few arti-cles—now what? It doesn't do much good to have a blog if no one is reading it, so you'll want to figure out how to get some traffic. After all, isn't that what this chapter is about—creating a successful blog?

The largest portion of your success as a blogger will depend on one thing and one thing only: consistency. I've talked to many successful bloggers and they've all had one thing in common: they blog a lot. Some of the most successful bloggers I've talked to blog every single day and have been doing it for many years.

But don't worry. You don't have to write a blog post every single day (although if you're just starting out it doesn't hurt to write two or three blog posts a week for the first year). What's more important than any-thing else is picking a regular schedule and being consistent with it. The frequency will determine how quickly you're able to become suc-cessful. I'd highly recommend blogging at a frequency of at least once a week. At that frequency, you'll add 52 blog posts a year. This is critical because, as I said earlier, a good portion of your traffic—most likely a majority of it—will be coming from search engines like Google. The more blog posts you have, the more traffic you'll get from internet searches (that is, as long as the posts are actually decent and not just a bunch of random words).

Unfortunately, being consistent alone isn't enough to make your blog wildly successful—although I'm pretty sure if you wrote a blog post every single day for several years it would be difficult not to be. You should also make sure you're writing quality content. There are two reasons why the quality of your content matters. First, and perhaps most importantly, the higher the quality of your content, the more likely people will come back to your blog or subscribe to it in their RSS reader or via email. You're going to have much more success building an audience when you're giving people something of value.

Another important thing quality content will do for you is provide you with the oh-so-valuable backlinks. Most search engines judge the quality of a web page based on how many other web pages are linking to that page. The higher the quality of your content, the more likely it is that it will get shared through social media and linked to from other websites. The more websites that are linking to your content, the more search traffic you're going to get on that content—plain and simple. You want to actually write stuff that people want to read and share.

Before you get all stressed out about this, don't worry. Your stuff doesn't have to be perfect. When you're just starting out, it will most likely be … well … pretty bad. But as long as you're trying to produce good content and not just throwing whatever comes to your mind on a page without any thought for formatting, organization, or typos, you'll be fine. Just publish the highest-quality content you can each and every week and you'll get better and better over time.

Valuable content can come in many different forms. Just sharing your experiences or an interesting story might help someone who comes to your blog or provide them with some entertainment.

If you do these two things—consistently writing and producing quality content—you'll most likely be successful. How do I know this? Because I give talks to software developers all the time, and whenever I do I ask developers to raise their hands if they actually have a blog and keep it updated each week. Out of a room of 100 developers, I'm lucky if I see a single hand. Just writing good content, consistently, will easily put you in the top 1% of developers—at least in terms of marketing yourself.

Landmine: I don't know what to write about

Many would-be bloggers never get started or end up quitting quickly after starting, because they either don't know what to write about or find they don't have anything to say.

The best way to combat this problem is to brainstorm many different ideas ahead of time and keep a running list of possible blog topics so that you always have a pool to choose from.

Also, don't be so worried about writing that stellar post or about what people will think. Sometimes you just have to write a post that you know won't be your greatest hit, but will get something posted to your blog. I've written many posts that I thought were horrible, yet turned out to be some of my most popular posts.

One technique that might help you think about what to write is to have a conversation, or even an argument, with someone about that topic. Often, I'll find that I can write the best about something that I had previously discussed in a conversation. Call up a friend and start debating and you'll find you have pages' worth to write about a topic.

Of course, there are some other ways you can make your blog successful. Let's talk about a few of those next.

Getting more traffic

When you first start out blogging, it's going to be difficult to get traffic to your blog. You won't be getting much traffic from search engines and it's unlikely anyone will be linking to you, so what do you do?

One of the first strategies I'd recommend is to start commenting on other people's blogs. Find other developers who are blogging about similar topics as you and write meaningful comments on their blog, and when you have the opportunity, link back to your blog. (Often when you register to leave a comment, your profile can contain a link to your blog, so you might not even have to do this directly.)

It will take some work to make this strategy effective, but it will also help you make connections with other bloggers, who will appreciate your thoughtful comments. (Just don't leave "spammy" comments that only link to your blog and don't add any real value to the conversation.) Try to write a few comments on different blogs each day, and, over time, you'll start to see some traffic flowing to your own blog from people who visited other blogs where you left comments. The higher the quality of your comments, the more likely that people will be interested in checking out more of what you have to say on your blog. (You can also write a blog post as a response to someone else's blog post. This can be a very effective strategy for getting traffic, especially if they in turn link back to you.)

Another good way to get some initial traffic is to, of course, share your blog posts on your social networks and put a link to your blog at the bottom of your email signature and anywhere you have a profile online. This won't generate nearly as much traffic as you might expect, but it's still worth doing.

You should also make it easy to share your content so that others will spread it. If you're using Wordpress.org, you can find many different plugins that add a share button to your content. Wordpress.org software even has some of this sharing functionality built in. You might even put a direct call to action at the bottom of your blog post asking readers to share the content or to subscribe to your blog.

Finally, if you're brave and you think your content is either good enough or controversial enough, you can submit your own posts—or have someone else submit them—to social news sites like Reddit (http://reddit.com) or Hacker News (http://news.ycombinator.com). A word of caution though: some of the people who hang around these sites are just plain mean. I've written posts that I've shared on Hacker News that have been torn to shreds by angry commenters who just wanted to stick people with forks. You have to have a bit of a thick skin to withstand some of that kind of abuse. But if you do end up having one of your blog posts become popular on one of these sites, you could get tens of thousands of views in a single day and many backlinks. Overall, it's worth it.

I can't guarantee you success

Well, I'd like to say I could guarantee you success if you follow everything in this chapter, but unfortunately, I can't. I can only say that by following the advice I give you here, you'll be much more likely to find success. There's a bit of luck and timing involved in having your blog become wildly successful, but it's rare to find a successful blogger who doesn't at least write good content consistently.

Taking action

- What are your favorite developer blogs? Take a look at some of the blogs you read and see if you can figure out how often those blogs are updated with new posts and the average length of each post.
- If you don't have a blog already, start one. Sign up today and create your first blog post. Come up with a schedule that you'll stick to for writing future blog posts.
- Commit to keeping your blog up for at least a year. It takes time and commitment to get results. At about the one-year mark is when most people start to see some traction.
- Create a list of running blog post topics. Every time you think of a new idea, add it to this list. Then when you need to write a post, you'll have plenty of ideas handy.

22

Your primary goal: Add value to others

Try not to become a man of success, but rather try to become a man of value.

—Albert Einstein

You can do everything right as far as marketing yourself and still not be successful if what you're doing only serves your own interests and doesn't add real value to others. You can write blogs posts, share your content on social media, speak at events, write books and articles, and promote yourself as heavily as possible, but if what you're saying and the things you're conveying don't help other people, everyone will ignore you.

We're all interested primarily in ourselves. No one wants to hear about your successes and why they should help you achieve more of them, but they do want to hear about how you can help them be successful. The primary way you're going to achieve success in your marketing efforts is to help others to do the same.

Zig Ziglar said it best when he said "If you help enough people get what they want, you will get what you want." This is the primary strategy that you should use in marketing yourself. It will be more effective than any other technique.

Give people what they want

To give people what they want, you have to know what it is that they want. But it's not so easy to figure out what people want, because if you ask them…they'll lie. They don't mean to lie. The truth is most people don't actually know what they want. They have a vague idea, but like a bride looking for the perfect wedding dress, they'll know it when they see it.

It's up to you, then, to figure it out for them. You have to be able to read the signs and see where things are going and then find a way to provide value to that area. If you have a following already, it's a bit easier. But if you don't, you have to go out and see what people are interested in. What topics are being talked about in internet forums related to your niche? What trends are you seeing in the industry as a whole? And perhaps most importantly, what fears do people have and how can you address them?

The content you produce should be squarely aimed at providing value in the areas you identify from your research. You might be particularly interested in a certain aspect of a framework or technology, but if your target audience isn't, it won't do you much good. On the other hand, if you strike a nerve with what you blog about or some content you create, you'll know it pretty quickly. If you can find a way to address a real need or concern with the content you produce, you'll be creating real value for others. You'll be giving them what they want.

Give away 90% of what you do for free

Some people balk at all the content I give away for free. Every week I produce three blog posts, a YouTube video, two podcasts, and other content that's all completely free. But I'm a firm believer that 90% of the content you produce should be completely free. There's nothing wrong with charging money for your hard work, but you'll find the most success when you're giving people solid value mostly for free.

Free content is much more sharable than paid content. If you're writing blog posts, producing videos, or perhaps a podcast, and you're giving that content away for free, someone is much more likely to share and spread that content than if you're charging money for a product. Sharing free content is as easy as tweeting a link or sending an email. You'll reach a much larger audience with your free content than you will with anything you charge money for.

By giving content away for free, you're giving people a chance to see how valuable the content you produce is without having to invest any money first. You might not even have plans to sell anything, but if you ever do, you'll have a much easier time convincing people to buy what you're selling if they know that the free content you're providing is of high quality. It will also give them a feeling of gratitude so that they may want to pay back to you some day by supporting a product you create.

It can seem like doing all this work for free is a waste of time, but you have to think of it as an investment in your future. By marketing yourself through creating value for others and giving it away mostly for free, you're creating future opportunities for yourself by building up a name for yourself as someone who provides value to others. It's hard to put a price on the value of building this kind of reputation, but it can benefit you in many ways. Your reputation may help you get a better and higher-paying job or more clients, or to successfully launch a product.

The fast track to success

Every time you set out to do something, whether it be creating a blog post, recording a screencast, or another activity, you should look at it from the perspective of how it's creating value for someone else. As I'm sitting here writing this book, I'm constantly thinking about how the words I'm writing are going to benefit you. How can I convey information that will be useful to you? How can I provide you value?

It's easy to fall into the trap of talking about yourself and trying to demonstrate why you're worthy, but you'll find much more success in solving other people's problems and genuinely being helpful. It does no good to tell someone why you're the best Android developer in the world, but if you can help that person solve the problem he's facing when writing his own Android application, he'll consider you great.

You should carry this attitude through whatever medium you use to market yourself. In the following chapters we'll talk about how to market yourself using many different mediums, but you won't be successful at any of them if you don't know how to connect with your audience by solving their problems and providing them value.

Offering more of yourself

You might think that altruistic motives would be a questionable way to get ahead, but it turns out some of the most productive people are the most helpful. Why? Well, personally, I believe it's a combination of factors. The more you help others, the more problems and situations you're exposed to and the more connections you make. People who are always helping others solve their problems often find that it's a bit easier to solve their own problems with all that practice, and when they really get stuck, they usually have several people to turn to.

It's not just me who believes this, though. I read an interesting article about a 31-year-old professor at Wharton School who is one of the most productive and helpful people around (http://simpleprogrammer.com/ss-giving-secret). He's one of the most prolific professors in his field, organizational psychology, and he's done some studies to show why helping people can actually help you get ahead.

Taking action

- What kind of content do you find most valuable? Is there a particular blogger whose blog posts you read every single week or a podcast that contains such valuable content that you don't ever want to miss an episode?
- What is the biggest value you can provide your audience or your niche? What kind of content do you think would be the most valuable to the audience you're trying to attract?

23

#UsingSocialNetworks

Today social media is a big part of many people's lives. Facebook, Twitter, Google+, and sites like LinkedIn are important for connecting with people and sharing information. As a software developer looking to market yourself, you need to have some kind of a presence on these social networks and learn how to manage the image you portray through what you share and how you share it.

Lately there has been a huge emphasis placed by social media experts on how important social media is to branding and marketing, and while I agree it's important, I don't think it's quite as effective as some people would lead you to believe. Regardless, though, if you want to have maximum exposure and engage your audience, you need to know the basics of using social media to promote your brand.

In this chapter, I'll help you develop a social media strategy, take you through each of the major networks, and show some ways you can use social media to spread your message.

Growing your network

The first thing you'll need to do to be able to make use of social media is to get followers, or basically get people into your network. It does little good to stand on the corner with a bullhorn shouting your message if no one is around to hear you.

There are many different strategies you can use to build up your social networks, and how you do it will generally depend on the particular network, but for most social networks the easiest thing to do is follow someone else or ask them to join your network. Seems pretty obvious, but there are many developers who sit out there and wait for people to follow them or interact with them. Remember, people will be more interested in you if you show an interest in them.

You can also gain followers by putting your social network profile links in places like your online biographies, at the end of your blog posts, or even in your email signature. Make it easy for people to connect with you and they will. And don't be afraid to ask, either. There's no harm in ending a blog post with a call to action to follow you on Twitter.

It can take some time to build a large network, so don't rush it. It can be tempting to buy followers from one of those shady services offering to increase your following in a matter of days, but most of the time, you're just wasting money getting fake accounts to follow you or join your network. Those fake accounts won't be worth anything, because they don't represent real people.

Using social media effectively

Your strategy with social media should be primarily focused on building an audience and moving the temperature of that audience from cool to hot. You want to get people to go from follower to fan so that they'll be more engaged in your content, share it with others, and actively promote you. That's how you'll build up a reputation in your industry. But how do you do that?

Again, it comes down to a matter of value. If you're consistently providing value to others by what you're sharing on your social networks, you're going to gain respect and credibility. But if you constantly post inappropriate, offensive content or content that's all about you and what kind of eggs you had for breakfast, you're likely to turn people away.

So, what do you post on social networks so that you can add value to others? The simple answer is anything that you'd find useful or interesting. Chances are that if you find it valuable, someone else will as well. Just make sure you set your bar reasonably high. If you're known as an excellent curator of information, especially about a particular niche, people will pay more attention to what you're saying on social networks and be more likely to share your content.

I try to provide a mix of useful content every week that I think is likely to interest the people following me in my social networks. I usually include some blog posts, news articles, inspirational quotes, tips and tricks related to software development, and some questions that challenge my followers and cause them to engage me in conversation. Table 23.1 highlights some types of content to share.

Table 23.1   Content to share via social media

Blog posts	Find popular blog posts or share your own.
News articles	Post interesting articles related to your niche if possible or software development in general.
Quotes	Famous quotes, especially inspirational ones, are usually very popular.
Tips and tricks	Any special knowledge you might have that someone else might appreciate.
Humor	Some humor is okay, but try to make sure it isn't offensive and is actually funny.
Engaging questions	A great way to engage your audience and interact with them.
Promotion for your own stuff	Do the least of this, but mix some of it in.

Obviously you should be posting any new blog post or other content you create, but if you're selling a book or some other product, or you're offering consulting services, you should put those kinds of advertisements into your social media streams sparingly. Just like you should be giving 90% of what you create away, 90% of what you send out should be valuable to your followers, not advertisements for you.

Staying active

One big challenge with social media is staying active. You'll lose a large amount of your effectiveness if you aren't consistently active on your social media accounts, but it can be a burden trying to manage Twitter,

Facebook, Google+, LinkedIn, and whatever other social networks you belong to while still getting actual work done.

You aren't going to be able to be extremely active and engaged on all the social media platforms unless you're willing to devote a large amount of time to those activities every day, so most likely you'll have to choose one or two platforms where you'll be the most engaged.

Personally, I don't like to spend a large amount of time on social media. I feel like it can easily suck up my whole day, so I try to avoid it as much as possible. But I still need to stay active, so how do I do it?

I currently utilize a tool called Buffer (http://simpleprogrammer.com/ ss-buffer), but there are many other tools out there that do the same thing. What Buffer does for me is allow me to schedule my social media posts all at one time. At the beginning of each week, I'll run through a checklist of the different kinds of posts I want to put out on my social media channels. I'll create a mix of different types of content, and I'll schedule all that content to be released at different times during the week. I may add more content during the week as I find something interesting to share, but every week I know that I'll be sending out at least two pieces of content each day on each of my social networks. I also make it so that whenever I post a new blog post or YouTube video, that content is automatically shared on all my social networks.

I'd highly recommend adopting some kind of similar approach for managing your own social networks so that you don't have to spend so much time each day trying to manage everything. I end up spending about an hour or less a week and I'm able to be pretty effective.

Networks and accounts

As a software developer looking to market yourself, you should have a presence on all of the major social networks, especially the ones that tend to be more tech-related or career-focused. You may also want to create special pages or profiles that directly represent your brand— although if you try to maintain personal and professional accounts, it can be a bit overwhelming.

I'd definitely recommend having a Twitter account as many developers utilize Twitter, and it's a great way to connect with people you might not otherwise be able to reach. You can mention someone in a tweet, even someone fairly famous, and there's a decent chance they'll reply back to you, because it requires minimal effort. The same person might have ignored an email from you, but replying to a tweet just takes a few seconds. I also find Twitter to be a great place to share blog posts and tech-related news. The limited size of messages helps to keep conversations short and to the point.

Next on my list would be LinkedIn. You should obviously have a LinkedIn profile, because LinkedIn is really the social network for professionals. On LinkedIn you can create an online version of your resume and connect with other professionals. It's a great site for networking and your professional content, like blog posts, will hit the right audience there. You can also utilize the groups on LinkedIn to make connections with people who are directly interested in or involved in the specific niche you're targeting.

Perhaps one of the most underused features of LinkedIn, though, is the ability to ask for endorsements from your connections. This is a great feature which you should definitely utilize. For every job you have listed on your LinkedIn profile, be sure to ask former coworkers or managers for an endorsement. It might make you feel a little uncomfortable to do so, but having endorsements on your LinkedIn profile can make a huge difference in how you're perceived. Endorsements provide social proof, which is a powerful tool for shaping your image. Think about the last time you shopped for something on Amazon. Did you read the reviews and look for products that were highly recommended? That's the primary way I shop online now—and I know the same is true for many others.

Facebook and Google+ aren't nearly as important as Twitter and LinkedIn, but I'd still recommend having a presence there as well. For either of these platforms you can either use your personal account or you can set up what's called a page, which is basically a profile for a business or a brand. You can also find valuable groups on both Facebook and Google+ that can connect you with your target audience and allow you to share directly to people who are interested in a particular programming language or technology.

> ### Taking action
>
> - How are you using social media right now? Take a look at your social media timelines and try to figure out what impression someone would have of you and your brand if they just read what you put out via social media.
> - Come up with a social media plan. Decide what kind of content you want to share on each network and put together a strategy for sharing that content each week. Pay attention to what kind of content you share that's most popular.

24

Speaking, presenting, and training: Speak geek

One of the most effective ways to connect with people and market yourself is through speaking or giving some kind of training. This medium might not scale as well as other mediums, but getting up in front of an audience and talking directly to them is one of the most impactful things you can do.

I know, for me at least, there's nothing more invigorating than stepping onto a stage and giving a speech or a presentation. There's something powerful about being able to connect directly with an audience and adapt based on a feedback loop that you can't get with other mediums.

Even if you aren't going to get up on a stage and speak at a conference, giving a presentation at work can be very helpful to your career. You create a great opportunity to be able to show how effectively you can communicate your ideas and to influence your coworkers and even your boss.

The only problem is, it isn't easy to just start speaking. You might be wondering how you can get started when you don't have any experience, or you might even be scared to do it. It's not easy getting up on a stage and talking in front of people—especially if you've never done it before.

In this chapter, I'm going to tell you why doing things like speaking and training is so important for your career, and I'll give you some practical advice on how to get started or take what you're already doing to the next level.

Why speaking live is so impactful

Have you ever gone to a rock concert or seen a band perform live? Why did you do it? You could have just bought the album and listened from home. You might even have better audio quality using your own headphones listening to a CD-quality album. The same goes for plays and live theater. Why not just watch a movie instead?

It's hard to explain, but there's a personal connection you get when you attend a live event that you don't get when listening to or watching a recording. There's something about hearing a presenter speak live that is more impactful than many other mediums—even if they contain the exact same content.

People who hear you speak are much more likely to remember you and to feel like they have a personal connection with you. We remember the times we saw our favorite band in concert, but we don't remember the times we listened to their albums.

Speaking is also an interactive medium—or at least you can make it one. When you speak at an event you can directly answer questions from the audience and get them to participate in your presentation. Interacting in this way can build large amounts of trust quickly and can help you create fans who will promote your message for you. Coincidentally, just now as I was typing this chapter, I saw a tweet from a developer who attended one of my talks on marketing yourself and now is doing everything he can to promote me and my blog to other people. I don't think I'd have made that same kind of connection with him if he hadn't heard me speak in person.

Many famous software developers who you probably know of boosted their careers by speaking. My friend, John Papa, is a great example. He started out doing a few small speaking gigs and now he's able to travel all over the world talking about various technologies. He's created many opportunities for himself by being known as a speaker.

Getting started speaking

Okay, perhaps I've convinced you that speaking is important and worth doing. But you might be wondering how you can get started, because that part can be a bit tricky.

Let me start off by saying that you aren't going to get a speaking gig at a major conference if you haven't spoken before and haven't built up a name for yourself. But you don't need to start there. It's better to start small and begin to perfect your skill of public speaking. It can take some time to get good at speaking in public, so it's good to get some practice.

One of the best places to start is by giving presentations at your own workplace. Most companies are happy to have their employees present on various topics, especially if the presentation is directly related to what you're working on. Offer to do a presentation on some technology that your team is using or to give training in some area where your team could use help. You don't even have to present yourself as an expert, but as someone who earnestly wants to help by sharing what you've learned. (In fact, you'll find that you should almost always take this approach. Too many people get caught up in being perceived as an expert instead of being honest and humble. Being a real down-to-earth human with real flaws and weaknesses will go a long way to building trust with your audience and will make you seem a lot less like a jerk.)

Another easy avenue for public speaking is code camps and user groups. There are usually many different user groups for software developers in most metropolitan areas. It usually isn't hard to find some user group nearby that you can attend. After attending a user group for a while, you can ask the organizer if you can present on a particular topic. Most user groups are always looking for new people to present, so as long as you have a topic that's interesting, you'll probably be given a shot. This is a great opportunity to speak in front of a smaller, more forgiving audience, and as a bonus, it's a good way to market yourself to local companies and recruiters in your area.

In addition to user groups, you can find yearly code camps all over the world. Most code camps will let anyone with any level of experience speak on a topic of their choosing. Take advantage of this opportunity and try to speak at at least one code camp every year. Most these events are low-pressure situations, because no one paid to get in them. You can relax, and if you mess up, it's not that big of a deal.

Finally, once you have some speaking engagements under your belt, you can start submitting to developer conferences. There's quite a bit of competition in this area and there tends to be a bit of a "good-old boys" system with some of the events, but once you break into the circuit, you can find many opportunities to speak each year, and for most of these events, you'll be completely reimbursed for travel and any other expenses. (Many software developers I know get to travel all around the world speaking at these events. They might not get paid to speak, but they get to go to all kinds of places they wouldn't get to go otherwise and to expand their audiences. These bigger events are also a great way to get business if you're a freelancer.)

Landmine: I'm terrified of public speaking

It's okay, many people are. The fear of public speaking is one of the most common phobias. But what can you do about it? Well, there are organizations like Toastmasters (http://www.toastmasters.org/) that you can join that will help you to get over your fear of public speaking in a comfortable atmosphere. You can also start very small by doing little things like standing up and talking in meetings or giving presentations to a smaller team of people you know well. As you get more and more comfortable, you can move on to more intimidating events.

You have to remember that as human beings we're very good at adaptation. If you do something enough, you'll adapt to it. Paratroopers who are first learning to jump out of planes are pretty terrified, but after doing many successful jumps, the fear eventually goes away. If you keep attempting to speak in public, the fear will dissipate over time as you adapt.

What about training?

Doing training, whether live or recorded, is another great way to build a reputation for yourself and even to make a little money. I've had quite a bit of success through producing online courses, and not just through the money they've brought me, but also through the reputation of being an expert in the industry.

It used to be difficult to get a job as a trainer or to get a training gig, but now almost anyone can put together some form of training online. Of course, you can still do traditional classroom training as well, but for most developers who aren't going to focus on making a career out of it, online video training is a much simpler and more scalable solution.

A great place to start out is to create simple screencasts that you can share on free video sites like YouTube. A screencast is just a recording of your screen while you teach something or show someone how to do something. If you can clearly teach a concept to other developers with your screencasts, you can easily build up a reputation for being a knowledgeable expert in an area. That reputation can translate into a better job or even freelance clients who seek out your expertise.

Even though you might start out giving training for free—and free training is a great way to promote yourself—you might eventually want to start charging for the content you're producing. There are a few different options you can choose from to charge for your video training content.

First, there are dedicated developer training companies like Pluralsight (http://simpleprogrammer.com/ss-pluralsight). Most of the online video training content I produced was for Pluralsight, but there are other companies that will pay you to produce content and give you a share of the profit in the form of a royalty payment. This is similar to writing a book. When you produce content for one of these types of companies, you usually are commissioned to produce that content and don't have to worry about marketing and selling, because you'll be integrated into their existing audience. Typically, sites like these will have some kind of an audition process, so there's no guarantee you'll be accepted, but there's no harm in trying.

If you want to go a more solo route, you can try creating content yourself and selling that content directly. I've had some success with this approach as well, as I have been selling my "How to Market Yourself as a Software Developer" (http://devcareerboost.com/m) training directly from my website. The only difficulty with this approach is that you'll have to do all your own marketing and you'll need to figure out a way to distribute the content and accept payment for it.

One hybrid option is the online education company Udemy (http://
simpleprogrammer.com/ss-udemy). Udemy allows anyone to publish
content, which is hosted on their platform, but they take a large cut of
the profit and you're mostly responsible for doing your own marketing
and acquiring your own customers. I know several software developers
who have been successful on that platform.

Taking action

- Come up with a list of all the user groups in your area. Also come up with a list of any code camps that you might be able to speak at. Offer to speak at one of these events on a topic you feel comfortable talking about.
- Take a look at some of the free and paid training you can find on the web for software developers. Take some notes and see if you can figure out what kind of things successful trainers are doing.
- Try to create your own short training in the form of a screencast and publish it on a site like YouTube.
- Create a list of topics you could speak about.

25

Writing books and articles that attract a following

If you want to be successful at writing, you have to connect with your audience. Hopefully, as you're reading these words, that's exactly what I'm doing right now—with you. I could have started off this chapter in a much different way, but I chose not to, because I wanted to create a more powerful connection by talking directly to you.

If I'm doing my job correctly, right now, as you read this text, you're starting to feel like I'm talking to you, not at you. Words aren't just information. Words are a powerful canvas to carry your voice to another person. Sometimes when you read what I write, it's more real than when I speak the same words to you. Through your words you can convey your voice, and if that voice is interesting, grabs your reader's attention, and provides them some value along the way, they'll connect with you and you'll win them over.

Why books and articles are important

Have you ever heard the phrase "He wrote the book on the subject?" Books, in particular, carry a certain weight to them. There's a certain amount of credibility a person assumes just by writing a book. It makes sense that if you want to be seen as someone credible in your industry, you should write a book. The same applies for a magazine article published in a software development magazine. Most people assume that if someone wrote a book or had an article published on a particular subject then they're probably an expert of that particular subject. If you're looking to market yourself, it certainly doesn't hurt to be seen as an expert.

But beyond the clout you generate from having your name on the spine of a bunch of bound pages of paper, a book is a vehicle for delivering your message in a very targeted and focused way. When someone sits down to read a book, you're getting their focused attention for a long period of time. A single book could take 10 to 15 hours of time to read. You'd be hard-pressed to find another medium where someone will devote that much time listening to your message. With a book, you have the ability to deliver your complete unabbreviated message to your readers.

Although magazine articles don't allow you to deliver quite the same amount of content to your readers, they also allow you to spend quite a bit of time delivering your message—typically much more than a blog post—and the circulation can be pretty large.

Books and magazines don't pay

Many software developers get confused about the reasons for writing a book, assuming that most book and magazine authors must make a large amount of money from their writing. The simple truth, though, is that you don't write a book to make money. You write a book to increase your reputation.

It's very rare for a book to make a substantial amount of money, and an author only keeps a small portion of the proceeds. Most magazines only pay a small stipend for an article that can take a long time to write and edit. Don't count on making a fortune directly from writing a book or magazine articles, unless you happen to get very lucky and knock one out of the park with a bestseller.

But just because you don't get paid directly, doesn't mean publishing isn't profitable. As I mentioned before, the real benefit to writing a book or magazine article is in the wide distribution and the credibility you get from being published. The publishing industry acts as a sort of gate-keeper for quality. If you can pass by that gatekeeper and make it to the other side, you'll find that there are all kinds of other lucrative opportunities that indirectly present themselves by becoming published.

Published authors find it easier to get invited to speak at conferences and can establish themselves as an authority in a particular subject area, which can lead to more clients and better job offers.

Getting published

I have to admit, this is my first traditionally published book, but I know from speaking with many other published authors that getting published isn't easy—especially for your first book. Not too many publishers want to take a risk on a completely unknown author, and there's a big risk that an author won't even complete a book—because it isn't exactly an easy task to do.

The best way to give yourself an opportunity to get published is to have a clearly defined topic that you know there's a market for and you can demonstrate your knowledge as an expert in that area. If you've created a niche for your brand, you'll have a much easier time doing this, because you can carve out a small area of expertise where there isn't much competition. The more focused and narrow your topic is, the easier it will be to prove your expertise in it, but the smaller your potential audience will be, so you'll have to find the appropriate balance that appeals to a publisher.

You should also do some legwork ahead of time to establish yourself in that market. I'd recommend starting with a blog and submitting articles for smaller magazines. You can build up to bigger and bigger publications as you establish a track record and your reputation in your area of expertise increases. Book and magazine publishers like to publish authors who already have a fairly large audience, because it means that they'll likely have guaranteed customers for the book. You can make yourself more appealing to any publisher by demonstrating how large your audience is.

Finally, you should have a solid proposal (or magazine abstract) that's well written and clearly outlines the purpose of your book, its target audience, and why you think it will be successful, and your own credentials that show you're the best person to write your book. The better case you can make, the better chance of your proposal being accepted.

> ### Landmine: I'm not good at writing
>
> Neither am I, but I'm writing this book. All throughout my school years, my weakest subject was always English. I was in all the advanced classes for math, science, and even history, but I was only average or slightly below average in English. I never imagined that I'd spend a large portion of my career writing—like I do now.
>
> What happened? Well, I just started writing every day. I started mostly with blog posts. At first my blog posts were horrible, but eventually I got better. I'm still no Hemingway, but I can now effectively communicate my thoughts and ideas in the written word—at least most of the time.
>
> My point is: don't worry about not being good at writing. It doesn't matter if you're good right now. What matters is that you start writing and you write consistently. Over time your skills will improve.

Self-publishing

Traditional publishing isn't your only option. More and more authors are finding success by self-publishing—especially if they have an existing audience. I self-published my first few books and was able to do well selling them on my own. I didn't have the resources and distribution of a large publisher, but I didn't have their overhead, either. I was able to keep almost all of the proceeds I made from the books.

Self-publishing is a great way to start out, because you can do it completely on your own and it's easy to do. It's also a good way to find out if you actually have what it takes to write a book before entering into a contract with a publisher that will have deadlines that you'll be required to meet.

There are many services you can use to help you self-publish your book. One popular service with programmers is Leanpub (http://simple programmer.com/ss-leanpub). This service allows you to write your book using a simplified formatting language called Markdown and then Leanpub takes care of formatting the book nicely, putting it up for sale for you, and collecting payments. They charge a fairly small percentage of the total price of the book.

You can also easily list your book on Amazon with the Kindle Direct Publishing program or even use a service like Smashwords (http://simpleprogrammer.com/ss-smashwords) or BookBaby (http://simpleprogrammer.com/ss-bookbaby) to have your book distributed to multiple marketplaces. These services can even help you convert your book to an e-book format.

Two good friends of mine are both self-published authors and they are able to make from $10,000 to $20,000 each year from the sales of their books. This can be some good supplemental income, as well as a great way to get your name out there and build some credibility—although traditional publishing will always carry a bit more weight.

Taking action

- Go through the Amazon best-sellers list for software development-related books and check to see what kinds of books are selling the best.
- Before you write a lengthy book, try to take on a smaller assignment like writing a magazine article. Look for some lower circulation software development magazines and submit an article abstract.

26

Don't be afraid to look like an idiot

If you really want to succeed at marketing yourself, you're going to have to learn to overcome one huge fear that most of us have—looking like an idiot.

It isn't easy to get up on stage and talk to a crowd of people. It isn't easy to write blog posts for the whole internet to see and comment on. It can be embarrassing to hear your voice on a podcast or to see your face on video. Even writing a book, to some degree, takes some guts—especially if you're putting all you've got into it.

But if you want to be successful at your efforts, you have to learn to stop caring about what people think. You have to learn how to not be afraid to look like an idiot.

Everything is uncomfortable at first

The first time I got up on a stage in front of people and had to deliver a presentation, I was sweating bullets. I was trying to hold my voice steady, but it kept cracking. I'd click a slide and my stuttering hand would click forward two slides instead of one. But do you know what happened? I got through it. I might not have done the best job. I probably didn't charm the audience with my charisma, but the time passed and eventually it was over.

The next time I got up on stage, I was still a mess, but I wasn't quite as nervous. My hands didn't shake so much. My shirt wasn't as soaked with sweat. And the next time was even easier than that. Now when I get up on stage, I take the microphone and confidently stride across the room, and the energy in the room empowers me and makes me feel alive. I never thought I'd be saying that the first few times I ever gave a speech.

The truth of the matter is that things change. Over time the things that made you uncomfortable become second nature. You have to give it enough time and be willing to go through that awkwardness until it stops being awkward.

When you first do something that makes you feel uncomfortable, you can't imagine how you could ever feel comfortable doing that thing. You're tempted to think that it just isn't for you or that other people have natural talents in a particular area, but you don't. You have to learn to overcome this kind of thinking and realize that almost every-one goes through the same kind of uncomfortable feelings when they first do anything challenging—especially in front of a group of people.

I'll be honest with you, most people don't make it. They give up early. They care too much about what other people think about them and they don't push hard enough to get through the difficult, awkward part to something better. That's why if you follow the advice in this book, you'll succeed where others fail. Most developers won't be willing to do what you'll be willing to do. Most developers won't be willing to bear looking like an idiot for a short period of time in order to achieve some-thing greater.

It's okay to look like an idiot

Okay, so perhaps you believe me that things will get easier over time. That if you just stick through it and keep going, if you keep writing blog posts, if you keep talking on stage, or making YouTube videos, that it will eventually not feel so uncomfortable and that it may even begin to feel natural. But how do you get to that point when your hands are shaking uncontrollably and you can't even hold the mic?

Simple. You don't even care. You don't care that you might be up there looking dumb. You don't care that someone might read your blog post and think that you're completely wrong and stupid. You don't care that someone might laugh at you, because you're ready and willing to laugh with them. Again, I know that's easy to say, but let's break it down a bit.

First, what's the worst that can happen if you end up looking like an idiot? It's not like physical harm is going to come to you because you made a fool of yourself. No matter how bad you blow it at presenting on stage, no one is really going to care that much. Sure, it might be a spectacle while you're up there blubbering away and sweat is pouring off of your forehead, but after it's over, chances are no one will even remember it.

Think about it this way. When was the last time you saw someone "biff it"? Do you even remember? Did you shout obscenities at him and boo him off the stage? Did you email him or call him on the phone as a follow-up to let him know how horrible a person he was and that he wasted your time? Of course not. So what do you have to worry about?

If you want to succeed, you have to learn how to swallow your pride and get out there and not be afraid to make a fool of yourself. Every single famous actor, musician, professional sports player, and public speaker at one time wasn't very good at what they do and had to make a conscious choice to get out there anyway and to do their best. The results will eventually come. You can't keep doing something and not get better at it; you just have to survive long enough for that to happen. The way you survive is by not caring. Don't be afraid to look like an idiot.

> I've missed more than 9,000 shots in my career. I've lost almost 300 games. 26 times, I've been trusted to take the game winning shot and missed. I've failed over and over and over again in my life. And that is why I succeed.
>
> —Michael Jordan

Take small steps (or dive right in)

If it were up to me, I'd take you right over to the edge of the pool and give you a nice hard push right into the deep end, because I know that's the fastest way to learn. But I realize not everyone appreciates being put in a sink-or-swim situation, so you might want to start off slowly by taking small steps.

If you're nervous about doing speaking, writing, or something else I mentioned in the previous chapters of this section, try to think of the smallest thing you can do that doesn't make you quite as nervous and start there.

A good place to start would be writing comments on other people's blogs. I realize even this task can be intimidating for some developers, but it's a good place to start, because it doesn't require you to write very much and you can contribute to a conversation instead of starting one.

Be prepared for criticism, but don't be afraid of it. It may turn out that some people don't like what you have to say or don't agree with you. So what? It's the internet, and everyone is entitled to their own opinion, so don't let it get to you. It's good to get used to a little bit of abuse, because even your most perfect work will be criticized by someone. You can never please everyone.

Once you're feeling a bit braver, write your own blog post. Write about a topic you already know about well or even write a "how-to." Don't start with an opinionated post, because those are the most likely to draw the internet trolls out of their caves to bludgeon you with their clubs. You'll probably find it isn't that bad and some people might actually like what you wrote. (Just don't let it go to your head.)

From there expand out further. Perhaps you can write a guest post for someone else's blog or you can be interviewed on a podcast. You might even join a club like Toastmasters (http://www.toastmasters.org/) to help you get used to speaking in public. Many people who never thought they'd be able to speak in front of a crowd go through Toastmasters and end up being excellent public speakers.

The point is to always be moving forward. It doesn't matter if you're taking little steps and slowly getting accustomed to the temperature of the water or if you jump right in and make a big splash in the deep-end. You're going to feel uncomfortable, you're likely going to be scared — possibly even terrified — but it will pass. If you keep on going and you're willing to face those challenges head on, if you're willing to look like an idiot—for a short period of time—you'll succeed where most people fail, and I guarantee it will be worth it.

Taking action

- Get brave. Today is your day. Go out and do something that scares you. Big or small, it doesn't matter. Force yourself to be in an uncomfortable situation and remind yourself that it's no big deal.
- Now repeat the first action item at least once a week.

Learning

Education is what remains after one has forgotten what one has learned in school.

—Albert Einstein

The world of software development is always changing. It seems that every single day a new technology is emerging and what you learned yesterday is now irrelevant.

In this rapid world of change, the ability to learn is extremely important. Software developers who choose to remain stagnant and neglect to develop their skills are soon left behind, miss future opportunities, and are relegated to work on legacy systems of the past. If you want to escape that fate, you need to learn how to learn.

In this section, my goal is to teach you how to teach yourself. I'm going to take you through a 10-step process I've developed to learn new technologies rapidly; it's the same process I used to create over 30 full-length developer training courses in under a year. I'll also give you some solid advice on finding mentors, mentoring others, and how to unlock your inner potential for absorbing information like a sponge.

27

Learning how to learn: How to teach yourself

There's nothing wrong with going to school and getting a good education, but if your education stops with graduation, you're going to be at a distinct disadvantage in life. In fact, if you constantly rely on someone else to teach you and never learn the skills to teach yourself, you'll be greatly limiting your opportunities to advance your skills and knowledge.

One of the most important skills a software developer can learn is the skill of self-teaching. Self-education is a vital skill in a world where new technologies are introduced every single day, and a typical web developer is expected to know at least three programming languages to even be eligible for a junior-level position.

If you want to be the best software developer you can be, you have to learn how to teach yourself. Unfortunately, self-education isn't a skill that's taught in schools. You could easily argue that the exact opposite is taught by systems designed to deal with the group rather than the individual. At its core, learning how to learn is a skill that you have to teach yourself.

Dissecting the learning process

Have you ever considered how you learn and what it truly means to learn something? We tend to learn things that we're interested in almost unconsciously. When someone tells us an exciting story, we usually don't have to take notes or try to memorize exactly what happened, yet most of us can hear a story and repeat that story back with little effort.

The same goes for something we do. If I show you how to do something, you might forget it, but if you do something yourself, you're much more likely to remember it, and if you actually teach what you're trying to learn to someone else, not only do you remember it, but you get a much deeper understanding of it. It turns out that the idea that we all have different learning styles is a myth (see http://simpleprogrammer.com/ss-learning-myth for more information). We all tend to learn best by doing and teaching. Active learning is a much more effective way to learn than any other way.

> *The great aim of education is not knowledge but action.*
> —Herbert Spencer

Think about it this way: you could read all the books you want about the proper way to ride a bike. You could even watch videos of people riding bikes. I could lecture you on the mechanics of proper bike riding, but chances are, if you've never ridden a bike before, the first time you get on a bike, you'll fall right over. You might know a lot about bikes. You might know a lot about the mechanics of riding a bike and what kind of bikes are best, but you won't really learn how to ride a bike until you actually put what you're learning into practice.

Why, then, do so many software developers pick up a technical book on a programming language or framework and read it cover to cover hoping to absorb all the information within? At the very best, by using that approach you'd amass all the information about your subject, but you still wouldn't have actually learned it.

Teaching yourself

If you want to learn something, what should you do? Well, ultimately, you'll learn best when you take action and you'll reinforce that learning and gain a deeper understanding when you take on the task of teaching what you learned to someone else. Your efforts on self-education should be focused on trying to get to the point where you can actually be involved and do something as early as possible.

I feel that the best way to learn something is to jump right in and start doing, before you even know what you're doing. If you can gain enough knowledge about a subject to start playing around, you can tap into the powerful creative and curious nature of your own mind. We tend to absorb more information and develop more meaningful questions about a thing when we're actively playing.

It seems a bit strange, but it should really be no surprise that play is a powerful mechanism for learning. We see it all throughout the animal kingdom. Baby animals tend to play a lot and through that play they learn important skills they'll need to survive. Ever watch a baby kitten learn to hunt mice? We, too, learn by playing, by actively doing without really knowing what we're doing.

To give you another example, when I was younger, I used to play a trading card game called Magic the Gathering. I'd play this game for hours, because it interested me. I was fascinated by the strategy required to beat your opponent using a combination of your wit, luck, and creativity.

At one point, I had memorized almost every one of the thousands of cards that existed in the game. You could name a card and I could tell you exactly what that card did and what its stats were. (I could probably still tell you that information for most of the cards.) Do you think I sat down and tried to memorize thousands of cards? No, I didn't need to. I was playing and having fun. That natural exploration and curiosity helped me learn so much information with so little effort.

Being able to tap into that ability to play around is a powerful tool you can use, not only to motivate you, but to greatly accelerate the pace at which you learn. Before you read a book on a subject, skim the book and dive right in and start playing around. Don't worry if you don't know what you're doing. Just have fun and see what kind of questions your mind develops as you experiment and explore.

Once you've played around and you have all kinds of questions, only then go back and read the text. Now when you go back to your reference material, you'll approach it with a greater desire to devour and absorb its contents. You'll have questions that you'll want answers to; you'll have an idea of what's important.

Then you can take what you've learned and reapply it to your play. See how the new tools you've learned about fit into your play and solve the problems you had. Explore new areas and unlock new questions that need solutions. Repeat this cycle over and over again as you inch forward in knowledge for the purpose of solving the problems you discover as you play. This way the information you acquire is meaningful to you, not just words on a page.

Finally, seal it all in cement by teaching what you've learned to someone else. At this point you should be busting at the seams, ready to share your newfound knowledge with anyone who will listen, because you'll actually be excited about what you're discovering—such is the power of play. Teaching might be as simple as having a conversation with your spouse about what you've learned or it might be writing a blog post. The key is to regurgitate that information in your own words and organize the thoughts somewhere outside of your head.

This is the exact concept behind the 10-step process I've developed that we're going to go over in the next few chapters. I've added a bit more formality and introduced a few preparatory steps to help you organize your learning before you begin, but the key guiding principle is this idea of learning through play, experimentation, and teaching what you learned to someone else. This simple process that comes naturally to us all, but somehow gets "taught" out of us, is the simplest and purest way to learn.

Taking action

- What is the last thing you taught yourself how to do? What process did you use to learn it?
- When was the last time you were really excited about a hobby or other interest? How much do you know about that hobby or interest? Did you make a concerted effort to learn about it, or did it come naturally through play?

28

My 10-step process

Over the years, I've been under immense pressure to learn new technologies, programming languages, frameworks, and other competencies very quickly. Often, this pressure has been my own fault, due to me jumping into things and getting in way over my head, but regardless of the source, it has forced me to develop a repeatable system for self-learning.

In the next few chapters I'm going to take you through a 10-step system I developed to learn anything quickly. Let's start off by talking about what exactly this system is and how it works.

The idea behind the system

Early in my career, I learned primarily by finding a book on the subject I wanted to learn about and reading through it cover to cover. Only when I had finished reading about the subject would try to actually implement what I learned. Using this process, I found that I was learning, but at a very slow pace, and I'd often have to go back through the book to fill in the gaps I'd invariably have in my knowledge about a subject.

When I had plenty of time and I was learning without a real concrete goal in mind, this approach was fine. I eventually learned what I was trying to learn and it wasn't difficult to read a book cover to cover—it just took time. But as I started to have more demanding reasons to learn—and to do it quickly—I found the approach I was taking wasn't going to work. Oftentimes, I didn't have time to completely read a book, and I found much of the material in a book was better suited for reference, not for actual learning.

Necessity forced me to look for better ways to teach myself what I needed to know in a compressed timeframe. In some cases, I had only a week or less to absorb enough information about a subject to be able to teach it to someone else. I found that the natural thing for me to do in that situation was to clearly define exactly what I needed to learn and to look for the best resources I could find to get exactly the information I needed while ignoring any additional information that wasn't required to meet my goal.

I discovered that there were three main things I needed to know to be able to learn a technology:

1 *How to get started*—What were the basic things I needed to know to get started using whatever I was learning?

2 *The breadth of the subject*—How big was the thing I was learning and what could I do with it? I didn't need to know every detail to start, but if I had a decent overview of what I could do and what was possible, I could always find more details later.

3 *The basics*—Beyond just getting started, what were the basic use cases and the most common things I'd need to know to use a particular technology? What was the 20% I could learn that would cover 80% of my daily usage?

Equipped with just these three things, I could be effective with a technology without having to know everything about it upfront. I found that if I knew how to get started, what I could do, and the basics, I could learn the rest of what I needed to know as I went. When I tried to learn everything upfront, I was just wasting my time, because what was actually important got mixed in with all the other little details. This new approach allowed me to focus on only what was important. I could rely on reference materials to fill in any gaps later when I actually needed more details. How many times do you read a technical book cover to cover and find that you only actually use a small portion of the technology that's covered in the book?

I used this technique to learn the Go programming language in a very short time period—just a few weeks. I focused on learning how to write code with Go as soon as possible. Then I got an overall idea of how big the programming language was and what kinds of libraries were available. I wanted to get an overall feel for what the language could do. Finally, I went through and learned the basics. I only expanded on those basics when I needed to dive deeper.

The 10-step system

It turns out that getting those three pieces of knowledge isn't as easy of a task as it might seem. Learning how to get started with a technology can be a challenge, and it's often difficult to find out what is the 20% you need to know to be 80% effective with a technology. Plus, I often had a hard time finding a compact description of the breadth of a technology. Often this information was spread throughout an entire book or several different books.

To solve these problems, I needed to do a bit of research ahead of time to make sure I could find the information I needed and organize it in a way that made the most sense for progression.

The basic idea of the 10-step process is to start by getting a basic understanding of what you're trying to learn—enough to know what you don't know. Then take that information and use it to define the scope of what you want to learn, along with what success will look like. Armed with that knowledge, you can find resources—and not just books—to help you learn what you want to know. Finally, you can create your own learning plan to chart the course you're going to take to learn your subject and filter the materials down to just the best ones that will help you achieve your goal.

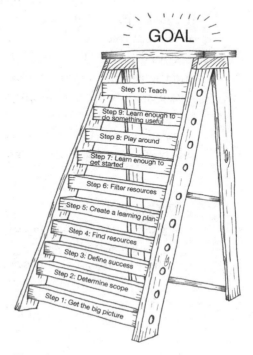

The 10-step system

Once you've done this legwork and know what you're going to learn and how you're going to learn it, you can take each waypoint in your learning plan and apply the process of "learn, do, learn, teach" (LDLT) to gain a deep understanding of the subject matter as you progress to your goal.

The first part of the 10-step process is the research portion and it's done once. But steps 7 through 10 are repeated for each module you end up creating in your learning plan. This technique ends up being effective because it forces you to clearly define a goal for what you're trying to learn upfront, and it constantly moves you in the direction of that goal by actually doing instead of just reading or listening to lectures.

I've been able to learn whole programming languages using this technique, in a matter of days. Thousands of other developers who've signed up for my video course on this 10-step process have had similar results (http://simpleprogrammer.com/ss-10steps).

Is this the only way to learn quickly? Is this some magical system? No. It's just a practical way to learn quickly by reducing down the volume of content to only what's important and to really make that content stick in your head by forcing you to learn through the self-discovery of play and the reinforcing power of teaching. As we go through the actual steps in the next couple of chapters, feel free to modify the system as you see fit, throw out what you don't like or don't find effective, and keep what works for you. Ultimately, you have to figure out how to educate yourself in a way that works for you—your future depends on it.

Taking action

Take a technology you know well and see if you can define

- How to get started with it
- The breadth of that technology
- The 20% you need to know to be 80% effective using it

29

Steps 1–6: Do these once

For the first 6 steps of the 10-step process, you'll focus on doing enough research upfront to make sure that you know exactly what you're attempting to learn and how you'll know you're done. You'll also pick out the best resources to help you achieve your goal and charting out a plan to get there.

These first six steps will only be done once for each topic that you want to learn about. Steps 7–10 will be repeated for each module you create in the learning plan you'll put together in step 5. Even though you'll only go through steps 1–6 once, they're some of the most important steps, because they'll set you up for future success or failure. During these six steps, you'll do all the prep work you need to prepare you to actually learn about your topic. The better the foundation you lay, the easier it will be for you to reach your goal.

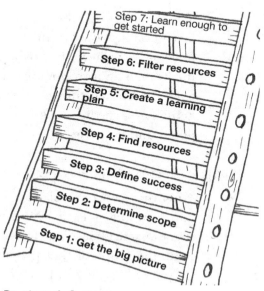

Do steps 1–6 once.

Step 1: Get the big picture

Learning is always tricky, because when you first start to learn about something, you don't know enough about it to really understand what you need to learn. Former U.S.

Secretary of Defense Donald Rumsfeld talked about "unknown unknowns," or basically what you don't know that you don't know.

Most developers crack open a book and start reading through it without even knowing what they don't know. They leave these "unknown unknowns" for later discovery. The problem with this approach is that you're very likely to learn the wrong thing or get in way over your head. It's important to at least understand a little bit about a subject before diving into it. Then you can figure out exactly what you need to learn and decide the best way to do it.

What you want to do in this step is to get the big picture of the topic you're trying to learn about. What is the 50,000-foot view of this topic? Can you learn just enough to understand what you don't know and how big this thing is?

Suppose you wanted to learn how to do digital photography. You might start out by searching the internet for everything you could find on the subject and skimming blog posts and articles about digital photography. You could probably have a good idea of how big the topic is and what kind of subtopics exist within a few hours of research.

To complete this step, do some basic research on the topic you want to learn about. You can probably accomplish most of this research using internet searches. If you happen to have a book on the subject, you might read an introductory chapter to skim through the material. Don't spend too much time on this step, though. Remember, the goal isn't to actually learn the topic here, but to just get a big picture of what it's about and how big it is.

Step 2: Determine scope

Now that you have at least somewhat of an idea of what your topic is and how big it is, it's time to narrow down your focus to determine what exactly you want to learn. In any project, it's important to determine the scope of that project so that you know how big it is and can prepare accordingly. Learning is no different.

If you were continuing with learning digital photography, at this point you'd want to figure out exactly how big the topic was and how you could break it down into a smaller scope. You can't learn everything about digital photography in any reasonable amount of time, so you'll have to decide what areas to focus on and what the scope should be. Perhaps you want to know how to shoot portrait pictures. That could be your scope.

One common failing point in learning is becoming overwhelmed by trying to tackle something that's too big. It's not practical to try to learn "physics." That topic is far too big and unfocused. You can't learn everything there is to know about physics in any reasonable amount of time—perhaps not in your whole life. You need to determine the scope of what you do want to learn. You have to take the information you gained in the previous step and use it to narrow your focus to a smaller area—something much more manageable.

Let's take a look table 29.1 to see some examples of how you might break down a big topic into a much narrower focus.

Table 29.1   Breaking down a big topic into manageable pieces

Original topic	Properly scoped topic
Learn C#.	Learn the basics of the C# language needed to create a simple console application.
Learn photography.	Learn digital photography for shooting portrait pictures.
Learn Linux.	Learn how to set up and install Ubuntu Linux and how to use its basic features.

Notice how each of these examples takes a broad topic like C# and narrows it down to a specific focus. We take a fairly unbounded topic and define a clear scope that has a focus. You'll also notice that in this step we put a reason for learning into a properly scoped topic. For instance, you want to learn photography, specifically digital photography, for the purpose of shooting portrait pictures. By stating the reason for learning, it can help define the scope, because people usually learn something for some particular reason.

For this step, take the information you gathered in the first step and use it to come up with an appropriate scope for what you want to learn about. Use your reason for learning a topic to help you determine what the scope should be.

You might be tempted to make your scope bigger and less focused, because you want to learn about different subtopics in your topic area, but resist the temptation and try to be as focused as possible. You can only learn one thing at a time. You can always come back later and learn about other subtopics that branch off of your original topic, but for now, pick one narrowly focused thing and go with it.

One last note about this step: use your timeframe to help you determine the scope. If you have just one week, you need to be realistic about what you can learn in that timeframe. If you have a couple of months, you might be able to tackle a bigger topic. Scope your topic down to the appropriate size that fits your overall reason for learning and fits into the timeframe that's available to you.

Step 3: Define success

Before starting any great endeavor, it's very important to define success. Without knowing what success looks like, it's both difficult to aim and to know when you've actually hit the target. Before you try to learn anything, you should have a clear picture in your mind of what success will look like. When you know what your target is, you can more easily work backwards from the goal to determine the steps you need to take to get there.

Again, if we follow the example of learning digital photography, you might decide that a good success criteria would involve learning to use all the features of your digital camera, being able to describe what they are, and understanding why and when to use each feature.

The goal of this step is to come up with a clear and concise statement that will define success for your learning endeavor. Depending on what you're trying to learn, this statement might look very different, but you want to make sure you have a specific set of success criteria that you can use to adequately assess whether or not you've met your learning goal.

Good success criteria are specific, not ambiguous. Don't make a vague statement about what you want to accomplish. Instead, list a specific result or thing you should be able to do once you've reached your goal. Table 29.2 shows some examples.

Table 29.2   Examples of bad and good success criteria

Bad success criteria	Good success criteria
I can take good pictures with my digital camera.	I can go through all the features of my digital camera and describe what they are, as well as why and when I should use each feature.
I can learn the basics of C#.	I can build a small application in C# that makes use of all the major language features.
I know how to use HTML to build web pages.	I can create my own homepage that displays my resume and sample work on the internet using HTML5.

Your own success criteria will be determined primarily by what you want to get out of your learning experience. Just make sure it's something that you can evaluate at the end of this process to be sure you met the objective. Good success criteria will also keep you on track by giving you a target to aim at.

Step 4: Find resources

Remember back in school when you had to write a report on a particular subject? What would happen if you wrote your whole report and only provided a single reference—just one book—where you got all your information from? You'd probably receive a big fat "F" on the report. Why, then, do so many of us do exactly that when we try to learn something today? We just read one book on a subject, or we have one resource we use for all of our research.

For the subject of digital photography, you might start with your camera manual, but you wouldn't want to stop there. You could probably find many different websites dedicated to digital photography or even your specific brand of camera. You could also do a search on Amazon for books on digital photography and even find experts whom you could ask for advice.

Instead of reading a single book on a subject, try to gather many different resources to help you learn. Resources can take many forms besides just books. In fact, today, with the wide availability of the internet and all the different content available on it, you can find many resources for almost any topic you want to learn about.

In this step you want to find as many resources as possible for learning about the topic you've selected. Don't worry about quality at this point. This is similar to a brainstorming step. Later on you'll filter your resources and select the best ones, but for now you want to get as many different resources as possible.

One of the best ways to do this is to jump on your computer and start searching for your topic. I usually start my searches with Amazon to see how many books I can find and then I'll search on Google to see if I can find videos, blog articles, podcasts, or other content that would be useful to me. You can even go "old school" and hit the library. The important thing is that you find a variety of different resources. You don't want to be biased by the viewpoints of a single source and you want to have access to as much information as possible.

RESOURCE IDEAS

- Books
- Blog posts
- Online videos
- Experts or people already knowledgeable about the topic you want to learn about
- Podcasts
- Source code
- Example projects
- Online documentation

Step 5: Create a learning plan

Ever notice how most books are broken up into chapters and those chapters usually follow a progression through the content? Good technical books lay a foundation of groundwork that's built upon in each subsequent chapter.

Now that you have some resources, you can use those resources to get an idea of what you should learn and in what order you should learn it.

By now you should have a good idea of what subtopics you might want to learn about in regards to digital photography. You need to skim through the material you have on digital photography and find a way to break down the topic into smaller sections.

For most subjects, there's a natural progression for learning. You start at A, work your way to B, and finally end up at Z. It does you little good to learn random bits and pieces of information. You need to find the correct path that will get you from point A to point Z in the least amount of time, hitting all of the major landmarks along the way.

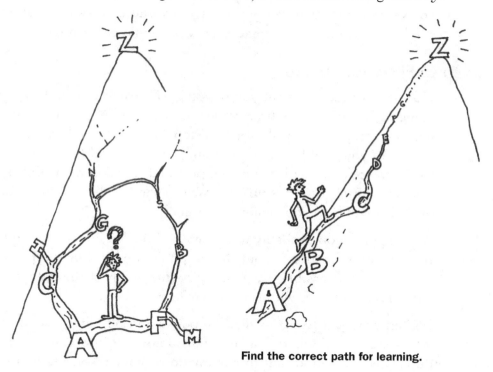

Find the correct path for learning.

For this step, you need to create your own learning path. Think of it as an outline for a book you'd write on the subject. In fact, your learning path will probably be very similar to the table of contents of a book when you're done. You basically want to end up with a series of modules you individually focus on learning until you reach your final goal.

A good way to create your learning plan is to see how others are teaching the subject you want to learn about. When I'm working on this step, I'll often look at the table of contents of several of the books I've chosen as possible resources from step 4. If five different authors have chosen to break up their content into the same sets of modules and the same ordering, chances are I should make my learning plan follow a similar approach.

That doesn't mean you should just copy the table of contents from a book and call that your learning plan. Many books will cover more than what you need to know to achieve your objectives, and many books will also be poorly organized. By looking at all the resources you've gathered, you can get a better overall picture of what content needs to be covered and what order you should cover it in.

Step 6: Filter resources

Now that you know what you're going to learn and what order you're going to learn it in, it's time to decide what resources you're going to use to accomplish the task. Back in step 4, you gathered together all the resources you could find on your subject. You used those resources in step 5 to come up with your own personal learning plan. But now it's time to whittle those resources down to the handful of most valuable ones that will help you achieve your goal.

At this point, you probably have plenty of books, blog posts, and other resources for learning about digital photography, but the problem is that you can't possibly utilize all of them. Much of the data is redundant and not all of it will fit your learning plan.

It's not practical to try to read 10 books and 50 blog posts on a subject—and even if you did, a large portion of that information would be duplicated. It's important to narrow down your resources to a smaller list of the best ones to help you achieve your goals.

Think of it this way: for step 6, you're the basketball coach making cuts for the varsity team. Sure, you'd like to let everyone play, but it just isn't possible. You've got to cut down your resources to a number that you can manage.

For this step, go through all the resources you've gathered in step 4 and figure out which ones have content that will help you to best cover the content in your learning plan. Also take a look at reviews and try to determine which resources are of the highest quality. I usually will look at the Amazon reviews for the books I'm considering purchasing and narrow it down to the best one or two books that I think will provide me the best bang for my buck.

Once you've completed this step, you're ready to move on to the first module of your learning plan. You'll repeat steps 7–10 for each learning plan module until you've made it to your destination.

Taking action

○ Pick a subject you want to learn about and actually go through the first six steps outlined here. You might want to start with something small, so you can get used to this process, but pick something. If you just read these steps, it won't do you much good.

30

Steps 7–10: Repeat these

Now comes the fun part. You'll repeat the next four steps for each of the modules you've defined in your learning plan. The goal of steps 7–10 is to actually learn the material by using my learn, do, learn, teach (LDLT) formula. You'll start off by learning just enough to get started. Then you'll play around to learn and gather questions through self-discovery. After that, you'll learn enough to do something useful. And, finally, you'll teach what you learned in order to fill in any gaps in your learning and cement the ideas in your head through a deep understanding.

Step 7: Learn enough to get started

There are two common learning mistakes that most people make, myself included. First, there's the problem of jumping in without knowing enough—acting too soon. Second, there's the problem of preparing too much before jumping in—acting too late. You want to strike a balance between the two and learn just enough to get started, but not so much that you don't get to explore on your own—where you end up learning the best.

Repeat steps 7–10.

For this step, the goal is to get just enough information about the topic you're learning about to be able to get started and to play around in the next step. For technologies like programming languages or frameworks, this step would involve learning how to create a basic "Hello, world!" program or set up your development environment. For something like photography, it might involve learning enough about a module on light to experiment on your own with various light sources and their effects.

The key to this step is to not go too far. It's easy to get carried away and start consuming all the resources you have on the module you're trying to learn, but you'll find the most success if you can avoid that temptation. Instead, focus on learning the minimal amount you'll need to get started and to be able to experiment on your own in the next step. You may want to skim material or read chapter summaries or introductions to gather enough information to have a basic idea of what you're doing.

Have you ever bought a new videogame and taken a quick look at the manual before you popped the cartridge in your video-game system and started playing? That's exactly what you want to do here. After you've played around a bit, in the next step you can go back and

Learn the basics quickly and start playing around.

read the manual in full. But for now, learn the basics and get right into playing the game.

Step 8: Play around

This step is both fun and scary. It's fun because you get to do exactly what the step says: play around. But it's scary because the step is completely unbounded. There are no rules. You can do whatever you want to do for this step. It's up to you to decide how to best execute this step.

Your first thought might be that this step doesn't seem important, but let's consider the alternative—the way most people learn. Most people will attempt to learn a subject by reading a book or watching a video about that subject. They'll try to absorb as much information upfront and then take action later. The problem with this approach is that when they're reading about their subject, they have no idea what is important. They're just following the path someone has laid out for them.

For this step, you might end up playing around with different light levels in your camera—assuming you're learning about how light affects digital photography. You might go outside and start adjusting the light levels or shooting in different conditions, without knowing what you're doing. You'll learn through discovery and also develop plenty of questions.

Now consider the approach I'm suggesting here, where you don't read everything upfront, but one of the first things you do is play and experiment on your own. With this approach, you learn by exploring and doing. As you play around, your brain naturally forms questions: How does this work? What happens if I do this? How do I solve this problem? These questions lead you in the direction of what's actually important. When you get back and find the answers to your own questions, not only will it be more rewarding, but you'll remember more of what you study, because what you learn will be important to you.

For this step, you want to take what you learned from step 7 and actually get started. Don't worry about outcomes. Just explore. If you're learning a new technology or programming language, you might create a small project during this step and test things out. Write down the questions that you have but don't have answers for. You'll have the opportunity to look for the answers to those questions in the next step.

Step 9: Learn enough to do something useful

Curiosity is a critical component of learning—especially self-learning. When we're children, we have rapid periods of learning driven mainly by curiosity. We want to know how the world works, so we ask questions and seek out answers to help us understand the world we're living in. Unfortunately, as we grow up, much of that curiosity tends to disappear as we start to take the world for granted. As a result, our learning slows down and we find education boring instead of fascinating.

The goal of this step is to bring that curiosity-fueled learning back. In step 8, you played around and hopefully came up with some questions that you couldn't find answers to on your own. Now is the time to answer those questions. For this step, you'll go through all the resources you gathered and learn about your module in depth.

Going back to the digital photography example, if you're playing around with light levels for the camera, this would be the point where you take all the questions you had while playing around and try to answer them by reading up on the subject. You might go through your resources and look up everything pertaining to light or any other questions that came up while you were playing around.

As you're reading text, watching videos, having conversations, or doing whatever else is necessary to consume the resources you've chosen, look for the answers to the questions you came up with in the previous step. This is your chance to really dig into the material and learn as much as you can.

Don't be afraid to go back and play some more as you discover answers to your questions and learn new things about your subject. Take as much time as you need to thoroughly understand your subject matter by reading and experimenting, and watching and doing.

Remember, though, you still don't have to completely consume every single resource you gathered. Only read or watch the parts that are relevant to what you're trying to learn right now. There are no golden stickers given out for reading a book cover to cover. Use the resources to help you teach yourself, driven primarily by the questions you've come up with by playing around.

Finally, don't forget about your success criteria that you defined in step 3. Try to tie what you're learning back to your ultimate goal. Each module you master should in some way move your forward toward your final destination.

Step 10: Teach

> *Tell me and I forget. Teach me and I remember. Involve me and I learn.*
>
> —Benjamin Franklin

Most people are afraid to teach. I know I was. It's easy to be filled with thoughts of self-doubt when you're considering whether you're worthy or not to teach what you know—or you think you know—to someone else. But if you want to learn a subject in depth, if you really want to gain understanding about a subject, you have to teach it. There's no other way.

In reality, you only need to be one step ahead of someone to teach them. Sometimes, in fact, experts who are many steps ahead of a student have a hard time teaching, because they can't relate to the student. They end up glossing over details that they think are simple, because they don't remember what it was like to be a beginner.

If you wanted to teach someone about what you learned about how light affects digital photography, you might create a simple YouTube video showing examples of different light sources and how they affect your shots. You could even do something simpler like explain to a friend or coworker how light affects digital photography—I'm sure plenty of people would be interested to have that conversation.

For this step, I'm going to ask you to move out of your comfort zone and teach what you've learned to someone else. It's the only way to know for sure that you've learned something, and it's a great way to fill in the gaps in your own learning as you try to explain it to others. It's a process that will cause you to really dissect and understand the topic you're learning about in your own mind as you organize the information in a way that will make it understandable to others. I've made the greatest leaps in my career and professional development and in my own understanding when I started teaching.

You can teach what you've learned in many different ways. You could write a blog post or create a YouTube video. You could even talk to your spouse about what you've learned and explain it to them. The important thing is that you actually take some time to take what you've learned out of your own mind and organize it in a way that someone else can understand. When you go through this process, you'll find that there are many things that you thought you understood that you didn't. You'll also begin to make connections that you didn't see before and simplify the information in your head as you try to condense it down and regurgitate it.

It may be tempting, but whatever you do, don't skip this step. This step is crucial to retaining information and developing more than a surface-level understanding of a subject.

WAYS TO TEACH

- Write a blog post.
- Create a YouTube video or tutorial.
- Give a presentation.
- Have a conversation with a friend or your spouse.
- Answer questions in an online forum.

Final thoughts

It takes dedication and work to learn how to educate yourself, but the rewards you'll gain over the course of your life by doing so are innumerable. This 10-step process isn't a magic formula that will make you instantly smarter, but it can help you go through the process of organizing your studies before you jump in to absorb more of what you learn about by using the natural curiosity mechanism that drives most of us.

If the steps in this process don't work for you or you feel the formality is unnecessary, by all means, throw them out. The steps themselves aren't important. It's the concept behind this learning process that really matters. The important thing is to develop a system that you can use to teach yourself—a system that you can consistently apply to get results.

Taking action

- Finish your learning experiment by executing steps 7–10 for each module of the learning plan you created in chapter 29.
- For now, don't skip any steps. See how the process works for you and then modify it.

31

Looking for mentors: Finding your Yoda

In almost all great movies or stories where a hero goes through the "coming-of-age" experience, the hero has a mentor, someone who imparts to them the wisdom needed to proceed to their goal, someone who challenges the hero to grow.

Having a mentor can be a huge asset to your software development career, because a good mentor affords you the benefits of experience without actually having to go through the ordeals of obtaining it. You can learn a great deal from the failures and successes of a mentor who has already blazed the path for you. A good mentor might be able to help you learn a technology much quicker than you could on your own.

But like most things in life, finding a mentor isn't easy. You might not have to get in an X-Wing and fly to the Dagobah star system, but you'll have to do some work. In this chapter, I'll give you some tips on what to look for in a mentor, how to find one, and how to convince a mentor you're worth investing in, so that it's truly a win–win situation.

Mentor qualities

Mentors can come in a wide variety of shapes and sizes. Paradoxically, it's often a mistake to judge a person's ability to help you by their own life. Some of the most successful coaches for professional sports teams couldn't play a sport to save their own life. Some celebrity trainers look like they've never stepped foot in the gym. And some motivational speakers live their own life in the exact opposite way of what they preach — they just can't seem to pull their own lives together.

Does that mean you should look for the most whacked-out, screw-job, failure you can find and ask to become their student? No. But it means you shouldn't discount someone because of what they've accomplished in their own life or how they look. The best teachers are often the ones who have fallen into the most pits.

If you want to find an example of this, go into an AA (Alcoholics Anonymous) meeting or perhaps even a local church. Often, you'll find that many of the mentors in those places are people who've failed miserably and then overcame their troubles and learned to help others do the same.

Okay, so what do you want to look for in a mentor? You should look for someone who has either done what you want to do — successfully — or has helped other people do what you want to do. If they've done it themselves, great. But the more powerful indicator is what they've done for others. The more people a person has been able to influence others for the good, to achieve their own goals, the more likely that person will be able to do the same for you.

We have to separate what we think about a person or what they say from the results they achieve. This isn't as easy of a task as it seems, though. When we're looking for help from someone else, we have to assume that we don't know what's best; otherwise we wouldn't need help. That means that whatever analysis we come up with is likely wrong. We have to trust that what we think is the way actually isn't, and rely on looking at the results a potential mentor has achieved instead of our own logic and reasoning.

Think about learning to swim. When you're first learning to swim, your mind is filled with all kinds of false information about how to swim and the dangers of the water. You might think that you can't float and that you'll drown. You have to trust someone who is teaching you how to swim that they know more than you do and your judgment about swimming is wrong.

When searching for a potential mentor, put aside your own judgment and reasoning and look at results. Look for someone who has accomplished what you're setting out to do or who is higher up the ladder than you. Look for someone who has helped others reach a level you want to reach—even if they haven't reached the level themselves.

FINDING A MENTOR CHECKLIST

- Have they done what I want to do?
- Have they helped someone else do what I want to do?
- What results do they have to show?
- Can you get along with this person, personality-wise?

Where to find a mentor

Now that you know what you're looking for, where do you actually find a mentor? You can't just go to a mentor store and rent one. (Well, actually you sort of can now—check out http://simpleprogrammer.com/ss-clarity and you can talk to mentors in different fields for an hourly rate. You can also hire coaches to coach you on various areas of your life.)

Your best option is either someone you personally know or a friend of a friend or family member. If you're willing to do a little research and ask around, you can probably find someone in your network of friends and family who would make a good mentor for whatever endeavor you're trying to pursue. Finding a mentor this way is optimal, because you're more likely to get the time of someone you already know or someone who you can be introduced to by a close friend or family member.

Sometimes, though, your personal network isn't large enough, so you need to look elsewhere. Before you fasten R2D2's seatbelt, you might want to check local groups in your area. There are often groups for all kinds of hobbies and pursuits. If you're looking for mentorship in software development, find a local group of software developers on a site like Meetup (http://meetup.com). You can also find many entrepreneurial groups to join in your area.

Most of these local groups will have a mix of people with different skill levels, but they're a common hangout for experienced veterans who either are trying to give back to the community or are looking for a new apprentice to mold to their will. Even if you can't find a good mentor in one of these groups, you're likely to meet someone who can point you in the right direction or who has the connection you need.

A really smart move, if you're interested in climbing the corporate ladder, is to look for a mentor in your own company. A senior person, perhaps even your own boss or your boss's boss, is a great person for a mentor, because you'll likely be schooled in exactly what you need to know to advance in the company. As an added bonus, having friends in high places has never hurt anyone's career.

Virtual mentors

But what if you can't find a mentor after exhausting all your options? Well, in some cases, you might want to consider creating your own mentor.

When I first got started in real estate investment, I didn't know anyone who had done anything like what I was attempting to do. I had no connections to other real estate investors and I didn't have the sense to find a group of real estate investors in the area, so I set out to create my own mentor—from books.

I found the best books I could find on real estate investing and learned as much as I could from my virtual mentors. I tried to understand what kind of decisions they had made and why they had made them, in addition to reading what they wrote.

Obviously a real mentor is a better choice, but when you're stuck, you can turn to the people who you'd have liked to have as mentors in real life. In fact, you may even be able to reach out to some of those people over the internet and actually get their advice.

In one of my favorite books, *Think and Grow Rich* by Napoleon Hill (Wilder Publications, 2007), Mr. Hill recounts how he was unable to find the mentors he wanted, so he imagined them in his head. He read books of famous people he wanted to be like and he imagined having conversations with them. He imagined what kind of advice they would give him and how he would respond. It might seem a bit looney, but

Maxwell Maltz, the author of *Psycho-Cybernetics* (Reprint, Pocket Books, 1989)—another classic book—suggests exactly the same thing.

Recruiting a mentor

Even if you're able to find the perfect-match mentor for you, there's no guarantee your mentor will want to take you on as an apprentice. In fact, chances are most highly successful people will be rather busy and not have much time to spare at all. So how do you convince a would-be mentor that you're worth taking a chance on?

One of the best ways to accomplish this task is by offering something in exchange for help. And one of the best things you can offer is your eagerness to learn and to ... well ... work for free. That's right. It's pretty hard to turn down free labor. If you're willing to help with boring tasks in exchange for learning the ropes, you'll find your mentor much more likely to accept your proposition.

Perhaps you don't have the time or the financial resources to work for someone for free. Perhaps you just need a little bit of help in one area of life you're pursuing or your mentor doesn't have the need for your help. What can you do then?

> TIP   Consider offering to buy lunch or dinner as a way of getting a possible mentor to give you some advice.

Be persistent. Most people stop at the first "No." Don't be that kind of person. Instead, be the kind of person who has to be beaten off with a stick—and even then, still comes back. Your tenaciousness won't always be rewarded, but you'll probably be surprised how often it is.

Taking action
- Before you can find a mentor, you need to know what you're expecting a mentor to do for you. Sit down and think about why you need a mentor and what you hope to get out of a mentoring relationship.
- Make a list of all the people you know who might be a good mentor for you. Ask other people to help you fill in the list with people they know. Use your network.
- Think of what you can offer a mentor in exchange for their help.

32

Taking on an apprentice: Being Yoda

Having a mentor is great, but sometimes being a mentor is better. No matter how far along you may be in your software development career, chances are there's someone who could benefit from your wisdom or advice.

It's important to give back to the community, not only because it's the right thing to do, but because it can also benefit you immensely.

In this chapter, we'll discuss some of the benefits of being a mentor and how you can choose which apprentices you should take on.

Being a mentor

Many developers don't think they have what it takes to be a mentor to someone else. Perhaps you're in the same situation. Perhaps you feel that you don't have the qualifications to coach or help someone else along their path.

I don't know anything about you, except that you probably like to write code, but I can almost 100% guarantee you could be a mentor to someone in some area. One of my favorite things to tell people is that they only have to be one step ahead of a person in some area of life to help them. Regardless of where you are in life or your own career, chances are there is someone who you're one step ahead of in some area, someone you can help.

Take a moment to consider who you are one step ahead of. Think about developers you know who are trying to learn what you already know.

How could you help those developers by sharing your knowledge, even if you aren't an expert yet yourself?

Being a mentor isn't about knowing the right answers all the time or being so sure of yourself that you couldn't possibly make a mistake. Being a mentor is about looking objectively at another person's problems and offering solutions they might not be able to see because they are too close to the problem. Often, you'll temper this observation with your own wisdom and experience, but sometimes just having an outsider's viewpoint is enough to help someone reach success.

I know that I've personally experienced someone who knew nothing about my problems mentoring me just by listening carefully to what I had to say and seeing the obvious things that I couldn't see. Sometimes all you really need to do to mentor someone is pay attention. Many high-paid life coaches do exactly that.

We all need help seeing the things that we can't see in our own lives, because we're a bit myopic when it comes to our own problems and situations. The great Tiger Woods is coached by a golfer who isn't as good as he is, but is able to see things Tiger cannot. To be a mentor you just need to be observant and patient. You need to lend a sympathetic ear to your apprentices, encourage them when they need encouragement, and kick them squarely in the pants when they need…motivation.

The benefits of mentorship

Let's be honest. While we like to think of ourselves as charitable, we all are motivated primarily by our self-interests. It's only human. I can appeal to your sense of community and charity by mentioning how mentoring others will be a chance to give back and to do good for others—and it truly is. But I also want to tell you about some real tangible benefits mentoring can have on your own life—not just the people you help.

We'll talk about this more in the coming chapters, and we've already talked about it a little bit in the chapters on the 10-step program, but teaching is one of the best ways to learn.

When you take on the role of a mentor, you often end up learning more than the person you're mentoring does as you revisit your own thoughts on a subject and see them through fresh eyes. When you act as a mentor, you're often hit with one of the most powerful questions: Why? Why is this true? Why should we do things this way? When you're forced to explore those why questions, you may find that you don't know why. You may find that, in your attempt to help someone else, your answering of that question gives you a much deeper knowledge of a subject or even completely changes your mind about it.

Mentoring is also a bit like playing the lottery. Every person you help on their journey is a person who might someday surpass you and end up benefiting you when the tables are turned. Every person you mentor is like a seed that you've planted. Plant enough seeds and one of them will grow into a great tree that may someday provide you shade. There have been many people I've mentored in my career who have ended up in the position to do me a huge favor later on. People remember a person who helps them in their time of need.

Now, I'll finally appeal to your charitable side and tell you that it will make you feel good. It's rewarding to know that you've made a positive impact on another person's life, especially a person who can't repay you. Mentoring someone else can give your own life new purpose and meaning as you find that true happiness is usually only experienced when you help others.

MENTORING BENEFITS

- Feeling of "giving back" and doing something for another person.
- One of the best ways to learn something in depth.
- Chance that someone you mentor will someday be able to help you.
- Growth opportunity. You grow when you help others grow.

Picking a "worthy" apprentice

One difficulty of being a mentor is finding an apprentice who is worth investing time in. As you progress in your career and become successful, you'll find that there are more and more people who are asking for your time and help, but not all of them are sincere. It's really easy to end up wasting your own valuable time helping someone who has no real desire to help themselves. For this reason it's important to choose an apprentice carefully. Don't throw your pearls to swine.

When deciding on an apprentice, look for base qualities that you know will lead to success. A person who has the right qualities and principles, though lacking wisdom or knowledge, will eventually succeed if given the right guidance. A person without them can be given all the help in the world, but it won't matter.

Look for a person who truly has a desire to learn and is willing to work hard to do it. Look for someone who isn't asking for your help out of laziness and unwillingness to put forth the effort required, but wants your help to accelerate their progress and to prevent making mistakes that could easily be avoided by the benefit of experience.

Taking action

- What are some areas in which you could provide mentorship to others? Make a list of topics that you're passionate about and have sufficient knowledge of to help someone else.
- Go ahead and become a mentor. Find someone who needs your help and help them. Just be sure that you find someone who meets the criteria of a good apprentice.

33

Teaching: Learn you want? Teach you must.

We've already talked about this topic in the chapters on the 10-step process, but I think this is such an important concept that it's worth exploring in a little more detail. One of the greatest ways to learn—perhaps the only way to learn anything deeply—is to teach.

This profound truth is so frequently ignored because many people feel intimidated—and often unworthy—of trying to teach someone else. This chapter is all about getting over that fear, understanding just how valuable teaching is, and exploring some ways you can start teaching to begin reaping benefits in your learning experience.

I'm not a teacher

One of the most common excuses I hear when I tell developers they need to teach is that they aren't a teacher and they don't know how to teach. Now, not all of us are trained in teaching methods, but everyone is capable of teaching. More often than not, the real issue isn't ability, but rather confidence. If I ask you to show me how to do something that you've mastered, most likely you can, without hesitation. But if I ask you to show me how to do something that you yourself are unsure of, this is a much more frightening prospect.

The problem with only teaching things that you feel you're an expert in is that part of the requirement of becoming an expert is teaching. It's very difficult to gain expertise in an area that you haven't taught to someone else. In fact, I'd challenge you to try to find a skill that you've "mastered" but you've never taught to someone else. You might be able to find a few, but I'd venture to guess most skills you've really mastered, you've done so partially through helping someone else learn them. The trick is that most of us teach without even knowing it.

Teaching has such a formal ring to it, but really teaching is just sharing some knowledge with someone else. You do this all the time and don't even realize it. How many times have you explained some concept to a coworker or demonstrated how to use some framework or library? You may not have gotten in front of a class with a chalkboard and ruler, but you were still teaching.

You don't have to have degrees and certifications to become a teacher and you certainly don't have to be an expert. You just have to be one step ahead of a person to successfully teach them. So, although you may think you don't have what it takes, the truth is that we're all teachers.

What happens when you teach?

We tend to overestimate how much we know about a subject when we first learn about it. It's very easy to fool yourself into thinking you really understand something—that is, until you try to teach it.

Have you ever had someone ask you a question—a simple one—and been stunned by your inability to articulate a response? You start off by saying "Well, obviously," but then the next words are "umm." It happens to me all the time. This common phenomenon often happens when we think we understand a subject, but we really only have a surface-level knowledge of it.

This is why teaching is so valuable. Teaching forces you to confront all the areas in your own knowledge that aren't deep enough to be able to adequately explain them to another person. As humans, our brains are good at recognizing patterns. We often can recognize patterns and solve many problems that fit into the patterns we've recognized without truly understanding what we're doing or why.

This kind of surface-level understanding can go unnoticed as we're able to function and do our jobs with it, but the moment we try to explain to someone else how something works or why we do something, the gaping hole in our understanding is exposed.

But this isn't a bad thing. We have to know where our weaknesses are in order to fill them in. By trying to teach something to someone else, you force yourself to confront difficult questions about your subject matter and to explore it more deeply until you go from merely learning about a thing to understanding it. Learning tends to be temporary, but understanding is permanent. I can memorize multiplication tables, but if I understand how multiplication works, I can reproduce the tables even if my memory fails me at some point.

When you teach, you're also forced to reorganize data in your brain. When you learn something initially, it usually comes in bits and pieces. The material you were taught may have been organized nicely, but when it goes into your head, it often goes in a much more disorganized manner. You grasp one concept, which leads you to the next, and bounces you back to the previous one as you finally get that part you didn't grasp before.

Storing data in your head in this way is inefficient and confusing. This is why when someone asks you a question that you know you know the answer to, your words often come up in a garbled mess. You know you know it, but you just can't explain it.

When you try to teach someone, you're forced to reorganize the data in your own head. The act of thinking about the best way to explain something and put it on paper, or into words or slides, causes you to put together the disconnected bits of information in your brain and reorganize them in a way that makes sense. You essentially have to reteach yourself before you can teach someone else. This is why teaching is so effective for learning.

Getting started

Perhaps, by now, I've convinced you that teaching is both something you can do and something you should do—especially if you want to actually have a deep understanding of what you know. But you might be wondering how you can actually get started teaching. It isn't exactly easy to step out there and act as an authority on a subject that you may or may not feel comfortable about.

I find that teaching is best approached from a humble perspective, but with an authoritative tone. What I mean by this is that when you teach, you don't act like the knowledge you have makes you in some way better or smarter than your student, but you do teach with confidence, firmly believing what you're saying. No one wants to learn from someone who is unsure of what they're saying, and they also don't want to be made to feel stupid when they are being taught.

It takes some practice to get this right—it's easy to step too far in one direction or the other. Just try to realize that your job in teaching is to help someone else, not to prove your superiority or to seek approval.

Think about some of the teachers in your life who were most effective, the ones who made you enjoy learning and made an impact on your life. What qualities did they have? What approach did they take to teaching?

Now, where to get started? Should you open up your own classroom and invite people to attend?

I'd recommend starting small and getting used to the idea of sharing your ideas. I always recommend developers start a blog (did you read section 2?), which is a great place to teach what you're learning without much pressure. As you learn about a subject, blog about what you're learning. See if you can distill the information you've acquired in a simple way. After all, that's exactly how my blog, Simple Programmer, got started. My original goal—and still the most important one—is to make the complex simple. When I started my blog, I wanted to take what I was learning and simplify it so other people could understand it better.

You don't have to stop with blogging, though. Another great step is to start giving presentations at local user groups or your own workplace. Just remember to keep that humble yet confident spirit—not arrogant—and you'll do fine, even if you aren't the best presenter.

Videos, especially tutorial screencasts, are another great way to teach, and it doesn't take much to get started. You can use screen-recording software like Camtasia (http://simpleprogrammer.com/ss-camtasia) or ScreenFlow (http://simpleprogrammer.com/ss-screenflow) to record your screen and provide a voiceover explaining what is going on. This kind of teaching will really challenge you and force you to think about the best way to present information, because it involves audio, visual, and actual demonstration.

Taking action

- Figure out a topic you can teach about and do it. You could write a blog post, give a presentation, or record a screencast, but do some form of teaching this week.

- As you're preparing to teach a subject, pay special attention to how your preparation to teach actually increases your own understanding of a subject. Pay attention to any gaps in your own knowledge that you wouldn't have discovered if you hadn't tried to teach.

34

Do you need a degree or can you "wing it?"

Long has the debate raged on among software developers about the value of a college degree. Can a software developer succeed in their career, in life, without a degree, or are they doomed to walk the earth ever searching, but never finding...work?

In this chapter, we'll explore the advantages and disadvantages of pursuing higher education. I'll also give you some tips for succeeding even if the roads in life didn't lead you to academia.

Do you need a degree to succeed?

I'm sure you know this is a very charged question. If you asked someone who has a degree they are likely to say "yes." Ask someone who doesn't have one, and you'll most likely get a "no"—unless they happen to be unemployed at the time. But what is the truth? Do you need one or not?

Well, I happen to have a degree in computer science, but I didn't start my career with one, so I've been on both sides of the fence. That doesn't make my answer infallible, by any means, but it does give me the perspective of having tried to get jobs and promotions in either situation.

From my experience, I've found that having a degree isn't required to succeed, but it's certainly a limiting factor that narrows down the number of jobs available to you and to some degree your advancement—especially in larger corporations. Not having a degree can end up causing you to be filtered out before your resume is even looked at by a human. Many companies, especially large corporations, filter job applications on education levels. In fact, some corporations have explicit hiring policies that require software developers to have a college degree. Again, that doesn't mean you can't get a job with one of those companies—there are always exceptions—but it certainly would make it harder to do.

I don't want to overemphasize the importance of a degree here, but I do want you to understand that not having one will limit your options. With that said, I firmly believe a degree isn't required to actually succeed.

I know many software developers who have had successful careers without ever getting a degree. Bill Gates is a great example of this. He didn't finish his degree, but look at him now. For a good portion of my software development career I didn't have a degree and I did just fine. In the field of software development, the most important thing is ability. If you can write good code and solve problems and you can demonstrate that ability, it will take you much further than a piece of paper that says you're "educated."

The thing that's different about software development, compared to many other industries, is that the field is constantly changing. Every day new frameworks and technologies are introduced. It's virtually impossible to adequately prepare a software developer for the real job environment in an educational institution. By the time textbooks are published and course curriculums are decided on, many things have changed.

Now, this doesn't mean that there aren't some core areas of software development that don't change. Many computer science degrees include courses on algorithms, operating systems, relational database theory, and other topics that are timeless, but the simple truth is that when you sit down at your desk to write some code, you rarely fall back on the skills you were taught in school. Most of the work we do as developers involves using new technologies and learning how to work with them. We rarely need to go back to our computer science roots.

Again, that doesn't mean that a basic computer science education isn't valuable. The ability to be able to dig deep into a problem and to understand it at more than a surface level can be very valuable. It's just that, for most developers, the more relevant indicator of success at a job is relevant experience.

Advantages to having a degree

We've already talked about some of the advantages of having a degree, but let's dive in a little deeper.

First, having a degree is going to ensure that you have a well-rounded education in software development. A computer science degree, or similar software development–related degree, won't give you all the education you need to be a good software developer, but most degree programs are going to at least equip you with the basics and a solid foundation.

You can, of course, learn these things on your own, but if you're self-taught, you may end up with some holes in your education that could hurt you later in your career. A computer science or related degree will equip you with high-level mathematics; understanding of programming languages, operating systems, and algorithms; and a few other key topics that you might not necessarily need to know to do your day-to-day job, but that will provide you a good foundation and deeper understanding of what you're actually doing and how things work.

Having a degree also helps you get started without experience. It's very difficult to break into the field of software development, especially without any experience. Having a degree, in that case, can make a big difference. It's very hard to convince someone that you can write code when you've never had a job doing it before and you don't have formal education.

A degree can also give you more options. There are some positions that you'll never get without a degree—especially in large corporations. And you'll have a hard time moving over to an executive position without a degree. If you decide you want to switch tracks and advance up the management track, you may want to get an MBA, which will require a lower degree first. Table 34.1 outlines a few benefits and drawbacks of having a degree.

Table 34.1   Benefit and drawbacks of a degree

Benefits of degree	Drawbacks
Well-rounded education in software development	Spend time learning when you could be earning
Get started easier without experience	Might be trapped in a way of thinking that's hard to break
More options; easier to move to executive route or management	

What if you don't have a degree?

Okay, so obviously having a degree isn't going to ever hurt you, and it could help you, but what do you do if you don't have a degree?

If you don't have a degree, you're going to have to rely more on experience and demonstrated proof of your capabilities. A degree gives an employer at least some confidence that you know something about software development, so without one you need to be able to prove your ability on your own.

The best way to prove your ability is through previous experience. If you were a software developer for the past five years without a degree, it's pretty likely that you can write code. But if you're just starting out, your job is going to be a bit tougher. You're going to have to prove that you can actually do what you say you can do. One of the best ways to do this is with a portfolio.

I'd recommend having a portfolio of your work, whether or not you have a degree or experience, but if you have neither, you better be able to show some code you wrote. One of the best ways to do this today is to contribute to—or start—an open source project hosting on a site like GitHub (http://github.com). GitHub is a service that hosts many open source projects. Someone can look at your GitHub account and see your contributions.

You can also put together some websites or applications you've created and bring the source code with you to a job interview. I always recommend that developers, especially ones starting out, create a mobile application, like an Android or iOS app. This is a good way to show a prospective employer that you have what it takes to build an entire app and deploy it.

Take a moment now and think about apps that you could create or how you could create some kind of a portfolio that you could bring to an interview. Do you already have some code or a project that you could use?

Another thing to consider, if you don't have a degree at present, is whether or not you want to get one in the future. When I first started out, I didn't have a degree. I ended up working hard to get my first few jobs, but then I got to a point where I had enough experience that a degree wasn't all that important. Still, I decided to pursue my degree after working for a couple of years, just so I could get that piece of paper. By going after my degree this way, I was still able to work, so in the end I actually ended up having about four more years of experience than my peers, but also had a degree. The only downside is that I had to spend my evenings studying for a few years. Even the cost wasn't a factor for me, because correspondence and night schools are usually cheaper. Plus, when you already have a job, the expense seems much less and you don't have to go into debt. Not only that, but some companies will actually pay some or all of the cost of your degree.

If you don't have a degree right now, you can pursue a similar route. You can keep your current job and get a degree by taking classes part-time. It's a good backup plan that may help you in the future.

One other course you may want to pursue is professional certifications. While not as powerful as a degree, they aren't nearly as expensive and can help you to prove competency in an area. There are professional certifications for Microsoft and Java technologies and for methodologies like Scrum. You can usually self-study for one of these certifications programs and take a fairly cheap test to become certified.

Taking action

- ○ If you don't have a degree, look into online or part-time courses you could take. See how much it would cost and how long it would take you to graduate.
- ○ If you decide to forgo the degree completely, make sure you have a good portfolio of your work. Spend some time putting together solid examples of your code that prove you know what you're doing.

35

Finding gaps in your knowledge

There is nothing wrong with focusing on your strengths, but sometimes your weaknesses, if not addressed, can be the limiting factor in your career or life in general. We've all got weaknesses. We all have gaps in our knowledge that prevent us from doing things as efficiently as possible. The more of these gaps we can find—and eliminate—the better off we'll be in the long run.

This chapter is all about finding those gaps in knowledge that are holding you back from reaching your full potential. We'll examine why those gaps exist, how to find them, and finally how to fill them in so that you aren't limited by what you don't know.

Why we leave the gaps

For a long time I didn't understand how lambda expressions worked in C#. Lambda expressions are basically anonymous functions that can be used to create a delegate in C#. You could use a lambda expression as a shortcut for declaring a function that doesn't have a name.

I kept seeing lambda expressions in C# code I was working with, and I could kind of figure out what was going on, but I didn't really understand it. I knew that if I took the time to understand how lambda expressions worked and what they really were then I could do my job better, but I just didn't have the time.

Eventually, it became readily apparent to me that I had a severe gap in my knowledge. Neglecting to take the time to thoroughly learn how lambda expressions worked was costing me hours of wasted time. I eventually decided to take the time to understand lambda expressions. It only took me a few hours of reading and experimenting with them before the concept clicked.

An observer, watching me work, would have immediately identified my weakness and how much productivity it was costing me, but even though it's apparent now, I couldn't see it at the time.

That's the problem with gaps in our knowledge. We tend to gloss over them and we tend to be too busy to stop and take the time to fill them in. We end up not really understanding what we're doing or do things in an inefficient way to avoid areas where we're weak or feel uncomfortable.

Even when we do eventually identify these gaps and understand the pain they're causing us, we still have a tendency to do nothing about it—even though we know we should. It's like avoiding going to the dentist when you have a toothache, because you don't want to be bothered with it.

Finding your gaps

Now, not all gaps in your knowledge are apparent. In fact, I'd say that most of them you're only vaguely aware of—if at all. It's often difficult to know what it is you don't know and it's easy to ignore.

One of the best ways to identify gaps in your knowledge that could be holding you back is to look at where you're spending the largest amount of your time and any repeated tasks you're doing. Often, you'll find that tasks that are taking you an inordinate amount of time are being slowed down by some gap in your knowledge. You might be fumbling through something because you lack a thorough understanding. That's exactly what was happening to me with lambda expressions. I was spending a large amount of time trying to debug or work with code that had them, instead of taking the few hours it would have taken me to understand them.

The same goes for repetitive tasks. Anything you're doing repeatedly is worth a thorough examination to see if there's something you don't know that, if you did, might increase your efficiency. Consider keyboard shortcuts. Perhaps you're using an application repeatedly, but you aren't working as efficiently as possible, because you have to manually drag a mouse around the screen and click. A possible gap in your knowledge could be keyboard shortcuts. Just spending the time to learn the keyboard shortcuts for an app you use for hours each day—hint: your IDE—could save you hours a week.

Another technique for identifying gaps in your knowledge is to always try to be aware of anything you don't understand or that isn't clear to you. You can keep a list of things you need to research or aren't clear about and keep track of how often those same subjects keep coming up. You'd be amazed how quickly that list can grow. Just be honest with yourself: if you encounter something you don't understand, you don't have to learn it right away, but add it to your list so you can at least identify gaps in your knowledge.

This technique works great if you're preparing for a job interview and need to identify what you need to study. Try to find as many job interview questions as you're likely to be asked at an interview. If you're looking for a Java job, perhaps you'll find lists of Java job interview questions. Go through all the questions, and put any concept that you don't understand or any questions you can't answer with complete certainty on your list. Once you're done, you'll have a nice long list of topics to study. It seems simple and obvious when I say it here, but many software developers preparing for a job interview have no idea what to study or how to figure it out. Completing table 35.1 can help you with this task.

Table 35.1 Checking for knowledge gaps

Areas to check for gaps	What are your gaps?
Where you're spending the most amount of time	
Repetitive tasks that could be improved	
Things that you don't fully understand	
Job interview questions you can't answer	

Filling the gaps

It does no good to identify all the gaps in your knowledge if you don't have a way to fill them in. Fortunately, just like the trip to the dentist, the actual work of filling in a gap, once you identify it, isn't as dreadful as you might imagine.

Really, the key to filling in a gap is identifying it. Once you know what a gap in your knowledge is and how it's holding you back, it's usually easy to figure out how you can fill in that gap. When I was able to figure out that not learning C# lambda expressions was holding me back, all I had to do was take the few hours needed to sit down and make a concerted effort to learn.

Just make sure you know exactly what it is you need to learn—and make sure the focus is narrow. If your weakness is that you aren't good at physics, you aren't going to be able to easily fill in that gap. But if you can identify that not understanding how springs work is what is actually causing you the trouble, you can spend some time studying Hooke's law (http://simpleprogrammer.com/ss-hookes-law) and you'll be good to go.

Often, you can fill in a knowledge gap very quickly just by being willing to ask questions. You might be a bit embarrassed because you don't

Find a gap and then fill it in.

know something, but if you can overcome that embarrassment and ask a question when you don't understand something, you'll find that you'll fill in many gaps in your knowledge with little effort. When you're having a conversation or discussion and you encounter something you don't understand completely, don't gloss over it—ask for clarification.

Taking action

- For the next few days keep a pad of paper with you, and any time you encounter something you don't understand, write it down.
- Make a conscious effort to ask questions—even if they're embarrassing—any time you don't understand something in a conversation.
- Identify some "pain points" in your day and figure out ways you can get rid of them by filling in some gap in your knowledge.

Section 4

Productivity

Amateurs sit and wait for inspiration, the rest of us just get up and go to work.
— Stephen King, *On Writing: A Memoir of the Craft*

I f I could distill this whole section into one piece of advice, I'd say "Do the work." But the problem is that doing the work isn't as easy as it seems. We all know we'd be more productive if we'd do what we know we're supposed to do, but a variety of reasons including laziness, lack of motivation, Facebook, and funny cat videos tend to foil our plans. How can we sit down and do the work we're supposed to do? How can we overcome our addiction to animated feline antics and kill procrastination dead in its track?

That's precisely what this section is about. I'm not perfect myself. (I spent way too much time delaying writing this opening.) But I've figured out quite a few techniques for being extremely productive, and in this section, I'm going to share them with you. Some of these techniques will seem pretty obvious—we all need gentle reminders—and hopefully some of these techniques will be not so obvious.

Ultimately, though, I can't make you a superproductive machine of performance and quality, although I can give you some effective tools to fight distraction, hone your focus, and click the X in the top corner of that browser window playing cat videos—as funny as they are.

36

It all starts with focus

There is no big secret to productivity. If you want to be more productive, you need to get more work done faster. Now, being productive doesn't guarantee you'll be effective. Producing a lot will make you very productive, but getting the *right* work done will make you effective. But for right now, we'll just focus on being productive; I'll assume you can solve the problem of choosing what to work on, once you can produce consistently.

How do you get more work done…faster? Well, it all starts with focus. Focus is critical to getting any task done. Right now, I'm focused on the task of writing this chapter. I've got my headphones on, I'm ignoring my email, I'm looking at my screen and typing, because I know this chapter could take me all day to write, or it could take me a couple hours. It all depends on focus.

In this chapter, we'll discuss what focus is, why it's so important, and—most importantly—how you can get more of it. Resist the temptation to flip the pages ahead, put your phone on vibrate, and let's get started.

What is focus?

Put simply, focus is the opposite of distraction. The problem is we live in a world that's so distracting that many people don't actually know what true focus is. It's easy to work an entire day and never reach a point of focus. The constant bombarding of emails, phone calls, text messages, distractions, and interruptions tends to rob us of focus and make us forget what it even feels like to be focused. Let me take a second to remind you what true focus is—in case you're having trouble recalling the last time you had it.

Remember the last time you were working a really hard problem? Perhaps you were trying to fix some bug or trying to figure out why your code didn't work. Time seemed to fly by as you forwent food, drink, and sleep laboring at your task. Anyone who dared distract you was greeted by an angry growl and you poured all your attention into a single task.

That's focus. We've all felt it from time to time, but the problem is that most of the time we aren't focusing. Most of the time, we're in quite the opposite mode of working—we're easily distracted and can't seem to settle down into the task we know we should be doing. Focus, like many things in life, is a game of momentum. It's harder to get focused, but relatively easy to remain focused once you've pushed the ball up the hill.

The magic of focus

I don't usually believe in magic pills, but I do believe focus is the magic pill for productivity. If I could buy focus, I'd whip out the credit card and max it out, knowing full well the return on my investment was all but guaranteed. Focus is that important.

The problem is, without focus, tasks end up getting stretched out over a very long period of time. Distractions that break our focus—or prevent us from ever getting it—end up costing us more than the time they take away. We'll discuss this more in chapter 41, when we talk about multitasking, but many tasks we take on have a context-switching cost. When we switch from one task to another, we end up having to regain some lost ground before we can begin again.

Focus is important, because it keeps us from having to keep laying that foundation over and over again when we're trying to work on a task. It can take some time to get everything set in our mind so that we can actually perform at our peak. Think of it like a car getting up to highway speed. It takes a few gear shifts before that car can maintain a highway speed. If you have to constantly stop and start, you'll be forced to go at a much slower speed overall. It takes time to get that car back up to highway speed again and shift it into fifth gear. But once you're there, you can cruise along with very little effort.

Focus helps you maintain speed.

I'm sure you've probably experienced situations where you were able to work very hard, yet it seemed effortless. In those situations it often takes some time to get to that point, but once you're there, you can really get a lot done in a short period of time (unless you're chasing your tail trying to track down an elusive bug).

Getting more focus

I probably don't have to take any more time to convince you of how important focus is. But you're probably wondering how you can get more of it. (No, sorry, I haven't figured out how to get it in pill form, but I'll let you know if I do.) In fact, it's pretty critical that you learn how to get focused, because most of the rest of this section will be of little help to you without the ability to stay focused. I can tell you all the productivity hacks and techniques in the world, but if you can't sit down and focus on a task, it won't do you much good.

Now is as good time as any to put this into practice. Is there some task you can pick up right now that will take you around 15–30 minutes? Put a bookmark in this book and do it now. But concentrate on doing it with complete focus. Don't think about anything else, just work on the task. See how that feels.

As I said before, focus has its own kind of momentum. If you want to get into a focused mode, you have to realize that it isn't an instant switch that you can flip. You'd be kind of a strange person if you could instantly flip into focus mode. I think you'd probably scare people when you sat down at your computer and in an instant your eyes glazed over as you started typing frantically.

To get into a focused mode, you have to push through the initial pain of contorting your mind to a single task. And unless your task is something you thoroughly enjoy doing, it's pretty painful—at first. But that's the key. You have to realize that the pain and discomfort is only temporary and doesn't really last that long.

When I first sat down to write this chapter, I felt a burning urge to check my email, urinate, and get some coffee all at the same time—and I don't even drink coffee anymore. My brain was doing anything it could to stop me from focusing. I had to subdue it and force my fingers to start typing. Now I'm in a zone where I could keep typing for hours—well, maybe half hours. The point is that I had to sit down and force myself to get going to get into a focused mode.

Most of the techniques I use to be productive are rooted in this backbone of productivity, reaching a point of focus. In chapter 38 we'll talk about the Pomodoro Technique, which is a formalized way to force you to sit down and work long enough on a task to build up the momentum that will take you to focus nirvana.

It's not as easy as it sounds

Now, I may have made it seem a little easier than it is. Focusing isn't as simple as just sitting down at the keyboard and typing. You've got to actively fight against the distractions that will come at you while you're upshifting to the high gear that will send you cruising. Fighting these distractions requires some forethought.

Before you begin a task, make sure you have done everything you can to protect yourself from interruptions—both internal and external. Silence your phone, close distracting browser windows, disable popups on your screen, and you may even consider hanging a sign up on your door or cubicle entrance that says you're busy. You might think I'm joking about the sign part, but I'm absolutely serious. Your coworkers and boss might be a bit resistant at first, but once you start producing like a madman, they'll understand—in fact, they'll want to buy some of your magic pills.

Okay, so you're ready to start working. You sit down at your computer and start typing. No distractions in sight, but wait—oh, what's that? You can't think of what to say. You feel like you just have to see if someone liked your post on Facebook. Stop it. Don't even think about it. Now it's up to you to use your willpower to remain glued to the task at hand. At first the focus will be forced, but eventually the momentum will build up and carry you through. Your goal is just to survive the first 5 or 10 minutes. If you can make it to 10 minutes, chances are you'll have enough momentum to continue. At that point, even a minor distraction will be unlikely to break your focus.

Taking action

- Think about a time when you were extremely focused. What did it feel like? What caused you to get into that focused mode? What eventually caused you to break the focus?
- Time to practice focus. Pick a task that will take you a half hour or more and block off the time needed to complete that task, giving it complete focus. Force yourself to concentrate on that task and that task only. Make a mental note of what it feels like when you're in the "zone."

37

My personal productivity plan

I've gone through almost all the major productivity systems out there. I've tried Getting Things Done. I've spent time using the Pomodoro Technique. I've used variations of the "Don't break the chain" technique from Seinfeld. (In this technique, you basically mark each day on a calendar that you successfully achieve doing some task. The idea is to make the streak as long as possible.) I've even tried list-based systems like Autofocus. After trying all these systems, I couldn't find one that worked perfectly for me, so I took some of the most useful things from all of them and combined them with some Agile processes to create my own.

In this chapter, I'm going to tell you the exact productivity plan I use to keep myself as productive as possible—the same plan I'm using right now to help me write this book.

Overview

The basic idea of my productivity plan is to plan out my entire week in small tasks that take no more than two hours. I use what is called a Kanban board to organize my week. The Kanban board is a simple board that has different columns that you can move tasks between. In the Agile world, Kanban boards usually contain columns for the various states some work could be in. Typically, there will be states like "not started," "in progress," and "done." But my Kanban board has columns for each day of the week. (Take a look at *Kanban in Action* by Marcus Hammarberg and Joakim Sundén [Manning, 2014] for an excellent book that talks more about the Kanban technique.)

I utilize the Pomodoro Technique to stay focused when I'm working on my tasks and to estimate and measure how long they'll take. We'll talk more about how that technique works in the next chapter.

Quarterly planning

My planning starts at the quarter level. I divide my year up into four quarters of three months each. When I plan out my quarter, I'll try to come up with one big project that I want to get done during that quarter and I'll also plan out some smaller goals. I'll also think about what things I'll do on a weekly or daily basis. This planning is usually done in a list in an application like Evernote. I'll create a high-level outline of what I want to accomplish during the quarter. This gives me a good idea of what my one major goal is and how I'll achieve it. It also keeps me focused.

Some of my quarterly goals have been things like writing this book, creating my How to Market Yourself as a Software Developer package (http://devcareerboost.com/m), and sometimes even just taking a big break.

Monthly planning

Every month, on the first day of the month, I print out the calendar for that month and try to plan out where I think work will fall on the days of the month. I can't be very exact here, but I can estimate roughly how much work I can get done that month based on how many days are available and any previous commitments I made. I'll simply take items from my quarterly outline and see what I can fit on the calendar.

I'll also plan out anything that I want to do on a monthly basis. For example, I batch-create all my YouTube videos for the month at the beginning of the month and that usually takes me a whole day.

Weekly planning

Every Monday morning, I'll start my day by planning my week. I was using a tool called Trello (http://trello.com) for the Kanban board I

Sample Kanban weekly schedule

use to organize my week, but lately I've been using Kanbanflow (http://simpleprogrammer.com/ss-kanbanflow) to create my Kanban board, because it has a built-in Pomodoro timer. My Kanban board has a column for each day of the week and also has columns for "today," for what I'm going to be doing that day, and "done," for any tasks that I've already completed. I also have a column called "next week" where I move any tasks that I couldn't get done this week or anything I know I need to do next week and don't want to forget.

I start off by going through the list of things that I need to do every week. I have a checklist I created in Evernote that lists everything I need to do each week. For me, it includes

- Writing a blog post
- Producing a YouTube video
- Creating a blog post about the video
- Recording two podcasts
- Creating a blog post about the podcast
- Getting my podcast transcribed and edited
- Writing a newsletter email
- Scheduling my social media content for the week

I schedule all of these tasks by creating cards in Trello or Kanbanflow. For each card, I estimate how long it will take in pomodori (which are each 25 minutes of focused work). I assume that I can get about 10 pomodori done each day. I make sure to add these tasks first, because I know they need to get done each week.

Once I've added the mandatory tasks for the week, I go through my calendar and see if there are any fixed appointments that will take up time during the day. For those days, I'll either create cards to represent those appointments—if they're work-related—or I'll reduce the number of pomodori I expect to complete that day.

Finally, I'll slot in whatever work I plan to get done that week. I'll add cards for each task I'd like to get done that week, filling in all the available slots. I usually leave myself a small amount of slack by only scheduling nine pomodori worth of work each day.

At this point I'll have a pretty good idea of what I can accomplish during that week. I find this prediction to be very accurate. I have the

Schedule your weekly tasks.

power to shift around cards to prioritize certain tasks that I think are more important and I want to be sure get done. I'm also able to see clearly where my time is going each week and I'm able to control where I spend that time ahead of time instead of looking back at where I actually spent the time in retrospect.

Daily planning and execution

Each day I'll start off by getting my workout done, before I sit down to work. I do this so that I won't have an interruption during my day that might break my focus. Once I'm ready to sit down and actually work, the first thing I do is plan my day.

To plan my day, I move the cards from the corresponding day into the "today" column and put them in the order of importance. I make sure that I work on the most important things first each day. I'll also adjust the tasks for that day and give them a bit more detail if what the task entails wasn't clear enough from the card. I want to make sure that I know exactly what I'm doing and what criteria I'll use to determine that a task is done before I start it. Doing this prevents me from procrastinating and wasting time during the day with tasks that aren't clearly defined.

Once I've slotted everything I plan to do for the day, I'll go back and make small changes to the schedule of the rest of the week. Sometimes, I'll get more done than I expected, so I'll need to move cards forward or add new cards to the board. Other times, I'll be behind, so I'll need to make adjustments and possibly move some cards to the next week.

Finally, I'm ready to work. I'll go over the Pomodoro Technique in more detail in the next chapter, but I basically use the Pomodoro Technique throughout the day to focus on a single task at a time and to work through my list.

Dealing with interruptions

There are many interruptions that can come at you during the day. As soon as you sit down, the phone rings. Your email notification pops up on your screen. Someone has liked your post on Facebook. Oh no, the world is coming to an end again, better check CNN and find out why. Some interruptions are unavoidable, but I've found that you can actually get rid of most of them if you're willing to put forth the effort.

I try to avoid interruptions as much as possible during the day, because I know they're the biggest productivity killers. I work at home in my home office, so this is a bit easier than in cubicle environment, but it's still a challenge. My phone is never set to ring. It's always on silent during the day. My wife and daughter also know not to disturb me while I'm working on a pomodoro. If they need my attention, they'll either send me an email or pop their head in the door so that I know when I'm on a break to come and see them—unless, of course, there's an emergency.

Another big thing I do to avoid interruptions is to basically ignore email during the day. During breaks, I'll often check email just to make sure there isn't something urgent that has to be dealt with immediately, but unless there's something truly urgent, I'll only reply to email at one set time in the evening. By batching up all my email correspondence at one time, I'm able to get through my email much more efficiently. (I'd probably be more productive if I could kick the habit of checking email, but I'm only human.)

I also either log out of or make myself unavailable on all the chat programs that can be a source of constant distraction. I find chat programs to be a complete waste of time. In most cases an email works better, because I can respond at my leisure instead of being interrupted while I'm trying to focus.

Breaks and vacations

Working like a machine on a tight schedule every single day isn't something that can be maintained in the long run, so I make sure that I have some time off and some weeks I'll do what I call "free work," which is basically a week where I don't use pomodori and I don't plan the whole week out. I just work on what I feel like working on during that week. Those weeks are usually pretty unproductive and I'm eager to get back to my system, but they give me a break from the monotony and help me to remember how important having a system is to being productive.

I also take a day off every once in a while to recharge or do something with my family. I just schedule my week around it accordingly. Tomorrow I'm taking my daughter to Disney World, so I'll be just doing three pomodori worth of work when we get home. I take a longer break every few months for a couple of weeks or a month at a time. During that longer break, I either queue up things like blog posts and podcasts, or I do the minimum I need to get done to keep up with my weekly commitments. I find that this kind of break is needed after working hard and being productive for an extended period of time. (After I finish this book, I'll be taking one of those breaks.)

Taking action

○ You don't have to use my exact productivity system, but you should have some kind of system in place to ensure you get consistent results. Make a note of what you're doing right now each week. See if there's some way you can develop a system that you can repeat on a monthly, weekly, and daily basis.

38

Pomodoro Technique

I've tried quite a few productivity techniques over the years, and although I use a combination of parts of different ones, the one that has the biggest impact on my productivity is the Pomodoro Technique® (http://simpleprogrammer.com/ss-pomodoro). If there's just one productivity habit that I'd encourage you to develop, it's the Pomodoro Technique.

I wasn't always sold on the Pomodoro Technique, though. The first time I tried it I thought it was far too basic to be effective. I didn't really see the point of it until I tried using it for a week and immediately began to see results.

In this chapter, I'm going to introduce you to the Pomodoro Technique and I'll show you why this fairly simple technique is so effective.

Pomodoro Technique overview

The Pomodoro Technique was created by Francesco Cirillo in the late 1980s, but it started to gain traction in the 1990s. The technique is actually very simple at its core—so simple that you might dismiss it at first, as I did.

The basic idea is that you plan out the work you're going to do for a day. Then you set a timer for 25 minutes and work on the first task you've planned. You work only on a single task at a time and give it your complete focus for the full 25 minutes. If you're interrupted, there are various ways of handling the interruption, but generally you strive to not be interrupted at all. You never want to break focus.

Pomodoro Technique process

At the end of the 25 minutes, you set a timer for 5 minutes and take a break. That's considered one pomodoro. After every four pomodori, you take a longer break, usually 15 minutes.

Technically, if you finish a task early, you're supposed to dedicate the remaining time to "overlearning." That is, you continue to work on the task by making small improvements or rereading material if you're trying to learn something. I tend to ignore this part and move on to the next task immediately.

And that's basically it. The Pomodoro Technique is really that simple. Francesco originally used a tomato-shaped kitchen timer to time the pomodori (*pomodoro* is Italian for tomato), but there now exist plenty of apps for tracking and recording pomodori. I use the built-in pomodoro timer in the Kanbanflow app (http://simpleprogrammer.com/ss-kanban flow) for tracking my pomodori. (In fact, I have one running right now.)

Using the Pomodoro Technique effectively

When I first started using the Pomodoro Technique, I didn't do it properly. I simply tried to do some pomodori during the day by setting a timer for 25 minutes. I didn't pay attention to how many I got done or do any estimation of how many pomodori a particular task would take me, so I didn't get much out of it. I figured that the whole technique was about focusing for an extended time period. I thought it was a good idea, but I didn't see why I'd need to do much more than remember to focus for 10–15 minutes to get into my work.

I didn't see the real value of the Pomodoro Technique until later, when I decided to apply a bit more rigor to my use of it. A friend of mine, and fellow software developer, Josh Earl (http://joshuaearl.com/), had been using the technique very effectively and convinced me to give it another try. What he was doing effectively was tracking how many pomodori he completed in a day—and setting a goal for how many to accomplish. It turns out this makes all the difference.

The real power of the Pomodoro Technique is using it as a tool to estimate and measure your work. By tracking the count of pomodori done in a day and having a goal of how many to accomplish in a day, you're suddenly given the power to truly gauge how hard you worked in a day and what your true capacity is.

Once I started applying the Pomodoro Technique in this way, I found that I was getting quite a bit more out of it than before. I was able to utilize the Pomodoro Technique, not just to stay focused during the day, but to plan my days and weeks, figure out where I was spending most of my time, and motivate myself to be as productive as possible.

Using the Pomodoro Technique, you can start thinking about your week in terms of a finite resource of pomodori. Want to get a certain amount done each week? Figure out how many pomodori you can do in a week and prioritize accordingly. You no longer have to feel like you didn't get enough done, because you can be sure of exactly how much you got done during a week by measuring the amount of pomodori you completed. If you didn't get done what you wanted to, but you completed your target amount of pomodori, the problem isn't doing enough work, it's one of prioritization.

Using the Pomodoro Technique in this way taught me the true value of prioritization. When I have only so many units of work I can assign to each week, I have to be careful with how I dole out those precious pomodori. Before using the Pomodoro Technique, I'd always imagine I could get a lot more done in a week than what was actually possible. I was overestimating my time and underestimating the length of time tasks would take me, but once I started using the Pomodoro Technique, I knew exactly how much time I had to work with during a week and I had a good idea how many pomodori tasks would take. I can't even begin to tell you how valuable that is. In fact, I know with a precise degree of accuracy how long it will take me to finish this book. I have a good idea how many pomodori each chapter of the book takes to write, and I know how many pomodori I'm willing to assign to the job each week.

Try it out yourself. Now is a good time to put down this book and try applying the Pomodoro Technique to some task you have to do today. Give it a shot and then come back and finish reading this chapter.

The mental game

So far I've only really talked about how the Pomodoro Technique can make you more effective by increasing your ability to plan, but the Pomodoro Technique is also very powerful because of the psychological impact time-boxing has on you.

One huge problem I've always had with my work is that I always feel guilty that I'm not doing more. It doesn't matter how much I work in the day, it seems like I can never relax. I always feel like I should be doing something. I'd sit down to play a videogame (one of my favorite pastimes) and I wouldn't be able to enjoy it, because I'd feel like I was wasting my time and should be doing more work. Perhaps you have this same feeling as well.

The problem stems from not being able to accurately assess how much you've accomplished in a day and not having a clear goal of how much should be accomplished. Perhaps, like me, you've tried to solve this problem by defining a list of things you wanted to accomplish for the day. This seems like a good idea until you hit a day when the tasks you estimate take way longer than they're supposed to take. You've been working like a dog all day, but you didn't complete the tasks on your list, so even though you've put in a herculean effort, you still feel like a failure. That sucks.

We can't necessarily control how long a task takes to complete. All we can do is control how much time we dedicate to the task—or any tasks—during a day. If you put in a hard day's work, you should feel good about yourself. If you've slacked off and it turns out you ended up getting everything on your list done because the tasks turned out to be easier than expected, you don't really deserve a pat on the back. Making a list of things is arbitrary; what really matters is the volume of focused work that gets done in a day.

That's exactly where the Pomodoro Technique saves the day. When you have a goal of x pomodori for the day and you get that goal done—a goal you can actually control—you know you did what you were supposed to do that day and you can give yourself permission to feel good about it—and more importantly—relax.

This realization has made a huge improvement in my working life and has helped me to get much more done while enjoying my free time. Once I've hit my goal for the day, pomodori-wise, I'm free to do whatever I want. If I feel like it, I might get more work done, but if I want to sit down and play a videogame or even waste time watching a movie or some other mindless activity, I can do it without guilt, because I know I've put in a hard day's work.

We've already talked about focus, so I won't drive too hard on that topic here, but there's a huge difference between doing focused work and unfocused work. The Pomodoro Technique also forces you to focus, so when you do a full day's worth of work using the Pomodoro Technique, it ends up being a lot more work than you might normally be used to. The good news is that you're more productive. The bad news is that you feel it. I'm not going to lie; it takes some getting used to. Focusing for a majority of your day is hard—probably a lot harder than what you're used to.

> **Landmine: I work in an office and I can't just focus for 25 minutes at a time**
>
> Just because you work in a regular office doesn't mean you can't start using the Pomodoro Technique. I often hear the complaint that the Pomodoro Technique sounds great, but I'm constantly interrupted throughout the day. Coworkers stop by my cubicle, my boss wants to talk to me; I can't just hold up my hand and tell them to wait 10 minutes until my timer dings.
>
> Ah, but you can. Well, as long as you give people notice ahead of time. If you're having trouble with too many interruptions, try telling your boss and coworkers what you're planning to do and how it will increase your productivity. Tell them that you'll never be unreachable for more than 25 minutes at a time and that you'll respond to any requests as soon as you've completed a pomodoro.
>
> I know this sounds a bit crazy and that no one would go for it, but if you present it in the right way, you'll be surprised how supportive many people will be. Just present your case to show how this will be best for the team and help you to be more productive overall, and you'll have the best chance of success.

How much work can you get done?

One thing I've discovered after using the Pomodoro Technique is that I have a definite cap on the amount of pomodori I can get done in a week or a day. That cap has grown over time and I've gotten better at focusing and used to the increased amount of work, but if I overstretch my bounds and exceed my capacity, I always end up paying the price.

The actual cap might be a surprise to you. You might figure that in a given average work day you have 8 hours, so theoretically, you should be able to do about 16 pomodori in that time, because each pomodoro takes about 30 minutes to complete. Realistically though, getting 16 pomodori done in a single day, even in 12 hours, would be a ginormous effort.

When I first started doing the Pomodoro Technique, I found it difficult to even get 6 pomodori done during a day. You'd be amazed how time just seems to disappear during the day and the amount of dedication and mental strain it takes to stay focused for most of your day. Now I set a goal of about 10 pomodori per day, which is still a very taxing effort. I often put in more than 8 hours to reach this goal and some days I still fall short.

My goal for the week is about 50-55 pomodori. If I hit that range, I know I'm doing well and I can count on making consistent progress each week toward my goals. If I go even just a little bit above that range, I feel it the next week. It hits me hard.

If you're going to adopt this technique, make sure you have a realistic expectation of what you can actually accomplish. Just because you work 40 hours in a week doesn't mean you can get 80 pomodori done. (If you're able to achieve that feat, I'd be utterly amazed, and, quite honestly, would fear for your mental health.)

And lest you think I'm a bit crazy or just lazy, examine this quote from John Cook about Henri Poincaré, a famous mathematician, theoretical physicist, engineer, and philosopher of science (http://simple programmer.com/ss-poincar), courtesy of Cal Newport's blog (http://simpleprogrammer.com/ss-four-hour):

> Poincaré...worked regularly from 10 to 12 in the morning and from 5 till 7 in the late afternoon. He found that working longer seldom achieved anything.

Many other famously productive people, like Stephen King, have said similar things about the maximum capacity of focused, productive work a person can hope to achieve in a day. You only have so much time—it's up to you to choose what to do with it.

Taking action

- Give the Pomodoro Technique a shot. For now, don't worry about setting a goal for how many pomodori to get done in a day, but try using the technique and chart how many you get done for an entire week.
- Once you have an idea of how many pomodori you can get done in a week, set a goal for the next week and see if you can reach it. Pay attention to how much work you end up getting done and how it makes you feel to accomplish the set number of pomodori for a day.

39

My quota system: How I get way more done than I should

I've already told you about the basic system I use to stay as productive as possible, but there's another part to it that I haven't talked about very much. This part of my productivity system is unique—as far as I can tell. I haven't ever heard anyone else talk about it or seen it in any productivity systems. I call it the quota system.

I use the quota system to make sure I make definite, measurable progress toward my most important goals on a daily and weekly basis. In this chapter, I'm going to tell you about the basics of the quota system and how you can use it yourself.

The problem

One of the major problems I had with all the productivity systems I tried is that none of them seemed to do a great job of addressing repeated tasks that occur every single day. I also wanted a way to handle big tasks that might take weeks or even months to complete.

I found that I have many different tasks that repeat each week. Every week I need to produce a blog post, several podcasts, exercise, and make progress toward my major goals. I even have daily tasks that I repeat every single day. I'm sure you have similar weekly and daily commitments.

I was always slipping on getting these kinds of repeated tasks done, because I'd either forget about something I was supposed to do or I'd end up not having as much time in the week as I had expected. I never quite got as much done as I planned and I always felt like I couldn't get traction, because I wasn't consistent.

Perhaps you've tried to do a workout program and you found that you just didn't get to the gym as much as you had expected. Maybe you have a blog and you'd like to update it regularly, but months go by without an update. You know that if you could just consistently blog, you'd see much better results, but even though you mean well, you never actually end up having the time to blog as much as you'd like.

Enter quotas

I began to realize that the only way to guarantee that I'd make consistent progress in something I was pursuing was to create a defined goal for how much progress I needed to make in a predefined time period.

I originally had some success with my workouts by creating quotas for how many times I needed to run in a week—three—and how many times I needed to lift weights during the week, also three. I decided that every week I needed to meet this quota of three runs and three weightlifting sessions.

I started applying a weekly quota of doing one blog post per week and added quotas for other things I wanted to make sure I got done regularly, like creating YouTube videos and podcasts. I created a quota for everything I did that I needed to do more than once. I quantified exactly how frequently I'd do any repeatable task. It could be once a month, four times a week, or twice a day. If I was going to repeat it, I was going to define how often, and I was going to make a commitment about it. Rain or shine, I was going to do what I committed to. I took these quotas very seriously.

What I began to find is that I was producing much more than I ever had before. And the best part was that I was doing it on a consistent basis, so I could measure and chart out my progress over time. I knew exactly how much volume I'd produce in a given amount of time.

One of the biggest successes I had with this system was in my production of Pluralsight courses. I set a quota for myself to get three modules done every single week. (A module is a 30- to 60-minute part of a course. Most of my courses have five modules in them.) By setting this quota for myself, I was able to complete over 55 courses in under three years, even while taking some time off. I quickly became the top producer and had three times more courses than any other author for the company.

QUOTA EXAMPLES

- I will run three times each week.
- I will create one blog post each week.
- I will write one chapter each day.
- I will get 50 pomodori done each week.

Try it yourself. Take some time now to come up with your own list of quotas. Think about what you'd like to accomplish each week or each month and write them down. You don't have to commit to it now, but just doing the exercise can be helpful.

How the quota system works

You might be wondering how this quota system works. It's actually pretty simple. Just pick some task that you do repeatedly and set a quota for how often you'll get that task done in a given interval. Your interval could be monthly, weekly, or daily, but you have to have a clear interval of time in which so much work must be done. If you have a large project, you need to find a way to break it into smaller repeatable tasks. For my Pluralsight courses, I was able to break the work into modules. For this book, I've broken the work into chapters. (By the way, my quota for this book is one chapter a day.)

Once you've defined what you're going to do and how often you're going to do it, the next step is to commit. This is the really important part, because without really committing, you aren't going to be successful. True commitment means you're going to accomplish what you committed to so far as it's humanly within your possible ability. It means there's virtually nothing, besides physical incapacity, that's going to stop you from completing the task.

This idea is the core of the system. You don't leave yourself any choice but to do what you set out to do. In your mind, failure can't be an option. Because if you're willing to let yourself slip once, you'll slip again, and pretty soon the "quota" won't mean anything at all.

The whole system falls apart if your commitment is weak, so you have to choose attainable and maintainable quotas. Don't commit yourself to something you know you can't do; otherwise you're setting yourself up for failure. Start with small commitments and make them bolder as you become successful at reaching them.

If a quota is too high, I only have one rule about it: you can't quit in the interval in which the quota must be completed. At one point I committed to doing five modules for my Pluralsight courses each week. I was able to meet the quota for a few weeks, but it was very difficult to do and required me to work on Saturdays and Sundays most weeks. When I decided to reduce the quota, I made sure I completed the quota of five for the week and then reduced the quota to three for the next week. I didn't stop midway and change the rules, because I knew that doing so would cause me to lose respect for the quotas in the future.

QUOTA SYSTEM RULES
- Pick a repeatable task.
- Define an interval in which that task must be done and repeated.
- Define a quota for how many times the task should be done during a given interval.
- Commit. Make a firm commitment to meet your quota.
- Adjust. Make your quota higher or lower, but don't adjust during an interval.

Okay, now is the time to act—to make your own commitment. Pick a task that you came up with a quota for and commit to it. Go through the quota system rules and apply the quota system to just one thing at first.

Why the quota system works

The secret of why the quota system works goes back to the story of the tortoise and the hare. It's better to work at a slow and steady pace than to go really fast at times but lack consistency and follow-through. A quote from one of my favorite books, *The War of Art* by Stephen Pressfield, describes it nicely:

He [the professional] sustains himself with the knowledge that if he can just keep those huskies mushing, sooner or later the sled will pull in to Nome.

The problem most of us face when it comes to long-term productivity is maintaining a consistent pace. Over time, small bricks put perfectly into place each day eventually build up a wall. It can be discouraging to focus on the large task at hand, but it's easy to think about just laying a single brick. The key is putting a system in place that ensures you lay that brick each day, week, or month.

The quota system also helps you overcome willpower weakness by presetting a course for you to follow, eliminating the need to make decisions. Because you've already precommitted to doing a task so many times during a set interval, you no longer have to make a judgment call of whether or not to do a thing—you know you must do it. Any time you're required to make a decision during the day, you're forced to tap into the limited reserves of willpower you have left. Eliminate the decision by making it mandatory, in the form of a quota, and you eliminate the willpower drain. (For an excellent book on this subject, check out *Willpower Instinct* by Kelly McGonigal [Avery, 2011].)

Taking action

- Make a list of all the tasks in your life that you repeat. Especially focus on things that you don't do consistently right now, but you know you'd benefit from if you did.
- Pick at least one task and commit to a quota for a specific interval of time. Take this commitment seriously. Try to keep the commitment for at least five intervals. Imagine what would happen if you continued the quota for months or years.

40

Holding yourself accountable

There are two kinds of motivation that can cause people to get work done: internal—the motivation that comes from inside us—and external—the motivation that comes from outside penalties or rewards.

Internal motivation is much more effective than external motivation. When we're motivated internally, we get much more done and we tend to do a better job as well. The trick is getting your primary motivation to come from inside you instead of from the outside.

That's what this chapter is all about. Motivating yourself by holding yourself accountable to…you. Making promises to yourself does you no good if you can't keep them. If you're interested in learning more about this topic in depth, you might want to check out Daniel Pink's book *Drive* (Riverhead Hardcover, 2009).

Accountability

Most of us show up to work each day and on time at least to some degree due to the fact that we're accountable to our employers. The accountability of having a job requires us to do certain things we might not otherwise do if it were left up to us. If you currently work for someone else and you've had the opportunity to work from home for a day, or perhaps you've ventured out on your own and worked for yourself, you've probably quickly realized how powerful this concept of accountability is.

The first time I had a job working from home I intended to get up early and work, but I didn't. I wasn't trying to be a slacker. I just wasn't used to being accountable to myself. I was used to an external entity influencing

233

my behavior. When it was up to me whether or not I worked, I chose not to work. Just basic human nature.

This experience exposed a critical flaw in my work ethic that was hurting me in terms of productivity. I was influenced by external motivations rather than internal ones. Being accountable to my employer kept me in check, but once I was out on my own, I didn't have my own sense of accountability to control my behavior.

It's important to develop a sense of self-accountability to be productive when no one is looking. You could also call this having character or integrity, because they're all part of the same idea. Without this sense of accountability to yourself, you're always dependent on external motivations to get you to perform. You become easily manipulated by a carrot promising a reward or a stick promising…a beating if you fall out of line.

Self-mastery is the art of self-motivation, and at the heart of self-motivation is self-accountability. You have to learn how to be accountable to yourself if you want to have predictable, reliable results that aren't dependent on someone else's influence.

Becoming accountable to yourself

I struggled with this problem of being primarily influenced by external motivation for quite a while. I had to learn some self-discipline to be effective at my job and productive when the results were totally up to me. Eventually, though, I did figure out how to tame the wild beast that was dwelling inside me.

To develop self-accountability, you need to first develop some kind of structure in your life. If you don't know what you're supposed to be doing, you can't really hold yourself accountable to anything. When you go to work, you usually have certain days you're supposed to work and a starting and quitting time. Even though some of these things can be flexible, they're rigid enough to be clearly defined. You know when you're in violation, so you can be held accountable by your superiors.

Think about how you'd schedule your life if you didn't have to do the activities yourself.

Make rules for yourself so you can develop structure in your life.

Steps for self-accountability

You have to put that same kind of structure in place in your own life, voluntarily, by making rules for yourself. You need to create your own rules that govern how you'd like to live your life, and you need to make these rules ahead of time, when you're able to think clearly and your head isn't clouded with bad judgment.

You probably have some rules you've already defined for yourself, like brushing your teeth every day or paying your bills on time. But it's a good idea to put rules around any areas of your life that are trouble areas for you or are critical to your success. This added structure can help you to stay on task and do what you're supposed to be doing rather than being ruled by whims and emotions.

Sometimes it can help to step outside of yourself and think about how you'd schedule your life and your activities each week if you didn't actually have to do the activities yourself. Imagine if you were playing a videogame where you had to plan the activities for your character for each day. How would you plan out and schedule the time? What kind of diet would you put in place? How many hours of sleep would your character get? Answers to these questions are good candidates for rules that you can use to hold yourself accountable.

External accountability

You may find that it's easy to violate your own rules when you're only accountable to yourself. It may help to have a little bit of external help in those situations. You can still define your own rules and, thus, the motivation is still internal—because you're the one making the rules—but you can have someone else help you enforce them.

There's no weakness in getting others to help you hold yourself accountable to something you've agreed to. It can be helpful to recruit an accountability partner—ideally someone who shares a similar goal. You can tell the person your rules or the goals you're trying to achieve and you can keep each other accountable by reporting your progress—both successes and failures—regularly to each other.

Often the thought of having to report a failure to your accountability partner can be enough to discourage self-defeating action. It can be the difference that's the tipping point in making a good choice over a bad one. You can also run important decisions by your accountability partner to ensure that choices you're making are truly in your long-term best interest and not shadowed by temporary bad judgment.

I have a mastermind group that functions as an accountability group. Our group meets weekly and we each talk about what we did each week and what we planned to do. By discussing our plans in the group, we hold each other accountable to follow through with them. No one wants to let down the group by not following through on their actions. Since I've started this group, my productivity has increased tremendously.

It can also be a good idea to make your actions as public as possible. I publish blog posts, YouTube videos, and podcasts every week. If I miss a week, I'll know that it won't go unnoticed, so I don't feel like I can be lazy and not do what I know I'm supposed to do. It can be helpful to expose your own work to public scrutiny, because it can motivate you to action due to either embarrassment or letting down other people who are relying on you.

The important thing is to make sure you have some kind of account-ability for your actions. You'll be much more productive when you're holding yourself to a standard you've created.

Taking action

- Decide how you'd like to live your life and spend your time and create some rules to help you ensure you're heading in the right direction.

- Create an accountability system that will help you to enforce your rules.

41

Multitasking dos and don'ts

Ah, multitasking. Some people call it a bane to productivity and others swear by it. More and more, though, the sentiment has turned toward eliminating multitasking completely.

I don't think it's quite that simple though. I think some tasks are suited for multitasking and others aren't. If you really want to maximize your productivity, you'll have to learn when to multitask, when not to multitask, and how to multitask effectively.

Why multitasking is generally bad

Most of the recent research on multitasking seems to indicate multitasking almost always results in reduced productivity even though multitaskers themselves may think they're increasing their productivity. Take a look at this article from the American Psychological Association to see a summary of some of that research: http://simpleprogrammer.com/ss-multi-task.

The reason for this seems to be rooted in our inability to truly multitask. For many activities we may think we're multitasking, but in reality what we're doing is constantly switching between tasks. This task-switching seems to be the culprit for the hit on productivity. The more you switch between tasks, the more time you waste getting your brain ramped up to work on a task. True multitasking means to do two or more things at the same time—and that can be effective, as we'll talk about a little later on—but most of the time, we're actually doing task-switching.

This makes sense when you consider how important focus is to productivity (as we talked about in chapter 36). When you multitask, you tend to break your focus and end up having to take time to get back into that task. You're also more likely to procrastinate or allow other interruptions to distract you when you aren't in that focused mode. If you consider that you're most productive when you're "in the zone" and it takes a period of focused work to get there, it makes sense that rapidly switching tasks wouldn't be effective.

Now, this is only true for certain kinds of work where you can't actually do two or more things at the same time or doing so breaks your focus. If you can actually manage to combine tasks together, you can get quite an efficiency boost, but we'll get to that a little later on. For now, let's talk about a more effective strategy for dealing with tasks that we'd normally try to multitask.

Batching is much more productive

I get quite a few emails during the day. I used to have notifications on my computer to tell me when a new email came in. Almost every time a new email came in, I'd stop what I was doing and read and respond to that email. It wasn't very efficient, because I was interrupting my focus all the time and I never got into "email mode" either.

It's pretty obvious in that case that I wasn't actually multitasking. I was simply interrupting whatever work I was doing to deal with email. I was task-switching. It wasn't possible for me to answer email while writing this book, for instance. I simply don't have enough keyboards or fingers to accomplish that task.

The way I handle email now is in batches. I might check my email a couple of times each day and answer any urgent emails. But in general, I process all of my email at a single time during the day. I go through my entire inbox and deal with it all at once. I'm much more efficient, because I'm not interrupting my other task and I can get into the "email zone" where I can deal with emails much more quickly than I can when I'm just opening my inbox.

What's my point in telling you this? Well, if you're having trouble with multitasking during the day because there are multiple tasks you have to get done, you'll probably be better off learning how to batch those tasks and work on a series of related tasks all at once rather than splitting them up throughout the day. Email is a great place to start, but anything that you do in small intervals is a good candidate for batching.

POTENTIAL AREAS TO BATCH
- Dealing with email
- Making phone calls
- Fixing bugs
- Short meetings

Batching related tasks instead of working on them at different times during the day has two major benefits. First, you don't break your focus on bigger tasks you're working on during the day. Second, you're able to get into a deeper focus on the tasks that you'd normally not spend enough time on to get into a focused mode. Answering a single email doesn't afford you enough time to get focused on that task, but answering 20 emails in a row can put you in the zone.

Take a moment now and think about some areas of your life that you might be able to batch together. What types of activities do you do a lot of but are spreading out over time? Can you set aside a bigger chunk of time and do those things all at once?

What about true multitasking?

Okay, so now that we've got the multitasking hate out of the way, let's talk about true multitasking, when you're actually doing two things at once, not just switching between tasks rapidly.

I get quite a bit of a productivity benefit out of doing true multitasking. It only makes sense that if you can combine two tasks and actually do them both at once, you'll be able to get much more done. The trick is figuring out what tasks can actually be combined without reducing the productivity on each task more than the overall gain.

I've found that it's possible to combine a brainless task together with a task that requires some degree of mental focus. Right now I'm listening to music on my headphones while I'm typing this chapter. Now, arguably listening to music itself isn't a productive activity, but it turns out that listening to music while writing makes me more productive at the task of writing. The music seems to help me get my words flowing and reduces the chances of other distractions stealing my attention.

How about a more productive example? I usually try to combine fitness activities with educational ones. When I'm at the gym lifting or running, I'll often listen to an audiobook or podcast. I've found that I can do a physical activity while listening to something educational without any negative impact. I've been able to get through many books by listening to audio versions while running or lifting weights.

But imagine what would happen if I tried to listen to an audiobook while writing this chapter. I'd either not be paying attention to the book, or I'd be unable to write. Our brains can't do two mentally taxing things at once.

The key is to find time during your day when either your brain or body isn't engaged. Driving in the car is a great time to listen to audiobooks. You don't have to focus to drive. You can almost do that on autopilot, so you might as well learn something while you commute.

It's too hard to do two mentally taxing things at once.

Flipping it around, I've got a treadmill that has a little shelf that I can put my laptop on. There's no reason why I shouldn't be walking while I'm typing replies to emails. I've found, though, that I can't do a good job of writing code while walking on the treadmill—unless I'm going very slowly. It seems there's a small tax of concentration that walking or another physical activity imposes. For that reason, I'd recommend reserving the least concentration-requiring tasks for combining with physical exercise. You'd probably also find it hard to solve difficult math equations while lifting weights—not that I've tried.

Taking action

- Cut out any multitasking that isn't true multitasking. Strive to work on only a single thing at a time during the day. The Pomodoro Technique is a great help.
- Batch together any smaller tasks that can be done at one time instead of multiple times throughout the day or week.
- Look for areas where you can implement true multitasking. Any time you're doing a non-mentally taxing activity, try to combine it with something else. Any time you're doing a mentally taxing activity, try and combine it with a physical activity.

42

Burnout: I've got the cure!

One of the biggest hindrances to productivity is the physical and mental state known as burnout. We all tend to get started on a project with large amounts of enthusiasm and energy, but after some time, even our most passionate endeavors can make us sick to our stomach at the very thought of them.

Most people call this state burnout, and they never get past it. It's unfortunate, though, because if you can manage to get past that burned out feeling, you'll find that renewed energy and rewards are just on the other side of the wall you're banging your head against.

In this chapter, we're going to talk about what burnout is, how it happens, and why I think burnout—in most cases—is just an illusion.

How you burn out

As humans we tend to get really excited and motivated about new things at first, but then as they become more familiar and time wears on, we tend to either take those things for granted or even grow to despise them.

It's a natural cycle in life and I'm sure you've experienced it many times before. Remember when your car was brand new (at least to you)? Remember how excited you were about driving it and how good it made you feel? How long did that last? How long was it before you didn't really care about your car anymore? How long before it got "old"?

You've probably experienced the same thing with a new job. I remember my first days of work at several different jobs. I was excited and hopeful, eager to get started. But it didn't take long for most of that enthusiasm to fade. It didn't take long before I eventually dreaded going to work and felt like I couldn't take it anymore.

What happens is that the newness wears off and reality sets in. If you're starting a new project or trying to learn a new skill, you eventually reach a point where your interest and motivation are low and the results you're seeing are increasing very slowly—or seemingly not at all.

Eventually you get to a point where you feel mentally and physically exhausted. You may try to deny the fact—or hide it—but eventually you know that you just don't feel excited about that job, project, work-out routine, and so on anymore. You feel as though you're burned out.

The harder you push, the more work you get done, the faster you accelerate the pace of this feeling of being burned out. That's why it's so hard to be productive. The more productive you are, the less you feel like being productive.

In reality, you're just hitting a wall

Now, most of us think of burnout as the end. We can't really see past it. We think that we've just lost our motivation and interest, so therefore we must move on and do something else.

We go out and look for a new job. We leave that book half-written. We drop the side project a few weeks from completion. We're off to search for something new—to find our real passion. Because if what we got burned out on was our real passion, we wouldn't have gotten burned out.

Sometimes we think we need to take a vacation. But often when we come back from vacation, we feel even more burned out than we did before. Not only have we lost motivation and interest, but momentum is gone as well.

The truth is that—in most cases—this feeling of burnout is totally natural and doesn't indicate a serious problem. The truth is that most of us, in any endeavor we pursue, eventually hit a wall, a point where our initial interest and motivation have dropped off and we aren't seeing enough results to rev them back up.

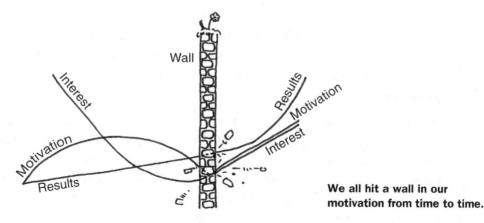

We all hit a wall in our motivation from time to time.

When you first start a new project, your interest is the highest. But just like that new-car feeling, the interest level drops down rather quickly. Interest seems to be fueled by hope and anticipation. We're most interested in things before we actually start doing them.

Motivation tends to start out low, but as you make progress doing something, your motivation level starts to rise. Early successes make you feel more motivated. Momentum pushes you forward.

Over time, though, the slow pace of results starts to wear on your motivation. You eventually find yourself at a point where your motivation and interest are both close to rock bottom. This is the wall.

On the other side of the wall

Unfortunately, most people never get past the wall. You only have to look around to see that this is true. How many people give up before they actually get good at something or before a project is completed?

Look at your own history. How full is your closet of half-completed projects, yellow belts, dusty guitars, and soccer cleats? I know I've hit the wall many times and I've failed to push through it. My own closet is filled with plenty of passions that ended in defeat.

But there's good news. Remember that cure for burnout I promised you? Well, here it is. It's pretty simple. Ready for it?

Push through the wall.

Yes, it's that simple. And yes, I'm serious. Take a glance back at the figure of interest, motivation, results, and the wall. Notice what happens right after the wall, if you can manage to get through it? All of a sudden, results shoot up extremely fast. Motivation and interest come right along for the ride.

Before you get too skeptical, let me explain what happens and why the wall is there. Like we discussed earlier, most people quit when they hit the wall. They don't try and go past it, because they feel like they're burned out. Before you hit the wall, the competition is fierce. There are many runners in the race. Everyone is enthusiastic and excited. The road is easy. No one has been filtered out.

But because so many people never get past the wall, the other side of the wall is very sparse. There isn't much competition. Most of the runners have dropped out of the race. Each runner on the other side of the wall gets a bigger share of the reward, because there are so few runners left.

If you can just make it to the other side of the wall, suddenly things will start to get easier and your motivation and interest will pick up again. We have a high level of motivation and interest in new endeavors we undertake, but we also have a high level of motivation and interest in things we've mastered. Starting to learn guitar is fun and easy. Sticking to the path and becoming good is long and boring. Becoming a great guitarist is the most fun and rewarding.

If you can grit your teeth and bear it, if you can push your way through the wall, you'll eventually find that you've "cured" your burnout by simply ignoring it. Pushing through the pain is the secret to overcoming burnout. You'll eventually hit more walls, but every time you push through one, you'll get a burst of renewed energy and motivation. Plus, the number of people you have to compete with gets fewer.

Pushing past the wall

Okay, so maybe you're a little unsure of what I'm saying. I mean, you really do feel burned out. When you wake up in the morning, you seriously don't feel like typing at your computer. You just want to get away to a cabin in the woods where you'll never have to see a computer again.

But perhaps…just maybe, you're willing to give it a try. Perhaps you're willing to see if there really is a pot of gold on the other side of the wall.

Good. Then let me tell you how to do it.

You've already gone through the first step, which is realizing that there's something waiting for you on the other side. Most people give up because they don't realize that things will get better if they just keep pushing through. Knowing that your efforts aren't in vain can help you to hold on and eventually make it through.

Unfortunately, though, that isn't enough. Trying to push on when motivation is at an all-time low is really difficult. Without motivation, you don't feel like pressing on. You feel like doing exactly the opposite. What you need is some structure. You might want to review chapter 40 on holding yourself accountable, but essentially, you need to create a set of rules for yourself that will ensure you keep moving forward.

Take this book, for example. When I first started writing it I was extremely excited. I couldn't imagine what could be more fun than sitting down and writing "my book" all day. It didn't take long for that initial excitement to wear off. But the fact that you're reading this proves that I made it through to the end. How did I do it when my motivation

You need to push past the wall.

and interest eventually faded? I set a schedule for myself and I stuck to it. Rain or shine, no matter how I feel, a chapter gets written each day. Some days it's more, but it's always at least one chapter.

You can adopt a similar approach to help push you through the walls you hit. Want to learn to play the ukulele? Set aside a certain amount of time to practice each day. Do this before you even start your first lesson—while you have the interest and motivation. When you eventually hit that inevitable wall, you'll have a structure in place to help you get through it.

Taking action

- Think about all the unfinished projects and endeavors you undertook but never completed or mastered. What was it that made you quit? How do you feel now about this thing?
- Decide that next time you take on a project, you're going to take to completion or mastery. Set up rules and constraints that will force you to overcome the walls you'll inevitably hit.
- If you're facing a wall of some sort in your career or personal life, try and push past it. Think about what might lay in store for you on the other side of the wall. Imagine that your motivation and interest will eventually return.

43

How you're wasting your time

We all do it. We all waste time. In fact, if we could learn to stop wasting time, by definition, we'd be as productive as possible. If you could maximize the hours of your day so that there was absolutely no time waste, you'd be operating at maximum capacity.

Unfortunately, you can't squeeze every minute out of every day—that's too unrealistic of a goal. But you can figure out the places you're wasting the most time and eliminate them. If you can get rid of your one or two biggest time wasters you'll be in pretty good shape. In this chapter, I'm going to help you identify some of the biggest time wasters in history, help you find your own, and give you some practical advice on eliminating them once and for all.

The biggest time waster of all

I'm just going to come right out and say it. Stop watching television!

Seriously, stop doing it as soon as you can. Put down the remote, turn off the TiVo, and find something else to do—anything else to do.

We live in a world where a majority of people waste a large chunk of their lives watching TV with no benefit to themselves or society. In 2012, a Nielson report showed that the average American over the age of two spends more than 34 hours a week watching live TV. But wait, that's not all. They also spend 3–6 more hours watching taped programs. Holy cow. Are you serious? Did I read that right? We're spending 40 hours a week watching TV? We're spending as much time as a full-time job every week glued to the TV. That's just insane.

Now, you might not watch much TV, or perhaps you don't watch as much as the average American, but it's pretty hard to ignore this kind of data. It indicates we all may be watching much more TV than we think.

Imagine what you could do with an extra 40 hours per week. If you want to start your own business, there you go, 40 hours. If you want to get ahead in your career, do you think you might be able to do it with about 40 more hours each week? How about getting in shape? I think 40 hours ought to be enough time.

Even if you're watching half as much TV as the average American, that's still 20 hours per week—a part-time job. Be honest with yourself and estimate how many hours of TV you're watching each week. Track it so you know for sure.

Take a moment now and track your own TV watching. Think about all the shows you watch and track how long you think you spend watching TV each week. Be honest with yourself. Add up all those hours over a year's worth of time.

Giving up the TV

I probably don't need to tell you why watching TV is such a waste of time, but you might need a little more convincing to give it up completely or at least cut it back.

The biggest problem with TV is that there's no actual benefit from the time you spend watching it. Unless you're purely watching educational programs, you're basically wasting time. Time would be better spent on literally just about anything else.

Not only is TV watching a time waster, but it also has the ability to influence you in ways that you aren't likely aware of. TV programs short-circuit the problem-solving part of your brain and lay everything out for you. Everything from your spending habits to your world view is directly influenced by TV. The more you watch, the more you're giving up control of your own mind and actions. The TV is literally programing you.

How do you give it up? I'll be the first to admit it's not easy. I used to watch quite a bit of TV every week. I had the habit of getting home from work and turning on the TV. (I even bought a little foldable table so I could eat dinner in front of it.) I grew up doing it, my parents did it, and when I became an adult, that's what I did. I was used to it. I felt like after a hard day of work I needed to relax and watch some TV. I needed my mindless entertainment.

I didn't start to back off watching TV until I started working on side projects of my own. I started out creating an Android application to help track my runs. I was setting aside a couple of hours each day to work on the app. I found that by replacing the time I was spending watching TV with working on this project that I enjoyed, I was getting a lot more done and I was feeling better about it.

After seeing these positive benefits, I wanted to reclaim more of my time, but I didn't want to give up some of my favorite programs. I decided to narrow down my TV programs to just one at a time. Instead of watching TV live or recording episodes on TiVo, I bought complete seasons of the shows I wanted to watch and I watched them when I wanted to watch them or when I had the time. I stopped letting the TV programming and weekly cliffhangers set the pace for my TV watching. (Even now, I'll occasionally buy a complete season of a TV program and watch it as if it were a movie.)

By finding something else to occupy my time and by breaking the control over my schedule that regularly scheduled TV programming had on me, I was able to eventually break my addiction to TV, freeing up 20–30 more hours per week.

Other time wasters

I primarily set my focus on TV, because for most people it's the biggest time waster. Just eliminating that one time waster can potentially double or triple your productivity—not to mention save you some money. But there are some other major time wasters out there that you might want to learn how to eliminate from your life as well.

One of the major ones today is social media. It's definitely important to have a social media presence, as we talked about in section 2, but it's easy to waste countless hours on Facebook, Twitter, and other social media sites when you're supposed to be working or you could be doing something productive.

One good strategy, which applies to email as well, is to batch up your social media activities to one or two times during the day. Instead of incessantly checking Facebook during the day, try only checking Facebook at lunch time or in the evening. Trust me, you won't miss out on much.

If you're working a corporate job, one major time waster that can make you less productive is meetings. I probably don't need to tell you about how much time meetings can waste. I've worked jobs where I was in at least two to three hours of meetings a day. Needless to say, there wasn't much time left over for actual productive work.

One of the best ways to stop letting meetings waste your time is to simply not go to them. I know this sounds a bit heretical, but I found that many of the meetings I was going to were meetings where I was an optional attendee or where my presence truly wasn't needed.

You might also be able to reduce the number of meetings you go to by getting the meeting organizers to cancel a meeting if the agenda in that meeting can be handled over email or another medium. I found that calling a meeting is often chosen as the default action because it's so easy to do. Try to use a meeting as a last resort if an issue can't be handled via a less time-consuming medium like email or even a quick phone call. (Check out the book *Rework* by Jason Fried and David Heinemeier Hansson [Crown Publishing Group, 2010] for some more details on how to streamline your meetings.)

SOME OF THE BIGGEST TIME WASTERS
- Watching TV
- Social media
- News sites
- Unnecessary meetings
- Cooking
- Playing video games (especially online games)
- Coffee breaks

> **Landmine: Are cooking, coffee breaks, and other things you like doing really wasting time?**
>
> Yes and no. It depends on why you're doing them. Things you consciously do for enjoyment aren't a waste of time if you're doing those things specifically because you enjoy them and not to avoid doing real work that you know you should be doing.
>
> I saw playing video games as a waste of time, but I love playing video games. Does that mean I give up playing video games completely? No. But it does mean that I don't play video games when I should be doing something else that needs to get done as a way of avoiding my work.
>
> The same goes for cooking. Perhaps you enjoy cooking and making healthy meals for yourself. If so, great, but if you're spending a large amount of time cooking when you could come up with a simple meal plan that would greatly reduce your time, and you don't particularly enjoy it, perhaps you should consider finding healthy ways to reduce your cooking time.
>
> The point isn't to cut out everything you enjoy doing in life, but to make sure that you aren't wasting time by doing things that you don't need to do and you don't enjoy or things that eat up all of your spare time.

Tracking your time

If you're having a problem with social media distractions, you might want to track just how much time you spend on social media sites. You can use a tool like RescueTime (http://simpleprogrammer.com/ss-rescue-time) to track what you're spending your time on during the day and generate a report that will show you exactly how much time you're wasting on social media sites and doing other nonproductive things on your computer. The best way to eliminate the time wasters in your life is to identify them. You have to know where you're wasting your time before you can start claiming that time back.

I'd recommend implementing some kind of time-tracking system to see exactly where your time is going each day. When I first started working for myself, I didn't understand where all my time was going. I felt like I should be able to get much more done in a day than what I was actually getting done. I started meticulously tracking my time for about two weeks and eventually was able to find out many areas where I was wasting the most time.

If you can get an accurate read on where you're spending your time, you'll be able to identify and eliminate your biggest time wasters. Try to figure out exactly how much time you spend on different tasks each day. Even track how long you spend eating meals to really get an idea of where your time is going.

Taking action

- For the next week, meticulously track your time. Get an accurate estimate of how you spend every hour of your day. Look at the data and see where your biggest two or three time wasters are.
- If you have a TV habit, try and kick it for just a week. Have a "no TV" week and see how you do. Keep track of what you spend your time doing instead of watching TV.
- Figure out if you can buy back more time by hiring someone to do your yard work or cleaning for you. (If you cut your cable, you might even be able to pay for these services from just those savings.)

44

The importance of having a routine

The true secret to productivity: small things done repeatedly over a long time period. Write 1,000 words a day, every day, and in a year you'll have written four novels. (The average novel is between 60,000 and 80,000 words.)

Yet, how many people sit down to write a novel but never complete even a single one? They don't realize that the only thing that's standing between them and their dream is routine. A routine is one of the most powerful ways to shape your life, become more productive, and achieve your goals. What you do every day adds up over time in every area of your life.

In this chapter, we're going to discuss the importance of having a routine and talk about some ways you can set up a routine for yourself to make you more productive and help you achieve goals that might currently seem out of reach.

Routines make you

Every morning I get up and either go to the gym to lift weights or go for a three-mile run. I've been doing this for years and I'll continue doing this for years to come. When I get back from my workout, I sit down at my desk and go through my daily routine. I know exactly what I'm going to do each day and each week. The routine changes from time to time, but I always have some routine that's pushing me toward my goals.

The routine I put in place a year ago shaped the person I am today. If my routine involved going to the donut store every morning instead of working out, I'd actually look quite a bit different than I do now. If my routine involved practicing kung fu every day, I'd probably be a pretty good martial artist.

The same is true for you. What you do every day defines and shapes who you are over time. There are many things you may want to change about yourself, but the trick is that it takes time and consistency to do it. If you want to achieve a goal, like writing a novel, developing an application, or even building your own business, you have to put in place a routine that slowly but surely moves you in the direction you're trying to go.

It seems like common sense when I write the words here, but take a look at your own life and goals; examine the dreams and aspirations you have. Are you making an active effort to progress toward them every day? Don't you think that if you created a routine that put you one step closer toward your goals, each day, you'd eventually achieve them?

Creating a routine

Now is the time to act. Not tomorrow or next week, but now. If you want to reach your goals, if you want to shape your future—rather than let someone else or circumstance shape it for you—you have to develop a routine that will guide you in the direction you want to go.

A good routine begins with a big goal. What is it that you want to accomplish? You can usually only focus on accomplishing one big goal at a time, so pick the most important goal you have right now. You know, that one that you'd like to do some day, but you've never had the time to get around to doing.

Once you've picked your big goal, it's time to figure out how you can make incremental steps toward that goal each day or week that will eventually get you there. If you want to write a book, how many words do you need to write each day to get it done in a year? If you want to lose weight, how many pounds do you have to drop each week to reach your goal?

This big goal will form the basis of your routine. You'll build your schedule around this goal. Most people have to commit 8 hours of their day to working at their job. There might not be much flexibility there, but you still have 16 hours left to schedule your day. We'll take another 8 hours off for sleeping, which leaves you 8 hours. Finally, we'll take another 2 hours off per day for eating. At worst you should have about 6 hours each day that you can allocate to what you want to achieve.

Now, 6 hours a day might not seem like all that much, but that's 42 hours a week. (And if you read the previous chapter on how you're wasting your time, you can probably guess what most people do with 40 of those hours each week. See how important it is to quit watching TV?)

Alright, so now that we know what we're working with, the next task is to actually schedule that time. You'll be most successful scheduling your routine around a five-day work week because you already have a routine around going to work each day. I'd recommend taking the first hour or two of your day and devoting that time to your most important goal. You might have to wake up a couple of hours earlier, but by utilizing the first hour or two of your day, you'll not only be more likely to stick to what you're trying to do, you'll also have the most energy.

With just that simple change, you'll move yourself each day in the direction of your most important goal. If you only schedule your progress on weekdays, you'll still move 260 steps each year in the right direction. If you're writing a novel and writing 1,000 words a day, you'll write 260,000 words in a year. (*Moby Dick* is 209,117 words long.)

Getting more detailed

So far we've only scheduled one thing into your routine—but it's the most important thing. If you only do this, you'll be pretty happy with the results, but we can do a bit better than that. If you really want to be productive, you need to be even more in control of your life.

I work from home for myself, so you can imagine that my routine is pretty detailed. I have a routine that defines what I'm going to do for most of the day. This routine enables me to get the maximum amount of work done each day. Most people I talk to are surprised to find out that I follow a routine each day when I have the flexibility to do anything I want. But that routine is critical to my success.

If you work for yourself or from home, you should definitely put together a routine that clearly defines what you're doing during the day, including what time you start working and what time you stop. The lack of flexibility will be more than made up for by the increase in productivity and the security of knowing you're making forward progress toward your goals.

But even if you don't work from home, you still need to develop a routine that encompasses the majority of your day. If you're working a regular 9-to-5 job, the good news is that most of the structure is already in place for you.

I'd highly recommend scheduling out your workday so that you know what you're going to be doing each day and each week. We talked about having a big goal that defines your routine, but you probably have many smaller goals you want to make progress toward as well. The best way to make progress toward those smaller goals is to schedule them into your routine.

Decide what you're going to do each day when you first start working. It might be checking and responding to your email, but perhaps a better choice is to start working on the most important thing you have to do each day. (Email can always wait until later.) Pick out a few tasks that you're going to repeat on a daily or weekly basis (see chapter 39 for details on a quota system that can help you with that). Schedule a time each day to work on those tasks so you can be sure they get done. When I worked in an office, I regularly had 30 minutes each day I dedicated to learning more about whatever technology I was working with. I used to call it "research time."

You should also schedule your meals and even create a routine around what meals you'll eat each day. I know it might sound a little bit crazy, but we waste a large amount of time deciding what to eat and cook and we end up eating poorly if we don't plan these things out ahead of time.

The more structured your day is, the more control you'll have over your life. Think about it: if you're always reacting to circumstances, if you're always handling things as they come up instead of planning them out, your environment is directing your life, not you.

Table 44.1 shows an example of a routine for a day.

Table 44.1   Example routine

Time	Activity
7:00 AM	Workout (run or lift weights)
8:00 AM	Eat breakfast (M, W, F: breakfast A; T, Th: breakfast B)
9:00 AM	Get to work and pick most important task to work on
11:00 AM	Check and respond to email
12:00 PM	Eat lunch (M, T, W, Th: bring lunch; F: eat out)
1:00 PM	Professional development time (research, improve skills)
1:30 PM	Work on secondary work, meetings, and so on
5:30 PM	Plan tasks for the next day; record work done from today
6:30 PM	Eat dinner
7:00 PM	Play with kids
9:00 PM	Read
11:00 PM	Bedtime

Landmine: Be careful not to be too obsessed with your routine

You should have a general routine you follow, but be flexible as well. You may miss a day or mess up your schedule. Don't forget that there are unpredictable events like your car breaking down that will potentially mess up your routine. You need to learn to take these events in stride.

Taking action

- What is your current routine? Track your daily activities and see how much of a routine you're already following.
- Pick one big goal and work it into your routine at least every week day. Calculate how much progress you'll make in a year if you make a daily step toward your goal.

45

Developing habits: Brushing your code

> We are what we repeatedly do. Excellence, then, is not an act, but a habit.
>
> —Aristotle

We all have habits—some good, some bad. Good habits propel us forward and help us grow. Bad habits hold us back and stunt our growth. Developing and cultivating good habits can help you be productive without conscious effort. Just like routines help us to slowly but surely build a massive wall a brick a time, habits also can move us forwards or backwards by an accumulation of our efforts. The big difference is that routine is something we can control, and habits aren't.

In this chapter, we're going to talk about the value of having good habits and how to develop those habits. We don't have control over our habits, but we do have control over forming and breaking them. Learning how can be one of the most effective things you can do in your life.

Understanding habits

Before we can dive into changing your habits and building new ones, we need to discuss exactly what habits are. I'll give you a brief overview here, but for a more detailed explanation, you might want to check out the excellent book by Charles Duhigg, *The Power of Habit* (Random House, 2012).

Habits basically consist of three things: a cue, a routine, and a reward. A cue is something that causes your habit to be triggered. It might be a certain time of the day, some kind of social interaction, a particular environment, or just about anything else. I've got a cue of buying popcorn whenever I'm in a movie theater.

Next up is the routine. A routine is something you do—the actual habit itself. A routine might be smoking a cigarette, going for a run, or running all your unit tests before checking in your code.

Finally, there's the reward. This is the anchor that actually keeps the habit in place. This is the good feeling you get from executing your habit. The reward might just be a feeling of satisfaction, a "ding" when you gain a level in World of Warcraft, or that sugary taste of your favorite treat.

Our brains are really good at forming habits. We automatically form habits around things we do. The more we do a thing, the more likely a habit will be formed. The strength of the habit is often based on the value of the reward. We like to do things that give us better rewards. Strangely, though, variable rewards are more addicting than a known standard reward. This is why you see so many people in casinos. Not knowing if you'll get a reward or how big that reward will be can create some pretty bad habits, also known as addictions.

Habits consist of three things: a cue, a routine, and a reward.

You probably have hundreds of habits that you aren't even consciously aware of. There is probably a particular routine you perform each morning when you get up. You probably brush your teeth every evening, and you likely have all kinds of habits that influence the way you work and how you work. That's what I really want to focus on in this chapter, because developing those habits is going to help you increase your productivity the most.

Recognizing bad habits and altering them

It's often easiest to start by taking bad habits and turning them around to create good habits out of them. If we can identify what our bad habits are, we can gain a double boost in productivity by taking negative habits and making them positive ones.

I've got a bad habit of immediately checking my email and then checking a few internet deal sites and my social networks when I first sit down to my computer each day. I'd venture to guess that you have some similar routine that you do each day as well.

Now, I'll be the first to admit that I'm still in the process of breaking this habit and changing it around—it's not exactly easy to do. But it serves as a good example of a bad habit that I know I could turn around and change into a good one.

Let's examine that habit and break it down into three parts. First is the cue. Sitting down at my desk seems to be the cue. Once I get in front of my computer first thing in the morning, the habit begins. Next comes the routine. The routine is checking email, seeing if there are any good deals on Slickdeals.com, checking Facebook, checking Twitter, and so on. Finally, there's the reward. The reward is two-fold. It feels good to check all the internet sites I like to check—sometimes there are likes on my posts or shiny new emails just waiting for me. I also feel a bit of stress relief, because I can distract myself from what I know I need to get done that day and take a few moments to relax.

I could try to stop this habit completely, but it would be rather hard to do. I'd be constantly tempted by its alluring call, and half the time that I'm doing the habit I don't even realize it; it's just automatic. But

It's important to have good habits.

instead of trying to completely eliminate it, I can change the routine. Instead of checking all those internet sites I like to check, I could leave the cue in place and have the cue direct me toward another action—a more productive action.

What if instead of checking internet sites the first thing in the morning, I decided to plan my day and cherry-pick the one task for the day that I enjoyed the most? I'd be able to get more work done and I'd start off with the work I enjoyed instead of the work I enjoyed least. Sure, I wouldn't be working on the most important thing first each day, but I'd be working on something productive rather than waste half an hour doing something completely unproductive.

It might take me awhile to make the switch to turn the bad habit into a good one, but eventually the good habit would replace the old bad habit and it would start to become part of my daily routine.

You can apply the same approach to bad habits of your own, but first you have to identify them. The best way to identify your bad habits is to try to find things in your life and routine that you feel guilty about. What are the things that you want to stop doing, but you always put off for another day?

Try starting small. Pick a single bad habit that you've been able to identify and don't try to change it right away. Instead, try to identify exactly what triggers the habit, what exactly it is that you end up doing, and what the reward is that motivates you to execute on that impulse. Sometimes, you might even find the reward is a phantom one—a promise you expect to be fulfilled but that never really is. Many people buy lottery tickets habitually because they think they might win, even though they never do.

Once you have a good handle on the habit itself, you'll find that you'll become much more conscious of it. You might even be able to break or change a habit just by examining it closely.

Next, try to figure out if there's some other routine you can substitute for the one you're currently doing for that habit. If possible, try to find something that you can do that will carry a similar reward or even the same type of reward.

Finally, the hard part is forcing yourself to stick with this new change of habit for a long enough time period for it to take over the old one. It helps to know that the new habit will eventually become easy and automatic as long as you can stick with the change long enough.

Forming new habits

In addition to changing old habits, you'll want to form new habits around the things you want to do. In the previous chapter we talked about the importance of having a routine, but you won't be very successful with a routine unless it's made up of habits that will keep you doing it.

You might be successful in forming new habits by just sticking with a routine long enough. I was able to develop my habit of running and lifting weights three times a week mostly by sticking with the routine for a couple of months. After a couple of months, I automatically felt compelled to get outside and run or to go to the gym, depending on what day of the week it was.

One of my favorite examples of forming a new habit comes from a blog post from John Resig, a developer I hold in high regard. In his blog post titled "Write Code Every Day," John talks about how he wasn't making any progress in his side projects until he created the habit of writing some amount of useful code for a minimum of 30 minutes each day. After implementing his new routine, it became a habit and it resulted in a huge productivity increase for him. You can read the full blog post at http://simpleprogrammer.com/ss-write-code.

The idea of forming habits is similar to that of creating a routine. Try to think of one big goal you want to accomplish and see if you can form habits that will move you in the direction of it. The more positive habits you have, the easier it will be to progress toward your goals.

Once you've picked out a habit that you'd like to develop, think of a reward that will help motivate you to start the habit. You might decide that you want to develop the habit of running all your unit tests before checking in your code. Perhaps you decide that if you run the unit tests before checking in your code, you'll give yourself a nice five-minute break to check your email. Just watch out to make sure the reward you give yourself isn't a bad habit in itself. I wouldn't recommend eating a candy bar every time you work out.

Next, figure out the cue for your new habit. What's going to trigger the habit? Make this cue something constant that you can rely on. A certain time of day or day of a week is a great cue that will ensure you don't put the action off until another time. If you can piggyback off of another habit, even better. I had a habit of reading a technical book for 30 minutes every evening to keep my skills sharp. I decided I could create a new habit of walking for 30 minutes a day by combining the two. Now when I want to read a book I feel compelled to walk on the tread-mill as well.

Taking action

○ Track your habits. What are the most influential habits that currently make up your life? How many of them would you consider good habits and how many would you consider bad habits?

○ Take one of your bad habits and try to turn it around into a good habit. Before you do it, visualize what the net result will be in your life one week from now, one month from now, and one year from now.

46

Breaking down things: How to eat an elephant

When eating an elephant take one bite at a time.
— Creighton Abrams

One of the main reasons for procrastination — which is the bane of productivity — is problem admiration: being so busy admiring the size of a problem that you don't actually try and solve it. When we look at tasks in their entirety, they can seem much larger and intimidating than they really are.

In this chapter, I'm going to talk about a productivity hack than can help you overcome procrastination: breaking things down. By breaking down big tasks into smaller ones, you'll find that you're more motivated to get them done and you'll make much steadier progress toward achieving your goals.

Why bigger isn't always better

The bigger a task, the more intimidating it appears to be. Writing an entire software application is difficult. Writing a single line of code is easy. Unfortunately, in the field of software development, we tend to encounter more large tasks and projects than smaller ones.

These large tasks or projects can psychologically hurt us and our productivity, because of our inability to see far into the future. A large task can seem almost impossible when you look at it in its entirety. Think about incredible feats like building a skyscraper or a bridge that spans for miles.

Many skyscrapers and bridges have been built, so we know it's possible, but if you look at any of these kinds of projects as a whole, it seems like no one could possibly accomplish them.

I struggled for a long time to complete a large project like building an application from scratch. I started many different applications, but never ended up quite finishing any of them until I started learning to break things down. It seemed that I'd always be enthusiastic about a project at first, but pretty soon I'd get bogged down in the details. I'd get caught up in thinking about how much work there was left to do and I'd never quite make it to the finish line. The bigger the project was, the more likely I was to fail.

I've found that I'm not alone in this regard. In my various roles in the software development field, when I've given out work to other developers, I've invariably found that the biggest indicator of the success of a project was the size of the task that I doled out. The bigger the tasks I asked someone to do, the more likely they were to not do them.

We've already talked about one of the reasons why this is true: the psychological burden of a large task. When faced with large problems we tend to spend more time thinking about the problem than taking steps to solve the problem. Humans tend to take the path of least resistance. When faced with a big task, checking your email or getting another cup of coffee almost always seems like the easier path, so procrastination ensues.

But procrastination isn't the only reason why bigger tasks aren't better. The bigger a task, the less it tends to be defined. If I ask you to go to the store and get me eggs, milk, and bread, that task is well defined and you know exactly what to do. Executing on that task is easy and chances are you'll execute correctly on your mission.

On the other hand, if I ask you to create a website for me, that's a much bigger, less defined task. You might not know where to start and there are many unanswered questions. You're less likely to know exactly what to do to get that job done. I could write up a description of what exactly creating a website for me means and what I expect, but that

level of detailed description would take some time to read and understand and there would be a high probability of error.

Big tasks also tend to be very difficult to estimate. If I ask you how
long it will take you to write an algorithm to find the biggest item in a
list, you can probably give me a pretty accurate estimate. But if I ask
you to tell me how long it will take you to implement a shopping cart
feature on a website, your estimate is probably going to be closer to a
wild guess than anything else.

Bigger tasks are mentally challenging, more likely to bring about procrastination, generally less descriptive, error-prone, and more difficult
to estimate than smaller tasks.

Breaking down things

Don't lose hope. There is a solution. It turns out that most big tasks can
be broken down into smaller tasks. In fact, almost every large task can
be broken down into an almost infinite number of easier smaller tasks.

Breaking down large tasks into smaller ones is one of the techniques I
use all the time to get more work done and to have more accurate estimates of how long the work will take me to do.

In fact, it's no coincidence how this book is structured. You may have
wondered why there are so many small chapters in this book. When I
set out to write this book, I purposely chose to create many small chapters broken up into several sections instead of a few large chapters. The
reason is two-fold.

First, you as a reader will have an easier time digesting this content. I
know that when I read books with long chapters, I'm more likely to
avoid picking up the book and reading unless I have enough time to get
through a full chapter. The task of reading a book with longer chapters
seems more intimidating, so I'm less likely to do it. Hopefully, you've
found that each chapter of 1,000–2,000 words is easier to read and less
intimidating than a much larger, less broken-up text.

Second, it's easier for me. I know that writing a book is a challenge. I
know that most people who sit down to write a book don't finish it. I've

sat down to write books myself and never completed them. Having small chapters that are each the size of a long blog post makes the task of writing a book much more manageable. Instead of having one big task of writing a massive book, I have 80 or so small tasks of writing chapters.

When you break down tasks into smaller pieces, those tasks become easier to do, your estimates for completing the tasks are much more accurate, and you're more likely to perform them correctly. Even if a smaller task is done incorrectly, you have more opportunity for correction before you get too far into a large project or undertaking. I've found that it's almost always a good idea to break down any large task into smaller ones.

How to break down things

It turns out that breaking things down isn't all that hard. Most tasks can be easily decomposed into smaller tasks by taking them one step at a time. The quote about how to eat an elephant is very true. The only way you can conceivably eat an elephant is by taking one bite at a time. The same goes for almost every large task. Even if you don't consciously break down a large task, you're still limited by time's linear progress. One thing must be done before another thing can be done and so forth and so on.

If you want to take a large task and make it less intimidating, you need to start by determining what steps need to be done to complete the task. If I'm given a large task to work on, the very first thing I try to do is figure out if I can chop that task into smaller sequential pieces.

I was recently working on a project for a client of mine to get their continuous integration system and deployment working for their code. This was a large task. The task seemed quite intimidating and difficult at first, but instead of trying to tackle it head on, I started by breaking down the task into smaller tasks.

It made sense to first start by trying to get my client's code to build
and compile from the command
line, because that would be necessary for creating an automated
build. The next task that made
sense was to have a build server
be able to check out the code.
Then another task could be created to combine the two—have
the build server check out the
code and use the command-line
script to compile the code.

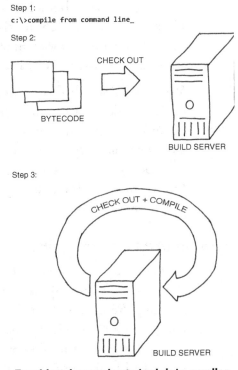

I broke down the entire project
into small tasks like these and
suddenly the insurmountable
beast looked like a little mouse.
Each little task seemed trivially
simple, even though the whole
project seemed like a very difficult problem to solve.

**Breaking down a large task into smaller
tasks makes more sense.**

One thing you'll probably find when you're trying to break down a
large task into many smaller ones is that you don't have enough information about exactly what you're supposed to do. Remember how I
said that bigger tasks are usually less defined? A critical step of breaking down a large task into smaller ones is identifying what information
is missing that's preventing you from creating smaller, well-defined
tasks. If you're having a problem breaking down a large task into
smaller ones, chances are it's due to lack of information.

This isn't a bad thing, though. It's much better to learn early on in a
project that you're lacking the information to complete it than it is to
find that out when you're already far into a large undertaking. When
you break down large tasks into smaller ones, make sure each small
task has a clear goal. Trying to identify these goals will often reveal
important information you might have otherwise missed.

When I work on Agile teams, I often try to use this technique to get the right information out of the customer. Customers often have a hard time stating exactly what they want when they're asking you to perform some large task like adding a shopping cart to their site. But if you can break down the large task into smaller ones, you can make it much easier for them to tell you what they want.

Breaking down problems

This same approach to breaking things down can be applied directly to code and problem solving as well. Many new developers get overwhelmed with trying to solve what they perceive as a difficult piece of code to write or a difficult problem to solve, because they try to tackle too big of a problem at once—they don't know how to break things down. (I have to admit, I'm still guilty of this myself from time to time.)

We naturally do some of this to manage the complexity in our code. That's why we don't have one large method with all the code in it. We break down our code into methods, functions, variables, classes, and other structures to help simplify it.

No matter how difficult a programming problem may be, it can always be decomposed into smaller and smaller pieces. If you're trying to write a difficult algorithm, instead of plowing ahead and writing code, it can help to break the problem down into smaller pieces that can be solved independently and sequentially. No matter how large and complex an application is, it can always be distilled into lines of code. A single line of code is never beyond the complexity level of any programmer to understand or to write, so if you're willing to break down a problem far enough, you can literally write any application with only the ability to write a single line of code.

Taking action

- What large tasks are you avoiding right now because the size of them intimidates you? Are you procrastinating on cleaning the garage, writing a blog post, or tackling that difficult algorithm?
- Pick a large problem you're facing now and see if you can figure out a good way to decompose it into smaller tasks.

47

The value of hard work and why you keep avoiding it

This chapter is near and dear to my heart. I feel like there was a huge turning point in my career—and my life—when I finally embraced the idea that hard work was necessary for success and not something to be avoided.

Everyone is always looking for a shortcut in life—some way to get out of doing the hard work required to succeed—myself included. We all want to find some way that we can enjoy the results of hard work without actually having to do it. I'd like to have this book be magically finished without me having to do the hard work of sitting down to write it.

The reality of the situation, though, is that everything that's worthwhile comes as a result of hard work. In life, and especially in your software development career, you have to learn how to sit down and do the work you don't want to do—and do it consistently—if you really want to see results.

In this chapter, we'll dispel some of the myths of the charlatans that promise you great rewards by working smarter instead of harder, and we'll tackle some of the motivational challenges behind doing hard work.

Why is hard work so darn...hard?

It's a mystery to me why some things are so much harder to do than other things. Why is it that I have no problem playing a videogame for hours at a time—which arguably may involve quite a bit of mental strain—but I can't seem to get myself to sit down and type out the words to a blog post? Does my mind really care what kind of work it's doing? I know that to my brain, the machine that runs the show, it's all work. Does my brain really care if it's mashing buttons on a videogame controller or mashing keys on a keyboard? But to me, one is work and the other is play. One is hard and the other is fun.

I've never met a person who really enjoys doing hard work. There are plenty of people who will say they enjoy hard work and most of us enjoy the work once we get into it or once it's finished, but hardly any-one ever wants to start doing hard work.

To be honest with you, I don't think I could give you a good reason why this is so. I can't tell you why it's much more difficult to get your brain to send the electrical signals to your hands to write the code to fix that bug you need to fix than it is to get that same brain to send those same electrical signals to your hands to type a comment in Facebook or the address of your favorite time-wasting website. But the reality is that certain work is hard and other work is easy.

It seems to me, though, that the work that we consider hard is the work that's most likely to benefit us. It's the work that's most likely to advance our careers or open up new opportunities. All the work that doesn't have any benefit always seems so easy.

I'll just work "smarter"

All the time now, it seems, I hear someone preaching the idea of work-ing smarter rather than harder. While I agree that we should work as smartly as possible, I don't agree that working smarter is a substitute for hard work. Everyone who promises greater results with less work is trying to sell you something, or they have forgotten how hard they had to work to get to where they are.

There is a major fallacy in the idea that smarter work can overcome harder work. It's true that to get ahead you have to work smart, but a hard worker will consistently pass a self-proclaimed smart worker any day. The truth of the matter is that if we want to actually see results from our actions, we have to be willing to work hard.

If you really want to be effective, you have to learn how to work both smart and hard. Being smart isn't enough. There is a certain amount of gumption that's required, a certain amount of perseverance in the face of obstacles that's necessary to actually succeed.

Hard work is boring

If I had to speculate as to why we avoid hard work, I'd say it's because hard work is generally boring. When I first started writing my blog I was excited about it. I was enthusiastic about this new opportunity to express myself. But over time, it became drudgery. If I didn't learn to stick with it, even through the drudgery, I'd never have seen the benefits of my actions.

The things that we perceive as difficult are actually the things we don't want to do because they aren't exciting or they aren't glamorous. It's very tempting to fly through life going from one passion to the next, only doing the things that interest you. As soon as something stops interesting you, you fly on to the next thing.

But there's a problem with this kind of thinking. The problem is that your peers who are willing to stick with a single thing over time will eventually surpass you. At first you may appear to be ahead of them. At first your passion for what you're doing will give you a temporary boost, but the person who is willing to put in the long, hard hours and do the boring work necessary to get a job done will eventually pull ahead...far ahead.

> *The race is to the driven, not to the swift.*
> —John Jakes, *North and South*

The reality

The reality of your situation, of all our situations, is that nothing comes easy. If you truly want to succeed, if you truly want to be successful, you're going to have to pull some all-nighters. You might have to spend a few years of your career doing 60- or 70-hour weeks. You might have to forgo watching TV or hanging out with friends for a few years to pull ahead. You can't cheat the system. You get out exactly what you put in. In one season you plant, in another season you reap. You never reap what you didn't plant.

But it doesn't mean that you'll never be able to take it easy. Success begets success. The more successful you are, the easier success will come. It's just that the first hill you have to climb is a long and steep one.

Few people ever make it to the top. Few people ever actually see real success. Most people go through their careers being mediocre. They aren't willing to put in the time and the sacrifice necessary to truly succeed. You could follow all of the advice in this book, but if you weren't willing to work hard, it would do you no good. No good at all. You have to be willing to work. You have to be willing to put the things you learn into practice to make them effective.

Working hard: How to do it

Okay, so at this point you might be wondering how it is that you can motivate yourself to actually sit down and do the work you know you need to do. I wish I had a magical answer that could suddenly make you the most productive person alive, able to take on any task without procrastination or protest, but unfortunately I don't possess a miracle to that degree.

What I can tell you, though, is that we all struggle with the same problems. We all have a tendency to procrastinate and to avoid the work that's truly important to us. Stephen Pressfield, the author of one of my favorite books, *The War of Art*, calls this mysterious force that throws these roadblocks in our way *resistance*. He claims that whenever we try to elevate ourselves to a higher plane of existence, resistance rears its ugly head and tries to keep us where we are.

We have to learn how to beat this resistance if we're ever going to succeed at whatever endeavor we're pursuing. But how do we beat this foe? How do we hold resistance's face to the mat and make him tap out? We simply sit at our desks and do what we're supposed to do. We all have to learn how to push through and just do the work. There's no easy answer.

I know that isn't what you wanted to hear. It isn't what I wanted to hear, either. But at least you know you aren't alone. At least you know it's just as difficult for me to sit down and write this book as it is for you to sit down and read it. At least you know when you're avoiding your work browsing Facebook instead, there are 100 million other people doing the same exact thing.

The question, though, is this: Are you going to be beaten? Are you simply going to decide that you're unable to focus and concentrate on your work, or are you going to push past those barriers and take resistance head on? It's a choice that only you can make. You just have to decide that you're going to do the work that needs to be done. You have to realize that the work must eventually be done, so it might as well get done now instead of later. You have to realize that the only way you're going to accomplish your goals, the only way you're going to reach your full potential is if you're willing to grit your teeth, bite the bullet, and get to work.

Taking action

○ What kind of hard work are you putting off? What kinds of tasks do you procrastinate because you don't ever feel like doing them? Pick one of those tasks and, without hesitation, do it. Get in the habit of not delaying, but immediately executing on work that needs to be done.

48

Any action is better than no action

> *Any action is often better than no action, especially if you have been stuck in an unhappy situation for a long time. If it is a mistake, at least you learn something, in which case it's no longer a mistake. If you remain stuck, you learn nothing.*
>
> —Eckhart Tolle, *The Power of Now*

I thought I'd end this section by talking about one of the worst killers of productivity: inaction. In your software development career, nothing is more deadly to your productivity than failing to take action. It's important to make wise decisions and to think things through, but often you don't have all the information you'd like to have and you have to just go ahead and make a choice—take action.

In this chapter, we'll talk about why taking any kind of action is almost always a better choice than taking no action at all, why so many people default to inaction, and what you can do about it.

Why we refuse to take action

So many opportunities are wasted and so many possibilities are squandered by the refusal to take action. It seems somewhat obvious. I mean, without taking action, how can you expect anything to happen? I think most people understand this statement to be true—it's pretty obvious. But why then do so many people choose not to take action?

I know for me—and I'd venture to guess for you, too—the reason is pretty simple: fear. Fear of being wrong. Fear of messing something up. Fear of not measuring up or failing. Fear of change, of doing something different.

Fear is probably the biggest reason that we refuse to take action when we know we should. But it's important that we don't let our fears trap us in. It's important we learn to overcome our fears and realize the truth that even though an action we take might not be the best one, it's almost always better than taking no action at all—the default choice.

Very few people regret actions they took based on the best knowledge they had available to them, but very many people regret not taking action—the opportunities they missed because they were too shy, cautious, or indecisive to go forward and do something.

What happens when you don't take action

I know a couple who are constantly plagued by their inability to take action. The husband is a very logical person and the wife is more feeling-oriented. A pretty common situation. But the problem they have is when it's time to make a big decision and to take action on that decision.

One time that couple decided it was time to upgrade the guest bathroom. They got a new tub installed, but then had the problem of deciding whether they should put in a shower curtain or a glass enclosure for the tub. One wanted a curtain, the other an enclosure. The debate raged on for years. Neither side wanted to give in or take any kind of action. Arguments were laid out, possibilities were discussed, but no decision was made. No action was taken.

This went on for years. My wife and I stayed at their house at least seven times over the last 10 years, and every time we stayed with them we had to use the master bathroom instead of the guest bathroom because there was no shower curtain or enclosure for the tub.

They went for years without being able to utilize a shower they had, inconveniencing their guests and themselves, because a decision couldn't be made; action couldn't be taken. This same couple is now in another epic battle over replacing the lawn, which threatens to last for the next decade.

Now, this couple could have decided to take some kind of action, even if it wasn't optimal and it would have almost certainly been a better outcome than not having a functioning shower for 10 years, but they didn't. Instead, they chose the default choice that most of us choose when we can't make up our minds—no action at all.

You might not have a shower without a shower curtain for 10 years, but how many choices in your life have you dragged out over time that could be solved today, in five minutes, if you would just take action? How many choices are you stuck on because you haven't found the optimal solution or you're afraid of making the wrong decision, so instead you're ensuring defeat by choosing to do nothing at all? How many hours, years, decades of your life are you wasting by not taking action?

Perhaps you want to learn how to play guitar. Maybe you aren't happy with your job and you want to find a new one. Perhaps your financial situation needs a major overhaul. Whatever it is you're avoiding, whatever it is that's plaguing you, but you refuse to take action on, now is the time to act. Now is the time to make a decision.

What is the worst that could happen?

What is the worst that could happen? You should always ask yourself this question if you're stuck on making a decision. Most of the time, the answer to this question is that you find out you were wrong and take another course of action instead.

Many times you'll need to be wrong quite a few times before you'll find the correct course of action to take. The longer you delay any action, the longer it will take you to go down all the wrong paths and finally end up on the correct one.

Most of the decisions we tend to get hung up on tend to be trivial. We're often trying to find the 95% solution that will take us 300% more effort rather than settling for the 90% solution that's more than good enough. We do this with life, we do this with code, and we even do this when we're trying to decide on a new television set. (Although for the third choice, you're arguably better off if you never do decide on a television set to buy; see chapter 43 on how you're wasting your time.)

Yet, some of these trivial decisions can have a big impact on our life if we choose to do nothing rather than risk a suboptimal solution or an outright failure. Consider what happens when you can't decide between two comparable algorithms for solving a problem in some code that needs to be completed to deliver a feature to an important client.

Perhaps both choices would produce an acceptable outcome, but one of those choices might be marginally better. What happens when you delay taking action so that you can gather more information and end up missing a deadline that results in you losing that important client?

In that case, it would have been much better to choose one of the algorithms, even if it wasn't the best one. By taking action, you might have even found out that one of the algorithms didn't work and had time to still implement the other. The choice to not make a choice—to delay action—resulted in the worst possible outcome.

Even some seemingly important choices—life-altering ones—are better off left to a random roll of the die than indecision and inaction. Many college students think that choosing a major or a career is a really important decision. While that decision may be important, it isn't nearly as important as choosing something, but how many college students graduate with unusable degrees or generalized majors because they couldn't make and commit to a real decision? Being paralyzed by indecision prevented them from taking action.

It's easier to steer a moving car

Often not taking action is like sitting in a parked car and turning the steering wheel. Have you ever tried to turn the steering wheel of a parked car? It's not easy to do. It's much easier to turn the steering wheel on a car when the car is in motion.

Yet, so many of us are sitting in the garages of our lives behind the wheel of a parked car, furiously cranking the steering wheel to the left and right trying to decide which direction we should go before we've even pulled out of the driveway.

It's better to just get in your car and start driving, so you're at least going in some direction. You can always turn the steering wheel and course-correct once the car is in motion—and it's much easier to do. As long as you're sitting parked in the garage, you might not turn the wrong direction, but you won't turn the right direction, either.

Once a car is moving, it has momentum. That momentum can carry you forward in the wrong direction, but it can be just as easily diverted with a turn of the steering wheel to the correct direction once you figure it out. And you might even start out in the correct direction to begin with.

Sometimes, when you're completely unsure about what to do, the best course of action is to do something and course-correct along the way. Sometimes, this will be the only way to proceed. You can't know where the left-hand turn that you need to make is if you never see it, because you never moved forward. You can't anticipate all the future actions you'll need to take and what might possibly go wrong until you start doing something.

Often, the only way to find out a direction is wrong is to go that direction. When the cost of being wrong is small, always opt to do something rather than nothing.

What can you do now?

Okay, so how can you apply this to your life right now? How can you start taking action today? Go through the simple checklist in table 48.1 and see if it can help spur you into action.

Table 48.1   Checklist for taking action

Checklist for taking action	Answers
What specifically is holding me back from taking action?	
If there is a choice I need to make, what is that choice? What options do I have to choose from?	

Table 48.1   Checklist for taking action

Checklist for taking action	Answers
What's the worst that can result from making a wrong choice?	
If I choose wrong, can I go back and try another choice? Will the cost of doing so be high?	
Is there a big difference between the choices? Can I get away with a suboptimal solution that I can take action on right away?	
Does the problem I'm facing lend itself to self-discoverability? If I start taking some action, will I be able to course-correct until I eventually find the right action to take?	
What will happen if I don't take any action? What will the cost be in time, missed opportunity, or money?	

Taking action

- Pick something that you know you should be taking action on and fill out table 48.1.
- Identify a past missed opportunity from not taking action; for example, buying and selling a stock, investing in a company, or starting a business.
- What would have been the worst outcome if things didn't go as you had hoped?
- What would have been the best?
- If an action goal is too complex to decide on today, what smaller decision can you make to still move forward? For example, if you're trying to decide whether to learn to play guitar or piano, could you make a decision to temporarily start learning one while you decide which one to take on for the long term?

Financial

Money is only a tool. It will take you wherever you wish, but it will not replace you as the driver.

—Ayn Rand

Software development is one of the most well-paid occupations available today, and in the future it's only likely to increase in value as more and more of the world is run on computers and software. But all the money in the world will do you little good if you don't know how to handle it. Plenty of lottery winners, movie stars, and famous athletes have made and lost millions because they lacked the financial intelligence to deal with their fortunes.

You can be a millionaire or live your entire life paycheck to paycheck—the choice is up to you and in great part is based on your knowledge of how to manage your finances and how the financial systems of the world work. Just a little bit of knowledge about how money works and how you can make the best use of it can go a long way toward securing your financial future.

In this section, we'll go over some of the most important financial concepts that are likely to benefit you as a software developer. We'll go over topics like how the stock market actually works, how to get started in real estate investing, retirement plans, and more, and at the end of this section, I'll share with you my story and how I used the principles and knowledge in this section to retire at the age of 33.

Now, I know what you may be thinking. You may be thinking "That's great, John, but I'm not really interested in reading about finances. I'm a software developer. I want to improve my career." But before you skip this section, think about it this way: how you manage your finances and the investments you make or don't make will have a major impact on your life, probably more so than any other thing, besides your health—which we'll also cover in this book.

In fact, many of the key decisions you make about your career will be in a very large part based on finances. The opportunities you have as a software developer will be equally influenced as well. A little knowledge here can go a long way. Even though you might be a bit skeptical, I'd encourage you to seriously consider how changing your financial situation could significantly alter your life and the decisions you make in your career.

After getting some feedback from the initial version of the book, I've decided to move some of the more basic and generalized chapters into the appendix at the end of this book. If you find that some of the things I'm talking about in this section are a bit over your head, you might want to visit the appendixes first and check out the basic financial information there.

49

What are you going to do with your paycheck?

Over the course of your career, if you work for 30 years and get paid every two weeks, you'll get exactly 780 paychecks. If you work for 40 years, you'll get 1,040. What you do with those paychecks over that time will determine how long you work, how much money you'll have when you retire, and whether or not you can even retire.

It's important to have an understanding of where your money is going each month and how that money is either working for you or against you for the future. In this chapter, we'll explore some crucial financial concepts related to your income that will help you better manage your money and think about it in slightly different terms than you might be used to.

Stop thinking short term

I've stopped a lot of coworkers from buying new cars by talking to them about one simple scenario that changes almost everyone's mind—or at least makes them seriously reconsider their choice.

Whenever anyone tells me they're going to buy a new car, I ask them how much they think it will cost. Usually the number is between \$20,000 and \$30,000, which is quite a bit of money. Most people I know don't have that kind of money lying around. In fact, most people I know would have to save for several years to come up with that kind of money. It seems that so many people will gladly trade it for a car, but would they really?

After they tell me how much the car costs, I usually follow up by asking how they're going to pay for the car. Almost always I get the response that they'll get a loan, and they tell me how low the payments will be because they're stretched over so many years. Usually this seems to make sense, until I ask the next, all-important question: "If you had a suitcase with $25,000 in cash in it, right now, would you take the suitcase full of cash and trade it for that same new car?"

Some people still insist they would, but most people realize that they wouldn't—that they'd rather have $25,000 cash than a new car. But when they can buy a $25,000 car for $30,000 stretched over four to six years with only $300-a-month payments, it seems like a much better deal.

I usually then talk about how much more enjoyment you could get out of buying a $5,000 car that will get you from point a to point b just as well, but will leave you with $20,000 to spend however you like over the next few years. I'm not saying I've never bought a new car in my life, but it's hard to justify it when you think about the situation like this.

The problem is most of us think about money matters in the short term rather than the long term. We think about what things will cost us this month versus what they will cost us overall.

When I first started my career, that was exactly how I thought about things. I remember thinking about how much money I made each month. I'd take that number and from it decide how I could live. The more money I earned each month, the more money I could afford to pay for rent. Then I could subtract out some food and basic living expenses, and whatever I had left over I could use toward a car payment. The more I had left over, the better the car I could afford.

I remember getting a raise at my job and immediately thinking about it in terms of how much more I could afford to spend each month. I remember thinking that my $500-a-month raise meant that I could afford about a $300-more-a-month car payment, after taxes.

That kind of thinking is very dangerous, because it keeps us living exactly at or above our means. It's a short-term way of thinking about finances that never lets us get ahead, because the more we make, the more we spend.

I have a friend who owns a payday loan business that loans people short-term loans to cover them until the next paycheck. He charges ridiculous interest rates for these loans, because people getting a loan from him are in a desperate situation—or at least, they're supposed to be.

One time I asked him about the kinds of people that get payday loans. I mentioned that it must mostly be poor people who can't make enough to live so they're always deferring to the future. His response surprised me. He said that most of his clients were at or below the poverty line, but that a good percentage of them were doctors, lawyers, and other highly paid professionals making well over $100,000 a year or more in income.

It turns out that making a lot of money doesn't make someone financially smart. The doctors and lawyers who were getting payday loans from my friend were trapped in the short-term thinking and same kind of mentality I had early in my career. They were literally living paycheck to paycheck, because they always made sure to spend whatever they brought in each month. The more money they made, the more money they spent. They would buy bigger houses and faster cars, all on credit, because that's what they thought they were supposed to do.

Assets and liabilities

There's another way of thinking, though, that doesn't require you to spend more money just because you make more money. You can think in the long term and think about what the actual costs of things are, not what they end up costing you each month in relation to your income.

This kind of thinking is based around the idea of assets and liabilities. There are many definitions of assets and liabilities floating around out there, but here are mine. An asset is something that has a higher utility value than what its maintenance cost is. That means that for something to qualify as an asset, it has to be able to provide more dollars of value than it costs to own.

A liability, on the other hand, is just the opposite. It's something that costs more than the value it provides. To keep the liability around, you have to shell out money, but you could never get as much money as you're shelling out.

Now, I realize these definitions don't exactly match the definitions an accountant would give for an asset or liability, but these definitions can help you to think about everything you own or buy as either an asset or a liability—something that either has a positive financial impact on your life or a negative one.

Let's look at a few examples of assets versus liabilities, according to my definition. Let's start with some clear examples of both, and then we'll get into some things that could fall into either category.

A clear example of an asset would be some stock you owned that paid you a dividend every quarter. That stock doesn't cost you anything to hold on to, but it gives you income every three months, just for owning it. The value of the stock itself may fall or rise, but if we look at it just in terms of the money it generates, it's an asset—by my definition.

An example of a liability would be your credit card debt. Having credit card debt doesn't give you any benefit. It just costs you money, because every month that credit card debt has interest that has to be paid on it. If you could get rid of it, you'd be in a better situation financially, no argument about it.

But things get a little trickier when you consider something like your house. Is your house an asset or a liability? One of my favorite authors about money management, Robert Kiyosaki, author of *Rich Dad, Poor Dad* (Demco Media, 2000), says that your house is actually a liability and not an asset, and in most cases I agree with him.

We all need a place to live. Regardless of whether or not we own a house or rent, we have to pay for some kind of shelter. Even if you owned your house outright you'd still be "paying for shelter" because you'd be using up a resource you could potentially rent out. When you own a house, you're essentially renting it from yourself.

If the cost of your house is more than the basic cost of shelter that you need, it's a liability to you. For most people, their house is a big liability, because they don't get the extra utility value out of their home that gives them more value than paying rent.

The same goes with your car. You probably need some kind of transportation, but if you are making payments on a car that doesn't provide you any extra real value than a much cheaper car would, it becomes a liability.

Table 49.1 outlines some main assets and liabilities to consider.

Table 49.1   Assets versus liabilities

Assets	Liabilities
Dividend stocks	Credit card debt
Rental real estate	House (if it's more than you need)
Bonds	Car (if it's more than you need)
Musical royalty rights	Monthly services
Software royalty rights	Equipment that loses value over time
Businesses	

Robert Kiyosaki is even stricter on these terms than I am. He calls anything that puts money in your pocket an asset and anything that takes money out of your pocket a liability. You certainly can't go wrong taking that viewpoint.

The key is to realize that certain things you buy generate income for you or generate more value for you than your initial investment, while other things you buy take away from your income or aren't really worth what you paid for them.

When you have this viewpoint, you're more likely to think in the long term rather than the short term. The money you make each paycheck is money you have to work for. The money your assets generate for you each month is money that you didn't have to work for. If you can use more of the money you have to work for to buy assets that generate money you don't have to work for, you'll eventually make more money while doing the same amount of work or less. If you spend money you work for to buy liabilities that cost you money each month, you'll go the opposite direction and be forced to work harder to make more money to continue to pay for the upkeep costs on those liabilities.

Take a moment and list your assets and liabilities. It doesn't have to be perfect, but try and identify your biggest assets and your biggest liabilities. Don't worry if you don't have anything in assets—most people don't.

Back to your paycheck

What does all of this have to do with your paycheck? Let me tell you a story that might make things a little more clear.

Back when I was 19 years old, I got a ridiculous opportunity that I definitely didn't deserve. I was offered a contracting position in Santa Monica, CA, working for a company that would pay me $75 an hour. (This was back in the early 2000s, when that was even more money than today.) This job would basically pay me at least $150,000 a year, assuming two weeks of vacation.

This was an incredible amount of money to make at my age, and I thought I was surely rich. While the opportunity was a golden one, it didn't take me long to realize that not only was I not rich, but I wasn't going to get rich anytime soon unless I made a lot more money.

I was living pretty frugally, so I ran the numbers to see how long it would take for me to reach millionaire status. If I made $150,000 a year, I'd have to pay about 30% of that in taxes, so that leaves $105,000. Then I'd need to live, and I could probably live frugally off of about $35,000 a year. So, that would leave me with $70,000 to save each year.

Then I calculated that if I was able to save $70,000 each year, it would take me just over 14 years to finally become a millionaire. Of course, 14 years later, 1 million dollars wouldn't be quite as valuable due to inflation. In fact, if you go to http://simpleprogrammer.com/ss-measuring-worth, you can punch in the numbers to see that 1 million dollars in the year 2000 would be worth $1.3–1.6 million today. I'd actually need to make more than that, but we'll assume that my salary would rise with inflation.

That was a bad day for me. I realized that I'd have to work hard at my job—the one I was lucky to get—for 14 more years, and during that time I'd have to live extremely frugally, saving as much money as possible to finally become a millionaire. And then what? Being a millionaire was nowhere close to rich. And it wasn't exactly enough to retire on. I'd need to have at least 2 or 3 million to retire comfortably.

It was at that point that I realized that if I wanted to actually be rich someday, not only would I have to not waste my paycheck on liabilities that would bring me down, but I'd also have to invest a significant portion of that paycheck in assets that would eventually earn me more money.

If you want to be financially successful, you have to learn how to invest. There's no other option. Even if you work your entire life and sock away as much money as possible, you'll never become rich or even financially independent unless you find a way to make your money work for you.

Taking action

- Follow the cash that goes through your hands every month. See how much money you start with and where that money goes. Does most of your money go toward liabilities instead of investing in assets?
- Calculate how much money you'd have to save each year to reach 1 million dollars in the bank or whatever number you'd consider to be financially independent. Can you possibly save that much money in your lifetime without investing?
- Start asking yourself "How much can I save?" rather than "How much can I afford?"

50

How to negotiate your salary

I'm often surprised how many software developers neglect to do any salary negotiations at all or make a single attempt at negotiating their salary and then give up and take whatever is offered.

Negotiating your salary is important, not just because the dollars will add up over time and you could end up leaving a lot of money on the table, but also because how you value yourself and how you handle yourself in a salary negotiation will greatly influence how you're perceived at the company you're working for.

Once you're part of a company, it's difficult to shake the first impression that has been pinned on you. If you handle salary negotiations in a tactful way that indicates your value while still respecting your prospective employer, you'll likely paint yourself in a more positive light, which can have huge implications on your future career with that company.

Negotiations begin before you even apply for the job

Your ability to negotiate your salary will be greatly influenced by your reputation. Think about a famous athlete or movie star—how much negotiation power does having a well-recognized name have for either of these professions? The same is true for software development or any other field. The more recognized your name, the more power you'll have when it comes to negotiations.

So what can you do to build up a name in the software development field? For some people it will happen by chance, but for most software developers it will require some careful planning and tactics. I highly recommend building a personal brand and actively marketing yourself as a software developer.

The basic strategy to do this is to get your name out there through as many different mediums as possible. Write blog posts, get on podcasts, write books or articles, speak at conferences and user groups, create video tutorials, contribute to open source projects, and do whatever else you can to get your name out there.

Because marketing yourself isn't the topic of this chapter, I won't go into details here, but if you're interested in learning more about marketing yourself as a software developer, you can check out my blog post on the topic at http://simpleprogrammer.com/ss-3-easy-ways, or if you want a real in-depth treatment of the topic, you can check out my "How to Market Yourself as a Software Developer" course at http://devcareerboost .com/m.

Just remember that the better job you do of marketing yourself and building a reputation, the easier it will be for you to negotiate. This might even be the most important factor. I've worked with software developers who have been able to literally double their salaries based on nothing but building up a bit of a personal brand and online reputation.

How you get the job is extremely important

The second biggest factor that will influence your ability to negotiate your salary will be how you get the job. There are many different ways to get a job and not all of them are equal. Let's examine a few different ways you might get a job.

First, you might get a job by seeing a job posting and cold-applying to that job posting with your resume and hopefully a good cover letter. In fact, many job seekers think this is the only way to get a job. This is, in fact, the worst way to get a job. If you get a job in this manner, it's difficult to have a good negotiating position, because you're in a much weaker position than the employer. You're the one taking all the initiative and asking for the job.

The person with the greatest need always has the disadvantage when negotiating anything. Ever played Monopoly? Ever tried to negotiate with someone who didn't really need anything from you, but you needed one of their properties to complete your monopoly? How did that go?

Another way to get a job is through personal referral. You know some-one who works at a company, they personally refer you for the job, and you end up getting offered the job. This is definitely a much better situation than just applying for a job. In fact, you should always try to get a personal referral when you're actively seeking a job. In this situation, the prospective employer might not even know that you're actively looking for a job—so your need is going to register as less. And because you got a personal referral, you already have some credibility. You're essentially borrowing the credibility of the person who referred you for the job. I'm sure you can figure out that the higher the credibility of the person who referred you for the job, the higher credibility you'll have. This credibility will greatly influence your ability to negotiate when given an offer.

Okay, so how else can you get a job? How about the best way possible? When the company that offers you a job finds you and comes after you by either directly offering you the job or asking you to apply for it. How the situation presents itself will influence your negotiating power. Obviously, your best situation would be if a company knows of you and directly offers you a position without even an interview. In that case, you'll be able to just about name your own price. But any time an employer directly seeks you out, you'll have a good position to negotiate from.

You might be thinking "Yeah right, an employer isn't going to directly seek me out, much less offer me a job without an interview." I'll admit, it's somewhat rare, but it does happen. The best way to make these kinds of opportunities happen is to build up a name for yourself and market yourself like I mentioned in section 2 of this book.

First person to name a number loses

Okay, so now that we've covered the preliminaries—which are actually the most important parts of negotiating your salary—let's get into the actual details of negotiations.

One important thing to understand is that the first person to name a number is at a distinct disadvantage. In any kind of negotiation, you always want to act second. Here's why: Suppose you apply for a job and you expect that the salary for that job is $70,000. You're offered the job and the first question you're asked is what your salary requirements are. You state that you're looking for something around $70,000. Perhaps you're even clever and say somewhere in the range of $70,000–$80,000. The HR manager immediately offers you a salary of $75,000. You shake hands, accept the deal, and are pretty happy—only there's one big problem. The HR manager budgeted a range from $80,000 to $100,000 for the job. Because you named a number first, you ended up costing yourself potentially as much as $25,000 a year—whoops.

You might think this is an extreme example, but it isn't. You have no way of knowing what someone else is expecting to offer until they tell you. Revealing your number first puts you at a distinct disadvantage. You can't go up from the number you state, but you can certainly be talked down. When you name a number first, you have no upside, but a big downside potential.

Oh, but you're more clever than that, you say. I'll just name a really high number. This can blow up in your face as well. If you name too high of a number, you might not even get countered, or you may get countered very low in response. It's almost always to your advantage to have the employer name a number first.

The only exception to this is when an employer is purposely going to low-ball you. This situation is pretty rare, but if you have a good reason to suspect this will happen, you may want to name a number first to set an anchor point. Why? Because if you get a low-ball number, it may be difficult to get an employer to come up very far from that number. Of course, in that situation, you probably aren't going to have much success no matter what you do.

What about when you're asked to name a number first?

Don't do it. Just say "no."

Yes, I know this is tough advice to follow, but let me give you some specific situations and some ways to deal with them.

First, you may be asked about your salary requirements before an interview or as a field on a job application. If you have a field on a job application, leave it blank if possible or simply put "negotiable depending on overall compensation package." If you have to name a specific number, put $0 and then explain why later.

If you're asked directly in a prescreening interview about what salary you require or are expecting, try to answer the same thing. Say it depends on the overall compensation including benefits. You may get a response stating what the benefit would be or that they just need a general number. In this case, you should try, as tactfully as possible, to turn the question around and ask a series of questions like the following:

- "I'd rather learn more about your company and understand more about the job I'd be doing before naming an exact number or estimate, but it sounds like you're trying to figure out if we're in the right range so we don't both waste our time—is that correct?"

Most likely you'll get a yes. Then follow up with something like this:

- "You must have a range that you've budgeted for this particular position, right?"

Again, you should get a yes. If you're brave, just pause here and don't say anything else. You may then get them to answer with the range, but if you aren't brave or they aren't volunteering any information, you can follow up with this:

- "Well, if you tell me what the range is, even though I don't know enough to state exactly what my salary requirements are, I can tell you whether or not the range matches up to what I'm looking for."

Now, obviously, this isn't easy to do, but if an employer is going to ask you to name a number, there's no reason why they shouldn't expect to name one as well—or even first. Try as hard as you can to get them to name one first.

If they absolutely refuse, you still have some options. If you have to name a number, name a large range and make it conditional on the overall compensation package, but make sure the lower end of the range is slightly above the absolute lowest you're willing to go.

For example, you might say, "I can't really name an exact figure because it's completely dependent on what the overall compensation package is, but I'd generally be looking for something between $70,000 and $100,000—again, depending on the overall compensation package."

What if you're asked about your current salary?

This is a tough one; technically it's none of their business, but you can't exactly say that. Instead, what you want to do is to turn the question around. There are a variety of different ways to do this, but here's one suggestion:

- ⊙ "I'd prefer not to say what my current salary is because if it's higher than what you expect to pay for this job, I wouldn't want that to eliminate me from being considered for this job—because I might be willing to accept less for the right position—and, if it's lower than what this job would pay, I wouldn't want to sell myself short either— I'm sure you can understand."

This is a pretty honest answer, which will most likely avoid the question without causing offense. You can also state that you'd prefer not to answer that question or that you're under a confidential agreement with your employer to not talk about exact salary numbers.

If you absolutely have to name a number, try to make the number as variable as possible by talking about bonuses or benefits that affect the overall compensation, or state it as the overall compensation package is valued at x dollars and add up what any benefits you're getting are worth.

When you have an offer

If you can avoid the salary question, you'll eventually get an offer and it will have a number on it. You can't really get an offer without a number, because it wouldn't be an offer. But negotiations don't end when you get an offer, unless of course you named a number and they gave it to you — whoops. (By the way, if you're in this situation, don't try and pull any stunts. If they give you what you asked, you pretty much have to either take it or leave it. If you name a higher number than you first asked, not only will it be in bad taste, but you'll likely get the entire offer pulled.)

Once you have an offer in hand, you'll almost always want to counter. What you counter with is up to you, but I'd highly recommend countering as high as your stomach will allow. You might think that by coming closer to their number, you'll be more likely to get a favorable response, but in general that approach will backfire. Pick a high number and counter back.

You might be worried that doing this will cause you to lose the offer completely. As long as you do it in a tactful way, it's unlikely that the offer will be completely taken off of the table. Usually, the worst-case scenario is they stay firm on their offer and tell you that you'll have to take it or leave it. If the offer does get pulled, you can always respond by saying that you made a mistake and after weighing everything you realized that their original offer was more than fair. (Not fun, but if you really need the job, you can always go down that road.)

The fact of the matter is that once you're offered a job, you aren't likely to get that offer pulled. Remember, an employer that has invested that much time in interviewing you and making an offer isn't going to want to start over again, so you can afford to be a little brave.

In most cases, when you counter, you'll get back another response with a slightly higher offer. You can accept this offer, but in most cases, I'd recommend countering just one more time. Be careful here, because you can tick people off. But one tactful way to do it is to say something like this:

○ "I'd really like to work for your company. The job sounds great and I'm excited to work with your team, but I'm still a bit unsure on whether the numbers will work out. If you can do x dollars, I can be sure and commit to it today."

If you do this right and don't ask for something too much higher, you can usually get a yes. Most employers would rather pay you a little bit more rather than lose you. Worst case, usually, is that they will tell you they can't go any higher.

I don't recommend negotiating beyond this point. If you're really brave you can try, but past a second counteroffer, you risk losing goodwill and souring the deal. You want to appear shrewd, but not greedy. No one likes to feel like they got worked or taken advantage of.

Some final advice

Know your numbers well. Research as much as possible what the salary ranges are at the company you're applying for and what the salary ranges are for comparable positions. There are some sites online you can use to get salary ranges, although they aren't always reliable. The better the case you can make for what your salary should be, the easier your negotiations will be. You're in a much better position if you can name exact number ranges and statistics that show why the salary you're asking for is justified.

A reason for the salary you're requesting is never because you "need" that much money. No one cares what you need. Instead, talk about why you're worth a certain amount or what benefit you can bring to the table. Talk about what you've done for past employers and why investing in you at the salary you're requesting is a good investment.

Get as many offers as possible at any one time, but be careful about playing them against each other. You're at a distinct advantage in any negotiation if you can afford to walk away from the deal. To be in this position, you may need to get multiple offers lined up, so you may want to apply for several jobs at once. Just be careful in playing different offers against each other. You can do it in a tactful way by talking about how you have a couple of offers you're currently considering and want to make the best decision, but be careful not to sound arrogant. Confidence is good, arrogance is bad.

Taking action

- Practice negotiating as much as you can so that you can get over the fear of doing it. The next time you go to a store and buy something, try to negotiate. Even if you fail, you'll gain some valuable experience.
- Carefully research salaries so that you know what you're worth. Try to find out what companies in your area are paying their employees and how your current salary compares.
- Try to get a few interviews, even if you aren't looking for a new job. You might find it easier to negotiate when you have nothing to lose (because you aren't looking for a new job anyway). Who knows, perhaps you'll find a better job by trying to practice.

51

Options: Where all the fun is

For a long time I thought the stock market was all about buying shares of stocks. I didn't understand that most serious investors do more than just buy low and sell high. I've found that I wasn't alone. Most people I talk to have no idea what an option is and how this investment vehicle allows you to apply the power of leverage to greatly magnify your potential gains—or losses—in the market.

It turns out that most people who invest in the stock market don't bother to understand how options work because they either deem them too complicated or they think it will take too much time. While it's true that options aren't exactly the easiest things to understand, as a software developer, you'll probably find they're much easier to digest than you might have first guessed.

In this chapter, I'm going to take you through a lightning-fast tour of options. I'm not going to give you a strategy for investing with these investment vehicles, but I'm going to try to give you a solid understanding of how they work. If you've never learned about options, I think you'll find this chapter fascinating. There's a whole world of trading just under your nose that you may have never even known existed.

Option basics

An option is exactly what it sounds like: the choice to do something or not to do something. The basic idea behind an option is to allow someone to pay for the option of either buying or selling a stock by a later date in the future.

> ### Landmine: Why should you care about options?
>
> Well, for a few main reasons. First, as a software developer, you already likely have the aptitude to understand options better than most people. Options and option theory are based on mathematics, and the way you calculate and trade options is very algorithmic. But after talking with many software developers, I've found that most of them don't really understand options. So, the purpose of this chapter is to quickly get you up to speed and then you can decide if you want to further your education in this area.
>
> In addition, understanding how options work tends to stretch your mind financially. Even if you never trade stocks or option contracts, having a good understanding of how all this stuff works will help you to think more strategically about everyday financial decisions. You may find that this chapter triggers a switch in your mind that changes the way you start thinking about leverage and risk, which are two key, defining characteristics of options.
>
> Finally, options are a lot of fun when you understand them. As a software developer, I find studying options and how they work very interesting, and I strongly suspect you might as well. But if you don't, don't worry, this chapter is fairly short—plus, you can skip it if you want to.

Let's dive into this a little to understand exactly how this works. Suppose that you wanted to invest in Microsoft because you think that with a new operating system release in the next few months Microsoft stock might really take off. You'd like to buy up thousands of shares, but there are two problems. First, you don't have enough money to buy thousands of shares of Microsoft, and second, you think there's a good chance that Microsoft stock might actually go down quite a bit if the new release is no good.

If you had to just buy the stock, you'd have to come up with quite a bit of money, and if you're wrong, it could be costly. But what if you could get someone who has Microsoft stock to agree to sell it to you a few months in the future—just after the new operating system release comes out—for just a little bit more than the current price of the stock? That's exactly what an option can do.

Sounds a little too good to be true? Well, it is. To get this option, you have to pay for it. You can purchase the right to buy Microsoft stock in the future, but to purchase that right, you'll have to pay a certain amount called a premium. If you do go ahead with the transaction and buy the right to purchase, say, 300 shares of Microsoft anytime within the next three months, you'll be able to purchase the stock and make a hefty profit if Microsoft stock happens to go above the price you were guaranteed to be able to buy the stock at (also called the strike price).

If it turns out that Microsoft doesn't spike up beyond your strike price or it even drops down in price, you simply choose to not exercise the option, meaning you don't buy the stock. In that case, you're only out the price of the option you bought.

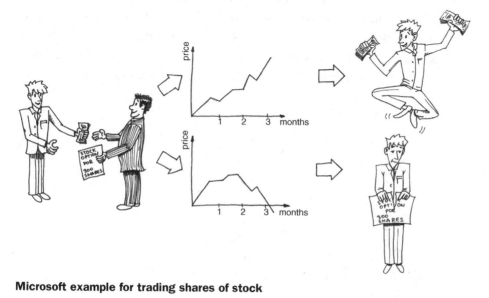

Microsoft example for trading shares of stock

Digging a little deeper

Options basically give you the option to buy a certain number of shares of a stock by some date in the future for a fixed price. But you can also buy an option that lets you sell a certain number of shares of a stock by some day in the future for a fixed price as well. This kind of option would allow you to make money if a stock dropped in value, just like shorting a stock does, which is discussed in appendix B.

An option that lets you buy a stock at a certain price within a period of time is called a call option. An option that lets you sell a stock at a certain price within a period of time is called a put option.

Not only does an option allow you to speculate on the movement of a stock, but it also gives you leverage. Imagine that stock in your favorite company, T-Mart, was trading at $100 a share. If you had $1,000 to invest, you could buy 10 shares of T-Mart. If T-Mart went up to $200, you'd be pretty happy, because you'd double your investment and now have $2,000.

But now imagine that you decided to take that same $1,000 and invest it in T-Mart, but through the use of a call option. Options are sold in contracts that have a size of 100. So for each option you buy, you're given the option to buy 100 shares of T-Mart. Let's imagine that the T-Mart option you want to buy is to be able to buy shares of T-Mart at $110 a share within three months. The price on that particular option contract might be $10 per share of the stock. It would cost you $10 ∗ 100,

The process of trading shares

or $1,000, to have an option to buy 100 shares of T-Mart stock at $110 within the next three months.

That same $1,000 that was originally buying you just 10 shares of T-Mart stock is giving you the ability to potentially buy 100 shares of T-Mart at $10 higher than the $100 it's trading at right now. If that T-Mart stock rises to $200 within the next three months, instead of making $1,000, you'll make quite a bit more. Let's calculate exactly how much.

If you were able to execute the option and buy the 100 shares of T-Mart at $110 a share, it would end up costing you $110 * 100 = $11,000. You're able to sell those shares at $200 each, so you'd get $200 * 100 = $20,000 for your shares. If you subtract out the cost of buying the shares ($11,000) and subtract out the cost of the option ($1,000) you're left with $20,000 – $11,000 – $1,000 = $8,000 profit.

The process of buying options

This example is a bit contrived. Things do have to work out in your favor, and if the stock price didn't rise above $110 within that three-month time period, you'd end up losing the entire $1,000 you paid for the option, but that's the power of leverage. Options give you the leverage to either make or lose more money much more quickly.

Selling options

You probably can already figure out that buying options can be a very speculative and risky move. If things don't go how you planned, you can end up losing a lot of money—quickly. But there's another side to options that allows you to make money in a wider variety of situations—just not as much.

Besides buying options, you can also sell options. Technically this is called writing an option, because you're creating an option contract that someone else can buy. When you write an option, you're taking the other side of the bet. Instead of betting that a stock will move in one direction, you're betting that it will either stay where it is now or move in the opposite direction of the option.

The tables are turned, though, when you're writing an option. When you write an option, you're the obligated party who must buy or sell a stock at a certain price. The good news is that you can charge a premium for that obligation.

Of course, writing options has its risks as well. In fact, writing options can carry much greater risks than buying options because your costs might not be known from the start. When you buy an option, you're paying a fixed price and you risk losing that entire amount. When you write an option, if the market moves against you strongly, your losses could be extremely high.

Fortunately, most options that are written are what are called covered options. This means that the option contract is backed by some actual stock or even another option that limits the potential loss for the option writer.

In a realistic situation, you might write an option on some stock you're already holding. Let's imagine that you already have 100 shares of

T-Mart and you decide that you don't think T-Mart is very likely to go up or down, but you'd like to make a little money while you're holding onto the stock. You decide to write an option to sell your shares of T-Mart at $110 within three months in the future. Right now the stock is worth $100 a share, so as long as T-Mart doesn't go above $110, this would be a good deal for you and whoever bought your option would end up having it expire worthless.

You can charge a premium for your option. Perhaps you could get $10 per share for selling your option. You write a single contract that controls 100 shares of T-Mart. When you sell that option contract, you immediately get $10 * 100 = $1,000 for it. No matter what happens, you'll get to keep that $1,000, but if the stock price goes above $110 (the only likely case in which someone buying the option would choose to exercise it), you'll have to sell them your stock at that price.

More complex options

Options can get much more complicated than just buying and selling them and writing them. Options can be combined together and combined with stock purchases to form all kinds of complex trading positions.

We won't be able to go into all the details of the complex kinds of options strategies in this short chapter, but I want to give you a basic idea of some of the possibilities, because it's fascinating how these tools can be combined together to create almost any trading position you'd like.

First, let's consider a simple use of options called a covered call. A covered call is when you buy some stock, but at the same time you sell a call option against that stock. Why would you want to do this? Well, if you're buying a stock that you know you're going to hold for a long time period—perhaps you want to collect a dividend from it—you might as well sell an option against that stock and make some money from holding it.

You might use this strategy if you didn't expect the stock you bought to go up in value quickly and you were willing to risk missing out on a large rise in value for some guaranteed income on the stock. You're basically trading some of your upside potential for less risk.

Another strategy is what's called a married put. This occurs when you buy a stock, but at the same time buy a put option on that stock that allows you to sell that stock. This strategy would allow you to get all the upside from a stock if it rises, but would mitigate some of the potential losses if the stock dropped, because you'd have the option to sell the stock for a certain guaranteed price. You might use this strategy if you bought a stock you were unsure of and thought it might either go up high or drop low.

Options can also be combined with different option spreads, as they're called. You can combine options of different kinds with different expiration dates to create many different kinds of trading positions that have various degrees of risk and potential gains for many different scenarios.

One of my favorite spreads is called the iron condor. In that spread, you sell options on both sides of a stock or exchange-traded fund (ETF) and you buy options a bit further out in price. You make some money off of selling the options and you spend some of that money to buy some protection for yourself by buying options that will limit your losses if the stock goes too high or too low. If the stock or ETF stays within a certain range of values, you get to collect the full premium. If you create a good iron condor, you have a very high chance of making money. Of course, if you're wrong, it can be very costly. (If you're interested more in iron condors, a good book I recommend is *Profiting with Iron Condor Options: Strategies from the Frontline for Trading in Up or Down Markets* by Michael Benklifa [FT Press, 2011].)

Taking action

- Look up a stock you're familiar with and see if you can find what is called an option chain for it. Most stock quoting sites have option chains that you can find.
- Take a look at the option chain and calculate how much it costs to buy an option on that stock that's one month in the future. Notice how the price of the option changes based on the different strike prices.

52

Bits and bytes of real estate investing

Of all the possible investments a person can make, I think real estate investment is by far the best. No other investment offers such a long-term guarantee of profit and allows so much leverage. But that doesn't mean real estate investing is easy. Real estate investment isn't something you can do with the simple push of a button, like you might do to trade a stock. Real estate investment also requires significant capital—which is one of the reasons I think it's so well suited to software developers who often are able to command higher wages than many other professions.

I'll admit, I'm a bit biased, because real estate investment is my primary investment choice, and the one that has made me the most money over the years. But whether you do decide to invest in real estate or not, you should know enough about it to understand how it works and what kind of opportunities it provides you.

Unfortunately, if you look up "how to invest in real estate" or some other similar query online, you'll most likely be bombarded with less-than-credible information promising you some kind of get-rich-quick scheme. The goal of this chapter is to cut through all of that unreliable and untrustworthy information and give you some real, practical advice on how real estate investing works and how you might get started.

Again, you might be asking yourself why I'm including a chapter on real estate investment in this book. Well, over the course of my career, I've gotten a lot of questions from fellow software developers about how to get started in real estate investment. Software developers tend to make fairly high salaries compared to many other professions, so they can often benefit from learning how to invest in real estate. I feel like I'd do you a real disservice if I didn't at least address the topic of real estate investment in this book and give you the basics you need to know to get started.

Obviously, in a short chapter on the topic I can't delve in as deeply as I'd like, but I can give you the ins and outs of what you need to know to explore the topic further on your own—should you choose to invest.

Why real estate investment?

Before we dive into how to invest in real estate, let's address the most important question: why. Why is real estate such a good investment, especially when it's a more difficult investment to get started in and requires much more upkeep than holding a stock?

It might sound foolhardy, but the biggest reason I'm going to suggest is stability. You've no doubt seen real estate prices greatly fluctuate, so you might be a bit incredulous about this idea, but let me try to explain it.

While real estate prices may fluctuate greatly, the kind of real estate I recommend investing in is rental properties, and the kind of income that's stable about those kinds of properties is...rent.

A good real estate deal stays a good real estate deal, because rental prices don't tend to fluctuate much. As long as you're able to secure a fixed–interest rate loan on a property, that property is very stable in terms of the income it can produce. If rents do change, they usually go up, not down.

So even though the overall price of a property itself may swing wildly, if you're willing to ride it out and hang on for the long term, counting on rental income instead of price appreciation, your investment is very solid and stable. I, myself, have ridden out some of the roughest patches in real estate history without so much as a scratch.

Real estate investment is also one of the only types of investments that allow a great degree of leverage with little risk. You can't find a bank that will give you a long-term loan on buying a bunch of stock where you'll only put down 10% and the bank will supply 90%, but it happens every day in real estate. You can even secure loans with no money down—but that's usually not a good idea.

This kind of leverage is extremely powerful. It can be dangerous as well, but the bank bears more of the danger than you do when the property is the collateral for the loan. Let's look at an example of how powerful this leverage is.

Suppose you buy a rental property for $100,000. You get a bank loan for 90% of the property cost and you put down a down payment of 10%. The property you've selected is what we call "floating," meaning the costs, including the mortgage, tax, and insurance, are covered by the rental income it produces. In this instance, we'll assume all that happens is that the costs are covered and there's no additional cash flow, or very little.

Just being in this situation is great. If you get a 30-year loan on the property, in 30 years, your $10,000 investment will be worth a minimum of $100,000 and probably a great deal more due to price appreciation. The tenants in your rental unit will essentially be paying your mortgage and you'll be getting a house for free—a good deal in my book.

But it gets better than that. The leveraged power of your investment allows you to benefit greatly from any price appreciation. It's not unrealistic for property prices to appreciate by 10% in two years' time. Suppose that your property increases in value after two years to $110,000—a 10% increase. Now, what do you suppose the return on your investment will be at this point?

Many people I talk to guess that the return would be 10%, but that's not quite correct. If you were to sell the property at this point, you'd get $110,000. Subtract from that the balance of the loan—we'll assume it didn't go down by much and say it's $90,000—and you get $20,000 left over. Your initial investment of $10,000 became $20,000. That's a 100% return on your investment, or 50% per year. Have you ever heard of anyone getting that kind of return in the stock market?

The power of leverage allows you to make high returns off of small price appreciations, with little risk. And because the collateral for the loan is the property, technically the most you can lose is your initial investment. (Although there is such a thing as deficiency judgments, but you can ignore that if you're willing to hold on to the property.)

Finally, let's talk about inflation again. Remember when we said that if inflation hit, the value of your debts would be reduced and the value of your cash in the bank would also be reduced? Real estate investment is one of the best hedges against inflation.

If you experience a high period of inflation, but you're holding a real estate loan, although your cash in the bank is diminished in value, your real estate loan is also reduced at the same time as its price is technically increased, along with the rents. What does this all mean?

Well, let's take the example of that $100,000 house you might have bought. In that case, let's suppose the rent is $1,000 a month and your mortgage and all other costs including taxes and insurance come to $1,000 a month. You're at a wash, or as we said before, your property floats. But if inflation rears its head, eating up your bank account, reducing your salary, it also raises...rent. You might be able to get $1,200 for your rental property while your mortgage and other fixed costs will stay at $1,000 a month. Now you're cash-flow positive $200, which is making up for some of the negative effects of inflation.

The property value also tends to rise with inflation. This isn't a real appreciation, because it's the devaluing of the dollar, but it acts as a hedge. The weaker the dollar gets, the higher the value of the property gets, because it's priced in terms of dollars.

To summarize, why is real estate a good investment? Because if you buy rental properties and rent them out with fixed loans, the income from them is very stable, you can use the bank's money to finance most of your property, thus giving you extreme amounts of upside through leverage, and when everything else is being hurt by inflation, your real estate investments are benefiting from it—acting as a hedge.

Okay, so how do I do it?

At this point, hopefully you're excited about the prospect of real estate investing—although you may still be a bit skeptical because I've promised such great things but haven't told you how to do them. I can't give you a step-by-step guide in this short chapter, but I can give you enough information to see how the process works and learn how to get started.

Smart real estate investment—not speculation—starts with an understanding that real estate investment is a long-term investment. If you believe you'll get rich quickly by flipping properties and buying foreclosed properties for pennies on the dollar, you'll get exactly the results you deserve.

Nothing in this world is free. To achieve the great returns possible through real estate investment, you need patience, diligence, and a whole lot of time. When I buy investment properties, I'm planning for the profits I will make 20–30 years out. I know that buying a rental property that's cash-flow positive or floating with a fixed loan will, at the very least, result in a fully paid-off property in 30 years. That's what I bank on and hope for, and everything else is a bonus.

The general strategy—or at least the one I recommend—is to buy rental properties that are either cash-flow positive or floating and to finance them using 30-year-fixed loans. This strategy carries very little risk and still has an enormous upside, if you happen to hit a real estate boon and prices rocket upwards, but it also virtually guarantees you paid-off properties in 30 years' time.

First step: Education

The first step in executing this strategy is market education. You make the most money in real estate investment when you buy—not when you sell. The better deal you can find, the better position you can begin with. Remember how we said that the stock market was very liquid? The real estate market is not. A very liquid market is usually efficient. This means that there aren't many situations where there's a disparity in pricing.

Because real estate isn't very liquid there's often a high disparity in pricing. What's the value of a stock at any given time? Everyone knows within seconds. It isn't debatable. Sure, you could say that a stock is undervalued or overvalued, but the quoted price ultimately reflects its real value at any given time.

Not true with real estate. What's the price of a house? Who knows? Ten appraisers can make an appraisal of the same property and each come up with different answers. Sometimes, if there's little good market data and comparable sales, those differences in price opinions could be huge.

What does this mean for you? It means that if you're smart and diligent, you can buy real estate for a heavily discounted price. You just need to be able to recognize a deal and learn how to make a good one.

To learn how to recognize a good deal, you need two things: practice and market education. The first thing you should do if you want to invest in real estate is to study the market. Get an idea of what prices properties are selling at. Look at how many square feet those properties have, how much they're renting for, the area they're located in, and any other factors that you can, until you get a feel for what's a good price on any piece of property.

At the same time as you're doing this, you should also be running mock scenarios of what would happen if you were to buy a property at a given price and thinking about what kind of offer you'd need to make to buy a property at a price that would be a good deal.

To do this you need to run all the numbers associated with a property. You need to estimate, based on the price, the cost of a mortgage loan on the property, along with any other expenses such as taxes, insurance, homeowner's association fees, utility bills, and any estimated maintenance on the property.

This exercise is somewhat tedious, but it's the best way to get a feel for what is a good deal and how that deal will work. You need to have confidence in what you're doing before you sit down and write that big check. My strategy for real estate investment is based on acting quickly.

Taking action

Once you have a decent feel for the market, it's time to act. When I'm ready to buy a property, I'll sign up to receive alerts from real estate agents on any new properties that meet my criteria. If I see a property that's a good deal, or one that I think I can make a low enough offer on to make it a good deal, I'll act immediately.

I'll often send an offer on a property, sight-unseen, to put the seller to an immediate test and make sure to grab a good deal before someone else does. I almost always make a low-ball offer—one that my real estate agent is embarrassed to present—because sometimes those offers get accepted as is or they get countered with offers that are only slightly higher than what I had offered.

That's not to say that most of my offers don't get rejected—they do. But it's a numbers game. Make 50 low-ball offers on properties and all you need is one seller to accept. You may be able to pick up a property for as much as a 50% discount on the real market value of it, because the seller is looking to get rid of the property or just doesn't care. You wouldn't believe how many sellers just don't care for whatever reason.

When I make a sight-unseen offer, I put in a contingency in the offer that says the offer is contingent upon my physical inspection of the property. This allows me to go back and do my due diligence on the property to verify the facts in the listing and make sure there wasn't anything major that wasn't disclosed. If the property isn't to my liking, I can back out of the deal at that point without any repercussions.

Assuming the property looks good and you've it tied up in a real estate contract, the next step is to get a home inspection done on the property. I always get a home inspection by the best and most detailed home inspector I can find. If there's a problem with the property, I want to know about it before I invest more money into it.

Assuming the home inspection clears, the next step is to obtain financing. You can also do this step before you actually even look for a property—this is called prequalification. Just like you want to find the best deal on a piece of real estate, you also should seek to find the best financing deal you can. I'm not going to go into the details of obtaining financing in this chapter, but make sure you shop around and compare rates and costs from various lenders.

Use property management

Finally, after you buy the property, my recommendation is to put property management in place. I highly recommend against managing a rental property yourself. In my opinion, it's not worth the effort or the headache. The best money I spend each month is to pay my property management company to manage my rental properties.

A good property management company will take care of almost everything concerning your rental property, including finding renters, executing a lease, screening tenants, taking care of maintenance issues, and collecting rents. But finding a good property management company can be difficult. Be sure you shop around and find the most honest property management company you can. I've fired at least three property management companies because of issues like incompetence, false repair costs, and plain negligence.

Expect to pay about 10% of the rental income to property management and make sure you factor that number into your rental calculations when figuring out your deals. A good property management company can make your real estate investments hands-off. This is necessary if you want to own many properties over time and still handle your full-time job.

Taking action

- Today, go out and buy a rental property. Good luck!
- Just kidding! Instead, look for a rental property listing in your area and practice running through all the numbers. Try different scenarios of various down payment amounts to figure out if it would be possible to buy that property and for it to be cash-flow positive or at least break even.

53

Do you really understand your retirement plan?

Sipping piña coladas on a beach with the waves crashing against your feet while you relax and read a book. That's how many of us envision retirement, but I'm surprised how many people take it for granted and assume it has to happen after the age of 60.

The truth is that a tropical beach retirement isn't guaranteed, nor is it only for those over the age of 60. (In fact, in chapter 55, I'll tell you exactly how I was able to reach a virtual retirement at the age of 33.) The reality of the situation is that if you want to have a successful retirement, you have to start planning for it and you have to start planning now.

Unfortunately, though, most of the advice I read on retirement is just plain wrong. I constantly hear advisors telling people to put their money in a retirement account and forget about it. While it's true this advice might serve a good majority of people, I'm guessing that you, as a software developer—and more importantly as someone who picked up this book—can do much better.

In this chapter, I'm going to attempt to change the way you think about retirement. A good portion of my advice will be U.S.-centric, because the United States has flexible retirement accounts like 401(k)s and IRAs, but the same kind of thinking and strategy I'll give you for dealing with those kinds of accounts should apply to planning any kind of retirement, even if you're relying on a company-provided pension, as people do in many other parts of the world.

Retirement is all about working backwards

The key to planning your retirement is being able to work backwards by calculating exactly the amount of money you need to live on each month and figuring out how you can guarantee that kind of passive income with at least a little buffer for some breathing room.

Many articles and books I've read on retirement make a big mistake in assuming that a retired person has the same financial requirements as a working person. I don't blame those financial advisors for making these kinds of assumptions, although I'd strongly caution against taking any advice from someone who has a job telling other people how to increase their wealth, but isn't wealthy themselves.

The truth is that there are certain expenses that are greatly reduced when you have an abundance of free time and you no longer have the requirement of saving money or commuting. Not only that, but most of us live lifestyles that are much more extravagant than what would generally make us happy.

It's easy to fall into the trap of thinking that you wouldn't want to decrease your lifestyle once you're retired, because you don't want to have to make a sacrifice after working so many years. You don't want to end up having to barely scape by in your later years. But the biggest factor that will determine how much money you need to retire is what your monthly expenses are. If you can reduce those monthly expenses now, not only will you not have to live at a reduced style of living later in life, but you'll also get there much quicker.

Think about it this way. If you "need" $8,000 a month to live, and so you think you need that much retirement income, you'll need to make above $8,000 a month to save anything for retirement, and you'll be burning through those savings at an $8,000 a month rate when retired.

But imagine if you could cut those costs. Imagine if you could find a way to live off of $4,000 a month instead. In that case, you'd be able to not only save money for retirement much faster, but when you got there, the money would last you twice as long, so technically, you could retire much, much earlier. The savings benefits you at both ends—it accelerates how fast you can save money and makes that saved money stretch further.

All of this is to say that the most effective thing you can do to save for retirement is to figure how to reduce your monthly expenses. No investment, no job, no raise, nothing else is likely to benefit you more than figuring out how to live on less. Frugality wins the day.

Calculating your retirement goal

Once you've come up with the monthly figure you need to live on to retire, you can officially "retire" when you reach that monthly income through passive income—that is, income you don't have to work for. You do need to make sure the passive income source will increase with inflation—one of the main reasons why real estate is such a good investment choice.

I don't like the idea of drawing down from savings. There's no reason why a person should have to draw down and diminish their savings in order to retire—not when there are so many ways to turn savings into passive income. At the very least, you could buy bonds that would yield a few percentage interest and have almost no risk at all.

How much money do you need to retire? It depends on your expenses, what vehicle you use for passive income, and what investment opportunities are available, but I'll give you a practical example that applies to the time of writing this book.

Suppose you had 1 million dollars right now. If you wanted to invest that money into real estate, I happen to know that you could buy approximately three four-unit rental buildings (that's fourplexes) that would bring in rents of about $2,400 a month each (based on a pretty conservative estimate). Now, you still have to pay taxes, insurance, property management fees, and other expenses on those properties, so assume that each property actually brings in $1,800 a month (again, a pretty conservative estimate). That means that 1 million dollars today could earn you $5,400 a month or $64,800 a year.

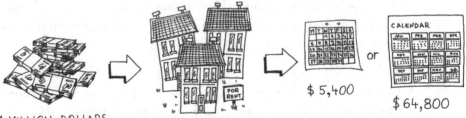

1 MILLION DOLLARS

$ 5,400

$ 64,800

Example of how 1 million dollars could work for you in real estate investing

The question then becomes, can you live off of $5,400 a month? If you can, you can call yourself retired, and the best part is that a real estate investment will keep up with inflation. Now, this could all change in time. Prices of real estate could go up, inflation could make 1 million dollars have much less purchasing power, and other unforeseen circumstances could happen, but in general, there will always be some kind of investment with a similar expected return.

To live off of passive income that's generated from some amount of capital, you first have to generate that capital. You can't live off of 1 million dollars if you don't have 1 million dollars. That's the tricky part. And here's where two paths can diverge—especially if you live in the United States.

Path 1: 401(k), IRAs, or other retirement accounts

The first and most obvious path to accumulate wealth over the long term is to contribute to a retirement account or some kind of pension plan. In the United States most employers offer a well-known retirement plan called a 401(k) that allows you to contribute pretax dollars from your paycheck to this investment account. Sometimes employers even offer to match a certain amount of your contributions.

For a majority of people given this option, it's the right one to take. Maxing out your 401(k) contributions will ensure that you're at least shielding a significant portion of your income from taxes, and the gains you make in the 401(k) account aren't taxed either.

I'm not going to go over the exact numbers, because I don't want to get too specific here. But if you're given the ability to save pretax dollars and not get taxes on gains you make, you'll be able to achieve a much higher return than you would otherwise.

The only downside to this path is that it's fully dependent on you deciding to wait to retire until you have reached the age of about 60. The strategy here is to save as much money in retirement accounts as possible and to have that money continue to grow and compound until you reach your retirement age when you can access the money without paying extra fees.

For retirement accounts, like 401(k)s, you have to pay a 10% penalty if you withdraw the funds early. That's why I say there are basically two paths to retirement you can take. If you go down the road of using a tax-deferred retirement account like a 401(k), you're in it for the long haul. You can't really change your mind; otherwise you'll pay a pretty big penalty for doing so. And because you'll be contributing to a significant amount of your income to your retirement account, you won't have much room do other kinds of investing.

But, again, I can't stress enough how advantageous any kind of tax-deferred retirement account is—especially if you have some kind of employer match—if you're planning on retiring at the age of 60 or above. If you're making a decent wage and you're making the maximum contributions, then as long as you start early enough, you're going to be in pretty good shape when you choose to retire. If you aren't interested in path two, which I'll explain next, you should definitely be maxing out your retirement accounts.

Landmine: What if you work for yourself?

If you work for yourself, you might not have access to a 401(k) or employer-provided pension plan, but in the United States, at least, you can still set up a tax-deferred retirement account. We aren't going to cover these kinds of retirement accounts in this book, because I don't want to sidetrack too far, but looking up information on IRAs and Roth IRAs is a good place to start.

Path 2: Setting up an early retirement or aiming to get rich

While I understand that most people are perfectly content to retire at the age of 60, I was never interested in waiting that long. I've always wanted to retire earlier in life, even if it meant more hard work earlier on and some significant risk. That's exactly what path two is.

Before we get into the details of path two, let's talk about why the two paths are pretty much mutually exclusive. The biggest reason is that retirement accounts can't really be touched until you reach a traditional retirement age. That means that if you plan to retire at, say, age 40, contributing to a retirement plan that's stashing away money you can't touch until you're 60 isn't going to do you much good at all.

You'll basically be diverting funds away from the investments that you could be making in order to retire earlier. Sure, it's possible to contribute to a retirement account for when you reach age 60 and to take some money and do something else like invest in real estate, but if you try to go down both roads, you'll probably be doing both strategies in a suboptimal way.

If you want to retire early, or you want to try to really strike it rich, you probably shouldn't be contributing to a retirement account. I know that advice sounds a bit crazy, but that's why I warned you. And that's why I say most people should just max out their retirement accounts — it's the safest way to go. But if you're like me and would rather shoot for the more aggressive and riskier goal of retiring young, read on.

To retire early, you need to figure out a way to build up a passive income stream that exceeds your monthly expenses and you need to be able to guard that income stream against inflation. You can't just put 1 million dollars into a U.S. treasury bill that yields about 2% and think that you'll be good. You might be able to make $20,000 per year with little or no risk, but inflation will eventually erode your initial capital and your profit.

If we go back to our example of taking a million dollars and investing it in rental properties that bring in about $5,400 a month, you can see that kind of investment would work much better, because you'd be protected against inflation and you'd get a much higher return on your investment.

The only problem is that it isn't exactly easy to earn a million dollars to invest in real estate, and investing in real estate isn't a hands-off proposition. You can get to the point where the investment is basically passive income, but it takes some time, work, and learning to get there.

But real estate isn't the only way to generate passive income that would fulfill your retirement requirements. You could utilize high-dividend-yielding stocks that would hopefully go up in value to combat inflation. You could create or buy intellectual property that you get royalties off of. This could be patents, music, books, or even something like a movie script. You could buy or start your own business and eventually hand the management of it over to someone else while you pull in the remaining profits.

As you can imagine, all of these kinds of passive income–generation vehicles carry with them huge risks, so you should definitely try to set up multiple streams of passive income. Even just acquiring one of these kinds of streams of passive income can be difficult, so, like I said, only choose this path if you're ready to do the hard work required to be successful.

Now, what about acquiring that million dollars—or more? You can't exactly invest without having the money, and if you're forgoing a traditional retirement account, you aren't going to have the tax advantages or time that would make it much easier to accumulate a large amount of capital.

This is where things get tricky. You have to be able to make small investments that pay off, and work your way up to larger and larger ones over time. You don't just start out by buying three fourplexes for 1 million dollars. Instead, you start off by saving up perhaps $10,000 to make a 10% down payment on a $100,000 property. Then you do it again, and again. Eventually, you might trade one or two of those properties up for something bigger.

You have to gradually work your way up, always with the goal of increasing your passive income. The more money you're able to generate from assets that you hold, the more progress you'll be able to make in buying more income-generating assets. What you're after is the snow-ball effect that occurs over time as you keep building up more assets that generate income that gives you more income to buy more assets.

There are three main ways to accelerate this process. First, and we already talked about this one, reduce your expenses. Buy the smallest house or rent the smallest apartment you can. If you can live with your parents for free, by all means do it. Get a used car, or figure out how to live without one. Cut your cable, don't eat out, and get used furniture; don't just be frugal — be cheap! The lower your living expenses are, the more money you'll have left over each month to invest. (I told you this wouldn't be easy.)

Next, make as much money as you can. Move to a big city like San Francisco or New York where the salaries are much higher if you can. If you're smart, you can find a way to live cheaply in an expensive city, which allows you to pocket the salary difference that's mostly due to the cost of living increase of housing. If you can start a side business, or do some freelancing, do it. The more money you generate, the more you can invest.

Finally, make the most profitable investments you can. Again, this one may seem obvious, but the more careful you are to make investments that will give you higher yields, the faster you'll be able to multiply your money. This will require careful research, learning to negotiate and to spot good deals.

Like I said, this isn't an easy route to go. Most people don't have the stomach for it, and I don't blame them. On my quest to early retirement, I slept on mattresses on the floor, worked 70-hour weeks, and lived in much smaller places than I could afford — and even then there was no guarantee of success.

What if I am stuck in the middle or close to retirement?

Not everyone is just out of college and able to clearly choose one path or the other. Perhaps you've already been investing in your retirement account for a long time, but now you're considering trying to get on the path to retiring early. Or perhaps you can't just get up and move to San Francisco to get a higher salary—you have a spouse and kids.

Don't worry, you can still set up a successful retirement, you'll just have to modify my advice to fit what's possible for you. I wanted to give you the extremes of each path so you could clearly see the difference, because you're better off going hard in one direction or the other so that you waste as little effort as possible.

And even though it isn't optimal, you can also walk the middle between the two paths. If you already are invested in your retirement plan and you want to keep doing it, you may still be able to generate enough income after maxing out your retirement account contributions to invest in real estate or some other income-generating asset.

Taking action

- Calculate your current monthly expenses. Figure out how much you could reduce those expenses by if you were willing to make some big sacrifices.
- Now calculate how much money you'd need to generate each month to retire off of your reduced expenses—make sure you leave a little buffer room.
- Figure out how much money you'd need to have at various rates of return, like 2%, 5%, and 10%, to have enough monthly income to retire.

54

The danger of debt: SSDs are expensive

Of all the financial mistakes you can make, the biggest one is to go into debt. Unfortunately, it seems that we're trained to accept debt as normal and often don't see how bad and destructive it can be to our lives.

One of the biggest struggles you may face in your career as a software developer—at least financially—is dealing with success. The more money you make, the better off you are, right? No, not always. In fact, I've found that many really financially successful people—especially software developers—end up going deeply into debt, because the more money they make, the more money they end up spending.

The only way you can really become financially successful is to make money off of your money. You have to be able to get your money working for you if you ever want to achieve financial freedom. If interest gives us freedom, it only follows to say that debt compels us to bondage.

In this chapter, I'm going to discuss just how destructive debt can be and point out some of the most common follies regarding it. We'll also discuss how not all debt is bad and how to tell the difference between good and bad debt.

Why debt is generally bad

We've already talked about this a little bit, but in general debt is bad, because it's the exact opposite of what is good—gaining interest on your money. When you're in debt, you're usually paying interest on your money. That means someone else is likely becoming rich at your expense.

It's almost impossible to be investing your money and making money off of those investments while you're in debt—unless, of course, that debt is actually being used to get a higher return than the interest you're paying on it, but we'll talk about that later.

When you're in debt, you end up paying more for a product or service than it would otherwise cost. This penalty compounds over time—especially if you pay less toward the debt than the interest that's being accrued. The longer you carry a debt, the more impactful that debt is on your bottom line. To see why, let's take a look at a simple example.

Suppose you buy a car for $30,000 and you take out a loan with a 5% interest rate to do it. Now, suppose that you pay off that car in six years. Over that six-year period, you'll pay $4,786.65 in interest in addition to the $30,000 your originally borrowed. That car will actually end up costing you $34,786.65.

But in actuality it will cost you even more than that. The $4,786.65 you paid in interest could have been actually making you money. You could have been getting interest on that money instead of paying it.

It's a bit difficult to calculate the exact amount, but the interest you could have made on that $4,786.65 over six years, if you put that interest payment each month into an investment that yielded 5% over that time period, would be around $2,000. So, in reality, that debt may have cost you close to $7,000.

Now, this might not seem like a huge amount of money, but all of this adds up over time. Especially if you have many different forms of debt that accumulate exponentially, so the interest rates you're paying are higher.

The more debt you have, the heavier a burden it is on you and the more it holds you back from ever becoming financially independent. When you have debt, you can't save money, and if you can't save money, you can't invest, either.

What's your current debt level? Add up all your debt and determine what your overall interest rate is and how much you're paying in interest each year to maintain your debt.

Some common debt follies

Okay, so maybe you're in debt. It happens. I was in debt once—I'm actually in debt right now—I owe about a million dollars in mortgages, but we'll get to that in just a bit. If you're in debt, though, you need to learn how to handle that debt properly so you can get it reduced as soon as possible.

The biggest folly I see concerning debt is saving money while holding debt, especially credit card debt. To me this makes no sense at all. I often hear the justification of needing an emergency fund or saving for the future, but there's almost no way to logically justify this behavior.

I've known people who had thousands of dollars of credit card debt, yet they had savings accounts with several thousand dollars in them as well. Don't be embarrassed if that situation describes you, but you need to do something about it right away. Let me explain why.

The problem is that, in most cases, the interest you're paying on the debt you have is costing you more than the interest you're making by having money in the bank—especially if that debt is credit card debt. Suppose you have $10,000 of credit card debt that you're paying a 15% interest rate on. That means you're paying $1,500 per year just in interest on that debt. Unless your bank is paying you more than a 15% interest rate on your money, you're much better off taking that money and using it to pay your debt.

Now, you might think this is pretty obvious advice, but I know that many people have car loans with moderate to high interest rates and choose to save money in the bank at the same time. Unless the interest rate you're getting on your car is close to 0%, this makes absolutely no sense. It's just a little more difficult to realize this, because car loans usually have lower interest rates than credit cards.

It may even make sense to pay off your mortgage on your house before putting money into savings. You'll have to run the exact numbers, and the situation is slightly different because once you've put money into a mortgage, you generally can't take it back out and you have to wait until it's entirely paid off before you actually feel the benefits of reducing the loan. But from a purely by-the-numbers view of the situation, if you can't get a return on an investment of your money greater than your mortgage interest rate, it makes more sense to pay the money toward your mortgage.

To illustrate the point: suppose you had a mortgage with a 7% interest rate. That means that you're paying 7% interest on the balance of your loan, every single year. Any money you pay toward the principal on your mortgage each year basically gives you a guaranteed return of 7%. (The numbers change a little bit based on the tax advantages you might get from deducting your mortgage interest, but if you're putting your money in a savings account, you're almost always better off putting it toward paying your mortgage.)

Perhaps the next biggest debt mistake I often see is paying off debt in the wrong order. The order in which you pay off your debt can make a huge difference in how long it takes to pay that debt down. Always prioritize your debt payments based on the interest rate. Make sure to pay off the most expensive debts first.

Again, this seems obvious, but I see many people making minimum payments on all their credit cards and other forms of debt. Don't do that. Instead, pour as much money as you can each month into your highest-interest debt and keep doing that until all of your debt is paid off.

Of all the debt mistakes, though, the biggest one by far is unnecessary debt—that is, taking on debt when debt doesn't need to be taken on. I'll pick on car loans again here, because one of the biggest mistakes people make is financing vehicles. It's so easy to go into a car dealership and buy a new car, saddling yourself with unnecessary debt.

The problem is having the order of things backwards. Typically, we do things in reverse order. Think about it this way. When you buy a car on financing you're essentially buying a car and then saving up for it. When you do things this way, it's like paying more for everything you buy.

Reverse the problem by saving and then buying things with cash. Yes, breaking the cycle the first time will be difficult, but once you break the cycle, you end up paying less for everything you buy. If you have a car that you've bought on credit, pay that car off. But when you do, don't buy a new car on credit; instead, break the cycle by keeping your old car and making payments into a "new car fund" account. Once you have enough money in that new car fund account (somewhere between four to six years) you can buy a new car with cash and immediately start making payments into your "new car fund" account again.

By doing things this way, you'll actually get a discount on your car instead of paying more for it, because the money you save for your new car can be accumulating interest over time for you, instead of for someone else.

Not all debt is bad

Even though I've painted a pretty ugly picture of debt, it doesn't mean all debt is bad. Debt can be good if you can use that debt to earn more money than the interest you pay on that debt.

I remember talking to a coworker of mine who figured out that his credit card company was running a special promotion where they would give him a 1% interest rate on a cash advance when he opened a new card or transferred a balance to it. He took out the maximum amount they would let him borrow and used it to purchase a 1-year CD that earned a 3% interest rate. At the end of the year, he cashed out the CD and paid off the credit card, making a nice profit off the bank's money.

Remember when I said that I still have over 1 million dollars in mortgage loans? It's a similar situation. I went into debt buying real estate because I knew I could earn a higher return on the money borrowed than the interest rate the bank was charging me. I'll eventually pay off that debt, but right now having that debt is actually making me more money than it costs me.

Buying a house isn't always better than renting, but in some markets, depending on the interest rate, it can be profitable to go into debt to buy a house, because you'll end up saving money that would have gone to paying rent.

In many cases a student loan falls into the same category. If you can get a loan so that you can get a degree that will help you to get a higher-paying job, that debt might be completely worth the investment. But be careful, because that's not always the case.

I often advise recent high school graduates to spend the first two years of their college education in a community college, and then transfer to a university to complete their degree. It's usually far cheaper to get your education this way. Far too many people go into excessive debt to get a degree from an expensive school that isn't likely to ever show a significant return on their investment and may even cause them to go bankrupt.

The bottom line is to make sure that before you take on debt, that debt is actually an investment that will yield you a higher return than the interest rate you'll pay on that debt. Only in an absolute emergency situation should you take on debt that isn't profitable.

Taking action

- Make a list of all your debt. Put that debt into two categories: good debt and bad debt.
- Prioritize the list of bad debt by interest rate. Calculate how long it will take you to eliminate all your bad debt.

55

Bonus: How I retired at 33

Ever since I started working, my goal has been to retire early. It's not so much that I didn't want to work or that I was lazy—although I definitely do have a lazy streak in me—but rather that I wanted to have the freedom to do what I wanted to do with my time…with my life.

If you have the same kind of aspirations—even if you don't want to retire as early as I did—you'll probably find my story pretty interesting. Until I did it myself, I always wondered how other people did it, and I often wondered if it was possible for a software developer to retire early without striking it rich by founding a startup.

In this chapter, I'll tell you my story. I'm not holding anything back. I'll tell you exactly how I did it and the mistakes and triumphs I had along the way.

What it means to be "retired"

Before we get into my story, I want to define what I mean by retired, because the word can bring up totally different images to different people.

When I talk about being retired, I don't mean that I play shuffleboard and eat breakfast and dinner at country diners, taking advantage of the early-bird special. (Although I did eat breakfast at Bob Evan's this morning.)

My definition of retirement also doesn't involve sitting on a tropical beach all year-round, drinking margaritas—although it certainly doesn't preclude that. I don't imagine retirement to be doing nothing—obviously I'm not doing nothing; I'm writing this book.

Instead, I define retirement as freedom. To be more specific: financial freedom. The ability to not be forced to spend your time in a way that you don't choose to spend your time due to financial constraints.

I've never aspired to get to a point where I never worked again, but I've always aspired to get to a point where I'd never have to work again—if I didn't want to. That's the point where I'm at now. I have enough passive income coming in that's protected against inflation that I can sip Mai Tais on the beach if I want to, but I can also work on the projects that interest me, the ones that I want to work on—and not necessarily because of financial reasons.

Now, I'll be the first to admit I'm not quite doing it right, so to speak. Doing things for the sole purpose of making money is a hard habit to break. I still spend quite a bit of time doing things that I don't necessarily want to do, but the difference now is that I'm at least choosing to do these things. Being free isn't quite as easy as it seems. But at the time that I'm writing this book, I've only been "officially retired" for about a year—I've still got a long way to go to figure out how I want to live and what it is I want to do with my life, now that I've finally bought it back.

How I got started

In chapter 50, I told you how I figured out that even though I was making around $150,000 a year in my early 20s, it would still take me about 15 years to even reach 1 million dollars—with a lot of sacrifice and patience involved. And even at that point, without a solid plan to fight inflation, I wouldn't really be able to "retire."

At first this was very disheartening to me. I really didn't want to have to work hard for the next 20–30 years, saving money and being frugal, with only the hope of being retired someday. I didn't like the idea of putting my life on hold until I reached 50 or 60 years old and then finally getting to do what I wanted to do.

This feeling of futility forced me to think hard. I've already told you how I got involved in real estate investing, and this was the primary motivator. I realized that real estate investment was my ticket out of the rat race. There was a chance that I'd still not be able to retire young, but at least I'd retire wealthy once my properties were paid off. I was willing to take the risk.

I'd like to say that I immediately started doing all the smart things that a person should do to prepare for early retirement. I'd like to say I cut my expenses way down to almost nothing, saving just about every penny I earned, and started making smart investments right away, but I didn't.

The truth is I was 19, I was making $150,000 a year, and I was in Santa Monica, CA, a few blocks from the beach. I went into a Dodge Viper dealership and found out that even though I could afford payments on a $70,000 car, the insurance for a 19-year-old driving a red Dodge Viper around Santa Monica would be just as much as the car payments. Whew, disaster averted.

I also had a short modeling and acting career—you have to do that when you live in Santa Monica.

Now, I don't want to paint the wrong kind of picture. I did make some financial mistakes—I ended up buying a new Honda Prelude for $32,000 on some pretty bad financing terms—but I was actually pretty frugal overall. I saved a majority of the money I was making and started to build up pretty decent savings.

Rental woes

Well, you know how that $75-an-hour job for a 19-year-old software developer who didn't really have any skills seemed too good to be true? It turns out it was—that job didn't last very long. After about a year and a half, the company I was contracting with began some restricting layoffs. The project wasn't going very well and throwing more expensive labor at it wasn't helping—surprise.

I had to find another job, but I couldn't find anything nearly as good as the golden opportunity that had found me a few years earlier. I ended up moving to Phoenix, AZ, to take a less lucrative contract position, but one that I couldn't complain about.

About that same time, my renters at my house in Boise, ID, moved out, having pretty much trashed the place, and I was supposed to get married about one week after I started my new job—fun times.

I ended up getting several different renters in the property I had in Boise, but there was always trouble. Rents were hardly ever paid, things got trashed. I even had a crazy neighbor across the street who videotaped all the illegal and crazy activities that went on at my property. One company offered to buy the house from me and asked if they could start renovating before the final papers were signed. They tore up the entire house and guess what? They didn't sign the papers. I had just about lost hope in the property and was ready to throw in the towel.

Perhaps real estate investment wasn't for me. I had one dilapidated property that I couldn't even keep rented out and that was costing me a fortune. What we call an alligator. How was I going to accumulate more properties and execute on my plan of becoming a real estate tycoon?

Gaining traction

I won't bore you with all of the details of what happened in the next few years. I ended up hanging on to my property in Boise, mainly because I couldn't get rid of it. I moved around the country, to Florida, up to New Jersey, and back to Florida. My wife and I had planned to live in Florida, but I couldn't find a job. Finally, I got a job working at Hewlett Packard (HP) back in Boise.

Through those years, I did a pretty decent job of saving money. My wife and I were frugal and I made pretty good money. We were able to save up around $20,000 by the time we moved back to Boise. It took us about two years of not really consciously deciding how much to save, but putting whatever was left over each month into savings—not the best strategy. (Now that I think about it, I'm wondering why I hadn't saved much more money in that timeframe.)

We ended up in Boise, looking for a place to live. We decided to buy a house that we'd be able to rent out some day. The plan was that we'd live in a house for a couple of years, and then we'd move into a new house and rent the old one out. We settled on the purchase of a town-house for about $120,000, which we were able to put about 10% down on. The townhouse would be able to rent for around $800 a month, so with our mortgage of around the same amount, I figured we'd break even every month. (Whoops, after taxes, insurance, homeowner's association fees, and repairs, it didn't quite work out that way.)

We saw that the townhouse next to ours was for sale as well and decided to expedite our real estate investment plan. We made an offer for the property next door, put another 10% down on it, and we had our second rental unit and third property overall. It was actually pretty terrifying buying that property—really the first property I bought completely for investment purposes.

At this point, I decided to hire some professional property management. I hired a property management company without doing much research and ended up getting a really incompetent company that just couldn't keep the properties rented and constantly had bogus repair charges. It would be awhile before I found a good one. (Okay, so the

Our home next to our rental in Boise

first property management company I hired wasn't exactly incompetent, they were just good at making money for themselves at the expense of their property owners.)

Grinding it out

The plan had been underway for several years now. I had acquired a few properties and was hitting my goal of buying one new property every year. I kept working my job at HP and saving as much money as possible to buy more properties. I actually ended up tacking home equity loans onto some of my existing properties to buy new ones, because I didn't have the cash saved up for a down payment. (A risky move, but it worked out for me because home equity loan rates were so low at the time.)

Because I was doing so much real estate investment, I decided to go ahead and get my real estate license, figuring that I'd be able to do my own deals and save myself quite a bit of money on real estate commissions. My wife and I both went through the real estate license course and passed the test—we were now officially real estate agents.

Around this time I had about six properties, but none of them were making money. In fact, at this time I was pretty far in the negative each month. I had miscalculated the real costs of the properties I had bought and I ended up having to pay around $2,000–3,000 out of pocket every month to maintain the properties. Most months my wife's entire paycheck would go toward covering our rental property losses.

Although this might seem like a really bad situation, even though I was paying sometimes $3,000 out of my pocket each month, a sizable chunk of money was going to pay off the principal on the loans, and having the properties was also giving me a pretty huge tax break. I was advancing…just slowly.

Short circuit?

Shortly after getting my real estate license, I made a somewhat crazy decision to leave my secure, high-paid job at HP and join one of my friends as a partner in his business selling trading card games online, as well as to partner with him on selling real estate. I also had a very short stint as a gumball machine operator after I finished reading *Rich Dad, Poor Dad* and decided that the only asset I could think of other than real estate and stocks was gumball machines.

Looking back in hindsight, I realize the primary motivator for making this decision was the desire to take a shortcut to real "retirement," not by achieving financial freedom, but by just "doing what I wanted."

Needless to say, it didn't work out. I was pretty immature and stupid. I didn't know how to hustle and work hard. I was a horrible business partner—I wanted to have my cake and eat it too.

I ended up leaving that venture and taking a full-time job again—but not before sticking my business partner with 20 gumball machines. Maybe entrepreneurship wasn't for me.

More grinding it out

For the next few years, I continued to grind it out at a regular job. My wife also started working a few years back and had gotten into the

I rented gumball machines for a while.

technology field, so she was advancing in her career and making more money. We both took all the money we made and invested in real estate.

I was still shelling out quite a bit of money out of my pocket every month to pay the mortgages on the real estate investments, but I ended up accumulating quite a few properties over the next few years. I had three single-family homes, one fourplex, two duplexes, and a couple of commercial office spaces that were all being paid down little by little each month.

I took a slight detour to try and be an entrepreneur again—and failed—when a couple of my friends who started a payday loan business offered to make me a partner and pay me a salary, if I'd build a new software system for them. Again, I was stupid and immature, and perhaps a bit lazy. The venture flopped after a year and I ended up looking for another corporate job.

It turned out that in all that time I was working, I never made as much money as I had when I got that golden job in Santa Monica at age 19. That is, until I took a job doing a contract for the state of Idaho. Here I was, about 10 years later, and I was finally making $75 an hour again. Only then did I realize how lucky I was to get that first high-paying job years earlier.

About this time, the real estate market was crashing—hard. Many of my friends who were investing in real estate were panicking and short-selling their properties. Fortunately, because I had bought all my properties with 30-year-fixed interest rate loans, the falling property prices didn't really affect me. Sure, my properties were worth a lot less, but what did it matter if my mortgage never changed and I still got the same rents?

What did affect me, though, were the loan limitations that banks started putting on new loans. My plan had been to acquire one property a year for 15 years and then to start selling the oldest properties and living off of the profit. But when they limited the number of loans a person could have to four, my plan was pretty much shot.

I ended up turning to commercial loans rather than residential loans to finance a big purchase I was going to make in Kansas City, MO. My friend who lived in that area was asking about how to get started in real estate investment, and when I looked into it, I found that prices were extremely low there, yet the rents were extremely high.

I was going to buy two fourplexes for $220,000 each—my biggest investment yet. But when I ran the numbers on this one, I knew that I was going to be putting at least $1,000 in my pocket each month, even with just 10% down. The problem was that I couldn't get a loan.

Finally, I got a lucky break and the bank that owned the properties agreed to give me the loan themselves in order to get the properties off of their balance sheets. They gave me some very favorable terms and the deal went though. Boom, eight more rental units added to my growing balance sheet.

The deal was still extremely scary. Here I was already paying out several thousands of dollars each month to pay the mortgages on my investment properties, the real estate market was dropping like a rock, and I was about to put about $50,000 down on two huge properties I had never seen. This investment was either going to make me or break me.

Turning a corner

With the purchase of those fourplexes in Missouri—sight unseen, by the way—things started to turn around. I was still pretty negative, cash-flow-wise, but now I had a pretty large amount of real estate that was being paid down mostly by tenants. I had pretty good confidence that I was going to be able to easily retire in 20 years, worst-case scenario. The best part is that when I did retire, it wouldn't be on a meager income. If all those properties were paid off, I'd be sitting on perhaps $100,000 a year in passive income.

I ended up leaving my lucrative contract job to work for a small company that afforded me the opportunity to work from home. I had always wanted to work from home, and I figured that even though I'd make less money, I'd have the freedom to move anywhere I wanted to and I'd also have much more time because I wouldn't have to commute.

When I started working this new job, I decided that I was going to start building my own software on the side. I wanted to find a way to get more passive income and I had reached a point in my career where I was pretty confident that I could build just about anything. I started learning Android development by creating an Android application that allows runners to run at a certain pace by telling them to "speed up" or "slow down" while they're running.

Shortly after taking this new job working from home, I was introduced to a gentleman who would end up changing my life, David Starr. Right now David is the chief operating officer at Scrum.org, but back then he was the chief software architect at a company my wife worked for.

A few years earlier, I had started my blog, and although it wasn't very popular, some of the articles were getting some attention, especially the ones I wrote on Scrum. David had seen some of my blog posts and I had talked to him at a Boise code camp. David had been doing some work for a new online training company called Pluralsight. He had heard about the Android application I had developed and mentioned to me that Pluralsight was both interested in having an Android application created and in having a course on Android development.

I wasn't sure I wanted to start developing Android applications for companies or to try and teach a course on Android development—after all, at this point I had a plan to start using my free time to develop Android applications and create passive income. My wife saw the bigger opportunity with Pluralsight better than I did and said "You better create a Pluralsight course," so I did.

The lucky break

Now, at this point my real estate investments were doing pretty good and I was actually starting to make some passive income from my new Android app that had just been mentioned in the popular women's fitness magazine Shape. I was also blogging a couple of times a week and reading quite a bit on software development and real estate investment.

Right before I got the Pluralsight opportunity, my wife got pregnant. I knew the time to get started with this course was pretty limited, so I auditioned for the course by submitting a demo module for it, and I was surprised to find that it was accepted. I ended up creating my first Pluralsight course in about three months.

The great thing about Pluralsight was that not only were they going to pay me for producing the course, they were also going to pay me royalties on the course. If developers subscribing to their service watched my course, I'd get a quarterly royalty check—again, I didn't see how valuable this was at the time, but my wife sure did.

Right after I finished that first course, we made two big decisions: we'd move to Florida so we could be near family because our child was going to be born, and I'd create an iOS version of my running application. (Okay, well the second one didn't seem like a big decision, but it turned out to be a huge one, because it led to me creating my second and third Pluralsight courses on iOS development.)

My daughter was born in April of that year and just four months later we all got into the car and made the long drive from Boise, ID, to Tampa, FL. The whole time I was either working on my iOS application or creating my Pluralsight course—not to mention working a full-time job.

My working conditions weren't exactly ideal either. I had what my wife and I call a "bed office." We were in a tiny two-bedroom apartment, so my desk ended up being against a wall in the bedroom, brushing right up against the bed. I literally spent all day and night in that room. During the days I worked my regular job and during the evenings I worked on my side projects.

When my first royalty check arrived (and I got a check for almost $5,000 for my single course), I knew that this was the lucky break that might be able to really accelerate my plans for retirement—if only I worked my butt off to make the most of it.

Hard work mode

I'm not sure how I actually survived the next few years. I can't imagine having the energy now to do what I did then, but I knew that opportunities like the one I had been given with Pluralsight only come once in a lifetime.

I spent the next couple years working an eight-hour day at my regular job, creating Pluralsight courses every night for four to five hours, and working more on weekends. In a period of about two and a half years I created 60 Pluralsight courses, with 55 of them in total being published. I recorded enough video for you to listen to my tutorials for over a week straight, 24 hours a day.

During this time I also kept blogging once a week, started a new podcast on fitness for developers called "Get Up and CODE" (http://getupandcode.com), and started creating weekly motivational You-Tube videos. I'd like to say that life wasn't hard and I was enjoying it the whole time, but the truth is it was miserable, hard work, and I just kept thinking about how someday I'd be free.

Multiple passive income streams

At this point, I now had multiple passive income streams; my blog was actually starting to generate some money from advertising and affiliate sales, I was selling my Android and iOS running apps, I had the Pluralsight royalty checks that were coming in and growing substantially every quarter, and I had actually seen a few positive cash-flow months on the real estate investments.

When we moved to Tampa, I immediately started refinancing all the properties I owned to reduce the interest rates. This ended up reducing my payments by over $1,600 a month. I also started putting almost all the money I was making from my Pluralsight courses and everything I was saving from my job into paying off some of the real estate properties.

My goal was $5,000 a month of passive income. If I could hit that point, I knew that I could officially retire. In January 2013, it was pretty clear I was at that point. I emailed my boss and told him the news. I was quitting—not because I found a better job or didn't like my job, but because I didn't need to work anymore. I was free.

A quick analysis

My story is a bit strange. It starts off a bit rocky and then it seems like I get this one lucky break and then—boom—I'm retired. While it's true that I did get a pretty lucky break and that lucky break accelerated my retirement plan, there's a bit more to it than that.

Getting the lucky break wasn't enough. I needed to have something to do with the money I was earning from my Pluralsight courses to actually retire. I could have earned 1 million dollars, or even 2 million dollars, but without knowing how to invest that money or having something like real estate to invest in, I wouldn't be able to retire. I'd still have to work because you can't live the next 50 or 60 years of your life off of 1 or 2 million dollars.

Investing in real estate was completely critical to my success. Pluralsight just ended up speeding up the real estate investment plan. If I never had the Pluralsight opportunity, I'd have still reached retirement within about 10 years of when I actually did—that would be around 43 years old, which still isn't bad.

I wouldn't even have had the opportunity to do Pluralsight courses if I wasn't marketing myself and getting my name out there. I was able to meet David Starr because of my blog and because I was speaking at code camps. I was also constantly trying to open doors. I was pursuing many different projects and I was investing heavily in my skills and my career. I'm convinced that if the Pluralsight opportunity hadn't come along, some other life-changing opportunity would have taken its place. In fact, I'm sure that's true, because I've actually had to turn down some of those other opportunities.

My point is that luck is required—I'm not going to pretend like I didn't get lucky—but to some degree, you make your own luck. If you're out there pounding the pavement, working hard, always trying to better yourself and those around you, you greatly increase the likelihood of getting lucky.

The final piece of the equation was hard work. There are many Pluralsight authors who have had the same opportunity I did. I'm not saying that they don't work hard, but I made an active choice to be the Pluralsight author with the most courses in the library. I busted my butt working late nights and weekends for years to make my dream come true.

It isn't enough to get an opportunity—even a once-in-a-lifetime one. You have to make the most of it, or it won't really matter.

Now, before I wrap this up, I want to mention what both my wife and I believe was a very important factor in our success. I don't know if you're religious. I'm not going to try and convince you of my religious beliefs in this book, because that's not what it's about, but I'd not be completely honest if I didn't mention that my wife and I are both Christian, and as part of our beliefs we contribute about 10% of our earning to charity.

Back when we first started on our journey, we decided to start tithing 10% of all the income we made—we actually give this income to a charity that supports orphan kids in India. When we first started making our tithes, the very next week my wife got a raise that exactly covered the amount of money we were now tithing. I personally think a large portion of our success was due to this commitment to tithe — which we maintain today.

Even if you aren't of the religious type, I think there is a somewhat logical explanation for this. I think the harder you hold on to money, the more difficult it is for you to make the smart financial investments you need to make to be successful. Tithing or giving away a fixed portion of your income to charity — voluntarily — changes the way you think about your money. The mental transition goes from owner to steward.

Well, I hope my story inspires you and at the very least gives you an idea of how it can be possible to retire early. Part of the reason I wanted to share my story with you is so that you could see how many mistakes I made along the way. I could have reached success much faster if I'd had the knowledge and experience then that I do now. Perhaps you can learn from some of my mistakes and avoid them yourself.

Fitness

The human body is the best picture of the human soul.
—Ludwig Wittgenstein

I t might seem a little strange to you that a book written for software developers would have a whole section dedicated to fitness, but I don't think it's strange at all. In fact, I think it's my duty to include this section, because I honestly don't see how you can be the best programmer you can be if you don't pay attention to your physical health.

I've seen the need for education and encouragement in the realm of physical fitness in the software development community for a long time. When I first started programming, the typical stereotype of a software developer was a nerdy, skinny guy with thick-rimmed glasses and a pencil protector. Today, the stereotype seems to have changed, but for the worse. Now, many people think of software developers as fat guys with a beard going down to their neck, wearing a stained white cotton t-shirt while eating pizza.

Obviously both of these stereotypes are wrong—there are plenty of software developers, male and female, who don't fit either of those molds—but the second stereotype scares me more than the first, because in a way I think that some developers start to think that they're supposed to fit it.

The goal of this section is to give you basic education on fitness and to encourage you to break out of the mold and realize that just because you're a software developer doesn't mean that you can't be healthy and perhaps even dashingly handsome or, if you're a female, strikingly beautiful. You can get in shape, you can be healthy, but it all starts with education and the belief that it's possible.

You might also wonder what makes me qualified to write about diet, nutrition, and physical fitness. I don't have any degree in nutrition, I'm not even a certified personal trainer, but what I do have is experience. I've been learning about fitness and diet since I was 16 years old. I entered my first bodybuilding competition when I was 18. I've also coached and helped many other people, including software developers, to get in shape, lose weight, gain muscle, and reach other fitness goals. While I'm not an expert, my knowledge in this area is fairly wide and it's tempered with experience.

I've also taken a couple of chapters that cover some of the basics of nutrition out of this section and placed them in the appendix. If you're interested in finding out exactly how calories work and how your body uses them, you might want to check there first.

56

Why you need to hack your health

Physical fitness is not only one of the most important keys to a healthy body, it is the basis of dynamic and creative intellectual activity.

—John F. Kennedy

How can I motivate you to get in shape? Let me see.... How about that you'll live longer because heart disease is the number one killer in the world, followed by stroke? How about that exercise has actually been shown to make you more creative and boost your mind? Vain? I've got answers there as well. Who doesn't want to be more physically attractive— I know I certainly do. Lifting weights and losing some fat can make you more attractive and give you more options for extending your...legacy.

And, let's face it, most software developers spend quite a bit of time at a desk, sitting down all day. As software developers, we stand to benefit greatly from learning how to get fit and healthy, because our jobs tend to push us in the other direction.

In this chapter, we'll take a more in-depth look at some of these reasons for getting in shape, and I'll try to convince you that you should start right away—as in now, not tomorrow or next week. Getting fit can make you a better software developer. Here's why.

Confidence

I'm not going to start by trying to appeal to your actual desire to be healthy. We all want to be healthy, and most of us have at least some idea of what we need to do to become more healthy, but we still pick up that slice of pepperoni pizza or make the late night Taco Bell run. Being healthy, by itself, isn't a strong enough motivator to get into shape—at least, not until your life is directly jeopardized, but we'll get to that in a bit.

Instead, I'm going to start off by focusing on one of the most important benefits of healthy eating and exercise: confidence. You might think confidence isn't that important, or perhaps you say "Hey, I've already got confidence, bro." But whether you already see yourself as having some extra to spare or you don't see why it's so important, I'll tell you why you're going to want to have it and have as much of it as you can get.

A study performed by researchers at the University of California at Berkeley's Haas School of Business showed that confidence was a better predictor of success than talent (http://simpleprogrammer.com/ss-overconfidence). There have been other studies that show a similar correlation.

But how can being fit gain you confidence? Simple: getting in shape helps you to feel good about yourself and the fact that you can accomplish the goals you set out to accomplish. That self-confidence carries outward and is projected in your conversations and interactions with others. Also, for a less scientific explanation: when you look good, you feel good.

Imagine how good you'll feel when you're fitting into those skinny jeans or popping the threads on the arms of your shirt. Feeling fit, feeling like you're healthy, changes the way you act. It changes how you view yourself and how threatened you feel around others and by their accomplishments, and it changes the way others see you and feel about you as well.

Much of this book is about going out and doing things that require some degree of confidence. It's difficult to conjure confidence by thinking about it, but almost every person I've ever trained in the weight room or helped to lose some pounds has suddenly found a confidence they didn't know they had.

Brain power

Is it really true that exercise can make you smarter? Well, I'm not sure about smarter, but a recent study at Stanford University showed that walking was able to substantially increase creativity—by about 60% (http://simpleprogrammer.com/ss-walking-creative). In the study, Dr. Oppezzo asked a bunch of students to complete some creativity tests. The tests involved coming up with uses for objects and other activities that could be attributed to creativity.

Students first sat at a desk and completed the tests, and then they were asked to do similar tests while walking on a treadmill. Almost all students showed a large increase in creativity. Even when the test was performed with students walking and then sitting down, the results still showed an increase.

What does this mean? It means that walking has a significant effect on at least one function of your brain—creative power—but I suspect that it also affects quite a bit more.

I can tell you from personal experience that the more I exercise and the healthier I am, the better I seem to perform at my work. I notice that I'm considerably better at focusing and being productive when I'm at my best physically. For my "Get Up and CODE" podcast, I've had the pleasure of interviewing guests like John Papa, Miguel Castro, and other well-known developers who've reported similar experiences.

I can't say for sure whether the actual exercise or body-fat percentage of my body causes chemical or structural changes in my brain that makes me smarter or more focused, or whether I just feel better and therefore work harder, but does it really matter which it is?

If you're always feeling tired and unmotivated to work or you just don't feel like you're performing at your peak, you might find that a change of diet and exercise can renew both your body and your mind.

Fear

I didn't want to pull the fear card right away, but I think it's still important to mention that if you're overweight and generally unhealthy, you're putting yourself at a considerable risk for all kinds of preventable diseases.

I run a podcast about fitness for developers called "Get Up and CODE" (http://getupandcode.com), and on that podcast I've interviewed many developers who eventually got in shape, not because they wanted to be more confident and increase their brain power, but because they felt like they were knocking on death's door.

In particular, I remember talking to Miguel Carrasco about his journey to fitness. He was a software developer who never paid much attention to his weight or his health until one day he had a really bad scare that put him in the hospital and forever changed his life.

He was driving his son home from daycare and all of the sudden his left hand started feeling numb. He figured maybe it was just cold outside or he had banged it on something, so he ignored it.

Later that evening, he went to lie down to take a little nap—which was strange for him, because he almost always stayed up late. His wife questioned him about his odd behavior and he said that the whole left side of his body felt really numb. His wife convinced him to rush to the hospital—fearing he had had a stroke.

When he got to the hospital, he found out his blood pressure was 190/140—which isn't good, not good at all.

It turned out he was okay. It wasn't a big deal. They performed some tests on him and let him go the next day, but monitored him and administered more tests over the next month. But that experience scared the heck out of him and forever changed his mindset.

I clearly remember Miguel telling me that it wasn't a workout program, a special diet, or going to the gym that caused him to lose the 73 pounds he lost in 180 days, but rather a state of mind. The scare caused him to take his health and fitness seriously, so much so that he quit his career as a software developer and became a fitness coach, motivating and helping other people to reach their fitness goals.

I don't tell you this story to scare you—okay, actually I do—but I hope that I can scare you through Miguel's story rather than through your own, when it may be too late. Miguel was lucky because his scare wasn't a big deal. His scare was a warning that kicked him into gear. But many people aren't so lucky. Sometimes you don't get a warning. Sometimes you drop dead of a heart attack or are seriously harmed in another way before you take things seriously. Sometimes it's too late.

Don't let it be too late for you. Get serious now. Don't wait until you have a health problem to start caring about your health. I know you might not have bought this book with the primary motivation of getting healthy, but seriously, if I help you get a better job or career, that's great and I'm happy for you, but if I can also help you to get in shape so you can be around a little longer to see your kids grow up, then I'll count this book to be a much bigger success.

Taking action

○ Before we get any further into this section, make a commitment to your health. Maybe you're already healthy and the following chapters are just review for you, but if you know that you need to get healthy, make a commitment to take your health seriously and to make a real change in your life. I can give you all the fitness and health advice I know, but if you aren't committed to change, it won't matter a bit.

57

Setting your fitness criteria

Regardless of your fitness goals, you'll never achieve them if you don't have them. Just like you have to know what the code you're writing is supposed to do, you need to know what kind of end result you want to achieve by all that sweat and starvation; otherwise you'll just be wasting your time.

In this chapter, we'll talk about how to set realistic and achievable goals for your fitness journey. We'll look at utilizing both short-term and long-term goals to achieve better results, and how long-term changes only occur through committing to a healthy lifestyle—not crash diets and four-hour cardio sessions.

As a software developer, prone to sitting at your desk for long periods of time and sometimes working crazy hours, it's especially essential that you define some explicit criteria for getting healthy, because it might be more difficult for you to live a generally healthy lifestyle—the odds will likely be against you.

Picking a specific goal

It's common to hear someone talk about starting a fitness routine or a diet with the goal of "getting in shape." While that may seem like a fine goal, it's not specific. After all, what does it really mean to be "in shape," and how do you know when you're in shape?

It's not that exercising and eating right without a specific goal won't still give you good results, whether you have a specific result in mind or not, but that not having a specific goal will make it much less likely that you'll stick with any program and see any real changes.

There are quite a few different goals you can pick for your fitness endeavors. Don't try and pick more than one at a time. If you want to lose weight, focus on losing weight, not on gaining muscle. If you want to improve your cardiovascular health by running, focus on that goal, even though you might drop some pounds in the process.

It's very difficult to achieve multiple fitness goals at the same time, because they're often in direct conflict with each other. For instance, it's difficult to gain muscle and lose fat at the same time, because you typically need to be in calorie surplus to gain muscle and in calorie deficit to lose fat.

POSSIBLE FITNESS GOALS
- Lose weight (fat)
- Gain muscle
- Increase strength (not necessarily the same as gaining muscle)
- Increase muscular endurance (for sports performance)
- Improve cardiovascular health
- Become better at some sport

Creating milestones

About six years ago, I tore my right pectoral (chest) muscle. I was doing some heavy dumbbell bench presses when someone offered to spot me. I accepted the spot, but immediately regretted it when the spotter tried to help me by pulling my arm outward instead of up. I remember distinctly hearing a popping sound as my limp arm fell to my side—the muscle was completely torn away from the bone. Ouch.

Needless to say, I wasn't lifting weight for a long time after that incident. I lost quite a bit of motivation, because I now couldn't even lift the bench-press bar, so I did what some would do in that situation—I stopped exercising and got fat.

At one point I weighed in at about 290 pounds. This was about 90 pounds over what I should have weighed—I'm 6 foot 3 inches tall. When I finally came to my senses and decided I had had enough of self-loathing and being fat, I realized I needed to lose about 90 pounds.

Losing 90 pounds seemed to be an impossible goal. How the heck was I going to lose 90 pounds and get back in shape? How long was it going to take? I realized that I wasn't ever going to feel motivated to lose 90 pounds, so I had to figure out how to make that huge task seem much smaller.

I came up with an idea. I'd make a small goal of losing 5 pounds every two weeks. I wouldn't worry about losing 90 pounds, even though that was my overall goal; instead, I'd focus on two-week periods at a time. All I had to do was get on the scale and be 5 pounds lighter than I was two weeks ago—that's it.

It took a lot of two-week periods, but I eventually lost the full 90 pounds I set out to lose—and even a bit more. I never missed my goal even once along the way. The key was breaking my big goal into smaller milestones that marked my way to success.

Once you've decided what your primary fitness goal is, you should figure out how you can create a series of milestones that you'll reach along the way to your final destination. If you're trying to lose weight, you might decide on a certain amount of weight you want to lose every week or two weeks—like I did. If you're trying to gain muscle, perhaps your milestones will be based around gaining a certain amount of lean weight on a similar interval.

Just make sure the milestones are achievable. If you set out trying to lose 10 pounds a week, you're going to get discouraged quickly when you don't come even close to hitting that number. It's better to commit to a less ambitious milestone that you can easily achieve than one that will be nearly impossible for you to reach. The momentum of success can help carry you forward and increase your motivation to reach your overall goal.

Landmine: What if you don't have time?

As a software developer, you might have a hectic schedule and you might even travel quite a bit, so how do you find time for diet and exercise and to pursue your fitness goals? There's no easy answer for this, but my best advice is to make it a priority. I used to create meeting requests specifically on my calendar for things like going for a run or lifting weights. If you're having trouble sticking with a plan, I'd advise you to do the same. No one has to know your 7:00 a.m. meeting is actually a run.

Measuring your progress

As you work toward your goal, it's very important to have a good way to measure your progress. You need to know, at regular intervals, whether or not you're heading in the right direction.

Think about the best way you can measure your progress toward the goal you're trying to achieve. If you're trying to lose or gain weight, one basic measurement is a scale. If you're trying to gain strength or muscle, you might chart your progress by recording how much weight you can lift and how many times you can lift that weight.

I try to avoid too many measurements, though; otherwise I can easily get overwhelmed. I usually try to pick one main measurement that I use to chart my progress and throw in some other measurements at longer intervals of time.

Perhaps the most common measurement is your weight on a scale. But you should be a little cautious with this measurement, because your bodyweight can fluctuate by a large amount from day to day depending on what you eat and how much water weight you're carrying at any given time.

I'd recommend weighing yourself every day, but only using a weekly measurement to actually chart your progress. I've seen my weight fluctuate by as much as 10 pounds in a single day. If you measure your weight once a week, instead of once a day, you're less likely to be thrown off by the big swings your body can go through from day to day.

Living a healthy lifestyle

Hitting a fitness goal can be a great feeling at first, but that great feeling can quickly deteriorate into hopelessness, depression, and eventually regression. Trust me; I've blown it plenty of times in my life after achieving a big fitness goal. In fact, many dieters who lose weight eventually gain it back, partially due to hormones that make them hungrier (http://simpleprogrammer.com/ss-hormone-weight), but also because they revert back to their old habits.

After reaching your fitness goal, your battle isn't over. You can quickly lose the progress you made if you don't change your actual lifestyle.

You can't live on a diet forever, so you have to find a way to live your life in a way that will maintain the level of fitness you worked so hard to achieve.

I'd recommend that after you reach any fitness goal you slowly taper off of the diet or program you've been on, rather than switching to "normal living." The goal is to make "normal living" somewhere in-between what you were doing to achieve your goal and what you were doing before that. Binge eating after losing 50 pounds will send you on the fast track to gain it right back, and perhaps more.

You have to figure out how to incorporate healthy habits into your life so that regular exercise and a healthy diet are normal parts of your life. It's not easy to do, especially if you do an extreme diet or fitness program, so even though you may lose weight a lot faster by starving yourself, you might want to try to incorporate a diet and exercise program that will only be slightly stricter than what you could do perpetually.

In the next few chapters, I'll give you some tools that will help you do that. We'll talk about how to figure out how many calories your body needs to maintain its weight, how to eat healthy, and how to exercise. With that information, you can learn to achieve your fitness goals, but more importantly, you can learn how to create a healthy lifestyle based on a routine you can continue for the rest of your life.

Taking action
- Identify one big fitness goal and write it down.
- Next list a series of realistic milestones to achieve that goal.
- Identify one action you can take to reach your first milestones.

58

Thermodynamics, calories, and you

If you want to lose or gain weight, you need to have an understanding of what exactly makes you pack on pounds or melt them off. Surprisingly, there's a huge debate in the fitness industry over whether or not the amount of your weight gain or loss is directly a factor of how many calories you eat versus how many calories you burn.

It seems like it would be a pretty easy thing to settle—I mean, to some degree we know that calories are responsible for changes in weight—but the debate about how much of an effect calories have isn't something that can be settled so easily.

I can't promise you an absolute, smoking-gun answer in this chapter, but I can give you some solid reasons why I tend to subscribe to the viewpoint that calories are the most important factor in gaining and losing weight. I'll also help you to understand what calories are and how to determine how many of them you burn in a day.

What is a calorie?

One of the first things we need to address, before you can understand exactly how calories affect your weight, is what they are. What exactly are calories and why do we care about them so much?

A calorie is basically a measurement of energy. To be specific, a calorie is the amount of heat necessary to raise one kilogram of water by one degree Celsius.

The food that you eat is the primary source of energy for your body. That's why it's measured in terms of calories. We also measure the amount of energy we expend in terms of calories as well.

For the most part, you can assume that all the calories that enter your body are either used or stored. Some calories go to waste, but human bodies are very efficient machines.

Different foods provide your body with different numbers of calories — and not just based on quantity. The same amount of broccoli will provide much fewer calories than an equivalently sized slab of butter.

Carbohydrates, proteins, and fats each provide a different number of calories per gram, so some foods are denser than others. Carbohydrates and proteins provide approximately four calories per gram and fats provide approximately nine calories per gram. And remember, because we can't digest fiber, calories that come from fiber sources can basically be discounted.

Losing weight is simple

If calories represent energy and your body can only get energy from food, then it's easy to figure out how to lose weight — just eat fewer calories than you burn. I don't think anyone will disagree that you'll ultimately lose weight if you eat fewer calories than you burn — the debate is over accurately calculating how many calories you actually burn.

The good news is that even though you can't know for sure how many calories you burn or consume in a day, you can make some pretty good guesses. And if you allow for a reasonable margin of error, you can almost guarantee weight loss or weight gain. The key is making a good guess.

Making a good guess starts with knowing how many calories you need to expend to lose some fat — I'm assuming you're interested in losing fat and not muscle. A pound of fat is worth, energy-wise, approximately 3,500 calories. If you want to lose a pound of fat, you have to burn about 3,500 more calories than you eat. Pretty simple. (By the way, this applies to both men and women.)

Only it's not quite that simple. Unfortunately, you don't just lose fat when you lose weight. It's true that if you have a deficit of 3,500 calories you'll lose weight, only not all of it will be fat, some of it will be muscle.

If you want to lose weight, you need to make sure that the calories you're consuming are fewer than the calories you're burning. The amount of calorie deficit you have will determine how much weight you lose. That means that if you want to lose weight, you need to know two things: how many calories you're consuming and how many calories you're burning.

How many calories are you consuming?

Calculating how many calories you're consuming isn't all that difficult. Most of the food we buy has a label that tells us how many calories per serving the food contains. For the foods that don't have a label, you can use an application like CalorieKing (http://simpleprogrammer.com/ss-calorie-counter) to look up the amount of calories a particular food has.

Unfortunately, food labels aren't always 100% accurate. You should plan for a 10% margin of error on packaged food labels. If you eat at a restaurant, you should expect a much higher margin of error—you can't trust a chef to measure everything perfectly. Adding a little more butter to a dish could increase the total calories by a large amount.

Also, the more complex the food you eat, the more difficult it is to accurately measure the calorie count. That's why I try to eat fairly simple foods when I'm dieting. I also try to eat the same foods frequently so that I don't have to keep looking up calorie counts.

How many calories are you burning?

Calculating how many calories you burn is a little more difficult, but you can get a good estimate.

Whether you're running a race or sleeping on the couch, your body burns calories. Your body requires a certain amount of fuel just to keep you alive. This base amount of calories is called your base metabolic rate, or BMR.

You can calculate your approximate BMR by a combination of your weight, height, age, and sex. This calculation will tell you how many calories you'll burn just to stay alive, so it's a good starting point in calculating how many calories you burn in a day—you know you at least burn that much.

To calculate your BMR easily, you can use an online tool: search for a BMR calculator or try the one at http://simpleprogrammer.com/ss-bmi-calc. For example, I am 6 feet 3 inches, I weigh about 235 pounds, and I'm 34 years old, so my BMR is about 2,251 calories per day.

Now, most of us don't just sit around doing nothing all day, so the BMR isn't exactly an accurate measurement of how many calories you burn. To get a more accurate estimate, you can use the Harris Benedict Equation shown in table 58.1 to calculate your approximate calorie burn based on activity levels.

Table 58.1   Harris Benedict Equation

Little to no exercise	BMR * 1.2
Light exercise (1–3 days per week)	BMR * 1.375
Moderate exercise (3–5 days per week)	BMR * 1.55
Heavy exercise (6–7 days per week)	BMR * 1.725
Very heavy exercise (twice per day)	BMR * 1.9

I run three times a week and lift weight three times a week, so by using the Harris Benedict Equation, I can figure that my daily calorie burn is 2,251 * 1.725 = 3,882 calories. But if I'm trying to lose weight, I drop myself one category lower to be on the safe side. A conservative estimate of my calories burned would be 2,251 * 1.55 = 3,489 calories.

Plug in your stats to figure out how many calories you burn each day. Before you do it, though, take a guess and see how close you come.

Utilizing calories to achieve your goal

Okay, so now you know how calories work and how to calculate how many calories you consume and approximately how many you burn. You can use this information to come up with a basic plan for losing or gaining weight.

Suppose I wanted to lose weight. Let's say I had a goal of losing about a pound a week. Using what you know now, how could I create a fitness and diet program that would allow me to reach my goals?

Well, first I'd want to start with the calories I burn each day. If I don't change my routine at all, I'll burn about 3,500 calories each day. If I don't eat anything all day, I'll lose a pound—I'll also be very grumpy.

If I want to lose a pound a week, that means I need a total deficit for that week of about 3,500 calories. If we take 3,500 and divide it by 7, we get 500. I need a calorie deficit of about 500 calories a day.

If I'm burning 3,500 calories each day, I can eat a max of 3,000 calories and I should be at a calorie deficit of about 500 calories. In theory this will work, but in reality, I might not see the results I expect.

A variety of reasons could cause me to not actually lose one pound a week, even though the numbers show I should. I could measure my food wrong and be off by about 100 calories at each meal, which could make my calorie count 300 calories higher than I expected. I could also not work out quite a much as I estimated, which could bring my calorie burn down—although I've already compensated for that a bit.

What I might actually want to do is reduce the calories I eat by about 10% or 250 calories, just to make sure that I'm going to meet my goal. That would mean that I'd try to eat around 2,750 calories a day and I could be pretty confident of hitting my goal.

You can apply the same steps to create a plan for yourself for losing or gaining weight. Be careful, though, because as you start to lose weight your BMR will drop, so you'll need to eventually reduce your calories further or increase your activity to keep losing weight.

Taking action

- Track the calories you eat for at least three days. This will give you a good idea of your basic calorie consumption. Before you do it, take a guess and see how close you actually end up.
- Calculate your BMR and use the Harris Benedict Equation to calculate approximately how many calories you burn each day. Compare that number with how many calories you eat. Are you on course to lose or gain weight?
- Utilize this information to come up with a basic plan, as far as calories and activity are concerned, for either losing or gaining weight.

59

Motivation: Getting your butt out of the chair

The hardest part of reaching any fitness goal isn't actually setting the goal, knowing how to achieve it, or even doing the work required to get there. The hardest part of reaching any fitness goal is getting and keeping the motivation to do it.

As a software developer, you're probably busy. You've got broken builds to worry about and bugs that need to be fixed. It seems like there's always some reason to put off working out and starting that diet until later. The only problem is that "later" never comes.

If you want to be successful with losing weight, becoming the buffest computer programmer in existence, or just getting healthy, you'll need to learn how to motivate yourself and stay motivated. This chapter is all about what it takes to actually stop thinking about your fitness plan, put it into action, and stick with it.

What motivates you?

We're all motivated by different things. What motivates you might not motivate me and vice versa. It's important to take some time to think about what kinds of things motivate you the most. What is it that makes you want to wake up and start your day? Conversely, what is it that makes you want to run away and hide?

If you can find one primary motivating factor in achieving your fitness goals, you can use that motivator to help get you out of your chair and start moving. If I asked you to go to the store to pick up something, you might not be that motivated to do it. But if I asked you to go to the store to pick up $1,000, you might be in your car and on your way before I could finish asking you. The right motivator can make a big difference.

Rewarding yourself too early

If you want to kill your motivation, make the mistake of rewarding yourself for a job well done before the job is…well…done.

Just last week, I did some work for a client that paid me up front. They paid me for about 24 hours' worth of work before I had actually done the work. Normally, I'd be motivated to get 24 hours' worth of billable time from a single client in a week, but this time, I wasn't motivated at all. Why?

It was because I already had the big, fat check in my bank account. I received the reward before I actually did the work, so I wasn't as motivated to do the work.

The same thing can happen to you. I see it all the time. It's common to buy a nice, expensive pair of running shoes or a brand-new treadmill to motivate you to start your new workout program. But while you might think that getting that new $400 blender is going to motivate you to eat healthy, the opposite happens. You already got the reward, so the motivation is gone. You can actually demotivate yourself by giving yourself the reward before you earn it.

Instead, try telling yourself that once you've been running consistently for three months, you'll reward yourself by getting a new treadmill and some running shoes. Tell yourself that if you can eat healthy for a whole week, you'll get to go on a shopping trip to Whole Foods and buy a bunch of healthy groceries. Always try to make it so that you have to earn a reward and you'll be much more motivated to reach your goals.

There's actually some scientific evidence to back up this viewpoint. For an interesting read on willpower, check out *The Willpower Instinct* by Kelly McGonigal (Avery, 2011). In this book, the author cites several studies that show that rewarding yourself before reaching a goal can make you feel like you already achieved the goal.

Motivation ideas

Even though you might have already come up with a great motivator to get you started on becoming a new, healthier you, that motivator may eventually lose its effectiveness—in fact, I know it will. I've lost my own motivation more times than I can count, and if you talk to anyone who has started and quit a diet, you'll probably find the same problem. You'll need to figure out some other ways to hack your motivation.

One good way to stay motivated is to post pictures all over the place that serve as reminders of what you want to look like. Those pictures can help keep you on track and focused on your goals. The next time you're looking at a piece of chocolate cake, Arnold Schwarzenegger will be staring you in the face saying "Are youuu gowving to eeeat dat caeek, you weenie?"

It can also help to chart your progress and constantly remind yourself how far you've come. Tonight I didn't feel like writing any more chapters in this book, but I reminded myself that I was on chapter 59 and it motivated me to continue. Sometimes just knowing that you've already traveled very far down a road is enough motivation to keep traveling down that road. Everyone hates to break a long winning streak.

Another powerful motivation technique is gamification. The idea behind gamification is simple: take something you don't like to do and make a game out of it. There are actually quite a few fitness applications that help you to gamify your workouts and healthy habits.

GAMIFICATION APPS
- Habit RPG: https://habitrpg.com/static/front
- Super Better: https://www.superbetter.com/
- Fitocracy: https://www.fitocracy.com/
- Zombies, Run!: https://www.zombiesrungame.com/

It can also help to get a lifting or running partner, or even to start a new diet program or challenge with a friend. Having someone to talk to and share your experiences with, good and bad, can make the journey seem more enjoyable and keep you motivated. I've always found that I'm more consistent in making it to the gym when I have a lifting partner.

Table 59.1 shows a few additional ideas for motivators that might help you stay on task.

Table 59.1 Motivators to stay on track

Listening to an audio book	I always have an audio book or podcast playing when I'm running or lifting weights. I find it's something I look forward to each day.
Watching TV on the treadmill	You might find more motivation to run if you allow yourself to only watch TV when you're on a treadmill.
Getting outside	If you like the outdoors, that can be a great motivation to get you going for a run.
Getting away from your kids	We all need a break and time for ourselves. Many gyms have day-cares that will take care of your kids while you work out.

Just get it done!

It's great if you can keep yourself motivated, but sometimes you just have to suck it up and stick with the plan, motivated or not. Try to make decisions ahead of time that commit you to a course of action that you want to take.

When you wake up in the morning and are feeling tired, it isn't a good time to decide whether or not you want to run. When you're at the office presented with free doughnuts, it isn't a great time to decide whether or not you want to stick to your diet. It can help to decide ahead of time that no matter how you feel, you're going to stay the course until some predetermined date in the future.

Try to remove judgment as much as possible from your life by planning things out far in advance. Know exactly what you're supposed to eat and do each day and you'll be less likely to make bad decisions and won't have to rely as much on motivation.

Utilize principles in place of motivation when your motivation runs out. When I'm tired and don't feel like finishing my run, sometimes I have to remind myself that one principle I highly value is that of finishing strong. Create a set of maxims to live your life by and stick to them when things get tough.

MAXIMS TO LIVE BY
- Always finish strong.
- Winners never quit and quitters never win.
- No pain, no gain.
- Time is short, if you want to do something in life, do it now.
- This too shall pass.
- A consistent process produces success.

Taking action
- Come up with a list of reasons why you want to get in shape or improve your health. From that list, identify the three biggest motivators. Print out those three motivators and put them in several places where you can see them every day.
- Pick a few motivation ideas mentioned in this chapter and incorporate them in your life. Perhaps try to find pictures of people who motivate you and post them where you can see them, or find a new fitness app that makes working out fun.
- Pick a reward to give yourself after you reach a certain milestone in your fitness journey. Chart your progress to the goal, and when you reach it, reward yourself.
- When tempted to break your stride, stop and ask yourself how you'll feel in three months, next year, and so on if you don't give up. That time is coming either way.

60

How to gain muscle: Nerds can have bulging biceps

Pssst! Hey, you. Yeah, you—over there. Do ya wanna gain some muscle? Well, do ya? Good. I can help—no illegal substances required. You just need to learn the basics of resistance training.

In this chapter, we'll talk about how to build muscle. It's not that hard as long as you're willing to put in the work. We'll cover what causes muscle growth and learn how you can stimulate muscle growth in your own body. We'll also go back to diet a bit and discuss what kinds of foods you should eat to maximize your "gains."

As a nerd—err … computer professional—having muscles can be a big advantage. Not only will you look and feel better, but you'll be able to break out of the stereotype given to many of our profession and that uniqueness might even help your career.

If you're female—look, I know that you don't want to look huge. I agree, it's not very attractive for a woman to look like the Incredible Hulk—but don't worry, lifting heavy weights isn't going to make you huge, unless you have a bunch of extra testosterone to go with it.

Whether you're male or female, everything in this chapter applies to you. Men and women don't need to lift weights differently. If you're a woman, lifting heavy weights will accentuate your figure and improve your physique. It's very, very difficult to get to the point where you look huge—you don't have the chemical hormones to do it. So, don't worry, lift heavy—and don't forget the squats!

How muscles grow

The human body is amazingly adaptable. If you grab rough things with your hands, they'll grow calluses to protect them. If you run long distances, your cardiovascular system will adapt to make it easier. If you lift heavy weights, your body will grow bigger muscles.

The trick is that your body is also very efficient—it doesn't grow muscle just because you want to look buff. You can stand in the mirror all day wishing you looked like Hercules, but if you don't actually lift heavy weight, nothing will happen.

If you do lift weights, but the weights aren't heavy enough—if they don't provide enough of a challenge to your body—your muscles will have no reason to grow, so they won't. The key is to progressively overload your muscles by increasing the amount of work you ask them to perform as they grow in response. You basically have to convince your body that you need bigger muscles before it will create them.

Growing in size is just one of the ways your muscles can adapt to being overloaded with work. Your muscles can also increase in strength and endurance. If you want to optimize your muscle growth—the size of your muscles—you have to give your muscles the proper kinds of stress.

Weightlifting basics

Getting started with weightlifting can be a little intimidating. There are all kinds of different exercises and it can be difficult to know what you're supposed to do. Fortunately, the basics are pretty easy.

First, we need to talk about some of the terms involved in lifting weights. When you lift weight, you usually break up the workout into different exercises. For each exercise you do a number of sets, and for each set you do a number of repetitions, or reps.

The definition of an exercise is pretty obvious, so we won't waste time talking about that. A set is basically one continuous session of performing an exercise. Reps are each one full cycle of the exercise.

Typically, you'll do a certain number of reps of an exercise and then take a rest. You'll call that a set. For each exercise you'll do a certain number of sets. Let's look at an example.

Suppose you were going to do a common lift called a squat, which is basically where you go from a standing position to a squatting position. Your goal might be to do 3 sets of squats of 10 reps each. That would mean that you would do 10 squats, then take a rest, and you'd repeat that three times.

Different goals

Remember how I said that your muscles can adapt in different ways? How your muscles adapt will be primarily determined by how you lift. Now that you know what reps and sets are, we can talk about how you can utilize reps and sets to achieve different goals with weight training.

Strength

If you do a small number of reps with a fairly high rest period between sets, you'll primarily cause your muscles to adapt by growing stronger. Naturally, muscles that grow stronger will also grow bigger, but the same-sized muscle can vary greatly in strength. Just because you're getting stronger, doesn't necessarily mean you're getting bigger — or at least not as big as you can with other training methods.

Typically, if gaining strength is your goal, you'll want to have reps that are in the one to six range. But limiting the reps isn't enough. You'll want to lift the heaviest weights you can for that rep range. The idea is that if you're targeting four reps, you physically can't do five with the weight you're lifting.

Size

The next goal you might have — perhaps the most common one — is muscle size. Muscle size growth is known as hypertrophy. Muscle size is primarily achieved by medium rep ranges with moderate rest times in between. To achieve maximum muscle size, you want to try to hit rep ranges between about 8 and 12. Again, this means that you lift the heaviest weight you can for that many reps. At the higher rep ranges, you'll feel quite a bit of burn before you actually hit muscle failure. As they say, no pain, no gain.

Endurance

Finally, you might be interested in increasing your muscular endurance. I'm pretty sure you can guess how to do that—increase the reps even further. If you train with very high reps and fairly short rest periods, you'll maximize your growth in terms of muscular endurance. That means that your body will adapt to be able to not tire out so easily when under a load.

To achieve muscular endurance increase, you want to have rep ranges above 12. You might do 20 reps or more to increase your muscular endurance. But be warned: if you focus on muscular endurance, you won't see much of an increase in size—you might even see a decrease. Consider the difference between sprinters and long-distance runners to get an idea of how this works.

Getting started

Okay, so now you might be wondering what kinds of lifts you should actually do and how to get started. The good news is it isn't as complicated as many fitness magazines and fitness gurus make it out to be. There are some basic lifts you can do that will get you the maximum benefit in the least amount of time.

Let's start by talking about how you might split up your routine in a week. I'm a big fan of a three-day workout routine, but you can adapt the basic plan I'm going to give you to exercise more frequently if you wish.

When you initially start out, you'll probably want to do lifts that target your whole body, but eventually you'll need to split things up so that you work certain body parts on certain days. (You need to increase the volume of the work you do so that your body continues to adapt.)

I divide exercises into three categories: push, pull, and legs. Push exercises are exercises where you're pushing the weight away from you. These exercises usually use your chest (pectorals), shoulders (delts), and triceps. Pull exercises are exercises where you're pulling the weight toward you. These exercises usually use your back and biceps. Finally, leg exercises work…well…your legs, of course.

Starting out, you might want to do push, pull, and leg all in the same day. Just do one exercise per body part—we'll get to what exercises in a bit. You'll be very sore the first time you lift weights. The soreness, known as delayed onset muscle soreness (DOMS), will come the next day and usually last around a week—don't worry, though; it gets better and less frequent if you stick with it.

Once you've been doing full-body workouts for about two to three weeks, you can progress to splitting up your workouts to either a two-day split of upper body and lower body or a three-day split of push, pull, and legs. Table 60.1 will give you some ideas.

Table 60.1   Splitting workouts between upper and lower body

	Monday	**Tuesday**	**Wednesday**	**Thursday**	**Friday**	**Saturday**	**Sunday**
Beginner	Push, pull, legs		Push, pull, legs		Push, pull, legs		
Intermediate	Upper body		Lower body		Upper body		
Intermediate to advanced	Push		Pull		Legs		

What lifts should you do?

Okay, so now that you have a basic plan and know how to reach your goals, you need to know what kinds of lifts you should do. In this section, I'm going to give you suggestions for what I think are some of the best all-around exercises you can do for each body part. I'm not going to go into the details of how to do each exercise here, but you can find pictures, videos, and full descriptions at one of my favorite internet sites for fitness, Bodybuilding.com (http://simpleprogrammer.com/ss-bodybuilding).

The general strategy for picking good exercises is that you want to do as many compound movements as possible. Compound movements are lifts that involve multiple joints. The more joints involved, the more muscles involved, so the bigger the bang for your buck. Many of the exercises I recommend here work different muscles, but have one primary muscle group that they work the most.

You'll also probably want to start with a low number of sets, perhaps just 1 or 2, and then eventually work up to about 3–5 per exercise. In general, I try to make a workout have about 20–25 sets total. That should take about an hour. More than that isn't necessarily beneficial.

Best all-around exercises

There are more exercises you can do and variations of these, but these are the staples that I add to almost any routine I create for myself or someone else. You can pick some of the best ones from these exercises.

PUSH
Chest

- *Bench press*—This is one of the core chest exercises. Learn how to perform this exercise correctly. You can also do this exercise in an inclined or declined position to target different parts of the muscle.
- *Dumbbell flys*—Another great chest exercise that can really help you to add size to your chest.

Triceps

- *Overhead triceps extensions*—I prefer to do these seated. I find them to be one of the best triceps exercises overall. They work the whole triceps and can really help you get bigger arms.
- *Cable pushdowns*—With this exercise you don't work as much of the triceps, but it targets the outer head of the triceps, so it can give you that nice horseshoe look.

Shoulders

- *Military press*—If you do this lift standing, it will work your abdominals as well. Just be careful with this one. You want to start with light weights and learn to do the exercise properly. Overall, this is one of the best shoulder exercises and a very good compound movement.
- *Side lateral raises*—With this exercise you hit the sides of your shoulders, which is a difficult area to grow. Even though this isn't a compound movement, I highly recommend it.

PULL
Back

- *One-armed dumbbell rows*—This is a pretty painful exercise—at least for me—but it will grow your back like nothing else. Do one arm at a time for maximum effect.

- *Pull-ups*—A staple for working your back and building big lats—you know, the sides of your back that give you that v-taper and make it look like you have wings. If you can't do any pull-ups, look for a machine that assists you until you can do them on your own.

Biceps

- *Alternating dumbbell curls*—This is one of the best biceps exercises, and really the only one you need if you're doing other back exercises, because biceps get worked by any back exercise. Just try not to swing your body and cheat, which is easy to do on this one.

Legs

- *Squats*—Oh, baby. This is the king of lifts. Nothing feels better than getting through your squats. This exercise activates almost all the muscles in your legs and even works your core. Learn how to do this exercise right and don't avoid it.

- *Deadlifts*—This is another good exercise, but it's somewhat difficult to learn. Take it easy and work your way up with the weights. This exercise works your whole body to some degree, but it's also very taxing. I recommend not going above five reps on this exercise. Definitely take the time to learn how to do it correctly, though, because it can really mess up your lower back if you don't. This exercise works your hamstrings and your lower back primarily.

- *Calf raises*—It's not that important how you do your calf exercises, but make sure you do some variation of these. You'll look weird if you have a huge body with tiny calves.

If you had to choose only a few exercises to do, here's what I would recommend, in order of value: squats, deadlifts, bench press, and military press. If you just do those exercises, you'll definitely see growth.

What about abdominals? Well, it turns out you don't need to worry about working those directly as long as you're doing the core lifts I mentioned in the sidebar. Squats, deadlifts, and military presses (standing) work your core as you try to stabilize yourself to do the exercises.

Make sure you look up how to do each exercise and learn how to do them correctly. Always start with light weights and work your way up.

What to eat

You can do a great job lifting weights and still not see any gains if you don't eat properly. Fortunately, it's not difficult to do. You just need to make sure you're eating a surplus of calories and that you're getting enough protein.

I recommend eating 1–1.5 grams of protein each day for each lean pound of your weight. If you weigh 200 pounds and you have a body fat percentage of around 20%, you'll have about 160 pounds of lean mass, so you should eat a minimum of about 160 grams of protein to make sure you eat enough to gain muscle mass.

Try to eat healthy foods so that a majority of the calories you eat go toward building muscle and not gaining fat, but you should know that gaining fat is inevitable. When you gain muscle, you also gain some fat with it—that's just how it is.

As far as supplements go, you don't need any. It can be helpful to have a protein shake right after your workout. You also can try out creatine if you like. It's one of the only supplements I've ever found to actually be effective. It can help you lift a little more weight and can make your muscles look fuller. Finally, you can take some BCAAs (branch chain amino acids) to help make sure you have enough BCAAs to build and repair muscle. But, again, you don't need any of these things, and everything else is almost certainly a rip-off.

Taking action

- Go get a gym membership and set up a personal lifting plan for yourself. If you feel intimidated, invest in hiring a personal trainer for a few weeks to get you started. But do something now. Don't wait.
- Go to http://simpleprogrammer.com/ss-bodybuilding and look up the exercises mentioned in this chapter. Watch the videos and learn how to do the exercises. Practice the movements without weight.

61

How to get hash-table abs

If there's ever one fitness question that everyone seems wants to know the answer to, it's "How do I get six-pack abs?" Abs seem to be the quintessential indicator of physical fitness and overall physical attractiveness. Having abs makes you part of a special club not subject to the normal laws of human interaction.

But how does one get abs? How does one transcend to that higher plane of physical fitness—the one reserved for swimsuit models, Hollywood celebrities, and ancient Roman statues? It's not easy, but the answer, surprisingly, has little to do with sit-ups or crunches.

In this chapter, I'll pull back the curtain, roll up the shirt, and tell you exactly how to get that washboard stomach you've been dreaming of.

Abs are made in the kitchen

I've got some good news and some bad news. The good news is you can stop doing those stomach crunches and grueling midsection workouts—they aren't working anyway. The bad news is that to get abs, you'll have to do something infinitely more difficult—you'll have to have the discipline to drop your body fat to a very low percentage.

Most people think you get abs by repeatedly working your ab muscles. While it's true that just like any other muscle, you can increase the size of your abs by working them with progressive resistance, most people don't have abs not because their abs aren't big enough, but because they can't see them.

You can do all the sit-ups, crunches, leg lifts, and other ab exercises you want and never see your abs if you don't significantly drop your body fat. Most people who lift weights have wonderful abs even without doing any direct ab training—I almost never work my abs directly. The problem is that the abdominal region, especially for men, is one of the main areas of fat deposits in the body.

Unless you're genetically gifted and happen to not store much fat in your midsection, you probably will need to have a very low body fat overall to even begin to see your abdominal muscles. Even if that weren't the case, from what we know about weight training, you can probably guess that crunches and sit-ups mainly build up muscular endurance in your midsection, because the resistance isn't enough to produce muscular hypertrophy.

If you want to get six-pack abs, your journey begins in the kitchen. We've already discussed quite a bit about how to lose weight, but there's a big difference in what you need to do to lose weight when you're 10, 20, or more pounds overweight and what you need to do to lose fat when you're already in pretty good shape.

Before you can even think about getting abs, you'll need to reach a point where you're already in good shape. If you follow the advice in the previous chapters, it won't be that difficult to do—it just takes time. But once you reach an average level of body fat, getting lower is going to require some strict discipline and probably quite a bit of sacrifice.

Your body doesn't want you to have abs

When we look at a picture of a fitness model with stunningly visible abs, we think "Hey, that person looks great." Our bodies, on the other hand, think about it a little differently. If your body had a mind of its own and could speak for itself, its reaction might be quite a bit different than yours. Your body would probably look at the same picture and say "Eek! That person is dying. He is starving to death. Why isn't his body saving him?"

You have to understand that your body is a very complex machine that doesn't care whether or not you look good in a swimsuit. Its chief concern is centered on the goal of keeping you alive. To your body, washboard abs are a serious problem. Washboard abs indicate that you're a few weeks away from starvation and death. You might be quite confident that you're going to have plenty of food to eat tomorrow, but your body prefers to be prepared for long-term disasters. That's why it stores fat. It wants to save it for a rainy day—just in case.

As a result of this selfish goal of keeping you alive, your body does all kinds of subversive things to halt your fat loss. Anytime you lose fat, you lose some muscle as well—it can't be helped—but when you're already at a low body-fat percentage, your body, in an evil plan to thwart your attempts to kill it, cranks up the muscle cannibalism to a higher degree. Your body basically throws more muscle on the fire to burn as calories to preserve its precious fat stores.

If you think about it, it makes perfect sense. Muscle requires a certain amount of calories every day to maintain it. The more muscle you have, the more calories you burn, so if you're short on calories and it seems like you're trying to kill yourself by starvation, your body kills two birds with one stone by utilizing your muscles for calories, thus getting some extra energy and reducing your overall energy requirements.

Not only does your body subvert your swimsuit-body transformation attempts by getting rid of your muscle, it also does some other nasty things like increase your amount of ghrelin, a hormone that makes you hungry, and decrease your amount of leptin, a hormone that makes you feel full. Basically, the more fat you lose, the hungrier you get and the more difficult it is for you to feel full.

I won't go into all the details here, but I think you probably get the point. Once you get below a certain threshold of body fat, your body starts kicking in all kinds of extra defenses in a crazy attempt to keep you alive.

What can you do about it?

Unfortunately, there's no magic bullet. Professional bodybuilders who get to extremely low body-fat percentages do it mostly by taking steroids and other drugs that you probably don't want to mess with, as they can be quite harmful and dangerous. In fact, if you're curious about some of the extreme cutting agents that some professional body-builders and fitness models use to get "cut," do a quick Google search on DNP. This extremely toxic chemical basically shuts down your mitochondria, halting that ATP cycle you learned about in grade school, and turns your whole body into a toxic furnace. (Disclaimer time: don't mess with DNP, anabolic steroids, or any other illegal substance to lose fat or gain muscle—it isn't worth it and you could die.)

But what about average, normal Joe who doesn't want to shut down his mitochondria? For you, the answer lies in being strict with your diet and sticking it out for a long time. If you want to drop your body fat low enough to see your abs, you'll need to carefully calculate your calories and make sure that you aren't losing weight too quickly or too slowly. It will take some discipline forged from Bethlehem steel to do it—especially with the increased hunger—but it can be done.

Not only will you need to dial in your diet and pretty much forgo any cheat meals, but you'll also need to make sure you're lifting weights as if you're actually trying to gain muscle. You can reduce the cannibalization of your existing muscle by a decent degree while losing weight if you continue to do heavy weight training, which can be difficult to do on a restricted-calorie diet. By continuing to lift heavy, you'll signal to your body that you still need to keep that muscle around.

You may also try what's known as high-intensity interval training (HIIT) training to lose fat. HITT is cardio that's done in very short, intense bursts—think running sprints up a hill or running as fast as you can for a minute or two at a time. This kind of cardio has been shown to burn fat while preserving lean tissue better than regular cardio sessions like running for long distances.

Overall, though, it's going to take a lot of discipline if you want washboard abs. You've literally got to fight your body in a battle to the death.

Taking action

- Search around on the internet and find pictures of people at various levels of body-fat percentages. See if you can figure out what body-fat percentage you'll need to be at to have visible six-pack abs. This number will differ greatly for men and women.

62

Starting RunningProgram.exe

Regardless of whether you're trying to lose weight or you want to improve your cardiovascular health, running is something you might be interested in. I know I'm not supposed to say this, but I'll be honest with you. I hate running. I've tried to like it. I've told myself that I'm having fun while I'm counting down the time I have left on the treadmill or glancing at my phone to find out how many miles I have left, but the truth is, I just don't like it.

Regardless, I do it anyway. I regularly run about three miles, three days a week—and I've been doing it for about five years. Even though I don't like it, now that I do it regularly, it has become a routine. But getting started wasn't easy. If you've never run before, you can't just head out your door and go for a three-mile jog. Well, maybe you can, but when I first started running, I couldn't even run a block.

In this chapter, we'll talk about why you might want to get started with a running program, how running might affect your body, and how you can get started doing it.

Why you might want to run

You'll have to excuse me if my viewpoint is a bit jaded, because I don't actually like to run, but even with my less-than-enthusiastic attitude about running, I can't ignore its many benefits. Obviously, I run for some reason besides torturing myself, right?

One of the biggest reasons why I run and why many people do is for cardiovascular health. Obviously, running isn't the only way to strengthen your heart and to increase your lung capacity—any form of exercise will do—but it's one of the easiest. It's pretty easy to get out there and run, no matter where you are.

Along the same line, running also provides a good way to burn some extra calories. Running alone isn't going to make you lose weight—most of your weight loss efforts should be focused on calorie restriction—but it can make an impact. Running has been shown to suppress appetite, so if you get hungry and go for a run instead, you can get a double whammy in getting closer to your weight-loss goals.

While I don't actually usually enjoy running while I'm running, I do feel pretty good afterwards. I find, and several studies back me up on this (see http://simpleprogrammer.com/ss-exercise-boosts, for example), that running makes you happier in general. Running is a good natural cure for mild depression and can make you feel better overall about yourself. If you've ever heard of runners' high, then you probably know that running can also actually lift your mood in a chemical way as well, although I usually don't run long enough to experience that effect—perhaps why I don't like running.

There are a bunch of other benefits, like strengthening your knees and other joints, increasing bone mass, reducing cancer risks, and potentially increasing your lifespan. (Some of these benefits are easier to prove than others.)

Getting started running

If you've never done any kind of distance running before, the idea of running for several miles can seem impossible. But almost anyone can get to the point where they can run a fairly long distance—even a marathon.

The key to being able to run long distances is using a schedule where you're increasing the amount you run over time. There are some standard marathon training schedules that can take you from barely being able to run three miles to running a full 26.2-mile marathon in about 30 weeks.

But before you can even begin to think about running a marathon, you need to get to the point where you can run three miles, or about five kilometers. That's a good starting point, and once you reach that point, you can enter many different 5K races and decide if you want to train for something more ambitious.

When I started out running again—after a several-year hiatus—I used a running program that has become popular lately, called Couch-to-5K. The original Couch-to-5K program was created by a running group called Cool Running (http://simpleprogrammer.com/ss-couch-to-5k).

The idea of the program is simple: you gradually increase the amount you run week by week. You start off by walking and running for just a short time and end up running a full 5K by the end of the program (although the increase isn't always so gradual).

The great thing about this program is that it's designed for someone who doesn't have any experience running and might not be in good physical shape. The program takes about two months to complete. For the program, you do a 20- to 30-minute running session three times a week.

When I did the program, I was able to find a mobile application that made everything extremely easy. The app kept track of where I was in the program and told me when to run and when to walk. You can find the official iOS version at http://simpleprogrammer.com/ss-c25k, and if you do a search on "couch to 5K," you'll find apps in all of the mobile app stores.

Advice for getting started

When you get started running, the most important thing is commitment. You can start doing the Couch-to-5K program and never actually make any progress if you don't consistently run three times a week. If you don't consistently run, you'll make backwards progress instead of forwards progress. It takes time to build your endurance and it doesn't take much time to lose it.

Also, don't worry too much about progress when you're first starting out. You'll probably have to start by mixing running and walking together for the first few weeks—there's a reason the Couch-to-5K program advocates that approach. Over time, you'll eventually increase the amount you can run and you'll reach your goals. You have to be persistent and patient. If you push it too hard, too early, you're likely to become discouraged and not continue.

Taking action

- ⚙ Go to Cool Running and check out the Couch-to-5K program: http://simple programmer.com/ss-couch-to-5k.
- ⚙ If you're interested in starting running, download the Couch-to-5K app and plan out the days you'll run each week on your calendar. Make a commitment to complete the program. You might get someone else to start the program with you. Having someone else do the program at the same time can help you be accountable and make it more fun.

63

Standing desks and other hacks

As a software developer, if you're anything like me, you're probably interested in any shortcuts or hacks that can help you reach your fitness goals faster or with less effort. I'm always trying to come up with a way that I can enhance my results and reduce my effort.

Over the years, I've come up with quite a few tricks I utilize in my daily routine that make losing weight, gaining muscle, and keeping up with my fitness goals a little easier. As an added bonus, most of these tricks will help you improve your overall health, because most of us spend way too much time sitting front of a computer all day. In this chapter, I'm going to share some of those tips and tricks with you.

Standing desks and treadmills

Have you ever thought that if you could just walk on a treadmill while doing your work you could burn so many extra calories? I have; in fact, I decided to give it an actual go. Right now, I happen to be sitting at my desk, but I have a treadmill just a few steps away with a shelf on it that can hold my laptop.

During the day, I'll often spend an hour or two walking on the treadmill at a very low speed while I'm working. By doing this, I'm able to burn quite a few extra calories each day with very little added effort. I keep the speed on the treadmill low enough so that I can easily walk and type or move my mouse at the same time.

Originally I planned on utilizing the treadmill desk all day while I worked, but it turns out that isn't very practical. While it isn't a huge amount of effort to work while walking slowly on the treadmill, it's some effort, and it isn't as convenient as sitting at my desk—especially with my big monitors.

I figured out that I could actually burn quite a few extra calories by slowly increasing the incline of the treadmill. Because the pace was the same, it was still easy to type and use the mouse or trackpad, but I was burning many more calories. I also could compact my time down to about an hour or so a day.

> ### Landmine: What if you don't work from home?
>
> Of course, to be able to do this you need to either work from home or have a very flexible working environment. For many, an easier alternative is a standing desk. A standing desk doesn't offer quite the same calorie-burning benefits of a treadmill desk, but you do burn considerably more calories standing up most of the day.

Plus, as an added bonus, apparently standing is much better for your health than sitting. There have been numerous studies that have shown that sitting for prolonged periods of time can be extremely harmful to your health (see http://simpleprogrammer.com/ss-health-sitting for an example).

Also, as an added bonus, if you do the Pomodoro Technique, like I do, you can take the five-minute break to do some stretching, pushups, pull-ups, or other exercise.

Food hacks

One of the most difficult things about getting into shape is dealing with food. Eating healthily normally requires quite a bit of cooking and preparing meals in advance. It's much easier to go out to a restaurant than it is to cook your own food, but if you want to be healthy, you have to do a large degree of cooking for yourself.

I'm always trying to find ways to make it easier for me to eat healthily, so I've developed quite a few food hacks that I find useful.

Eggs in the microwave

The first "hack" I have for eating involves eggs. Eggs are an excellent food to eat, because they are high in protein and you can control the total calories and fat by adjusting how many whole eggs you eat versus egg whites. The only problem with eggs is that separating egg whites from yolks and cooking eggs is a big pain.

I've figured out a way to make things much simpler, though. First, instead of buying whole eggs, you can buy egg substitute, which is basically egg whites. You can buy this in cartons at the grocery store. Although the egg substitute has to be refrigerated, it's a great way to get an almost pure protein source that's pretty convenient.

But what about cooking it? Well, I've found that I can actually cook eggs and egg whites pretty good in a microwave. At first I was skeptical about doing this, but it turns out that once you get good at microwaving eggs, you can get to a point where you can barely distinguish them from eggs cooked in a pan—as long as you're okay with scrambled eggs.

Most days, the first meal I have is microwaved eggs with frozen spinach. I'll first take some frozen spinach and put it into a microwavable container. Then I'll heat that in the microwave for a couple of minutes until it's thawed. Next, I'll pour in the egg substitute, real eggs, or a combination of both. (I find adding at least one real egg tends to make things taste a bit better.) Finally, I'll microwave the eggs for a minute or two, mix them around, and then microwave them again until they are a decent level of firmness.

My final step is to add some cheddar cheese or salsa to the eggs. I'll use low-fat cheddar cheese if I want to keep the calories down. I can make this meal in less than 10 minutes, and it's portable because it doesn't involve many ingredients. The spinach makes a great filler that adds quite a bit to the eggs, so I'm not as hungry—plus, spinach is pretty good for you as well.

Most of my hacks are based on trying to get a lot of protein without having to do much cooking, because I'm usually either trying to gain muscle or preserve muscle when losing weight, and both of those cases require a high-protein diet.

Plain nonfat Greek yogurt

My next food hack is to utilize plain, nonfat Greek yogurt as another highly portable, no-cooking-required protein source. I've found that the plain, nonfat Greek yogurt that you can find at most grocery stores is almost pure protein with very little calories.

The only problem is it doesn't exactly taste great. The flavored Greek yogurts taste fine, but they're full of sugar, so they aren't healthy at all. But don't worry; I have a solution for you.

It turns out that if you put a little lemon juice, vanilla extract, or other low-calorie flavoring and add a little bit of calorie-free artificial sweetener—my favorite is Truvia—you have a pretty good–tasting yogurt that's extremely high in protein and low in calories.

You can even add your own fresh fruit or frozen fruit if you like. Adding a little bit of fruit will add quite a bit of flavor, but very few calories.

Frozen meats

As far as meats go, I've found a couple of nice solutions as well. I've always hated cooking chicken. Not only is it time consuming and difficult to do, but I'm horrible at it. I know that chicken breasts are one of the staple foods of bodybuilders, but I don't like them and I just can't seem to cook them.

Fortunately, though, I've found that I can buy frozen precooked teriyaki chicken breasts, or, even better but slightly more fatty, teriyaki chicken thighs. I've found a few different brands, but in the United States, I've found Tyson to be the most common brand, and I've been able to find these items at bulk-item stores like Costco, Sam's Club, or BJs.

For a quick, tasty, and healthy meal, I'll just pop a couple of frozen chicken pieces in the microwave and I'll be ready to eat in minutes. While freshly cooked chicken might be slightly healthier, the convenience of this precooked chicken saves me from instances where I might be tempted to run out and get fast food. Plus, it tastes great.

Along the same lines, I've also been able to find frozen turkey meatballs. I got the idea for this food item when I read about Ryan Reynolds eating mostly turkey meatballs when he was getting in shape for one of his roles. It seemed like a good idea, so I looked into it and it turns out that turkey meatballs offer a good balance of protein, carbohydrates, and fat.

You can find turkey meatballs at most grocery stores. They are extremely convenient as you can pop a few in the microwave and be ready to eat in a few minutes.

Taking action
- See if there are any of the hacks mentioned in this chapter that you can apply to your own life to make it easier to reach your fitness goals.
- Take a look at your current schedule and fitness plan and identify the most annoying and time-consuming parts of your routine. How can you develop a hack that can make things much easier?

64

Tech gear for fitness: Geeking out

I don't know about you, but I'm a big gadget geek. I love using technology to make my life easier. As I sit here typing this chapter, I'm basking in the glow of five monitors that are hooked up to my single computer. Why? Well, I like to say it makes me more productive—and to some degree, I'm sure it does—but, in reality, I just like having a lot of screen real estate. Something about technology motivates me—especially when it comes to fitness.

This chapter is all about the tech gear that can help you achieve your fitness goals or just make your journey a lot more fun. We're entering a time period where we can know much more about ourselves and how our bodies work than ever before. This self-knowledge is known as the quantified self. In this chapter, I'll help you navigate your way through all the technology and pick out some of the most useful gear to help you find your quantified self.

Step counters and pedometers

I thought it would be appropriate to start out by talking about step counters and pedometers, because they're some of the most common pieces of tech gear that you're likely to see today.

I'm a big fan of having some kind of step counter because it can help you to identify how active you really are, and just knowing how active you are can result in changes in your behavior to help you become more active.

There are many different kinds of wearable step counters and pedometers available today, but perhaps one of the most popular—especially in the developer world—is the Fitbit (http://simpleprogrammer.com/ss-fitbit). There are many different kinds of Fitbit models available, but basically Fitbit tracks the number of steps you take in a day. You can automatically sync your Fitbit with your phone and have instant access to your data.

If you don't already have a Fitbit or a similar device from one of Fitbit's competitors, I'd strongly suggest getting one. They're fairly cheap, but the insight they can give you into your daily activities is priceless. I'd recommend getting one of the models that takes a watch battery and lasts several months on that single battery, because I found that when I was regularly wearing a Fitbit the biggest hassle for me was remembering to charge it.

I've also found that eventually you might want to stop using a step counter. I used a Fitbit regularly for a little over six months, but I stopped wearing it when I realized I could estimate my own step counts because I was so familiar with my routine and the readings I was getting from my Fitbit.

Wireless scales

One of my favorite pieces of tech gear is a wireless scale I got from a company called Withings (http://simpleprogrammer.com/ss-withings). What's cool about this scale is that it automatically uploads my data wirelessly to the cloud, whenever I step on it. It seems like a small and simple thing, but it's amazing to easily have the complete history of my weight available to me without me having to do anything except step on a scale.

Not only does it track my weight, but it also tracks my body fat percentage. While the accuracy of the body fat percentage reading is questionable, what I'm more concerned about is how it changes over time. Even though I might not get a completely accurate reading, I can see relative changes and know if I'm going up or down.

I'd highly recommend a scale like the one I got, because it can make you much more aware of your current weight and what direction it's going. They say that what gets measured gets improved, and even though you may already step on a scale every day, when you can see the changes over time on a graph, it can really motivate you to move that graph in the right direction.

Combo devices

One exciting area of technology for fitness that isn't even close to mature yet is the combo devices that are slowly being introduced. These combo devices can measure multiple data points through various sensors and give you quite a bit of information about yourself.

I had the chance to interview the CEO of a new startup called Angel (http://simpleprogrammer.com/ss-angel) that's making a combo device that will measure your heart rate, blood oxygen level, activity, and temperature. He told me about all kinds of different ways that devices like his Angel device could change the way we not only measure our fitness level, but all areas of our health.

Having all this data available to you can help you to optimize your workout and know much more about how what you're doing is affecting your body. I can't wait to get my hands on an actual Angel device to try it out.

Google and Apple are also heavily invested in this area. At the time of writing this book, Apple is rumored to be making a smart watch that will most likely have an array of sensors related to fitness and health. And Google has created a special version of the Android operating system designed to be run on smart watches. I predict that in the future we'll eventually have smart watches that will be able to give us all kinds of data about how many steps we take in a day, what our heart rate is, and anything else that can be measured.

PUSH strength

Another device that I'm really excited about (even though it's not out yet at the time of writing this book) is PUSH (http://simpleprogrammer .com/ss-push-strength). I also had the opportunity to interview the

CEO of this company for my "Get Up and CODE" podcast and I was able to learn quite a bit about this unique idea for a fitness device.

What I found interesting about the PUSH device is that it isn't a device that tracks your steps and your activity, but rather is designed to improve your weight-lifting workouts. You basically put this device on your arm or leg while you're lifting weights and it tracks your reps and sets. But it also tracks things like the amount of force and power you generate, how good your balance is, and how fast you're moving the weights around.

For me this kind of data is like a goldmine. It's a big hassle trying to track reps and sets when I'm lifting weights and I've always wondered how the speed at which I lift a weight affects the results I get after the workout.

Headphones

One major piece of tech gear for my workouts is headphones. I often listen to podcasts or audio books when I'm working out, so I like to have a good set of headphones that I can plug into my phone.

The biggest problem I have, though, is with the wired headphones. I can't seem to use earbuds or anything else that has a wire. I end up pulling the wire when I'm running and violently yanking the earbud out of my ear. Plus, when I go to grab my earbuds they're always a tangled mess.

Fortunately, I've been able to find a good pair of wireless headphones. I've bought many different kinds of wireless headphones, but I've found that the AresX (http://simpleprogrammer.com/ss-headset) works best for me. These headphones are basically like wireless earbuds, but they're connected by a sturdy cable that's just flexible enough to hold the headphones together and still not interfere with my movements.

I'd definitely recommend investing in a good set of headphones. The Bluetooth technology we have today makes it easy to get decent sound from wireless headphones, and they're easy to connect to a smartphone. With a good set of headphones, you can make use of some of that dead time you have working out. You might also want to get a subscription to Audible (http://simpleprogrammer.com/ss-audible) so you can listen to audio books.

Apps

And let's not forget about apps. There are tons of fitness apps available for all kinds of different purposes. I won't even try to name most of them because there are so many, but I'll give you a good idea of what kinds of apps you might want to look for and some of my favorites:

There are running apps that track your runs. I actually created an Android and iOS app that was originally called PaceMaker and now is called Run Faster (trademark dispute). This app tracks your runs and helps you keep a certain pace by telling you to "speed up" or "slow down" while you're running. But even though I created the app, I'll be the first to say that there are far better apps out there for tracking your runs. (Run Faster is really good for keeping you on pace, though.)

One of my favorite run-tracking apps is called Edomondo (http://simpleprogrammer.com/ss-endomondo). It's the primary run-tracking app that I use now. It has many different features that allow you to see quite a bit about your runs—including split times and elevation changes.

Another type of app I utilize is one to track my weight-lifting workouts. I used to use a pen and a notebook, but it's much easier and more convenient to have an app that can track your workouts, tell you what to lift next, and let you know what you lifted previously. If you aren't tracking your weight-lifting workouts already, you definitely should start.

I've tried a few different ones of these kinds of apps, but I haven't been terribly excited with any of them. The biggest problem I've had is trying to actually create the workouts—which is time consuming—and sharing those workouts with others. (I lift with my wife and I don't like having to manually reenter the whole workout program in her phone as well.)

I've finally settled on using the Bodybuilding.com app (http://simpleprogrammer.com/ss-bb-mobile). The reason why I like this app is because it allows me to create the actual workout online through the website and I can save and share that workout with anyone. It could still use a bit of work as the app isn't all that intuitive, but once I figured it out, I found that it works nicely.

Spirit

If you do not conquer self, you will be conquered by self.
—Napoleon Hill

Throughout the pages of this book we've talked about how to improve your career in a practical sense, how to using marketing to open doors and release the floodgates of opportunity, how to expand your mind through learning and teaching, how to be productive through a focused effort fueled by persistence, the basics of finance and how to think in a way that causes your wealth to work for you rather than you working for your wealth, and, finally, how to strengthen and shape your body. But there's one missing link that ties it all together.

If we were simple machines it wouldn't matter. But the truth is we aren't simple machines—we're human beings. We're not just a body connected to a mind. We can't just give ourselves instructions and expect them to be carried out. There is another force that drives us, a powerful force that can send us on the path to success or drive us into the ground. You can call this force what you will, but for the purposes of this book I call it spirit.

This section is all about that intangible connection between the mind and body that motivates us to action and ultimately controls whether or not we live up to our potential or fall back helplessly believing ourselves to be a victim of circumstance. In this section, my goal is to equip you with the tools to conquer the greatest enemy you will ever face—yourself.

65

How the mind influences the body

Everything in this book so far has been mostly backed up by at least some scientific evidence, but now we're about to reach into the realm of the unquantifiable. What I have to say on the upcoming subjects will mostly be a combination of my experience and my opinion.

Why should you take seriously anything I have to say on these subjects? A fair question, for sure. I could tell you that what I'm saying here is what I believe has led me to the success I've been able to experience in my life, but perhaps you don't want to be like me—or you aren't very impressed. In that case, a much stronger argument is to be made in saying that the ideas I'm about to give you in this section aren't entirely my own.

Many of the concepts in this section are derived from great works by authors much more famous and successful than me. But, more importantly, some of the ideas that came from these books—specifically the idea that the mind is a powerful influencer of the body—have been the hallmarks of success of some of the greatest minds of the 20th century.

I've made a habit every time that I've had the opportunity to speak to a famous or extremely successful person to ask them what single book has influenced them the most in life. Surprisingly, an unbelievable number of them have answered the same two or three books—the books I'll mention in chapter 69, "My Personal Success Book List."

It starts with the mind

There's almost nothing you can do without believing you can do it. It's amazing how much your mind influences your body and your ability to succeed. It's easy to quickly dismiss the idea that if you can believe it, you can achieve it, but there is some serious truth to that idea. At least, the converse of that idea holds more truth: if you don't believe it, you're sure not to achieve it.

You have to learn how to harness the power of your mind, to gain mastery over it, if you want to be able to put into action even the smallest plan that you devise. But it isn't an easy task. You can't just will yourself to believe something. Have you ever sat and tried to do it?

Give it a try now, if you like. Try to believe that elephants are pink. Can you convince yourself of it? Even if your very life depended on it, could you change such a simple belief? There is almost no trick you can conceive to get your mind to believe some arbitrary piece of information.

That doesn't mean that you could never believe that elephants are pink. A compelling piece of evidence could instantly transform your mind — but it's unlikely you'll ever find a piece of evidence compelling enough to force you to believe such an illogical fallacy. In fact, your mind is so powerful that even if you were presented with compelling evidence that completely contradicted your current belief on the color of elephants, you might still go on believing what you currently believe, what's comfortable to you.

You can see that the power to master your mind isn't quite as easy to obtain as it would seem. To some degree we're victims of the biological processes of our brains. But we aren't animals, we're humans, so we have the power to conquer this basic biological process because we have consciousness; we have the freedom of choice, of freewill.

I may not be able to convince myself that elephants are pink, but I can, in time, with repeated affirmations, change many of my beliefs to my own liking. I have the power to shape my own thoughts — as do you.

But what good is it to change what you believe? Why does it even matter if you possess an exceptional ability to alter your own thoughts and ways of thinking? Does the physical world change to meet your own perception of reality?

This is where things get interesting. I won't answer you outright with a "Yes," because if I did, you'd likely stop reading this book and throw it in the trash bin. Of course, your physical reality isn't molded entirely by your thoughts and beliefs...right?

Well, before I answer that question, let's take a step back. Let's think about how the physical world is actually altered. Suppose there's a block on a table and you'd like that block to be moved to another location. If you don't believe it's possible, you won't even try. But if you do believe it's possible and you believe that you can move your hand, pick up the block, and place it in a location off the table, then you can use your mind to control your body to perform the actions. Technically, what you believe does have the power to shape your reality—it's just an indirect shaping that requires the use of your body.

It's a mystery how consciousness is able to send signals to our nervous systems to move our limbs. Sure, we know how the chemical and physical process works, but we don't know what sparks it. We don't know how the intangible minds we all possess are able to directly manipulate the physical world—how we actually fire that first neuron.

Now, I'm not naïve; I know that plenty of people will tell you that we indeed do know how this happens: that we're just bags of chemicals interacting with our environment, forever on autopilot, a chain of chemical reactions that are completely based on the circumstances of our environments. But if you believe this is true, how is it, then, that you're able to make the choice to read this book? How is it that I'm able to write it? Either a complex set of chain reactions made both of the actions inevitable—neither of us had a choice, we're just along for the ride—or there's something else, something that we can't identify that gives us ... freewill, the power of choice.

The mind and body connection

When I use the words mind and body, I'm defining the mind as the nonphysical part of your body. Whether you call it a spirit or a mechanical mechanism of consciousness, it's distinct from the lower functions of the body, including the brain.

This distinction is important, because when I say that the mind influences the body, I also mean that it influences your brain. We don't have to look far to prove this. The placebo effect, in which the brain thinks it's receiving some drug but actually gets a sugar pill or some other substitute, is well documented. Just like Dumbo's feather gave him the power of flight, your mind can influence your body in ways that you don't have conscious control over.

Because we know that our minds are capable of manipulating the universe through the power of thought, realized as action through our bodies, we also know that what we believe or what we think has the ability to influence our physical reality.

In the most literal sense, this means that what you think becomes reality—at least as far as it's within the power of your body and mind to make it so. This principle is embodied in many different forms and philosophies. One popular one is the law of attraction that states that "like attracts like." If you think negative thoughts, negative results will result and vice versa—but more on that in the next chapter.

You may have also heard of the popular book by Rhonda Byrne, *The Secret* (Atria Books/Beyond Words, 2006), which is a bit too mystical and hyped for my taste, but still hits on an important truth that has been revealed in many ways in the past and will continue to be reinvented and discovered in the future: the same basic truth that people who are able to change their beliefs and control their thoughts through active mindfulness are able to bring into reality that which they think about.

I really don't mean to get all mystical on you here. I'm a practical person; thus I believe there's a practical explanation for much of the way this mechanism works, but at the same time I won't pretend that there isn't a somewhat mystical component to it that can't be ignored.

Your beliefs become your thoughts,
Your thoughts become your words,
Your words become your actions,
Your actions become your habits,
Your habits become your values,
Your values become your destiny.

— Mahatma Gandhi

Regardless of how the mechanism works, it's important to understand that what you think in no small way influences and shapes the reality you live in. You don't even need to read this chapter to see the truth in this statement. Simply look around you.

When you think about the people you interact with every day, do you notice certain patterns of thinking that result in certain patterns of behavior and results? Do you know many successful people who maintain a negative attitude about life and lack a personal conviction and belief in themselves and others? Do you see people in your life who are constantly victims, but not due to any external force—although they constantly claim it to be so? Even when you reflect on your own life, how often has the thought you've feared the most or worried about excessively somehow defied all odds to actually come true?

If you truly want to shape the direction of your life and control it, you have to learn to harness the power of your mind, the power of thought. Regardless of whether or not I've convinced you about the mind and body connection in this chapter, if you at least believe in the slightest degree that your mindset and beliefs can have a positive or negative impact on your life, the next couple of chapters will offer you some practical advice on how you can shape your mindset to be the shape most productive for your growth.

Taking action
- Look for connections between the mind and body. Try to find instances in your own life where what you've thought has influenced your reality in either positive or negative ways.
- What was your mindset the last time you experienced a great success?
- What was your mindset the last time you encountered a major failure?

66

Having the right mental attitude: Rebooting

Let me ask you a question: would you classify your thoughts as mainly positive or negative? This goes beyond being labeled as an optimist or pessimist. There are plenty of optimists who outwardly expect and hope for the best, yet internally harbor all kinds of negative thoughts and emotions that directly sabotage their efforts.

It turns out there's actually scientific evidence to support the idea that positive thinking—being more than just an outward optimist—can improve your health, increase your lifespan, and provide all kinds of other benefits in your life. And—perhaps more importantly—the converse, negative thinking, can have the complete opposite effect. Thinking negatively can actually harm you and hamper your efforts to succeed in life (see http://simpleprogrammer.com/ss-negative-thinking).

This chapter is all about having the right mental attitude. We'll look into what it actually means to have a positive attitude, why it's so important for your well-being, and how to develop a positive attitude so powerful that it's actually infectious.

What is positivity?

I'm sure you probably are aware of what it means to have a positive attitude, but the phrase is thrown around so often that it starts to lose its meaning. Besides, if your attitude is generally negative—which, let's face it, is the case for most of us—it doesn't hurt to have a gentle reminder of what exactly it means to be positive and why it's so important.

Many people outright reject the idea of positive thinking, because they're convinced that unrealistic optimism is destructive. Often I hear the phrase "I am realistic" thrown around in opposition to the idea that one should fill their heads with visions of rainbows, unicorns, and tropical beaches.

On the contrary, I'd say that positive thinking isn't in contradiction with being a realist. In fact, positive thinking, applied, is the ultimate form of realism because it's the belief that you have the power to change your reality, that you aren't a victim of your circumstances.

The root of positive thinking is this belief that you're greater than your mere circumstances. It's the view that there are good things ahead, because regardless of the situation, you have the power to change and alter your own future. It's the supreme belief in the power of human achievement as a powerful force in the world. It's the belief that you can somehow tap into that power, that that power lies within you — perhaps dormant — but no less real.

The positive attitude comes from an accumulation of these kinds of thoughts that over time have the power to change you from the inside out. When you possess a positive attitude, you don't live in a fantasy world separated from reality, but instead live in an optimal world — one where you see the best possible future — which you seek to bring into reality.

On a more practical level, positive thinking is all about choosing to think good thoughts rather than bad thoughts. Every situation that you encounter in life is open to your own interpretations. Situations don't present themselves as "good" or "bad." You interpret a situation and decide whether it's good or bad. A person with a positive attitude tends to interpret more situations as good than bad, not because those situations are objectively one or the other, but because they recognize that it's within their power to choose.

Here's a story I have always liked that illustrates this point better than I can. I don't know the origin of it:

There once was a farmer. One day the farmer's only horse broke out of the corral and ran away. The farmer's neighbors, all hearing of the horse running away, came to the farmer's house to view the corral. As they stood there, the neighbors all said, "Oh, what bad luck!" The farmer replied, "How do you know this is bad?"

About a week later, the horse returned, bringing with it a whole herd of wild horses, which the farmer and his son quickly corralled. The neighbors, hearing of the corralling of the horses, came to see for themselves. As they stood there looking at the corral filled with horses, the neighbors said, "Oh what good luck!" The farmer replied, "How do you know this is good?"

A couple of weeks later, the farmer's son's leg was badly broken when he was thrown from one of their new wild horses that he was trying to tame. A few days later the broken leg became infected and the son became delirious with fever. The neighbors, all hearing of the incident, came to see the son. As they stood there, the neighbors said, "Oh what bad luck!" The farmer replied, "How do you know this is bad?"

At that same time in China, a war broke out between two rival warlords. In need of more soldiers, a captain came to the village to conscript young men to fight in the war. When the captain came to take the farmer's son, he found the young man with a broken leg, delirious with fever. Knowing there was no way the son could fight, the captain left him there. A few days later, the son's fever broke. The neighbors, hearing of the son not being taken to fight in the war and of his return to good health, all came to see him. As they stood there, each one said, "Oh what good luck!" The farmer replied, "How do you know this is good?"

The positive effects of positivity

Remember when I said that positive thinking had some real, tangible, scientifically proven effects on your life? I wasn't kidding. Here's a list of confirmed effects that positive thinking has been shown to have. These results were derived from actual scientific studies (see http://simpleprogrammer.com/ss-negative-thinking for more information):

- Friendship development
- Marital satisfaction
- Higher incomes
- Better physical health
- Longer lifespans

These scientifically provable results are enough to convince me that I should find a cure for the Mondays, but there are other results that are more difficult to prove with scientific studies. I know for a fact that my attitude directly affects my performance at work. I've measured it in terms of my own productivity. I know that when I have a positive attitude, I'm more ready to deal with any obstacles I face and to see them as challenges to overcome rather than negative circumstances thrust upon me.

Besides, if there were no other reason to think positive than that it feels good, would it be worth it? Doesn't it feel better to experience positive emotions rather than negative ones? Isn't that really the goal of our lives when we take out all the mortgages, aspirations to greatness, soccer practices, television shows, and late-night snacking? Don't we just want to be happy? If so, why fight it?

How to reboot your attitude

Merely wanting to be positive isn't enough. You can desperately want to have a positive attitude while at the same time condemning yourself for the hopelessness of your aspiration.

Remember how I said that you can't easily change what you believe? Well, it's true, you can't very easily change your view on the world from a negative one to a positive one—although, strangely enough, it seems it's a much easier path in the other direction.

Change your thoughts

If you want to change your attitude, you must change your thoughts. If you want to change your thoughts, you must change your patterns of thoughts. Your patterns of thoughts are defined by your habits, and thus we go back to the staple way of changing anything significant in your life—develop a habit for it.

But how does one develop the habit of positive thinking? Much in the same way that one develops any habit—through a meaningful and committed conscious repetition until subconscious controls take over.

You may not have the power to respond to an event with a positive thought. It's difficult to will yourself to accept that rear-ending that car in front of you when you fumbled to check a message on your phone was "all for the good" and that "it could have been worse." You may even be tempted to shout an explicative and think…gasp…a negative thought.

But you do have the power to create positive thoughts, at will, when you choose. Right now you can stop what you're doing and think a positive thought. Go ahead, pretend like we're all sitting around at the Thanksgiving table, and think a happy thought. Easy enough. The key is to actively and purposefully try and do this throughout the day. The key is to remind yourself that even though you might not have control over your immediate reactions to any situation, you do have control over how you consciously choose to think about the experience.

The more you put into practice this kind of thinking, the more you will yourself to conjure up positive pictures and look for silver linings, the more it will become a habit. In time you'll be more likely to respond to any incident or possible misfortune in a positive way. You can train your brain to view things from a positive perspective rather than a negative one.

Meditation

I'll admit that I'm not a big meditator, although, I'd like to devote some serious time to developing it as a habit. Some studies have showed that people who meditate are more likely to experience positive emotions, so you also might try meditation as a way to increase your positive mojo.

Play more

I'm sure you've heard the adage "All work and no play make Johnny a dull boy." It turns out it also makes him quite negative and resentful. I personally can trace many of my negative emotions and lines of thinking to forgetting to play. I find that when I take some time to have fun, it's much easier to be positive. Probably not a big shocker, but something to consider as well.

Books

I'll also recommend some great books in chapter 69 that will help you to develop a positive attitude. If you're looking for something right now, try *The Power of Positive Thinking* by Norman Vincent Peale (Touchstone; Reprint edition, 2003).

The point is that positive thinking doesn't come by chance and it isn't something you can force overnight. It takes a concerted effort to move your mind in a positive direction. But it's an effort worth undertaking. Not only will you be more likely to live a longer, healthier, and more successful life, but you'll definitely live a more enjoyable life and you'll probably make life more enjoyable for the people around you as well.

Taking action

- ◎ Capture your thoughts. Writing helps you to understand what's going on in your head and to focus your mind on what you want it to be focused on. Keep a thought journal this week. Every time you get a chance, write down what you're thinking about and whether it's positive or negative. Make these entries anytime something significant happens in your day. Also create entries throughout the day on somewhat of a regular interval.

- ◎ Examine your thought journal. Is it mostly filled with positive expressions of thought or negative ones? Where do the negative ones derive from? What about the positive ones?

- ◎ Commit to actively trying to control your thoughts and to summon as many positive ones as possible. When a situation happens to you, take a moment to realize the universe isn't against you and is rather ambivalent to you—you'll be less likely to take things personally that way. Then force yourself to find the silver lining. Don't merely remove negative thoughts, but replace them with positive ones.

67

Building a positive self-image: Programming your brain

It isn't enough to think happy thoughts and have a good attitude. Sure, you'll see much more success by changing your attitudes from negative ones to positive ones—not to mention health benefits—but to truly be successful at what you wish to accomplish in life, you have to learn how to program your own brain to achieve your goals.

> *People who are unable to motivate themselves must be content with mediocrity, no matter how impressive their other talents.*
>
> —Andrew Carnegie

Your true battle is against mediocrity—and it begins in the brain. What you think about yourself has an amazing power to both limit you and fuel you forward.

In this chapter, we'll examine how you can program your own brain to create a positive self-image that will allow you to set your brain on auto-pilot to achieve your goals.

What is self-image?

Self-image is how you see yourself when you strip away all of the things you've been told about yourself and get rid of all the lies and deceptions you may use to trick yourself into feeling adequate.

It's quite possible to not even truly be aware of your real self-image, because to a large degree it's buried deep within your subconscious mind. You can tell yourself and others all kinds of half-truths about what you think about yourself, but you can't fool your subconscious mind. Deep down, we all have an image of ourselves that's the ultimate reflection of our brain's view of the reality of ourselves.

This self-image is powerful, because your brain tends to not allow you to do anything that would violate its assessment of self. This places artificial limitations on you that are difficult to overcome, simply because you may not even be aware that they exist.

Consider the boy who believes he's no good at pitching a baseball. Does he ever become a great pitcher? Most likely he doesn't. He certainly never does unless he learns to change his self-image to see himself in another light. His brain places a mental restriction on itself that causes him to conform to its view of his self-image.

You probably have similar limitations that you may not have even noticed—you may have taken them for granted as unchangeable, implacable, facts—just the way life is. Are you clumsy? Lazy? Not good at math? Bad with people? Do you have a short attention span? Perhaps you're shy or reserved?

While all of these things might seem like character traits that are as much part of your DNA as your height or eye color, they're not. There are certain physical characteristics that you can't change about yourself, but many of the other things you imagine to be true about yourself are manifestations of your own self-image that you've acquired, in many cases by random chance.

Perhaps when you were little you hid behind your parents at a dinner party and you heard words like "Little Johnny is a shy boy." Up to that point you may have not been shy at all, but because of that one moment, your brain suddenly latched onto the idea and implanted that into your self-image.

Your self-image is difficult to change

It turns out you do have the power to alter your own self-image. You've already been introduced to the idea in chapter 16, "Fake It Till You Make It." The concept behind faking it until you make it is that if you repeatedly do a thing and act as if you are already what you want to be, you'll eventually become what you want to be.

It seems like a simple concept—and to be completely honest, it is—but we hardly ever think in those terms and sometimes it can be difficult to believe that we can actually change the characteristics about ourselves that we believe are intrinsically part of us.

It's almost as if we have some sick, sadistic pull that causes us to embrace our weaknesses and limitations as a critical piece of who we are. Ask a person who has a short temper if he'd like to change, and there is a pretty good chance he'll say "no." To him, it's as if you're asking him to give up an arm or a leg, because he believes so deeply that being short-tempered is an intrinsic part of himself and releasing himself from that shackle would be tantamount to the highest treason he could commit against himself. That's how powerful your subconscious mind is in holding onto your view of self-image.

But the truth of the matter is you aren't your propensity to feel awkward in social situations or to lose your temper at the drop of a hat. You're not those things any more than you're the clothes that you wear. In fact, the clothes that you wear can have a dramatic impact on your perception of self. You may have noticed that you feel and act differently when you're wearing shorts and flip-flops than you do when you're dressed up in a suit.

Altering your self-image—if only temporarily—isn't all that difficult. The difficulty is in believing that it's possible and in having the desire to actually go through with it. If you can accept that you're able to change some of the core beliefs you hold about yourself, then you'll be able to alter your self-image to your own liking.

Imagine the power of being able to be anything you want. Imagine being able to go from a shy, socially awkward person to a social butterfly, charming and dazzling without a care in the world. Imagine being able to become the leader you dreamed of being or actually becoming good at sports.

It's all possible, and I know it for a fact, because I've altered my own self-image in many ways. When I was younger, I always saw myself as a dork. I won't say a nerd, because although I thought myself to be smart, I never really studied or took an active interest in academics. I was also socially awkward, and I had the tendency to get picked on and was extremely shy—to the point of being afraid to make a simple phone call to talk to a stranger.

Something happened around my sophomore year in high school. I can't tell you exactly what it was, because I don't know. It may have been blind luck or frustration that caused me to have the thought that I could decide who I wanted to become and then simply become it.

The transformation wasn't immediate, but it was rapid. I threw out my old clothes and bought a new wardrobe fitting for the person I wanted to be. I started lifting weights. I joined wrestling and track. (I had never really played sports much before, because I thought myself to be unathletic.) I decided that I'd no longer be shy, so I pretended to not be shy. I forced myself into awkward situations. I constantly reaffirmed and told myself who I now was. I held a mental picture in my head of myself, but in my new form.

Amazingly, it stuck. I still became a computer programmer, of course, but after high school I went into modeling and acting. I went from shy to the complete opposite of shy. I went from unathletic to a person who runs and lifts weights every single week. And even to this day, I'm refining the picture of the person I want to be and taking control of my self-image to have it work for me instead of against me.

Reprogramming your brain

How can you set out to purposely reprogram your brain? To change your self-image like I did so long ago? The formula is relatively simple. It just takes time and persistence to execute it properly.

It begins with having a clear picture of what you want. Your brain has an amazing ability to seek out whatever goals you put before it. You just have to imagine those goals clearly enough for your brain to be able to guide you down the path you need to go.

Picture the ideal you. Set in your mind a firm picture of what you'd like to be if there were no constraints placed upon you. Imagine yourself more confident, walking boldly into rooms. Imagine yourself running and leaping with grace instead of tripping over your own feet. Imagine yourself inspiring others or being highly fashionable. Don't place any artificial limits on yourself except those of physical characteristics that could obviously not be changed. (For example, it does no good to imagine yourself taller, unless doing so would make you feel more confident. Just don't expect it to make you grow.)

Once you have this picture set in your mind, your next task is to start acting "as if." Act "as if" you were already what you desired to become. Talk, speak, dress, and brush your teeth like the person you want to be. Don't pay attention to reality. Don't pay attention to what people say about your "changes"; instead, pretend like you're already at your desired goal and that your behavior is a natural extension of this new personality.

You'll also want to give yourself plenty of positive affirmations that plant the seeds of this new way of thinking deeply into your subconscious mind. It turns out that positive affirmations aren't just mumbo-jumbo that crazy self-help people spout. Your brain will actually start to believe something if you tell yourself it enough times. Remember how we talked about how difficult it is to change your beliefs? You can change them if you're persistent and deliver a consistent message.

I'd recommend finding quotes and images that remind you of the new mental state you want to have. Fill your day with positive affirmations that confirm and reinforce your new beliefs. Spend time mentally visualizing yourself as what you want to be. Many sports athletes do the exact same process to improve their performance. Before competing in a major event, they'll do a mental rehearsal. They'll actually play the event in their mind and see themselves succeeding. Studies have shown this kind of fake practice can actually be as beneficial as real practice. I read a story about how a professional football team, the Seattle Seahawks, have meditation sessions where the players are told to visualize success.

Most importantly, though, watch what you say. What you say about yourself, you believe. Your subconscious mind is still that impressionable child hearing your voice and it believes what you say. If you say you're clumsy or forgetful enough times, your subconscious will believe it.

Taking action

- Make a list of all the things you are, good and bad. Try to think not only about how you perceive yourself, but also how you think other people perceive you. This list might not be totally accurate—many aspects of your self-image are buried deep in your subconscious—but it will give you a good place to start.

- How many of those aspects on that list do you perceive as unchangeable? Why? Think about whether or not those things are permanent or just limitations you've placed on yourself because of what you believe.

- Try to change at least one aspect of your self-image that you find to be negative. Use the advice in this chapter to do it. Try the "fake it till you make it" approach and use positive affirmations to reinforce your new belief.

68

Love and relationships: Computers can't hold your hand

I debated whether or not I should include this chapter, because I'm not a relationship expert, and this book isn't really about finding love. But I thought that I wouldn't be true to the software developer's life manual if I didn't at least address this topic.

There are so many things to say about love and relationships that it would be pretty difficult to cover it all in a single chapter, so I've decided to condense down this chapter to the most important and most relevant issues that are likely to plague someone in the software development world—male or female.

Why software developers sometimes have a hard time finding love

I'll fall back to the stereotypical software developer again to try and address this issue. Of course, I recognize, like all stereotypes, that the particular stereotype of a nerdy, socially awkward software developer might not apply to you, but if it does—or if at least part of it does—you'll probably relate to some of what I have to talk about here.

Forever alone

There's a popular meme on the internet called "forever alone." It basically signifies this idea of feeling like you're alone and that you'll never find "love." In my experience, many software developers, especially in their younger years, can relate to this meme.

Unfortunately, identifying with this meme and feeling might actually be exacerbating the problem. It's kind of weird how human love and relationships work. It's really a game of cat and mouse. At any given time, one person is chasing and another is being chased. As long as the sides switch occasionally, there isn't a problem. But when one person is always doing the chasing, the other person tends to keep running further and further away.

It's the chasing too hard that's often the problem that many people face. When you go out there and you try too hard, you end up reeking of desperation. That desperation causes repulsion that tends to cause a nice hit to self-esteem, causing further desperation. It's a vicious cycle that many people are stuck in and don't know how to get out of.

Many people in this situation tend to wear their heart on their sleeve. They start projecting their feelings of pain and loneliness to the rest of the world. "If only they could feel my pain and realize how they are hurting me, then they'd understand." You've seen those Facebook posts where people make a desperate plea for attention and compassion by letting the world know how sad and alone they are.

As I'm sure you can figure out, this kind of behavior has the opposite effect of what is intended. When you tell the world that you're weak and fragile, people tend to avoid you. To put it bluntly, it's not an attribute that anyone really finds attractive.

Understanding the game

Love is a game. It's true. No matter how hard you try to opt out of the system, you can't do it. Many people think "I don't want to play the game. I'm just going to be myself and be honest about how I feel." While I can understand this sentiment, because you're reading this chapter, I have to ask you how that's working out for you.

Now, don't get me wrong. I'm not advocating dishonesty and being a sleazebag, but you also might not want to be too forthcoming and direct in your actions if you're trying to attract a member of the opposite sex. What I mean by this is that you might need to realize that you're indeed playing a game and think a little bit about the strategy you're employing.

For example—and I'll use examples from the male perspective, because that's the only one I have—you might approach a girl you find attractive who you've had your eye on for many weeks and say "I love you. I've loved you since the moment I first saw you." Now, this might seem like a romantic thing to say, pouring your heart out to your newfound love, but it's pretty likely you'll get a negative reaction from that course of action. In terms of the cat and mouse game, it's not very strategic.

I don't have to be a psychologist to tell you that, in general, we want what we can't have and also what other people find desirable. The more available you seem to be, the more desperate, the less likely you are to be wanted. I'm sure you experienced this in the playground in school. Did you ever run around chasing other kids trying to get them to play with you? Life is just a big playground. If you want to make someone run away, chase them.

Sitting down, doing nothing, and waiting for your love to come to you isn't a good strategy, either. You could be waiting a pretty long time. Instead, the solution is to project confidence in your actions and to approach someone in an easy-going but self-assured manner. "I feel good about who I am, I don't need you, but I think you're interesting and I'd like to get to know you better." (Although I wouldn't use those words verbatim, either.)

The trick is that you have to actually mean it. You have to have enough confidence in yourself to really believe that you don't need another person to make you happy. You have to really believe that you add a benefit to other people's lives by being in them. This doesn't mean you think you're God's gift to…fill in the blank, but it does mean that you have enough respect for yourself to only show up where you're wanted and to only want to be with people who want to be with you.

This doesn't mean that success is guaranteed—it isn't—but you'll have a much better shot at finding your true love if you can be aware of the subtle psychology of run and chase that seems to govern most relationships. And this doesn't just apply to love. It applies to all kinds of relationships. Be a desperate and needy kind of friend and you'll likely find yourself friendless. Approach a job interview as someone starving on the street, looking for a handout, and you'll find the same kind of revulsion.

So, all I have to do is be confident, right?

I know, I know, easier said than done, right? It's not exactly easy to suddenly decide to be confident. It's also pretty difficult to fake confidence. So what is a guy—or a gal—to do?

You might start off by going to the two previous chapters and work on programming your mind to be the positive kind of confident person you want to be. There's no reason why you can't become a truly confident person—it just may take some time and work.

You also may want to pay attention to the section on fitness, because getting fit is a great way to build your confidence without even trying. I've seen many people transform mentally as a by-product of their physical changes by lifting weights and trimming down.

Also, consider what it means to be confident and what it looks like. There's an element of bravery involved. If you're willing to approach someone you find attractive right away, without debating and delaying, it shows a great deal of confidence. In some circles this idea has been dubbed the "three-second rule." Basically, the idea is that from the moment you see someone you'd like to meet, you have three seconds to execute on that impulse; otherwise your hesitation will project a lack of confidence and things are more likely to go south. I'll admit, this isn't exactly an easy rule to follow, but what have you really got to lose by trying it out? Which brings us to the next and final thing I have to say on this topic.

It's a numbers game

People are strange. They like all kinds of things. It only takes a few searches on the internet turning up some really weird results to figure out that's true. Why am I saying this? Because it means that no matter how strange you are, no matter what flaws you perceive yourself to have, even if you don't have a perfect smile and chiseled abs, there is probably someone out there who'd like you—a lot. In fact, in this whole wide world, there are probably many potential matches for you, as bizarre as you may be or not.

What this really means is that it's all a numbers game. Too many people make the mistake of picking out a single person and putting them on a pedestal, obsessing over that one perfect girl or guy who would finally make them "happy." It's not only ridiculous to assume that there's just that one person out there, but it's not strategic either. Your odds are much better if you widen your search.

We'll talk about this more in chapter 70, "Facing Failure Head-on," but don't be afraid to fail. Have lots of failures. Get rejected. Big deal. What is the worst that could happen? You've got to be like that door-to-door salesman who is willing to have a hundred doors slammed in their face to make one sale, knowing that all you need to do each day is make that one sale.

Besides, all those rejections eventually lead you to that one person who does want to be with you—which is a lot better than being with someone who doesn't. And isn't that the whole point anyway?

Taking action

- Think about some of the ways that you may be projecting feelings of desperation. Take a look at your communications with others, your social media, how you interact with your friends. Do your words and expressions show confidence or neediness?
- What attributes—nonphysical—do you find attractive? What is it that you find repulsive?
- How wide is your net? Are you giving yourself enough chances to find your "true love?" Get out there and crash and burn a few times just to see what it feels like. Once you recognize that it's not that bad, you'll be able to approach people with more confidence, because you won't fear the outcome.
- Take real steps to improve your self-confidence by doing something like starting a fitness program or involving yourself in some other activity that will make you feel better about yourself.

69

My personal success book list

There have been many excellent books that have greatly influenced what I believe and how I behave. I try to spend at least some time every day reading or listening to the audio version of a book that will improve my life in some way.

When I first started my career, I spent a large amount of time reading software-development–focused books. Now, I spend more of my time reading books that have a wider application.

I've made it a habit of asking any famous or highly successful person who I've met what one book he or she would recommend that everyone should read. Through this quest, I've uncovered many impactful books that have literally changed my life.

In this chapter, I'm going to give you the list of the best and most influential books I've ever read—both on the software development and non-software development side.

Self-help and inspirational books

The War of Art by Steven Pressfield (Black Irish Books, 2002)

I'll start with one of my favorite books of all time. This book gave words to a frustration I long held in regards to work and why it's so difficult to just sit down and do it.

In this book, Pressfield identifies this mysterious force we all encounter when we sit down to try and do anything meaningful. He says this force, resistance, is the secret and ambivalent destroyer of all of our attempts to traverse from a lower calling to a higher one.

Just by identifying this common enemy within us, we start to gain power over it. If you're having trouble with procrastination or just finding the motivation to go forward and do what you know you should be doing, you'll find this book immensely useful.

How to Win Friends and Influence People by Dale Carnegie (Reprint, Gallery Books, 1998)

This book is another one of the most influential books I've ever read. This book changed my personal views in many ways and has helped me achieve success in dealing with people that I hadn't thought possible before.

Before I read this book, I was a staunch believer in negative reinforcement to modify the behavior of others. I felt compelled to enforce my own strict disciplinarian standards on others. I believed that when someone was wrong, it was important to tell them so; that the best way to motivate a person was through the threat of punishment.

After reading this book, my views changed 180 degrees. I realized that negative reinforcement was almost completely futile—that the only way to get people to do what you wanted was to compel them to want to do it.

If there is any book on this list you must read, this is the one. I firmly believe everyone should read this book. I've read it at least a dozen times, and every time I go back and read it again, I gain a new insight.

Think and Grow Rich by Napoleon Hill (Wilder Publications, 2007)

This first time I tried to read this book, I put it down in frustration. The second time, I got a little further, but again thought the book was a bit too crazy for my liking. Finally, after speaking to multiple highly successful people who recommended this book—some who completely attributed their success to it—I decided to read it again.

This book is a little strange. It basically purports that if you believe a thing and you hold onto and reinforce that belief, it will become reality. I'll warn you, there isn't much science to this approach. The book doesn't even try to come up with the science to explain it, but by whatever means this works, I've seen it work in my life and many others will swear by it as well.

The idea of a mastermind group actually originates from this book. There are many other important concepts in this book that will help you to learn how to change your own beliefs, which may have a powerful effect on your life.

Psycho-Cybernetics by Maxwell Maltz (Reprint, Pocket Books, 1989)

In many ways this book reminds me of *Think and Grow Rich*, but a scientific version of it. This book was written by a plastic surgeon who discovered that when he changed people's faces, it actually changed their personalities. This caused him to do research into self-image and to discover some important ways that our self-image has the power to completely change our lives for the good or the bad.

I found this book to have some very good insights on how the mind works and how it affects our bodies. This book is full of all kinds of practical applications of methods to change your attitude, your self-image, and your beliefs for the positive.

The Power of Positive Thinking by Norman Vincent Peale (Reprint, Touchstone, 2003)

This book is a bit religious, so be forewarned, but the overall message of this book is very powerful. The idea that positive thinking can have a profound impact on your life is one that I adamantly subscribe to. If you're trying to develop a more positive attitude, this book can certainly help you do that.

Atlas Shrugged by Ayn Rand (Reprint, Signet, 2005)

You'll either love this book or hate it, but either way, it will make you think. This book is fiction—and it's long at around 1,200 pages—but it asks some very serious questions about life, economics, and work.

Software development books

Code Complete by Steve McConnell (Microsoft Press; 2nd edition, 2004)

This book completely changed the way I wrote code. After I read this book was the first time I felt like I was writing and understood what good code was. The examples in this book are primarily written in C++, but the concepts transcend any individual language.

This book is a complete guide to writing good code and structuring that code at a very low level. While many software development books focus on higher-level design, this is one of the only books I've found that focuses on details like how to name variables and structure the actual code inside of an algorithm.

If I ever own a software development shop, this book will be required reading by all developers I hire. This has definitely been the most influential software development book I've ever read.

Clean Code: A Handbook of Agile Software Craftmanship by Robert Martin (Prentice Hall, 2008)

Reading this book was an absolute joy. *Code Complete* taught me how to write good code; *Clean Code* refined that knowledge and helped me understand how to take that knowledge to a complete codebase and design.

This book is another book I consider required reading for any software developer. The concepts in this book will help you to become a better developer and to appreciate why simple and understandable is better than clever.

Head First Design Patterns by Eric Freeman, Elisabeth Robson, Bert Bates, and Kathy Sierra (O'Reilly Media, 2004)

It might seem a bit strange that I'd recommend this book over the classic *Design Patterns* book, but this book does an excellent job of making design patterns approachable and understandable.

Don't get me wrong, the *Design Patterns* book is a great book and introduced the idea of the classic design patterns in software development, but this book does a much better job of explaining them. If you're going to read one design patterns book, read this one.

Investing

The Millionaire Real Estate Investor by Gary Keller (McGraw-Hill, 2005)

If I had to recommend one book on real estate investing, this would be it. This book explains exactly why real estate investing is such a good idea and how to get rich from it, and it gives you an exact plan for doing so.

This book contains plenty of charts that show you exactly how real estate investment pays off over the long run and it isn't filled with a lot of "fluff."

Rich Dad, Poor Dad by Robert Kiyosaki (Demco Media, 2000)

This was another life-changing book for me that changed the way I looked at money and finance. This book changed my view of how money works and what it means to have a job and work for someone else. After reading this book I clearly understood how important it is to create assets and to reduce your expenses.

My only complaint with this book is that it doesn't really tell you how. Still, there's valuable advice in this book—and Kiyosaki's entire *Rich Dad* series—and I'd highly recommend it.

No-Hype Options Trading: Myths, Realities, and Strategies That Really Work by Kerry Given (Wiley, 2011)

Lots of financial books promise ridiculous returns and make outrageous claims, but this one doesn't. Instead, it presents the facts and helps you realistically understand how options trading works and some practical strategies you can employ to make money, along with the inherent risk those strategies will incur. I'd highly recommend this book if you're looking into getting into options trading, or just want to understand it better.

70

Facing failure head-on

Fall down seven times, get up eight.

—Japanese Proverb

As we approach the end of this book, I want to give you one last piece of advice that I think has the potential to benefit you more than anything else in this book. You could have all the skills in life that should make you successful, but if you lack one important skill, perseverance, it will all be worthless, because at the first sign of trouble, you'll give up—and we all will face some amount of trouble in our lives.

On the other hand, you could be severely undereducated about your profession and have horrible social skills and financial knowledge, but if you're incredibly persistent, it's my belief you'll eventually find your way.

As a software developer, this trait will be especially important to you, because you're likely to face a large number of difficulties in your life and career. Developing software is difficult—that's likely one of the reasons you're drawn to it. In this chapter, we'll talk about the importance of persistence and why it's critical to develop the ability to face failure with the unflinching face of determination.

Why are we so afraid of failure, anyway?

The fear of failure seems to be a built-in instinct for most people. We prefer to do what we're good at. We avoid the things that show our incompetence or lack of skill. We seem to have this innate fear of failure.

I even see it in my three-year-old daughter. My wife is teaching her to read, and she's making great progress, but you can tell when she reads a word that she's unsure of; she'll say that word very softly. The words she knows she shouts out with confidence. Give her a challenging word or some other task that isn't quite matched with her abilities, and, instead of trying, she has the inclination to give up. "You read it, Mommy."

This same phenomenon is magnified in most adults. Most people, when faced with a significant challenge or the immediate and likely prospect of failure, will avoid that situation. This response makes sense when turning down the option to fight with a 300-pound gorilla of a guy at a nightclub who is likely to knock your block off, but it doesn't make much sense when faced with the task of speaking on a stage or learning a new programming language—there's no real harm that can come to you from failing in those cases.

If I had to guess why most people are so afraid of failure, I'd have to say that it's probably based around the idea of protecting our fragile egos. Perhaps we're afraid to fail because we take failure a bit too personally; we think that our failure in a particular area is a reflection of our own personal worth.

I think this fear of bruising our egos is also aided by the simple misunderstanding about the nature of failure. We tend to think, and to be taught, that failure is a bad thing. We don't view failure in a positive light, but instead think of it as the end. The word failure itself implies a dead-end path, a final destination, not a temporary bump in the road to success. We picture in our heads an island where people who have failed are sent. They sit there on the beach hopelessly downtrodden with no hope of rescue; their lives are failures; they are failures.

Even though we know failure isn't the end, we seem to feel like it is. We tend to take ourselves a bit too seriously and attach some pretty heavy stakes to messing up. Because we aren't trained to view failure as the path to success—in many cases the only path—we avoid failure at any cost.

Failure isn't defeat

Failure isn't the same thing as defeat. Failure is temporary, defeat is permanent. Failure is something that happens to you—something that you can't completely control. Defeat is something that you choose—a permanent acceptance of failure.

The first step in letting go of the fear of failure is to realize that failure isn't the end—unless you choose to make it so. Life is difficult, you'll get knocked down, but it's up to you to decide whether or not you're going to get back up again. It's up to you to decide that most things worth having are worth fighting for. It's up to you to realize the joy and enjoyment of an accomplishment that comes, in a great part, from the difficulty and struggle of achieving it.

Have you ever played a videogame that was really difficult? Remember that rewarding feeling when you finally beat that final boss? You may have failed many times along the way, but how good did it feel to finally succeed? Contrast this with that videogame that was equally difficult, but you entered a cheat code to give you infinite lives or make you invincible. How fun was that? Was there any joy in that accomplishment?

Continuing on with the videogame example, what would have happened if you threw down the controller in frustration the first time you died? Wasn't it to some degree the knowledge that you did fail so many times but finally succeeded that made the whole experience enjoyable? If that is the case, why do you avoid and regard failure in life as if it's a permanent state? You don't expect to pick up a videogame controller and beat a videogame perfectly without ever falling in a pit or getting singed by a fireball, so why do you expect to go through life without experiencing failure?

Failure is the road to success

Instead of fearing failure, embrace it. Not only is failure not the same as defeat, but it's also a necessary step on the path to success. Few worthwhile things that you'll do or accomplish in life will be done without at least some small failure along the way.

The problem is that we learn to view failure in such a negative light. When you go to school and you get an F on an assignment, it isn't viewed as progress. You aren't taught to think that failure was a learning experience that would take you closer to your goal. Instead, you're taught to see it as a wholly negative thing.

Real life doesn't work that way. I'm not saying you shouldn't study for you exams and that you should strive to get Fs for the learning experience and character-building opportunities, but what I'm saying is that in real life failures are usually necessary milestones that take us closer and closer to eventual success.

In the real world, when you fail at something, you learn from that experience and hopefully grow. Our brains are trained to work this way. If you've ever tried to learn how to juggle, or play baseball, or do any other physical activity that requires coordination, you know that you fail a lot before you succeed.

I remember when I was first learning to juggle. I'd throw three balls up in the air and all three of them would hit the ground—not a single one in my hand. I could have thrown my hands up and said, "I can't juggle," but for some reason I was persistent. I knew that other people had learned to juggle and that I could also learn, so I kept at it. After hundreds, perhaps thousands, of dropped balls, I eventually stopped failing. My brain made minor corrections over time and was learning from the repeated failures I was experiencing. I didn't control this process. All I had to do was keep trying—and to not be afraid to start trying in the first place.

Learn to embrace failure

Again, I'd have to say that if you take nothing else from this book, take the following advice: learn to embrace failure, to expect it, to accept it, and to be ready to face it head-on.

It isn't enough to just lose your fear of failure, but you should also be seeking out failure. You need to put yourself in situations where you're all but guaranteed to fail if you want to grow. We often stagnate because we stop doing things that are dangerous or challenging to us. We find a comfortable place in our lives, shut the doors to our cabin, batten down the hatches, and weather out the storm, never stepping back out into the rain.

Sometimes, though, you need to get a little wet. Sometimes you need to be willing to put yourself in an uncomfortable situation that will force you to grow. Sometimes you need to actively go out of your way to find those situations, knowing that the harder you steer your ship into failure, the stronger the wind of success will blow you in the opposite direction.

How do you embrace failure? How do you convince yourself to jump into that choppy sea? It starts with accepting failure as a part of life. You have to realize that you're going to face a lot of failure in your life and that for the most part it's unavoidable. You can't do everything perfectly the first time. You're going to make mistakes.

You also have to realize that it's okay to fail. It's okay to make mistakes. You can try to avoid them, but never at the cost of missing out on an opportunity just because you're afraid of the ego-crushing blow of failure. Once you realize that failure is okay, that failure doesn't define you but rather how you respond to failure does, you learn to stop fearing it so much.

Finally, I'd suggest overexposing yourself to it. Go and do things that make you uncomfortable. Earlier in this book we discussed the idea that you shouldn't be afraid to look like an idiot, and I'd say the same thing about failure. In fact, sometimes the two are deeply connected. Go out there and purposely put yourself in difficult situations that will inevitably result in some kind of failure. But the key is to not give up— let your failures fuel you forward, onward to success. Experience enough failures and the fear of failure itself will lose its power over you.

I'll leave you with these final words, in regards to failure, from *Think and Grow Rich* by Napoleon Hill:

> *Most great people have attained their greatest success just one step beyond their greatest failure.*

Taking action

○ How is the fear of failure holding you back? Think about all the activities in life that you'd like to do but you're afraid to do because of the temporary embarrassment or ego bruising of failure.

○ Make a commitment to do at least one thing that you've been avoiding because of your fear of failure. Don't do it half-heartedly, either. Many people "attempt" something knowing they're going to fail, and do so in a way that gives them the personal distance to not really feel like they failed because "they weren't really trying." Really try. Really fail.

71

Parting words

Well, this is it. We've finally come to the end of this book. I say we because I hope that reading it has been as much of an adventure for you as writing it has been for me. When I first set out to write this book, I had no idea how difficult it was to write a big, long book like this one. I just knew I wanted to write a book that would share some of the important lessons I've learned over my career as a software developer—not just the lessons about how to write good code and advance my career, but the things I've learned about being a better all-around human being. The lessons I've learned about how to maximize the value I get out of my life and how to provide a benefit to others at the same time.

I'm not a genius. I'm not even an old man reflecting back on his decades of life experience, giving you the benefit of 50 years of wisdom, so don't take what I have to say in this book as gospel. This book is really about me sharing my experience and the things that have made me successful so far in my life. Hopefully you find some of those things useful, even though you might not agree with all of them—and that's okay.

That's sort of the point of this book. You shouldn't take what anyone says as gospel. No one has a monopoly on the truth. Reality, to a large degree, is what you make of it. That doesn't mean that you can ignore blatant truths about the world and go about your daily business, but it does mean that you can decide what kind of life you want to live and how you want to live it. If you can learn the basic principles that govern things like success, finances, fitness, and your own mental state, you can use those principles to shape your reality.

Hopefully after reading this book, you've come to the conclusion that the narrow, straight path that you may have been told you have to live by—the one that tells you to get good grades, try not to mess up, go to college, get a job, and work for 50 years hoping to retire—isn't the only path you can go down. Sure, you can take that path if you want, but if you're reading this book, I assume that you think life is more than working a 9-to-5 job that you grow to hate.

Hopefully this book has made you realize that you have a world of opportunities at your disposal, from ways that you can manage your career to get more out of it, or even take it in a completely new direction, to ways that you can learn to actually build your own personal brand and market—allowing you to take your software development career to a level you never thought possible and to impact other people's lives at the same time.

Hopefully this book has taught you new ways to learn and absorb information and has given you the confidence to be part of something bigger than yourself—to not just learn things for the sake of learning them, but to share what you learn with other people who'd benefit from your knowledge, no matter where along the path you may happen to be.

Hopefully this book will inspire you to be more productive, to more carefully manage your time and make the best use of it, and to see the value in hard work and taking action—even when sometimes you feel like you lack the motivation to go on.

Hopefully this book has inspired you in some way to take better care of your health and fitness, to realize that you can actually get in shape, and that just because you may be a software developer, doesn't mean you can't also be an extremely fit and athletic person if you want to—or at the very least take active control of your health.

And finally, I hope this book has helped you realize how powerful and important your mind is as a tool that can either boost you forward or destroy you before you've even had a chance to apply anything you've learned, to realize that you have the power to become what you want to be, and that you can shape yourself through the power of positive thinking and consistency.

Yes, these are lofty goals for any book—especially a book that's somehow supposed to be related to software development—but if I've improved your life in at least one of these areas in some small way, then I'll consider it a win.

I have one small favor to ask of you before you put down this book. If you found this book helpful to you and you think someone else might benefit from it, please share it. I don't say this to drive up the sales of this book—although I'm certainly interested in doing that—but because I set out to write this book not so much to make a profit—there are many other ways I could have spent 500 hours that would have been much more profitable—but to do what I think we should all strive to do as not just software developers, but as people: to help others.

Thanks for taking the time to read this book and I sincerely hope that you've found some lasting value in it.

John Sonmez, http://simpleprogrammer.com

Appendix A

If you can write code, you can understand finances

Let's be honest, most software developers don't know much about finances. That might not apply to you, but I know that when I first got started in the world of software development, I had no clue how the world really worked. I didn't understand anything about how the stock market actually worked—besides buying and selling stocks. I didn't understand how mortgage loans and banks operated. I had no clue what an option or a derivative was. And I only had a vague idea of how insurance companies made money.

I'm not sure why I hadn't learned most of these things—I suppose because they aren't really taught in school and it's not the kind of things your parents teach you, either. But I started with a desire to own a house instead of rent, and ended up giving myself an education in all things financial, which has turned out to be a huge benefit for me.

That kind of financial knowledge has been so extremely beneficial to me that I'd like to pass on some of that knowledge to you as well. It turns out that even though some things about the economic world are quite complex, most of it is really simple—it's just that hardly anyone takes the time to understand how things work.

In appendix B, we're going to pull back the veil and expose how the world of economics really works, what actually happens when you trade a stock, how banks make mortgage loans, and where they get the money to do it. But before we can get into all of those details, it's important to have a basic understanding of money itself and how finances work in general.

In this appendix, I'm going to go over the basics of financial systems and help you understand exactly what that dollar in your hand means and how it got there. This basic knowledge will help us to move forward and talk about more complex topics and hopefully will help to change your mind-set about what money is and how it works. If you're already well-versed in economics, there might not be any big, amazing revelations in this appendix. But if you're like me—or rather like I was—you'll probably be surprised to find out how different money is from what you think it is, and you might never see it the same again.

What is money?

We'll start off with the most basic—yet most important—of questions: what is money? That dollar bill you're holding in your hand represents something more than a 99-cent cheeseburger at McDonald's—although, that cheeseburger analogy isn't all that far off, because money really represents utility.

Before there were currencies, people traded to get what they wanted. I have two cows I'll give you for five of your goats. I've got some wheat, but I sure could use some leather. The problem with trading is that you need to deal with someone who has what you want and also wants what you have. This is sometimes a hard combination to find, especially if you have exotic tastes.

It's much easier if you have some intermediary that has value to everyone. Then you can trade with anyone and not have to worry about whether you have an exact match between wants and needs. Money is basically that intermediary. It represents some future utility or value. A dollar bill by itself doesn't have value, but the fact that I can trade a dollar bill for a cheeseburger makes it valuable.

Types of money

For money to have value, there has to be a limited supply of it. Early monetary systems were commodity-based. That means that they were based off of something that was valuable and limited. That way, the money itself had value apart from its use as a trading tool. By making money out of intrinsically valuable and rare things such as gold and silver, it ensured the money itself was rare and had value.

To understand this concept better, think about those stories you've heard about prisons where the prisoners would use cigarettes as currency. That's a perfect example of a commodity-based monetary system. Cigarettes had their own value, but they could be used as an interchangeable tool for trading within that closed system.

The problem with commodity money is that it doesn't scale very well. It's difficult to scale commodity-based money quickly, because you have to be able to produce more of that commodity to increase the money available. The U.S. monetary system used to be commodity-based when the dollar bill was backed by gold. This was called representative money, because the dollar bill represented a certain amount of gold, but it worked exactly the same way. Back when the U.S. dollar was backed by gold, a dollar bill was essentially equivalent to having the amount of gold it represented. That meant that to print more dollar bills there would need to be more gold mined to back that money.

Eventually though, the United States left the gold standard behind and instead transitioned to what is called a fiat money. Fiat money is basically money that's issued by a government that doesn't have a direct relation to a specific commodity. Unlike commodity money, fiat money has no real value; it's just paper—or whatever material it's made of. Fiat money has a perceived value because people believe it's worth a certain amount. The amount fiat money is worth is based primarily on two things: how much of it is available and how well the economy of the government that issued and guaranteed the money is doing.

Inflation and deflation

You might have guessed that fiat money is pretty finicky. The value can change easily based on certain perceptions, and because it isn't tied to any specific tangible object, it can be greatly manipulated in value.

It turns out that fiat money is especially vulnerable to inflation and deflation. Inflation is when the value of the money becomes less in relation to what it can buy. When we have a high period of inflation, your nice, fat developer salary might stay the same from a pure numbers perspective, but its actual value decreases because everything else got more expensive.

Deflation is the exact opposite. When deflation happens, your money becomes more powerful. It suddenly can buy a lot more for the same amount. You'll recognize deflation by prices dropping. In deflation periods, the value of things aren't dropping, it's just that your money is worth a lot more.

Did you know inflation and deflation affect your mortgage? That's right. The amount of money you owe is especially subject to inflation and deflation. We talked about this in chapter 52, but let me give you a quick example of how inflation affects any debt you have.

Let's pretend you have a $100,000 mortgage. Imagine that we have a high period of inflation. At the end of that period of inflation, whether you pay anything down on your mortgage or not, you'll actually end up owing a lot less money. Yes, your mortgage balance might still be $100,000, but because the dollar just became less powerful, that $100,000 became a smaller debt.

Confused? Don't worry, you'll understand once we take it back to cheeseburgers. Suppose that cheeseburgers cost $1 each when you first got your loan. You essentially owed 100,000 cheeseburgers. After a period of high inflation the dollar became weak, so the prices of things rose, so now that $1 cheeseburger actually costs you $2 to buy. The value of the cheeseburger might have appeared to change, but a cheeseburger is still a cheeseburger. It still has as many calories and is as tasty as it was when you got the loan.

But now look what happened to the amount you owe. Instead of owing 100,000 cheeseburgers, you now owe just 50,000. Inflation actually reduces your debt.

Unfortunately, though, it works the other way as well. Suppose that you had a high period of deflation instead. You might be pretty excited to find out that you could now get scrumptious cheeseburgers for just 50 cents instead of $1, until you realized that you now actually owe 200,000 cheeseburgers instead of 100,000. Deflation increases your debt.

What does this little example teach you? Actually, something practical that you can put into use right away. If you have debt, inflation reduces that debt while deflation increases it. If you have money in the bank, or someone owes you money, inflation makes your money and future money less valuable, while deflation makes it more valuable. In periods of high inflation, you're better off investing your money and taking on some debt, because it loses value in the bank, but debts decrease as inflation increases. In times of deflation, you want the opposite. You want to eliminate as much debt as possible and hoard money in the bank, because money goes up in value without you having to do anything.

Central banks

By now it should be pretty obvious to you that large inflation or deflation is bad for any monetary system. Wild swings can make people skittish and can cause all kinds of behavior that isn't good for an economy, like excessive borrowing and hoarding.

Fiat currencies need special care and handling to prevent inflation and deflation—or at least to keep them from becoming too extreme. That's where the role of the central bank comes in to play.

In the United States we have a central bank known as the Federal Reserve. The Federal Reserve is charged with the task of maintaining the currency of the United States. The Federal Reserve has a bunch of different tools it can use to help curb swings in inflation or deflation or to help stimulate or slow down the economy.

You've probably heard of some of the things the Federal Reserve and other central banks use to manipulate the currency and the economy. At a basic level, most central banks can issue more currency. They can essentially print money. Printing money has exactly the kind of effect you might imagine. It causes inflation. If there's more money circulating around, all of that money has less value.

Several different economies have gotten into big trouble by printing too much money. Mexico and Japan come to mind, but many currencies have felt the pain of trying to solve problems by printing more money. It only works temporarily.

Central banks can also reduce the circulation of money by selling government securities. These securities can be sold in exchange for money, which is then kept out of circulation. If you guessed this would cause deflation, you're absolutely right.

But the power of a central bank doesn't stop there. Central banks can also control what are called reserve requirements, which are the rules that banks in that country must follow in terms of how much of the percentage of deposits in those banks must be held in reserve. Increase the reserve requirements and banks can't lend out as much money. Decrease it and they can. The more money banks lend out, the less it's worth—inflation, and vice versa.

You also may have heard about central banks like the Federal Reserve lowering the discount rate. This discount rate doesn't directly affect your mortgage rates, but it controls the interest rate that banks pay to borrow money. This affects the amount of money in circulation by effectively making money cheaper or more expensive.

What about "regular" banks

I don't mean to scare you, but there is much more money floating around in the economy than what actually exists. If you, I, and everyone else all decided to go to our banks to pull out all the money we had deposited, the entire economic system would collapse. There is literally not enough money in the banks to give everyone back the money they have on deposit, so it's a good thing we don't all take our money out at once.

Banks work by taking deposits and lending money out based on those deposits. We talked about how central banks set policies on how much money a bank has to keep in reserve, and that's the primary factor that determines how much money a bank lends. Typically, though, when you deposit $100 in your bank account, the bank lends around 90% of that out.

The entire banking system "banks" on the idea that not everyone needs access to all their money at once. Banks primarily make money by taking our money and lending it out to other people and businesses at a higher rate than the interest they pay you.

As you can imagine, this could be a risky business because you can't exactly predict when large depositors might ask for a sizable chunk of their money back. For that reason, banks have their own interbank networks where they can loan each other money when they need it. Banks can also borrow money from the government, but they typically pay a higher rate for doing so.

Did you know that MasterCard and Visa aren't actually the companies you pay your credit card payments to? Nope. It's actually banks. Banks are involved in all kinds of lending, from mortgages to car loans and even credit cards.

One thing that I always found confusing about banks is what they do when they loan out all the money they have. Do they just tell their employees to sit tight and wait for 30 years until they get the money back from the mortgages? It turns out that, at least in the United States, banks sell most of the mortgages they originate primarily to two companies called Fannie Mae and Freddie Mac. These two companies guarantee they will buy any loan as long as it meets a certain set of underwriting requirements they set. (That's why you have to jump through so many hoops when you apply for a mortgage loan.)

Banks are able to create the loan and then sell the loan to one of these companies to get their money back and get paid for a certain amount of the value of the interest charged on that loan. This allows them to continue to make new loans and loan out money without tying up all of their cash.

The basics of finances

Now that you understand the basic underpinnings that define how the economy and money work, you're set up to understand everything else that's built on top of it—and, more importantly, how it affects you. Almost all financial matters are based on risk, returns, and liquidity. How much money or interest do you stand to make on your money? How risky is an investment? How easily can you transfer money from one form to another?

There are all kinds of markets and economies that exist based on these factors. Some people make money trading bonds, which are usually low-risk, low-return, and liquid. Other people invest in stocks that are high-risk, high-return, and also liquid. I prefer to invest in real estate, which is low-risk, high-return, and about as far from liquid as you can get.

Taking action

○ To better understand how money works and how it's affected by inflation, do the following exercise:
  ○ Look up the price of white bread from 10 years ago and calculate how much bread you could buy with your current annual salary.
  ○ Now look up and see how much bread that same salary will buy you today.
  ○ Assuming the value of white bread remained the same over time, is your salary worth more or less than it was 10 years ago? Can you buy more or less bread?

Appendix B

How the stock market works: Rules of the system

Hopefully by now you understand the need to invest. Saving money isn't enough, unless you're willing to be very frugal and wait a long time. You have to put your money to work so that it makes more money.

One of the most common ways that people invest is in the stock market. I prefer real estate, but for many people the stock market is an easier way to invest because stocks, bonds, mutual funds, options, and future contracts are much more liquid than real estate properties.

Regardless of what you decide to invest in, it's important to understand how the stock market works. As a software developer, you'll probably have an easier time understanding the intricacies of the stock market, because much of it's based on math and computers—especially today. You may even have a distinct advantage in investing and trading, because you may have better-than-average abilities to analyze complex data and you can understand the kinds of algorithms involved in trading.

In this appendix I'll go over the basics of the stock market. If you've ever bought or sold a stock, you'll probably be familiar with some of what we'll cover here, but I'm going to go a little deeper and explain how the stock market actually works—why you have a bid and an ask price for each stock and what's actually happening behind the scenes when you trade a stock.

> **Landmine: Why is there an appendix about the stock market in this book?**
>
> You might wonder why I'm including an appendix about the stock market in this book. It's a fair question. I mean, certainly you can go somewhere else to find information about the stock market and how it works—and you could—but will you? And will you recognize how important it is to know how this complex financial system works? Don't get me wrong. It's not like I don't think that you most likely know the basics of how the stock market works, but I've found that few people know exactly what's going on behind the scenes—which is what I think is important. Plus, if you want to be able to get into the interesting stuff—the stuff that you can utilize your programmer brain to have an advantage over the general population with—you'll need to understand the basics.

The purpose of the stock market

To really understand the stock market, you need to understand what its purpose is. The stock market exists to make it easier for investors to buy and sell shares of a stock, but what exactly is a stock?

A stock is a percentage of ownership in a company. For a company to become publically traded on the stock market, it has to first become incorporated. Becoming incorporated makes a company its own legal entity. It essentially acquires many of the attributes of a person. A corporation can own real estate and other property, enter legal agreements, get credit, sue, and be sued in court. There are all kinds of laws in each country and region regarding corporate entities.

Why would a business want to become a corporation and sell its shares on the stock market? The biggest reason is to raise capital. When a corporation initially sells its shares on the stock market, also known as an exchange, this process is called an initial public offering (IPO). During an IPO, a corporation can sell a certain percentage of itself to raise money. If a corporation divides itself into 1 million shares and sells each share for $10, that corporation will raise 10 million dollars during its IPO.

That money can be used to further grow the business by hiring more employees, purchasing equipment, or even buying other companies. And the best part is that money doesn't have to be paid back. The

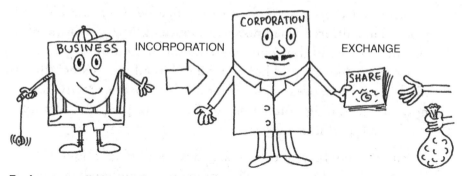

Businesses sell shares of stock to gain capital.

corporation is now owned by shareholders who vote on major decisions about the company. Having a controlling interest in the corporation, by owning a majority of the shares of the stock, allows a person or entity to control that corporation.

This finally takes us back to the stock market. Without an open market for trading shares of different companies, it would be difficult to buy and sell shares. It would also be difficult to decide what the prices should be. The stock market makes shares of stock very liquid, because they can be easily traded. Contrast this with real estate, which requires much more work to buy and sell.

What happens when you trade a stock?

If you've ever traded shares of a stock on the stock market, you're probably familiar with the basics of the stock market. Each stock has a value that fluctuates over time. You can buy or sell shares of a stock at the current value. But the stock market is actually quite a bit more complicated than that.

It turns out that individual stocks don't have a single value associated with them. In fact, each stock that's quoted on the stock market has what's known as a bid and an ask price. The bid price is the price that you can sell a stock at—it's essentially the price others are bidding for that stock. The ask price is the price you can buy a stock at—it's basically the price others are asking for shares of that stock.

It turns out there's actually a difference between the bid and the ask price. This difference is known as a spread. Many factors influence the size of the spread, but one major factor is the liquidity of the stock. A stock that's more liquid has a smaller spread, but a stock that's less liquid has a larger spread. The liquidity of a stock is mostly determined by how much trading volume it has. The more people who trade a stock, the more liquid it usually is.

Right off the bat, you can see how knowing about the difference between the bid and ask prices of a stock could be beneficial to you. If you buy and sell a stock immediately, you're almost guaranteed to lose money. As soon as you buy a stock, you've essentially taken a loss equal to the size of the spread. If you bought a share of a stock at $20 and the spread was $1, that would mean that the most you'd be able to sell that stock for, at that moment, would be $19. This is one of the reasons why investing in the stock market can be tricky. You're starting off at a disadvantage.

You may be wondering how those bid and ask prices are set and what determines how liquid a stock is. The answer to that question is market makers. Market makers are traders who create liquidity in the stock market by always being willing to buy or sell a particular stock. In most stock exchanges, there are specific market makers for each stock. These market makers set the bid and ask prices for a stock and make their money by collecting the difference.

If I sell a share of a stock for the ask price of $19 and at that same moment you buy that stock for the bid price of $20, the $1 difference is collected by the market maker. You don't trade stocks directly with other traders in the stock market; instead, everyone goes through market makers who set the bid and ask prices and keep the trading flowing.

Without market makers, the liquidity of the stock market would suffer. If everyone was trying to sell a particular stock and no one wanted to buy that stock, you'd have a difficult time selling shares of your stock. You might have to severely discount the price of your shares to get a buyer or you might have to wait a very long time. In today's market, most trades happen instantly thanks to market makers.

How to make money in the stock market

You might be wondering how you actually make money in the stock market. Buy low and sell high, right? Well, at a basic level it's that simple, but it can get much more complicated.

Most stock market trading is based on speculation. Investors are speculating that a stock's price will either go up or down. It's pretty obvious that if you buy a stock and its price goes up, you'll make money—that is, if you sell it before it drops again—but you can also make money when a stock goes down by a process called shorting.

When you short a stock, you borrow shares of that stock and sell those shares. This puts you in what is called a short position. You eventually have to cover that short position by buying back shares to replace the ones you borrowed. If you buy back those shares at a lower price than you sold the borrowed shares for, you make money.

Think of it this way. Let's suppose I borrowed your iPad. Now, suppose I sell your borrowed iPad for $500. (What a good friend I am.) A couple of days later, you ask for your iPad back, so I go out and buy a replacement one, but I pick up the replacement one for $450. In that exchange, I'd net $50 profit. Shorting stocks works exactly the same way.

You can also make money just by holding certain stocks. Some stocks pay what's called a dividend. A dividend is basically some extra profit the company made that it's sharing with its shareholders instead of reinvesting in the company. Usually, only big companies pay dividends.

The process of shorting stock

Dividends are a pretty safe way to make money on stock, but, as I'm sure you can imagine, the returns usually aren't that high. The lower the risk, the lower the potential returns.

Indexes, mutual funds, and ETFs

Trading shares of stocks is pretty simple in itself, but investing in the stock market goes much deeper than just trading single stocks. You also need a way to measure the performance of the stock market as a whole so that you can understand what direction things are going.

Indexes serve the purpose of providing a general measurement of a selection of stocks in the stock market. In the U.S. market, the most widely known index is the Dow Jones Industrial Average. The Dow, as it's often called, shows the collective stock price of 30 large publically owned companies based in the United States. You can get a general idea of whether the stock market is going up or down by just looking at the Dow.

There are many other indexes, such as the S&P 500, which can also tell you quite a bit about the overall direction of the market. Some indexes are industry-specific. There are indexes for the technology sector of the market and other sectors that help gauge the temperature of those sections of the market.

It turns out that buying the stocks in the major indexes in equal parts is a good general strategy for investing in the stock market, because over time most of the major indexes have averaged around 10% returns per year. But, unfortunately, you can't just buy an index. That's where mutual funds and ETFs come into play.

A mutual fund is a special program that's funded by investors and managed by a professional trader who buys different stocks across the market. Mutual funds usually focus on different investment strategies, but many mutual funds spend a large amount of their money buying the stocks in the major indexes to reduce their overall risk.

A mutual fund allows you as an individual investor to have a diversified portfolio with little money. If you wanted to buy a bunch of different stocks to make sure that you were getting close to the average of the stock market and weren't subject to any one stock's fluctuations in pricing, it would cost you quite a bit of money, but with a mutual fund, you pool your money with many other investors, which makes it possible.

Up until 1993, at least in the United States, mutual funds were your only options for pooling your money and buying the stocks in an index like the S&P 500 or the Dow, but exchange traded funds (ETFs) now allow an individual investor to have some of the same advantages as investing in a mutual fund. ETFs are like indexes that you can buy and sell shares of. An ETF is traded like any other stock in the stock market and is basically an investment fund that holds stocks and other assets that mirror a particular index as closely as possible. There are even ETFs that mirror the price of gold, so you can essentially trade gold on the stock market without ever having to own any real metal.

Taking action

- Go online and find the price of a popular stock that interests you. Pay careful attention to the bid and ask prices. Determine what the size of the spread is. Compare several different stocks of various size companies. See if you can spot any trends.

Appendix C

Garbage in, garbage out: Diet and nutrition basics

There are quite a few things you can do to get healthy and fit, including many different exercises or programs that you could embark on. But nothing is going to matter as much to your health and fitness as what you eat.

Whether your goal is to lose weight, gain muscle, or refactor your body to a healthier state, diet and nutrition is the most effective tool to do it. Think of diet and nutrition like writing code. You can have all kinds of tools at your disposal and apply all kinds of methodologies, but you'll never create any kind of application if you don't focus on writing good code.

In this chapter, we'll go over the basics of diet and nutrition. I'll give you a brief introduction to the basic components of food and you'll learn a bit about how your body processes what you put into it.

Basic components of food

Before we can get into the details of a healthy diet and nutrition, you need to understand what the basic components of food are.

Everything you eat can be broken up into three main categories: carbohydrates, fats, or proteins. Your body uses each of these components in various ways, but the main fuel source for your body is carbohydrates. Your brain and the rest of your body utilize a simple sugar called glucose for fuel.

Your body is very efficient at breaking food into glucose that can be used by the body. When you eat a meal, your digestive system breaks down that food into glucose, which is absorbed by the stomach and small intestines and released into your bloodstream.

After this happens, a hormone called insulin is released from your pancreas. Insulin makes it possible for your body to utilize and store the glucose in your bloodstream. Insulin in your bloodstream enables other cells to absorb glucose and either use it immediately or store it for later usage.

Diabetics have problems with their insulin production or sensitivity. Type I diabetics are unable to produce their own insulin, so they have to inject it artificially. Type II diabetics' bodies aren't as sensitive to insulin as they should be, so they require more insulin to do the same job.

Without insulin, your blood sugar levels would rise very high and you'd eventually die. That's why it's critical that diabetics monitor their blood sugar levels.

Even though your body primarily needs glucose, which mainly comes from carbohydrates, that doesn't mean your body doesn't need proteins and fats as well.

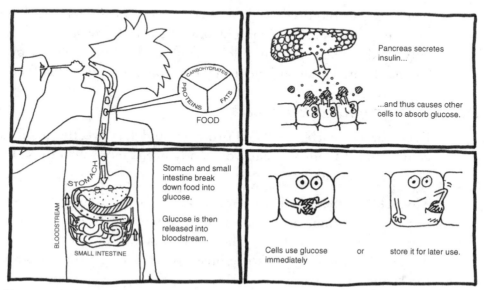

How your body breaks down food

Your body utilizes proteins to build and repair muscle, as a catalyst for certain chemical reactions, and for a variety of other functions including energy—if needed. But just like carbohydrates, proteins must also be broken down.

Proteins digested by your body are broken down into amino acids, which are the basic building blocks of life and many chemical reactions in the body. But proteins can also be converted to glucose through a process known as gluconeogenesis. This process isn't very efficient, though, so when the body has to use proteins as fuel, it actually ends up requiring more calories to do the job, which is great if you're trying to lose weight.

Fats are also broken down by the body into fatty acids, which can be directly packaged away by cells for future use in a form called triglycerides. Fats are also directly converted into fuel when they're broken down into glycerol, which can be converted to glucose.

Fats are the most concentrated form of energy—while proteins and carbohydrates provide about four calories worth of energy per gram, fats provide approximately nine.

Fats are also required by your body to produce what are known as essential fatty acids. You might have heard of omega-3 and omega-6 fatty acids. They're required by your body, but can't be produced directly by it. These fatty acids have to come from ingested foods.

Other things your body needs

Even though carbohydrates, proteins, and fats are the main components of most foods you eat, your body needs more than those building blocks to function.

Most of the other nutrients your body needs are commonly classified as vitamins. Vitamins are small molecules your body needs to carry out certain chemical reactions. There are about 13 different vitamins that your body needs yet can't produce, so it has to get them from various food sources.

In most cases, you can get all the vitamins you need from the food you eat, as long as you eat a large enough variety of foods. This is one of the reasons why you can't typically eat the exact same foods every single day.

I'm sure you have heard of scurvy, which is caused by a vitamin C deficiency. Vitamin C is required to create collagen, which is needed for various functions of your body. Commonly, sailors would get scurvy because their diet consisted of only cured meats and dried grains — once the fruits and vegetables ran out.

In addition to vitamins, your body also needs fiber to aid with the digestive process. Fiber is basically parts of plant foods that your body can't digest or absorb. Fiber can either be soluble or insoluble. Soluble fiber dissolves in water and can help lower cholesterol and glucose in your blood. Insoluble fiber is critical to proper digestion.

And let's not forget minerals. The body requires many minerals to function properly — salt, for instance, is required to maintain the proper level of fluid in your body's cells. Other minerals like calcium and iron are necessary for your body to function properly.

And last but not least, let's not forget about perhaps the most vital component your body needs: water. Water makes up about 60% of your body. Water is vital for many functions of the body and you can't live without it for long at all — perhaps three to five days at the most, but I wouldn't suggest testing it.

It all starts with diet

No matter what fitness goal you have, diet is probably the most important component of it. Burning fat, gaining muscle, or performing any physical activity is entirely dependent on the fuel you provide your body, but most people tend to put a heavier emphasis on exercise than nutrition.

This is unfortunate, because you can work hard at achieving a fitness goal, but if you don't have the proper diet and nutrition, all that hard work will be a waste. I've seen many people who could run marathons, but were still overweight, because they didn't realize how important diet was to their health and fitness levels.

You can spend hours at the gym lifting weights or run for miles, but without a proper diet, you'll never see the results you're looking for. It's important to understand how what you eat affects your body's performance and how it gets fuel.

Overall, calories are the most important factor in your physical makeup. Eat more calories than you burn and you'll gain weight; eat less and you'll lose it.

After that, the ratio of the types of calories is probably the second most important factor. Different ratios of fats, carbohydrates, and proteins will affect your body differently. Don't eat enough protein and your body will break down existing proteins—muscle—to get the amino acids it needs. Eat too many carbohydrates—especially simple sugars—and your body will have to work extra hard to produce enough insulin to reduce the sugar in your blood.

Finally, food sources have a measurable effect on your body. It not only matters what you eat, but where the food you eat comes from. Highly processed food tends to have lots of simple sugars and preservatives that can reduce the nutritional quality of the food and cause you to crave more of them while not feeling satisfied. Not all carbohydrates are created equal. There's a big difference between eating a sweet potato and eating a bunch of processed white sugar, even though both are carbohydrates. (We'll talk more about the differences in appendix D.)

Taking action

- Try to figure out the current calorie count of the foods you eat in a day and the ratio of proteins, carbohydrates, and fats in your diet. This may vary from day to day, but try to track a few days to get an idea.

Appendix D

How to eat healthy: Pizza is not a food group

Regardless of what your fitness goals are, basic, healthy eating is going to help you get there. Unfortunately, defining healthy eating isn't as easy as you'd think. It turns out that there are many different opinions on what exactly healthy eating is.

Not too long ago, we were told that fats and dietary cholesterol were bad; eating eggs for breakfast every day was considered unhealthy. But today we know that isn't true. In fact, the high-carbohydrate, low-fat diet recommendations of the past have been found to be incorrect. It turns out many of the things we thought were unhealthy were actually perfectly okay—in moderation, that is.

Rather than confuse you about the speculation and debate on the fringes of the healthy eating debate, I'm going to give you some solid, difficult-to-disagree-with advice on how you can eat healthier, and give you some reasons why certain foods are considered healthy while others aren't.

For the most part, food is food

It turns out we give a little too much emphasis to whether certain foods are healthy or not. For the most part, our bodies don't care where they get their carbs, proteins, and fats from, as long as they have what they need.

I'm not saying that some foods aren't technically "better" for you, but for most people, focusing too much on the specific foods they eat is a premature optimization. What I mean by this is that you shouldn't be thinking about whether this food or that food is healthy. You should instead be thinking mostly about macronutrient ratios and calorie counts.

Macronutrients are basically carbohydrates, fats, and proteins, and we've already talked quite a bit about calorie counts in chapter 58. The sources of macronutrients and calories aren't nearly as important as the amounts.

You might be skeptical — I know, it seems too simple — but a nutrition professor, Mark Haub, did a little experiment involving Twinkies that you might be interested in (http://simpleprogrammer.com/ss-twinkie). In Mark's experiment, he ate one Twinkie every three hours instead of eating regular meals. He also had some other "junk food" like chips, snack cakes, and cookies — Oreos specifically.

Here's the catch, Mark restricted his diet to 1,800 calories a day. Even though he was eating "junk," he was carefully controlling his calorie count. His maintenance calorie amount was about 2,600 calories a day, so he was in a deficit of around 800 calories a day.

After two months, he dropped his weight by 27 pounds. Not only did he lose weight, but his bad cholesterol dropped by 20% and his good cholesterol increased by 20%.

To be fair, he did drink a protein shake each day and ate some vegetables, but two-thirds of his diet consisted of junk food. Obviously eating a bunch of junk food isn't considered healthy, but quantity is the most important factor in healthy eating. And for restructuring your body — gaining muscle or losing fat while retaining muscle — the ratio of what kinds of macronutrients you eat is pretty important as well.

Wait, isn't this a contradiction? Didn't you just tell me that calories are the most important? Well, for just losing or gaining weight, yes, but if you want to gain muscle or lose primarily fat, you need to think about what you eat, not just how much.

Should I just eat junk food?

Perhaps you're thinking that you should follow Mark's example and just eat junk food. I wouldn't recommend it, and not because junk food is unhealthy. I wouldn't recommend it primarily because you'll be really hungry.

Here's the thing: not all foods have the same caloric density. Typically the high-fat, high-sugar foods that we consider "junk food" are bad for us simply because they are so calorie-dense. You don't have to eat much cheesecake to consume a large amount of calories, but on the other hand, you can eat a huge amount of broccoli and hardly consume many calories at all.

Whether some foods are healthier for you or not doesn't matter nearly as much as the quantity of foods you consume. You're much likelier to consume more calories when you eat unhealthy foods simply because they taste better and they're denser in calories. Because being over-weight is a bigger factor in our overall health than the foods we eat, it makes much more sense to focus on losing weight—by whatever means possible—rather than getting too caught up on what foods are healthy.

That means, for the most part, that it's really up to you. If you're trying to lose weight and you're trying to hit 1,800 calories a day, like Mark was, you can eat three meals of healthy foods daily or you can have one Outback Steakhouse Aussie cheese fries (2,140 calories total). Your choice. I prefer to eat mostly healthy food, because I don't like being hungry all the time.

But what exactly are "healthy" foods?

Oh, you mean you want to know what foods aren't as calorie-dense and might provide some other nutritional value than just calories? Okay, I can help you out.

Like I said before, it's subjective and we don't actually know with 100% accuracy what foods are healthy and which ones aren't, so we can focus primarily on caloric density and make some pretty decent assumptions about the rest.

With that in mind, some of the healthiest foods, or at least the ones that aren't all that dense in calories, happen to be fruits and vegetables. Most fruits and vegetables have high fiber content and also contain a lot of water. Remember that fiber calories basically don't count, because those calories can't actually be digested by your body. And, of course, water doesn't contain any calories, either.

It also turns out that for some vegetables, in their whole form, your body has to spend quite a bit of calories to digest them—this is known as the thermic effect. Proteins actually have the highest thermic effect—requiring about 20–30% of the calories they contain just to digest them—which brings us to the next category of healthy foods: proteins.

Foods that are high in protein are usually not very dense—unless they also contain a high amount of fat. That's why a chicken breast, which is almost all protein, is generally considered healthier than a nice cut of marbled steak—delicious, but pretty calorie-dense. Regardless of the actual density, in terms of calories, all proteins require quite a bit of energy for your body to digest and convert to usable calories.

Proteins are also essential in building and maintaining muscle. Remember that your body needs certain amino acids to produce and repair muscle tissue, so if you're trying to lose weight and want to keep your body from losing muscle, having a large amount of protein in your diet is a good thing. The same goes for gaining muscle. If your goal is to gain muscle, you'll see the most success with a diet that's high in protein.

What foods contain protein? Mostly meats, eggs, and milk, although, there are certainly vegetarian sources of protein as well, like beans, lentils, tofu, and nondairy milk. The best protein sources for dieting are usually lean protein sources, because they won't have as many calories. Chicken breasts, turkey, fish, and egg whites are great sources of lean protein.

Next on our list come carbohydrate sources that are considered complex carbohydrates. This would be carbohydrates that are a bit more difficult for your body to break down. These carbohydrate sources typically contain fiber and have a higher thermic effect. Sweet potatoes, brown rice, and oatmeal are good examples. Foods that contain processed sugar aren't as good, because the simple sugars are easily moved directly into your bloodstream. Those kinds of foods tend to be denser in calories.

Body has to spend 20–30% of calories to digest.

Usually not very dense caloriewise.

High in fiber.

Different foods have different caloric densities

We also need fats, and some fats are considered healthy while others aren't. Don't get me started on this topic. We've been told for a long time that saturated fats are evil, but a huge study involving over 350,000 people in 2010 that was published by the American Journal of Clinical Nutrition showed no conclusive proof linking saturated fat to heart disease or strokes (http://simpleprogrammer.com/ss-saturated-fat).

Even though saturated fats may not be that bad, it turns out that unsaturated fats can actually help lower bad cholesterol levels and triglyceride levels. You can find unsaturated fats in foods like fatty fish and nuts.

Overall, what are "healthy" foods? In general, the foods that are the healthiest aren't processed—whole foods like chicken, vegetables, fruits, sweet potatoes, brown rice, eggs, oatmeal, nuts, and fish. Again, these foods aren't necessarily a lot healthier than other types of foods, but in general, you'll find that these foods are less dense calorie-wise and provide the basic nutrients you need.

Taking action

☻ Look up the amount of calories per serving for a green vegetable like broccoli versus processed food you might find at a fast-food restaurant or some packaged food in your pantry. Actually measure out and physically compare the difference in volume of the healthy food versus the unhealthy food. Which do you think would make you more full for the same amount of calories?

☻ The next time you need to make a food choice, think about whether you'd rather have a little of something tastier or a lot of something not quite as tasty.

Index